More Praise for *The Fourth Star*

"A detailed inside analysis of four contemporary generals and the decisions that went right and wrong for them as their careers headed for Iraq . . . A big strength of this book is that the writers take a military point of view rather than sharpshooting from the clueless perimeter." —*New York Post*

"Fascinating, full of political intrigue and provocative inside information . . . the book's interwoven portraits of intertwined careers depict reluctant changes in the Army from Khe Sanh to Kabul." —*Army Times*

"Timely and poignant . . . paints intimate portraits . . . the authors magnificently connect the story lines of Abizaid's clash with Pentagon leadership, Chiarelli's challenges on the battlefield with Petraeus's 'surge' counterinsurgency strategy, and Casey's determination to win the war." —*Roll Call*

"[Provides] fascinating insight into today's Army . . . a real window into the military mind." —Fareed Zakaria, CNN

"Jaffe and Cloud draw intimate portraits of four members of the Army's high priesthood, and the implication is clear: The future of the Army is up for grabs. In *The Fourth Star*, America's wars from Vietnam to Iraq provide a backdrop for the high-stakes battle for the U.S. Army itself. If you care about winning tomorrow's wars, then read this book." —Nathaniel Fick, author of the *New York Times* bestseller *One Bullet Away*

"Insightful . . . a perceptive look at intelligent, capable generals trying their best." —*Kirkus Reviews*

"A fascinating, intimate look at the men who are leading our wars and trying to change America's largest institution, the U.S. Army. A must-read for students of history, leadership, and engrossing prose." —Dana Priest, Pulitzer Prize–winning author of *The Mission*

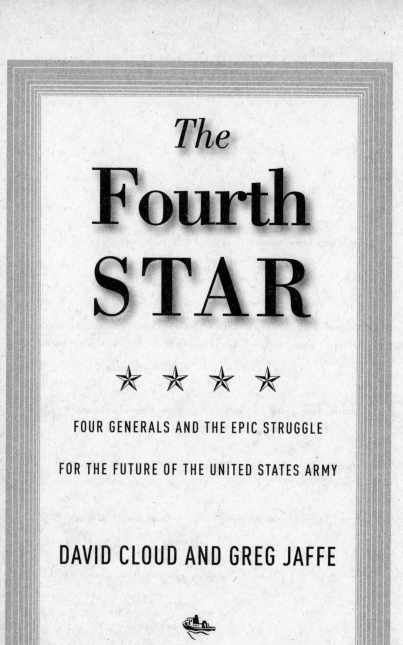

The
Fourth
STAR

★ ★ ★ ★

FOUR GENERALS AND THE EPIC STRUGGLE

FOR THE FUTURE OF THE UNITED STATES ARMY

DAVID CLOUD AND GREG JAFFE

THREE RIVERS PRESS • NEW YORK

Published in the United States by Three Rivers Press, an imprint of the Crown Publishing
Group, a division of Random House, Inc., New York.

www.crownpublishing.com

Three Rivers Press and the Tugboat design are registered trademarks of Random House, Inc.

Originally published in hardcover in the United States by Crown Publishers, an imprint of the
Crown Publishing Group, a division of Random House, Inc., New York, in 2009.

Library of Congress Cataloging-in-Publication Data

Jaffe, Greg.
The fourth star : four generals and the epic struggle for the future of the United States Army /
Greg Jaffe and David Cloud.— 1st ed.
Includes index.
1. Iraq War, 2003—Biography.   2. Casey, George W.   3. Abizaid, John P., 1951-
4. Chiarelli, Peter W.   5. Petraeus, David Howell.   6. Generals—United States—
Biography.
7. United States. Army—Biography.   I. Cloud, David.   II. Title.

DS79.76.J338 2009
355.0092'273—dc22
2009015591

ISBN 978-0-307-40907-2

Printed in the United States of America

Design by Leonard W. Henderson

10 9 8 7 6 5 4 3 2 1

First Paperback Edition

The Fourth Star

CHAPTER ONE

Age of Anarchy

Along the Cambodia–South Vietnam border
June 29, 1970

The helicopters descended onto the hilltop clearing, wave after wave, a vast armada of American power. Out of them tumbled soldiers with rifles and rucksacks, returning from the invasion of Cambodia. They were mud-caked and sodden after three days of monsoon rain, but many were grinning and snapping pictures with their buddies. A few flashed peace signs for the television cameras, happy to have survived this madcap ordeal. The United States and its South Vietnamese allies had crossed into Cambodia precisely two months earlier on President Richard Nixon's orders, setting off the biggest protests of the war at home. Nixon had promised that every soldier would be out by the end of June, and they would be. The last of the rear guard would be flown back into Vietnam by six that evening.

Major General George Casey, commander of the 1st Air Cavalry Division, stood at the edge of the landing zone. The White House wanted the operation dressed up as a major victory, so Casey, sad-eyed and handsome, was there to brief reporters ferried out from Saigon for the day, along with a group of congressmen on a fact-finding mission. The facts were these: In eight weeks of combing through the Cambodian jungle, U.S. and South Vietnamese troops had captured vast stores of munitions, rice, and other supplies in so-called enemy sanctuaries that had long been off-limits. They had fought several battles and reported killing or capturing more than 10,000 Communist troops. But the invasion and the secret bombing that preceded it had destabilized Cambodia and achieved little that would help gain victory in Vietnam. The operation marked the beginning of the slow American pullout from Southeast Asia, a last push before the Army, bloodied and tired after five years of combat, began going home for good. Casey didn't exaggerate the gains. The enemy, he knew, would recover and the war would go on. But, he told the reporters, the operation had bought some time for their South Vietnamese allies, who soon would have to stand on their own. "I've done two tours over here," he yelled over the roar of the helicopter rotors, and going into Cambodia "was an opportunity we thought we'd never have."

He was a good soldier doing his duty, as he had for decades. After Pearl Harbor, Casey had withdrawn from Harvard University and enrolled at West Point, receiving his commission too late to see action in World War II. In Korea, he commanded an infantry company, earning a battle-field promotion to captain at Heartbreak Ridge, along with a Silver Star, the Army's third-highest honor. He went on to work as a personal aide to General Lyman Lemnitzer, a future chairman of the Joint Chiefs of Staff, and then returned to Harvard as a military fellow from 1965 to 1966. He spent most of the remainder of the decade commanding troops in Vietnam and seemed sure to ascend to four stars. Already he was being talked about as a future chief of the Army, as his West Point classmates had foreseen in 1945 when they predicted, "He will be the Army's best."

A week after the withdrawal from Cambodia, Casey climbed into the copilot seat of his Huey helicopter at 1st Air Cav headquarters and took off, flying east. He was headed for the U.S. base at Cam Ranh Bay to visit wounded soldiers. It was raining and visibility was so poor that his chief of staff, Colonel Edward "Shy" Meyer, had urged him to cancel the trip, but he wanted to see his men before they were transferred to hospitals in Japan. The helicopter's path took it across Vietnam's mountainous central highlands. At about 10:00 a.m. his Huey flew into a dense cloud and disappeared. A second helicopter flying behind crisscrossed over the shrouded peaks, looking for any sign of the general's craft, but finally had to break off when its fuel began running low. The American military headquarters in Saigon ordered a massive search. Not wanting to alert the Viet Cong that a high-ranking general was unaccounted for, it held off making a public announcement until a few days later.

On July 9, the *New York Times* put the story on the front page: "The United States Army disclosed today that Maj. Gen. George W. Casey, who directed the withdrawal of the last American ground troops from Cambodia on June 29, has been missing since Tuesday when he took off in his helicopter. An intensive search is under way, an Army spokesman said."

✳   ✳   ✳   ✳

Casey's son, George junior, was sitting in the apartment that he and his new wife, Sheila, shared on Pennsylvania Avenue in Washington, D.C., near the Capitol when the phone rang. It was his mother. "Your father's helicopter crashed. He's missing," she told him. As they spoke George tried to sound optimistic, as painful as it was, but when he hung up and told Sheila the news, he was matter-of-fact. "Mom's hopeful," he said. "But you don't go down in one of those helicopters and survive."

He knew the Army. He had grown up with it and, even at age twenty-two, had its fatalism about death. Born in Japan on an Army base, he spent his childhood years moving every two years with his parents from one installation to another, an experience that had turned him into a jokester who made friends easily and applied himself as little as possible. He was, in that respect, completely different from his father. The Caseys were Boston Irish, and George junior had more than a little Irish mirth about him. It was the younger George who supplied the entertainment at the family's formal Sunday dinners. The table was set with linen napkins, china, and silver candlesticks. George and his brother, Peter, were expected to wear coats and ties. The three Casey girls, Joan, Ann, and Winn, and their mother wore dresses. Their father quizzed his brood about current events, which in an Army house in the mid-1960s usually meant the war or the protests that were just beginning in college towns such as Berkley and Cambridge.

When their father brought up Vietnam, George would usually make a joke and shift the conversation. Once he came to dinner in a coat and tie but no shirt, causing his sisters to erupt in peals of laughter.

His younger sisters were far more emotional on the subject—proud of their father, but also angry that the war pulled him away. George's teenage sister Joan responded to one of her father's Vietnam queries by declaring: "I'd go to Canada before I'd go to Vietnam!" A few months later she wrote a high-school essay on growing up as an Army brat and how their itinerant life, moving every two years and crisscrossing Europe in a beat-up station wagon, had drawn the family closer. When her father read it, she recalled, he began to cry.

Outwardly George, the eldest of the five Casey children, seemed the least bothered by the war. In the spring of 1966 he had applied to go to the United States Military Academy at West Point, mostly to please his father, but his math grades had been too low to get in. He enrolled instead at Georgetown University, just a few miles from his parents' brick colonial in Arlington, Virginia, across the Potomac River from the Georgetown campus. He signed up for the Army's Reserve Officer Training Corps program, played football, and always seemed to have the remnants of a six-pack stashed in his dorm room. George and his friends—Irish kids from Boston, New York, and New Jersey—crashed parties, hung out at the Tombs, a popular Georgetown bar, and squeaked by in class. At first they gave little thought to Vietnam. "We rooted for the Americans the way you'd root for the bobsled team at the Olympics," recalled Ray O'Hara, one of George's closest college friends.

George would always remember the Sunday afternoon in 1968 when he and O'Hara went downtown to check out the war protests by the White House. George threw on his Army jacket to ward off the chill. As he moved through the throngs of protesters he noticed that many in the crowd were wearing green field jackets identical to his. To them it was some sort of counterculture statement. Feeling uncomfortable, Casey took his coat off and tucked it under his arm. A few minutes later someone threw a garbage can at a police officer, and a melee erupted. George and his friend took off, unsure what they were doing at the protest in the first place.

The anger over the war was remaking the Georgetown campus. When

George entered in 1966 male students still wore coats and ties to class and more than 900 of his classmates were enrolled in the university's ROTC program. By the fall of 1969, the coats and ties were gone and only sixty stalwarts were left in ROTC, including George. None of his friends had stayed in the program. "It was something I did by myself," he recalled. As he walked across campus one day in uniform, a group of protesters handing out antiwar pamphlets started to shout at him. One of his closest friends circled back and flipped over a table, sending the antiwar propaganda flying.

During his senior year, George worked at a bar, attended classes sporadically, and cruised around town on his motorcycle, which he had nicknamed Brutus. He scored mostly C's and D's, but figured his grades didn't matter. When he was done with college he'd almost certainly be off to Vietnam, where his father was already on his second tour. George promised Sheila, the tall, pretty girl from Immaculata College he had started dating his junior year, that he wasn't going to be a career soldier like his dad. After his required four-year hitch, he planned on attending law school.

In April 1970, his dad came home from Vietnam to see his family before taking command of the 1st Air Cav. His new assignment meant a promotion. On April 30, he pinned on the second star of a major general at a promotion ceremony at the Pentagon. That evening, the Caseys hosted a party at their house to celebrate. The guests were mostly other middle-aged officers and their wives, but George stopped by with a few of his college buddies. They stayed in the kitchen at first, drinking beers and watching the older guests through the doorway to the living room. An oil painting of West Point's granite chapel hung on the wall.

It was the same night that Nixon announced the invasion of Cambodia in a speech from the Oval Office, and when the address began, everyone clustered around the tiny television set. Only ten days earlier, Nixon had announced he was pulling an additional 150,000 troops out of Vietnam, on top of the 100,000 already due to come home. Now standing before a gigantic map of Southeast Asia, he declared that he was widening the war to attack staging areas in Cambodia used by the North Vietnamese to funnel supplies into the south. It was an angry, deceptive speech that portrayed the United States as violating Cambodian neutrality with great reluctance and only in a supporting role to South Vietnamese troops already flowing across the border. He didn't mention the secret bombing campaign that had already been under way for months. The speech, however, was about more than just Vietnam and Cambodia; Nixon tried in his maudlin way to address the dark mood that had taken over the country.

"My fellow Americans, we live in an age of anarchy, both abroad and at home," he began. "We see mindless attacks on all the great institutions which have been created by free civilizations in the last 500 years. Even here in the United States, great universities are being systematically destroyed. Small nations all over the world find themselves under attack from within and from without. If when the chips are down the world's most powerful nation, the United States of America, acts like a pitiful, helpless giant, the forces of totalitarianism and anarchy will threaten free nations and free institutions throughout the world."

The president's words drew a cheer from the military men around the television set who believed they were finally striking back at the enemy's supply lines across the border in Cambodia. Nixon didn't say so, but everyone at the Casey house knew it was the 1st Air Cav, the Army division that George Casey Sr. would take command of when he returned to the war, that was spearheading the attack into the "Parrot's Beak," an area along the South Vietnam–Cambodia border only thirty-three miles from Saigon. Nixon's gambit might have pleased the military men, but George's college friends were disgusted. He was expanding the war that they all hated only weeks after announcing a drawdown of troops. George's friends began to argue with the elder Casey, insisting that Vietnam was lost and the invasion would only lead to more deaths. The Caseys' teenage daughter Winn, who was sitting at her father's feet as the argument grew louder and more emotional, ran to her room and slammed the door. After a few minutes, her father walked upstairs to check on her.

"How could those people talk to you like that?" she sobbed.

"Those boys stand to lose their lives if they go to Vietnam," he replied. "They are entitled to their opinions."

George had become expert at navigating the middle ground between his Georgetown friends and his family. He generally supported the war, but he wasn't the kind of person to get in arguments or begrudge his friends their opinions. Neither was his dad. One of the reasons the younger Casey had invited his friends to the promotion party was that he wanted them to meet a soldier who believed in the war yet did not consider opposition to it an act of treason. He also wanted his father, who had spent most of the last three years at war, to meet his friends.

In the days after the speech college campuses around the country exploded. ROTC buildings were attacked or burned. At Kent State University, a unit of Ohio National Guard soldiers opened fire on a crowd of students, killing four of them. At Georgetown, like most colleges, there were protests and violence, and the school responded by canceling final exams. Amid this tumult George's family said goodbye to his father, who was heading back to Vietnam. On a warm spring day George, his mother, and his father climbed into the family's Mustang convertible for the hour drive to the airport. In the car with the top down and the wind whipping their hair, George broke the news that he had asked Sheila to marry him. Mrs. Casey and George's two youngest sisters were going to move to the Philippines later that summer to be closer to his father. So they were planning on having the wedding in mid-June, before his family left for Asia.

George and his mother walked his dad to the gate at Baltimore-Washington International Airport, hugged him one last time, and then watched as he disappeared down the carpeted ramp to his plane. "You've done this so much that it must get easier," George said, turning to his mom. His mother, who had always remained stoic for her children when their father was heading out to war, for once didn't bother to disguise her anguish. "No," she replied. "It just gets harder."

✳   ✳   ✳   ✳

A little more than two months after the elder Casey returned to Vietnam his family got the news that his helicopter was missing. On July 11, arriving for the lunch shift at the Capitol Hill saloon where he was tending bar that summer, George noticed his father's picture on the front page of the *Washington Post*. He didn't need to read the story. Although no one had called him to deliver the news, he knew what the article said. They had found the wreckage and his father was dead.

George met the casket at Dover Air Force Base in Delaware and escorted it to Washington. On July 23, 1970, his father was buried with full military honors. The day began with a funeral mass at Holy Trinity Church in Georgetown. The elder Casey was one of the highest-ranking soldiers to die in Vietnam, and much of official Washington was there. George junior, wearing the gold bars of a second lieutenant on his shoulders, read a Bible verse before nearly a thousand mourners packed into the pews, among them senators, congressmen, generals, admirals, and a personal representative sent by Nixon. "Perhaps it is fitting, if this illustrious commander had to die on the field of battle," said General Lemnitzer, the former chairman of the Joint Chiefs, in the eulogy, "that his final mission was to visit the wounded and hospitalized soldiers of his division. Such was the man, General George Casey."

As the funeral party gathered at Fort Myer's Old Post Chapel, adjoining Arlington National Cemetery, a summer storm sent generals in their blue dress uniforms and white gloves scurrying for cover. The pallbearers were all generals, five of them former 1st Cavalry Division commanders. The procession moved through the stone gate into the cemetery, and George junior, his mother, and his four siblings walked behind the flag-draped casket. Ahead of them, a soldier led a black stallion, its saddle empty except for the cavalry boots inserted backward in the stirrups. At the grave site they huddled under a small canvas canopy as a military band played taps. As he stood saluting, Casey's raised elbow poked out from beneath the tent and water sluiced down his arm onto his pants leg and shiny black shoes. After the funeral the guests gathered at Quarters One, the brick mansion where General William Westmoreland, the Army chief of staff, lived. The house was set on a sloping hill at the intersection of Grant and Washington avenues, with the cemetery off on the right and the marble monuments of Washington spread out in the distance. The graying general, a World War II hero who had commanded U.S. forces in Vietnam until the setbacks of 1968 had led to his reassignment back to the States, circulated among the guests, making small talk. To Sheila, who had grown up outside New York City in a family with no connection to the military, this world of funerals and generals that she had entered by marrying George seemed alien and scary. She retreated to the house's sun porch, away from the bustle. A few days later the Caseys visited Westmoreland's sprawling Pentagon office, where the general presented George with his father's framed medals.

In the space of just a month or so George had graduated from college, married Sheila, buried his father, and received his commission. His family dealt with the loss in different ways. After the funeral his sisters unpacked their belongings, which had already been loaded into shipping crates bound for the Philippines, and moved back into the Arlington home. Winn, who had been planning to go to college in Boston, stayed with her mother and commuted to nearby Mount Vernon College, a two-year girls' school. Later she recalled hearing her mother quietly sobbing in her bedroom at night. George's life seemed the least disrupted, outwardly anyway. He reported as planned for six months of training in Fort Benning, and then he and Sheila shipped off to Germany, where Casey had been assigned to an airborne infantry brigade.

✳ ✳ ✳ ✳

Sierra Nevada Range
June 1969

After three days of battling a low-grade forest fire, John Abizaid's thin face was streaked with soot and dirt. His crew boss called him over. "We've got to get you to a phone right away," he said. "Your dad wants to talk with you about West Point." Abizaid wasn't sure what that meant. He had applied months earlier to the United States Military Academy but hadn't been accepted. He was planning to go to the University of Idaho on a Navy ROTC scholarship. When he finally reached the nearest pay phone, an hour away in Las Vegas, his father told him that there was a spot for him at West Point if he could get there in three days. Abizaid had always been a long shot. His high school, which had only twenty-four students in the senior class, wasn't especially demanding and his SAT math scores were low. But the Vietnam War had sapped interest in the military academy at the exact moment that the Army decided it needed more cadets to fill the quotas for Vietnam. Abizaid hung up the phone and hopped on the first bus he could find headed in the direction of the small house that he shared with his widowed father and sister in the tiny California town of Coleville, six hours away.

The next morning he and his high school principal, who had agreed to accompany him across the country, boarded a plane in Reno bound for New York City. It was the first time in as long as anyone could remember that someone from Coleville was going to West Point, and the first time Abizaid had been east of Montana.

His father was a mechanic whose family had immigrated to the United States from Lebanon in the 1870s. John's mother died of cancer when he was eleven. Shortly after her death, the elder Abizaid, who suffered from often crippling bouts of emphysema, moved the family from the lower-middle-class neighborhood of Redwood City, near San Francisco, to Coleville, a town of cinder-block buildings at the base of the snowcapped Sierra Nevada. The doctors thought the dry air would be good for his health. Some days his coughing fits became so severe he seemed in danger of suffocating. At age sixteen, John rushed him to the hospital in Reno, a two-hour drive over the mountains, where the doctors drained fluid from his lungs and told him to prepare for the worst. His father survived, but his condition was a constant worry.

The highlight of the elder Abizaid's life had been World War II, when he served as a machinist on Navy ships chasing German subs in the Caribbean and patrolling the South Pacific. Abizaid loved his father's stories about surviving a hurricane while on submarine escort duty and searching small Pacific islands for Japanese troops. He was impressed by the camaraderie and the sense of purpose in the military; before the men went ashore in small reconnaissance parties they made a pact to fight to the death. Among his fellow students at Coleville High, whose fathers worked as alfalfa farmers and sheep ranchers, Abizaid stood out for the scale of his ambitions. In geography class he drew imaginary countries and labeled them "Abizaidland." He quarterbacked the high school's eight-man football team, earned good grades, served as student council president, and began dating his future wife, Kathy, the dark-haired daughter of the local district attorney. Everyone knew he wanted to be a soldier, even if that meant shipping off to Vietnam. Whenever he got the chance he would talk to soldiers from the area home on leave. One fall evening during his senior year he spotted a sergeant with a 101st Airborne Screaming Eagles combat patch on his uniform in the stands at one of his football games. After the game, Abizaid's father thanked the sergeant for his service, and then Abizaid quizzed him: Where had he fought in Vietnam? What was it like? Why had he joined the Army? By the late 1960s Abizaid's father had become deeply disillusioned with the war, arguing heatedly to his American Legion friends that sparing the tiny nation from Communist rule wasn't worth the cost. His eldest son disagreed. But it wasn't Vietnam that drew him to the military; it was the opportunity to get out of Coleville.

Abizaid's Coleville education had left him woefully behind most of his West Point classmates in math and science. He finished his first year ranked 228th out of 1,206 cadets but each year managed to raise his standing, and by his last year he was third in his class. West Point opened new worlds for him. His favorite professor at the school was a twenty-six-year-old Army captain named Michael Krause who had earned a doctorate in history from Georgetown University and served a year as a combat advisor in Vietnam. Krause spoke fluent French and German, quoted Franz Kafka, and had the German diplomatic records of World War I in his personal library. When he learned that Abizaid had taken correspondence courses in German throughout high school, he set him to work combing through the documents for a research paper. Abizaid's final work relied heavily on arcane diplomatic cables from German ambassadors to Berlin and concluded that the Allies had missed opportunities in Bosnia to curb German aggression prior to World War I. Krause remembered it as the best undergraduate work he saw at West Point.

Compared with the other straight-backed cadets, Abizaid was short and even a bit slump-shouldered. But he had an easygoing swagger and didn't take West Point or the Army too seriously. After their first year the cadets were sent out on night patrols in the forest near campus to hunt for a guerrilla force played by Army sergeants. The exercises had been developed by General Westmoreland in the mid-1960s when he was superintendent and the Vietnam War was just beginning to ensnare the Army. Westmoreland had grandly dubbed the exercise "Recondo," a hybrid of reconnaissance and commando. The training, however, didn't live up to its inflated moniker. To the twenty-year-old Abizaid it seemed like little more than blundering around in the forest at night, something he had done regularly back home.

Midway through a monotonous patrol, he slipped away from his group and fired a volley of blanks from his M-16 into the air. The burst of fire sent his fellow cadets scrambling in all directions. Sergeants, who were leading the training, screamed at them to take cover in a dark thicket of bushes. Abizaid emerged from the darkness, flopping down next to his best friend Karl Eikenberry, and told him with a big grin that he had ambushed his own patrol.

When Abizaid arrived at West Point, his hope was to graduate and be sent to Vietnam. Four years later, it looked like the closest he would get was the silly "Recondo" training. The Army that he saw as his ticket to something bigger was now seen by most of his generation as either a last resort for people without options or a symbol of everything that was wrong with the United States. Nowhere was that more clear than at away football games, where Abizaid's company was in charge of the color guard. Before marching onto the field for a game against Boston College he and his fellow cadets conducted drills on how to protect the flag in case fans from the opposing team tried to grab it. As they filed into the stadium prior to the game, the cadets clustered around the colors in a tight knot, pointing the bayonets on their unloaded rifles outward, just as they had practiced. No one tried to take their flag. Instead, the rowdy and intoxicated crowd greeted them with chants of *"Sieg heil."*

✶   ✶   ✶   ✶

Seattle, Washington
1970

The telephone calls came late at night and never lasted more than a few seconds. On the line was an Army officer from Seattle University's ROTC department informing Pete Chiarelli which of three secret locations to show up at the following morning for drill. The department had adopted the procedure after getting anonymous threats that cadets marching in their uniforms on the campus athletic field would be firebombed, and at the time it didn't seem so far-fetched. Some days the downtown campus was literally ablaze in antiwar protests. In January, a bomb went off outside the Liberal Arts Building, where Chiarelli took many of his classes. In March, someone set fire to Xavier Hall the same day Barry Goldwater was scheduled to give a campus speech. After the Cambodia invasion in April, more than a thousand protesters marched in downtown Seattle, the first of several large and at times violent protests that spring that drew students from Seattle University, the University of Washington, and other schools. The ROTC programs seemed a likely target of the city's most radical protesters.

In the spring of 1970, Chiarelli was finishing his sophomore year, commuting to school every day from his parents' house in the hilly Seattle neighborhood of Magnolia. He would arrive before dark in his uniform and march for an hour before changing into civilian clothes for class. He had friends who joined the protests, but that wasn't for Pete. He supported the war and may have been the only student on campus who was disappointed when his draft number came in that year at 247, too high to have to worry about being sent to Vietnam. "I was just praying for a low number so I could justify to all my friends why I was still in," he would say later. Some ROTC cadets quit the program when they received high numbers and they no longer had to worry about the draft, but Pete actually enjoyed ROTC, especially the grueling summer training when cadets reported to Fort Lewis, the big Army base near Seattle. When he wasn't training that summer, Chiarelli drove down to Portland to see Beth Kirby, a Seattle University classmate he was dating.

He had wanted to enlist in the Army after graduating from high school in 1968 and go to Vietnam, but his father had vetoed the idea, insisting on college first. "If you're going to go into the Army, that's fine, but I want you to go in as an officer," he told his son. The son of Italian immigrants, Pete Chiarelli (he and his only son shared the same first name) served in a tank battalion in the Army's 3rd Infantry Division, which fought its way across North Africa, Italy, and northern France, and finally into Germany. In 1945 he won a Silver Star for helping to remove a stuck tank under enemy fire. His ability to speak Italian and his heroism helped him secure a battlefield commission as an officer even though he never attended college. After the war, his life went the way of many citizen soldiers of that era: he got married, went back to his old job at Serv-U-Meat, a commercial butcher downtown, and raised a family. He kept his framed Silver Star citation in a closet along with a picture of himself posing atop his tank, and rarely talked about his three years fighting across Europe. Anyone who really knew him realized that the war had been the adventure of his life. In his father's later years, Pete bought him journals and tried unsuccessfully to get him to write about his experiences in Africa and Europe while he was watching Mariners games on television.

Still, the Army remained a big part of his father's life. The elder Chiarelli and his wife, Theresa, played bingo on Wednesday night at Fort Lawton on Puget Sound, and they socialized at the officers' club. An Army reservist, he spent two weeks every summer drilling at the Presidio Army base in San Francisco, sometimes packing the whole family into the car and turning it into a vacation. On one of their summer jaunts, they stopped at a ranch in northern California to visit with the parents of a soldier from his dad's small tank crew. They had fought across Europe together. In the waning days of the war the young soldier was riding with his head sticking out of the turret and was shot in the head by a German riding past on a bicycle. The war was long over, but his dad wanted to say a few words to the parents about their son and how he had died. Pete's hazy memories of the trip stuck with him for decades. His father's rarely discussed wartime experiences seemed secret and exciting—especially when compared with his life as a butcher in Seattle. Rummaging in the garage one day as a teenager, he came across a yellowed clipping from the local newspaper about his dad winning the Silver Star during action in Germany. As he pored over the account, one paragraph brought him up short: his mother's name was wrong. The yellowed newspaper said that his father had been "married to Dorothy Chiarelli."

The sixteen-year-old Chiarelli bounded back into the house to confront his father: "Dad, this is not Mom! Who is this?" The elder Chiarelli revealed that he had been married to another woman before the war. When he came back to the United States his twin brother broke the news to him that Dorothy was living with another man in Seattle. Pete's mother, Theresa, who was Canadian by birth, had also had her own wartime heartbreak. She had been engaged to a Canadian Air Force pilot who was shot down over northern France in 1944.

By the time Pete Chiarelli graduated from Seattle University in 1972, few young officers were going to Vietnam. The Army was coming home, and American involvement would soon be over. Although he was a mediocre student, Chiarelli had impressed the officers in charge of the ROTC program, winning an award as the Distinguished Military Graduate of the program that year. With Vietnam winding down, his interest in the Army had lessened. He owed the Army four years in return for his ROTC scholarship, but Pete thought he wanted to become a lawyer. He applied to law school at the University of Washington but was rejected. Never good at standardized tests, Chiarelli scored poorly on the admission exam, despite three attempts. Crestfallen, he shifted course. He and Beth married in August and the next month they loaded his Chevy Camaro and headed to the Army's armor school at Fort Knox, Kentucky. Chiarelli spent the next three months learning to be a tank commander, just as his father had been.

✻ ✻ ✻ ✻

Cornwall-on-Hudson, New York
1970

As a kid Dave Petraeus used to sneak onto the West Point campus with his friends during the summer and play on the lush athletic fields until someone came along and ordered them off. In winter, he and his friends went skiing on the West Point slopes. His hometown, six miles away, was full of West Point professors and Army families. Reamer Argot, the son of an officer who lived near the Petraeuses' modest Cape Cod home, remembered Dave as the "alpha dog," the kid who led the pack of neighborhood boys and was usually up for anything. Several of his teachers at Cornwall High School were retired West Point instructors and now formed an informal recruiting network, steering local teenagers with the stuff to handle the rigors of cadet life to West Point. They urged Petraeus, a star on the school's championship soccer team and a top-notch student, to seek an appointment.

A wiry 150 pounds, Petraeus barely looked old enough to be out of junior high school. His family had no ties to the Army. His father, Sixtus Petraeus, a Dutch seaman until World War II, when he emigrated to the United States, worked for the local power company. His mother, who had attended Oberlin College, was uncertain about sending her only son into the Army with the Vietnam War still under way. But when West Point became one of the few colleges to recruit him to play soccer, Petraeus decided to give it a try. The full scholarship was attractive to a family of limited means, and if he didn't like it, he could always transfer before his junior year without owing the Army anything. He made the drive with his parents to the academy in late June and said goodbye, plunging into the chaos of Beast Barracks, the eight-week hazing ordeal plebes are subjected to before classes even start. Dave didn't have much trouble. He was meticulous and serious, the kind of cadet who knew a lot of the tricks for making life slightly more bearable, like where to send away for anodized brass uniform buttons and belt buckles that would keep their shine indefinitely—sparing you a few minutes of late-night polishing and maybe the unwanted attention from some upperclassman bracing you for not having gleaming buttons.

He did well during his plebe year but not spectacularly, earning a class rank of 161st out of more than 800 classmates. "I thought, 'Okay, he's like me, an A or B student,' " recalled Dave Buto, one of his plebe-year roommates. "But his second year he took off." Petraeus raised his class rank into the sixties. He gravitated toward others like him—hypercompetitive guys who enjoyed pushing each other to do better. At West Point, where cadets were ranked, graded, and assessed every day of their four years, he was in his element. The first time he went for a run around campus with his roommate, Chris White, they started out at a moderate jog, but the pace kept increasing, until after about five miles both of them were running flat out, neither wanting to admit he could not keep up. They finally pulled up outside the dormitory, panting and exhausted. "You're insane. I'm never running with you again," White said, more than a little serious. "I wanted to slow down, but you kept speeding up," Petraeus answered, grinning.

Petraeus wanted to go even faster. White told him that the Army paid to send the eight top graduates of the military academy every year to medical school on scholarship. His roommate was going for it, so Petraeus decided he would, too. Not because he had decided he wanted to be a doctor, but because aiming for the top appealed to him. It was even more exclusive than being a "Star Man," a cadet who was entitled to wear a small star on his collar for finishing in the top 5 percent of his class. Though room assignments rotated every three months, Petraeus and White received permission to be roommates several times during their second and third years. Almost every night they requested "late lights," permission to stay up an hour past the ten o' clock curfew, so they could study an hour longer before racking out. Petraeus made every second count. He persuaded his roommate to stop taking showers before bed, arguing it was more efficient to get up a few minutes early than to waste precious study time at night. When he got tired, Petraeus walked in circles in his dorm room to prevent himself from falling asleep.

He made a perfunctory call that spring to another nearby college to see if they were interested in offering him an athletic scholarship, but by then he had pretty much decided to stay on at West Point. As time went on, other cadets noticed that Petraeus became more and more serious about all aspects of cadet life—academics, military training, and the little details that separated the guys who were intent on excelling from those who resented the academy's tyrannies and just wanted to make it through.

As firsties (as seniors are called at West Point), cadets pick classmates to write a few words summing up their four years at West Point for the yearbook. Petraeus asked Chris White to compose his. "Peaches came to the Mil Acad with high ambitions," White wrote, using the nickname Petraeus had acquired as a kid and brought with him to West Point. "Unlike most he accomplished his goals. Dave was always 'going for it' in sports, academics, leadership, and even in his social life. This attitude will surely lead to success in the future, Army or otherwise." The reference to his social life was as an inside joke. Petraeus was dating Holly Knowlton, the daughter of the West Point superintendent, Lieutenant General William Knowlton. They had met on a blind date, attending a Saturday football game. She was pretty and smart and in her own way just as driven as Dave. "This is the girl you are going to marry," John Edgecomb, a fellow cadet, recalled telling Petraeus. A senior at Dickinson College, Holly was fluent in French and finishing her honors dissertation on the novelist François Mauriac. It was a whirlwind romance. By second semester, Dave and Holly were often seen on the campus tennis courts or driving around town in the superintendent's car.

By then he had abandoned his plans for medical school. He had done well enough to become a Star Man, finishing forty-third in his class, and was intent on becoming an infantryman. In his usual way he had picked the most demanding path. In May 1974, a few days before graduation, he and the rest of his class filed into South Auditorium. Each cadet stood and announced which branch of the service he was entering. Those at the top of the class had their pick, and called out "engineers" or "artillery" or "aviation" or "armor." Since Vietnam, the popularity of the infantry, the branch that did the most fighting and dying in Southeast Asia, had plummeted, and even with the Army gone from Vietnam it had not recovered. (For a class motto, one of the suggestions had been "No More War '74," but the class settled on the more patriotic "Pride of the Corps '74.") When Petraeus's turn came, forty-three of his classmates already had declared their branch selections. Only one had chosen the infantry. Petraeus became the second, and when he announced his choice an admiring cheer went up from the ranks. To young men who had been told since they entered Thayer Gate four years earlier that their job was to prepare to lead men in combat, anyone who went into the infantry voluntarily was worthy of special recognition. A few weeks later Petraeus received his commission as a second lieutenant and married Holly in the West Point Chapel. At the reception afterward, the young couple and their guests cruised up the Hudson River on the superintendent's yacht, basking in the early-summer twilight.

✳   ✳   ✳   ✳

Mainz, West Germany
1971

Lieutenant George Casey arrived at his first Army post carrying his father's dress blue uniform in his bags, along with the flag that had covered the casket. He was in that respect not that different from the entire Army, which was coming home from Vietnam broken and defeated. His new home, a U.S. base on the west bank of the Rhine River, was populated mostly by green officers like himself or soldiers recently back from the war, short-timers finishing the last six months of their enlistments. Sergeants and other noncommissioned officers, critical to maintaining order among the troops, were retiring in droves, exhausted by the repeated deployments. Casey's first platoon was supposed to have thirty-five soldiers. Instead it had nine, and he soon discovered four of them had heroin problems.

A few months after he arrived, a gang of soldiers tore through the enlisted barracks beating their fellow soldiers with heavy chains, sending several to the hospital. Later a senior sergeant was shot by one of his own men in front of the post exchange. The base commander responded by ordering the lieutenants to guard their own men. Casey sat in the barracks from 9:00 p.m. to 3:00 a.m. two times each week with a loaded .45-caliber pistol on his lap until his soldiers returned from a night of drinking, drugs, and brawling in Mainz. When his shift was over he headed to the small apartment he shared with Sheila, grabbed a snack and a quick nap, and then head back to the base for 5:30 a.m. calisthenics.

Officers around him were regularly relieved of their command. In the space of a year, Casey's battalion commander and three of the four company commanders in his unit were fired for incompetence or abusing their troops. The other battalions were just as bad, if not worse: "The price of Vietnam has been a terrible one. In terms of casualties, in terms of national treasure of both men and dollars that have been spent," said General Michael Davison, the commander of the U.S. Seventh Army in Germany. "We had to wreck the Seventh Army in order to keep Vietnam going."

Sheila hated military life in Germany. Her husband was constantly gone, either babysitting his troubled troops in the barracks or drilling with them in the field. Just as irritating was the 1950s-like formality. The base commander's wife bossed her and the other spouses around as if she were a colonel herself, assigning them to shifts in the base thrift store. "I hope you can look back on your time here as your best assignment in the army," the woman told George and Sheila one evening at a mandatory cocktail party.

"If that is true, we are out of here now," she whispered to her husband.

Amid the chaos, Casey excelled. His platoon was rated the best of more than seventy in his division in field tests where troops conducted mock attacks and fended off ambushes. His soldiers loved him. He was quiet, confident, and steady. Because he had grown up in the Army, he knew instinctively how to relate to troops. His platoon sergeant, Ed Charo, had returned from a tour in Vietnam angry and frustrated. "Vietnam ruined me because of what I saw wrong there. There was no loyalty. The officers were all in it for themselves and didn't care about their men," he recalled. "They treated their NCOs like dirt." Charo concluded that Casey was different. He questioned his platoon sergeant relentlessly about what he'd learned in combat and even invited him over for Sunday dinner with Sheila and their infant son. He urged Charo, a demanding taskmaster, to lighten up on the troops. The end of the draft meant that the Army was converting to an all-volunteer force, and many of the recruits who joined in those years did so because they couldn't get other jobs. Most had little interest in staying in the military.

"He was the first officer who treated me with respect and took me into his home," Charo recalled. "I asked him to be my daughter's godfather and he agreed to do it. What officer would do that for an enlisted man?"

In 1973, Casey and a handful of other high-performing officers in Germany were chosen to lead a newly formed airborne battalion in Italy. Although he hoped Sheila might like their new post better, he assured her that he wasn't interested in making the Army a long-term career. Sheila, however, could tell that he loved being a soldier and had no plans to leave the service. At boozy formal dinners, Casey was usually at the center of the hijinks. He'd push aside the dinner tables and organize raucous indoor rugby games with his peers. At one such game he was running through the dining hall with the rugby ball when a fellow officer tackled him and the two men went flying through a first-story window. Casey, cut and bruised, returned to the fray.

He rarely talked about his father and bristled when fellow officers referred to him as "General Casey's son." When a friend introduced him that way once, he snapped, "Don't ever call me that again." In 1973, Lieutenant Joseph Tallman, whose father, also a general, had been killed in Vietnam only a few months earlier, joined the battalion. Unlike Casey, Tallman had been a superstar in college, finishing as the top cadet in his West Point class. But he struggled in the real Army, disgusted with the low standards, second-rate equipment, and poorly motivated troops. Casey figured he might be able to help the young lieutenant deal with his loss.

The two soon realized that they had little in common. To Tallman everything about Army life seemed to drive home the injustice of his father's death a year earlier. Casey was just the opposite. For him the military had become a comfortable refuge from his family's tragedy. One evening after dinner at Casey's apartment, Tallman recalled watching Casey set his young son atop the refrigerator in the kitchen. The toddler, at his father's prodding, yelled, "Airborne!" and then launched himself like a paratrooper into his father's outstretched arms. "It was like George had shut the door on his father's death and it was gone," Tallman recalled. "He didn't dwell on it at all."

In 1974, Casey finished first in his class at Ranger School, a grueling eight-week hell of mock attacks and all-night marches on minimal rations in the forests, mountains, and swamps of Georgia and Florida. Many young officers go through the ordeal shortly after getting their commissions, claiming the coveted black and gold Ranger patch to prove their toughness. Casey initially had passed on it, figuring that since he wasn't going to make a career of the Army, there was no point in putting himself through the agony. But there was a culture of competitiveness in the Army, and even an easygoing guy like Casey could not escape it. So there he was, one of the older guys at the course and sore all over, but he had proven something to himself. When he put his mind to it, he was a damn good soldier.

One day near the end the course he was on the phone with his mom when she mentioned that there was a new second lieutenant named Dave Petraeus getting ready to start Ranger School. Go by his quarters and introduce yourself, she asked. She had been talking to his mother-in-law, Peggy Knowlton, who had mentioned that her daughter Holly had just married this young West Point graduate. After the course, he was headed off to the 509th Parachute Infantry Battalion in Italy, the same unit George had just left. As a favor to her, Casey tracked him down and they chatted for a few minutes about Vicenza and the Ranger course. Like Casey, Petraeus was on his way to finishing first in his class. Casey handed Petraeus a few 509th patches for his uniform and wished him luck.

Their careers would intersect repeatedly over the next thirty years, but they could not have been more different. Petraeus was always the striver who saw the Army as a summit to be conquered and the stars of a general as the ultimate prize. His fellow officers often saw him as distant and calculating. Casey was content to be a good solid officer. After Ranger School he headed off to Colorado to be an assistant logistics officer in a mechanized infantry battalion, about as unglamorous an assignment as you could find.

✯   ✯   ✯   ✯

Fort Carson, Colorado
1977

Casey was out in the field training his company in a mountainous section of Fort Carson in Colorado when his first sergeant said he had an urgent call. Casey took the call in a nearby shack. "You've been selected for a mission with the highest national priority," said the voice at the other end of the line. "I need to know if you want to do it."

"What is it?" Casey asked.

"I can't tell you over the phone," the voice said.

A buddy of Casey's had recently been selected to try out for the new counterterrorist unit, dubbed Delta Force, and he quickly figured out that he was getting a shot as well. Before he agreed to go he said he had to talk with his wife about it. "I need to know by one this afternoon," the voice replied. He phoned Sheila and described the curious call. He couldn't say what he was getting into, mainly because he didn't know for sure himself, but it was unmistakably something new and different. "I need to go do this," he told her. She could tell there was little use in trying to talk him out of going.

The chance to join Delta had not come as much out of the blue as it appeared. A few weeks earlier Lufthansa flight 181, bound for Frankfurt and full of German tourists heading home from Majorca, had been hijacked by four Palestinian terrorists. Four days later, after the plane landed at Mogadishu, Somalia, and the hijackers tossed the pilot's lifeless body onto the tarmac, a German counterterrorism unit, called Grenzschutzgruppe 9, stormed the aircraft. The operation was a miraculous success. Three hijackers were killed and the fourth was captured. Except for a few minor injuries, all eighty-six passengers escaped unscathed. In Washington, President Jimmy Carter sent a note to the Pentagon asking if it had a counterterrorist force like the Germans had. At the time an Army colonel named Charlie Beckwith was attempting to start up just such a unit, but he had been getting a lukewarm response from the Pentagon bureaucracy. President Carter's note kicked the effort into high gear. Beckwith told the Army chief of staff that his top priority was finding the right soldiers. That led him to Casey, who had impressed his superiors with his toughness.

Delta Force was the Army's attempt to come to grips with the new threat of international terrorism. In the Middle East and other volatile regions, political extremists were increasingly exploiting the shock value of televised terror. Airliner hijackings and bombings in the airports and nightclubs of Europe were happening with frightening regularity. How this threat would expand in coming decades was hard to discern, but the unit that Beckwith was assembling revealed how the Army saw the problem. Delta Force was to be a small, top-secret team that would rely on speed and stealth instead of mass and firepower. The unstated assumption was that terrorism did not pose a fundamental danger to the country. It could be handled by a small band of commandos who trained relentlessly in the special techniques of rescuing hostages and killing terrorists.

Casey reported to Fort Bragg in North Carolina in late November, one of just over a hundred soldiers invited to compete for a handful of slots in the new unit. They had been told to assemble at the base stockade, which had been cleared of prisoners and turned into a makeshift headquarters and barracks. For the first few days they slept in the empty prison cells, a fitting indicator of how they would be treated during the two-week selection process. As he looked around, Casey realized that he knew almost none of the other candidates. This was a Special Forces show, and Casey sensed that the SF officers were cutting each other slack.

Beckwith had spent a year as an exchange officer training in the jungles of Malaya with the Special Air Service, Britain's elite commando unit.

Later he commanded an elite reconnaissance unit in Vietnam that spent weeks tracking enemy guerrillas in the remotest parts of the jungle. He inflicted the same hunger, fear, and confusion that he'd felt training with the British commandos and in Vietnam on the men vying for a spot in his new unit. Beckwith began the ordeal with characteristic stealth. Most of the first week was spent on basic conditioning drills and psychiatric testing. Then the instructors announced they were starting the "stress phase." Casey was told to pack a rucksack weighing at least forty pounds and climb onto a truck with a dozen others and drive deep into Uwharrie Mountains National Forest, in rural North Carolina. Once there, he was handed a map and an AK-47 rifle and told to wait at the edge of a nearby clearing for instructions on what to do next. An instructor gave Casey an eight-digit coordinate and told him to hike there as quickly as he could. "Do not use any roads or trails," the instructor told him. "You are being judged against an unannounced time standard."

Some days Casey and the other soldiers started before dawn and went until sundown, hitting a half-dozen rendezvous points on the map. Another instructor, bearing new map coordinates, met them at each stop. "Show me where you are and show me where you are going," the instructor directed. Then he would tell them to hike as fast as they could. One day, exhausted and confused by a fold in the map, Casey accidentally started running along the wrong creek. When the brush on either side of the creek became too thick to navigate, he began marching through the water. After about thirty minutes he stumbled onto a nearby road and flagged down a farmer passing by in a pickup truck. His uniform was soaked, his face was scratched and bleeding, and the butt of his AK-47 rifle had broken when he fell. As Casey asked for directions, the farmer stared at him in disbelief. "Boy, you is really lost," he said. A few hours later the instructors saw Casey running in the woods and drove him back to the camp. Each day in the forest he was told to add a few more rocks to his rucksack. Each day a few more soldiers quit or were sent home.

On the last day of the tryouts the pack weighed fifty-five pounds. He and his fellow troops woke at 3:30 a.m. for a forty-mile hike through the wilderness. A few miles into the march Casey's feet began to throb and swell. To prevent blisters he had been slathering tincture of benzoin, a toughening agent, on his feet. Now he was pretty sure the medicine was causing an allergic reaction. For twelve hours he walked, stopping only to cut the back of his boot off in an effort to relieve the pressure on his Achilles tendon. As he grew more fatigued he began screaming at himself not to give up: "You pussy! You pussy! Keep going, goddamn it, you pussy!"

When he finished the hike his feet looked like raw hamburger. Back in the stockade and thoroughly exhausted, he phoned Sheila to let her know he had made it. Fewer than 20 of the 100 men who tried out survived the ten-day course. Soldiers in Delta would be gone for weeks or even months on secretive, dangerous missions. "Join Delta and we'll guarantee you a medal, a body bag, or both," Beckwith told the recruits. Casey had promised his wife when he left for the tryouts that he was doing it just to test himself; he wouldn't join up. After he was chosen he started wavering. Sheila bluntly told her husband that she couldn't live with the uncertainty. The first Army ceremony she had ever attended was her father-in-law's funeral, and the image from that day of Casey's grieving mother, a forty-two-year-old widow with five children standing in the pouring rain, had never left her. Now that she and George had two young boys, it was even harder to shake. "It is one thing getting hit by a bus crossing the street," she blurted out to him over the phone. "It is another thing to get hit while standing in the middle of the road." Casey badly wanted to accept the spot in Delta, but not at the expense of his marriage. He hung up the phone and informed the Delta officers that he was bowing out. He returned to Fort Carson to the sleepy unit that was at the bottom of virtually all of the Army's war plans. Beckwith, not one to hand out compliments to those who declined tough assignments, pulled Casey aside before he departed to offer some words of reassurance. "You are going a long way in this man's Army," he told him.

✷ ✷ ✷ ✷

The Army had a long way to go. It was still trying to pull itself out of its post-Vietnam nadir. The bedlam Casey had seen in Germany had been replaced by a mania for discipline that was nearly as crippling. Sometimes he'd grab a seat at the back of the theater at Fort Carson and watch the generals grill the lieutenant colonels on how many rules infractions each unit had accumulated that month. Commanders reeled off the statistics, detailing every AWOL, insubordination, and drug infraction. Meanwhile, the Army was burying the memory of Vietnam as much as possible. It removed virtually all of its war college classes on counterinsurgency warfare from the curriculum. Field exercises modeled after Vietnam were jettisoned as well. Instead it focused on preparing to fight an enemy it knew—the Soviet Union.

Even at that type of warfare, the Army wasn't very good. At the National Training Center, a 1,000-square-mile training ground in the Mojave Desert, tanks and artillery cannons faced off in laser-tag battles against a mock enemy meant to resemble the Soviet army. After each fight, the soldiers who ran the training center critiqued the visiting units. In his first test, Casey quickly realized that he and his raw troops had no idea what they were doing. Casey, riding with the senior intelligence officer from his unit, got hopelessly lost. The two officers tried calling for help, but their antiquated radios didn't work. After the fight, his brigade commander called the officers together and chewed them out. "You all are a bunch of dumb asses," he screamed. "That was the sorriest excuse for an attack I have ever seen." Casey agreed. "We don't know what the hell we are doing, and this has got to change," he told himself.

CHAPTER TWO

Abizaidland

Their life was the land, their families, and Allah.
Nothing could change that, and I had the distinct impression
that nothing ever would.

—JOHN ABIZAID

Amman, Jordan
Fall 1978

W ell, we have finally made it to the Hashemite Kingdom of Jordan," John Abizaid declared in a letter home on September 15, 1978. Just writing those words was exciting. At last, he and his family were where he had longed to be—in the Middle East with two years ahead of them to explore. Abizaid, whose great-grandfather was Lebanese, had been fascinated by the region since he was a cadet at West Point, but it had been a difficult journey to get there—a year in the 82nd Airborne Division, three years in the Rangers, and six months studying Arabic with his wife, Kathy, at the Defense Language Institute. The Army had to be convinced that sending one of its brightest young officers to the Middle East was worthwhile. He had won an Olmsted scholarship, which paid for a handful of officers each year to study abroad, but the seven other winners that year had all gone off to Europe—to the University of Geneva, the University of Grenoble, the University of Heidelberg, and other venerable institutions. The poster child for the program was Robert "Bud" McFarlane, a Marine artillery officer in Vietnam who had studied Cold War strategy in

Geneva and who would go on to become Reagan's national security advisor. That wasn't the path Abizaid had chosen. The last time an Olmsted Scholar had proposed going to the Middle East, it was to Hebrew University in Jerusalem. Abizaid was the first to go to an Arab country.

He had ditched his initial plan to study in Egypt when the university he contacted failed to respond to his letters seeking admission. His backup was Jordan, the impoverished kingdom in the heart of the Middle East, surrounded by wealthier and more powerful neighbors. Even with his scholarship in hand, getting there hadn't been easy. The University of Jordan had accepted him, which was better treatment than he received in Egypt, but the school seemed at best indifferent to having an American officer join its student body. The U.S. embassy discouraged him, warning about his safety and telling him it would offer him no special assistance. Kathy was pregnant with their second child and had never traveled outside of the United States. She was wary about moving to a part of the world that made news mostly for terrorist hijackings and brushfire wars. Her parents back in Coleville panicked when they learned their pregnant daughter was moving to the Middle East. "Wouldn't Germany be easier?" she wondered. It had taken a while, but Abizaid had convinced her that this could be the adventure of their lives.

The Jordanian capital, perched in the hills above the desert, was a backwater, with none of the opulent skyscrapers and elegant hotels that were beginning to appear in Baghdad, Cairo, and the oil-rich ministates of the Persian Gulf. The city had absorbed thousands of Palestinian refugees, who had come in waves across the Jordan River after the founding of Israel in 1948 and the Six-Day War in 1967. Dilapidated slums spread out into the distance. On a clear day, the city of Jerusalem could be seen to the west. Arriving in Amman ten days ahead of Kathy and their young daughter, Abizaid rented a dank basement apartment and registered for classes at the university, a short walk away. He quickly felt at ease. It took Kathy longer. When she stepped off the plane in Amman's tiny airport, the heat and the long journey from San Francisco to New York to Greece and now Jordan had left her feeling woozy. As she collected her bags in an atmosphere she would later recall as "absolute chaos," an unknown Jordanian man approached her. "I take baby now," he said, grabbing the toddler and rushing off. Kathy screamed and went running after him until the unknown man passed the child over the customs barrier to John, who was waiting with his daughter's favorite blanket.

When she saw their apartment, which John had dubbed the "Führer bunker," she cringed. They didn't have the money to live in a westernized enclave like most of the embassy staff and other American expatriates, but Kathy had been hoping for something slightly more comfortable. The basement apartment had concrete floors, no windows, and little furniture beyond two beds and an old couch. The arrival of an American family in the neighborhood created a minor sensation. Night after night neighbors appeared at their door, bearing food and offering welcomes. Kathy discovered that her months of Arabic-language training were almost useless. She could make out only bits of what her guests, who spoke an unfamiliar Jordanian dialect, were saying. She and John learned they were expected to ply them with tea, sludgelike Bedouin coffee, and frequently dinner as they discussed family, politics, and life in the United States for hours. A few weeks into their stay their American-made washing machine overflowed, flooding the apartment. Kathy was trying to contain the water when her landlady appeared for her daily visit. She pushed past her disheveled, pregnant, and obviously angry tenant, asked how everyone was doing, and began mopping up without apparent concern. "Fifteen minutes later we were sitting sipping tea as she advised me on the proper way to cook rice," Kathy wrote in a letter several weeks later. "My feelings were difficult to describe. I was irritated at the house she had rented us and her unceasing advice, but glad to have the company." This was the "Arab way of dealing with life's daily annoyances," she concluded. "One does what one can, and then turns to more important things like tea and company."

John's classes didn't commence until the second week in October, ten days later than scheduled. There was no explanation. It was just the way things worked. When Abizaid scheduled meetings with professors, they often showed up late or not at all. Keeping up with lectures conducted in Arabic was a trial, especially until he adjusted to the local dialect. "It is quite a surprise for the Arabs to see an American taking a course with them in Arabic and they will always marvel at my ability to understand what is going on in class," he said at the time. "If they were ever able to look beneath my confident expression of understanding they would see the stark terror of a student who understands much less than they think he does."

Many mornings after John left for the university, neighborhood women arrived at the apartment, offering to help Kathy with washing and cooking. They peppered her with questions: Why wasn't her mother here? How could she allow her four-year-old daughter to freeze in only a sweater? Why weren't her sisters married? "Don't worry. God will bless you with a son," they reassured her after their second daughter was born. Soon Kathy was communicating in rudimentary Arabic and teaching them English in return. "There were times when both Kathy and I would curse as our doorbell rang, yet open the door with a huge smile," Abizaid recounted in an early report to his scholarship sponsors. "Thankfully this period has now passed. We are now members of the neighborhood and very comfortable."

Even a newcomer to the Middle East, such as Abizaid, could see that the region was undergoing tumultuous change. In January 1979, as he was getting ready to begin his second semester, the shah of Iran, America's strongest ally in the area, was driven from power. The return of Ayatollah Ruhollah Khomeini to Tehran a month later marked the first successful takeover of a major Middle Eastern country by Islamists. Khomeini's ascendance unleashed a wave of political unrest across the region. In Jordan, which was ruled by King Hussein, a non-Palestinian monarch from the Hashemite tribe, the Iranian revolution revived the Palestinian nationalism long repressed by the regime's security services. Abizaid was studying in the history department one day when he looked out the window and saw demonstrators marching toward the five-story building and chanting Khomeini's name. A Jordanian friend urged him to leave, worried about what might happen if the mob found an American on campus. As Abizaid raced down the back stairs he could hear the demonstrators growing louder and angrier as they denounced the king. Another group of students, outraged at the insult, was massing to avenge his honor. Emerging from the back door, he threaded his way through the angry throng and sprinted home to find Kathy peering over the concrete wall surrounding their apartment. As Abizaid came through the front gate, a convoy of riot police in armored vehicles sped by in the direction of the university. A few minutes later they heard automatic weapons fire. The police were firing over the demonstrators' heads to break up the melee.

"Order was restored, certain activists disappeared from campus, and we completed the year in calm," Abizaid wrote, describing the episode in a letter to the American administrator of his scholarship program. "In all truthfulness experiences such as this are worth as much as classroom study."

He found his fellow students more assertive and angry, emboldened by Khomeini's rise. When sixty-six Americans were taken hostage in Tehran that November, many students skipped classes to celebrate. Almost overnight women began donning head scarves and the campus took on a more Islamic identity. Abizaid saw the signs of religious radicalization as ominous for the United States. "It was inevitable that something big was coming our way in the Middle East. You could just sense it," he recalled years later.

After registering for a course on Islamic history, he spent hours poring over the required reading—verses from the Koran, which many other students already knew by heart. By the end of the semester he had eked out a passing grade and gained deeper insight into the power of the new Islamist movement. "I cannot say that I mastered the finer points of Islamic law nor understand the historical background of certain Islamic practices today. I can only say that I now understand that Islam is much more than a religion. It is a way of life that guides Muslims in every aspect of their lives," he wrote in December 1979.

When school wasn't in session, Abizaid traveled, studying the region and its many conflicts. He and a fellow officer drove out into the Yemeni desert to watch the hit-and-run battles between the U.S.-supported North and the Soviet-backed South during that country's civil war. In Sudan, the U.S. embassy enlisted him to negotiate the return of one of its vehicles, which had been claimed by a warlord after it broke down and was abandoned on the side of the road. In the winter of 1980 he traveled with a team of U.S. diplomats and officers to a dirt airstrip at the base of a soaring desert escarpment near the Oman-Yemen border. There he met a British lieutenant in command of a motley group of Pakistani soldiers and local tribesmen, clad in colorful garb, who were attempting to put down an uprising against the sultan of Oman. As he wandered through the dirty camp, he was amazed that a few dozen British officers oversaw the wide-ranging effort—fighting insurgents, overseeing aid projects, and advising the sultan's government. Abizaid envied the small detachment of British soldiers, who actually seemed to be achieving something, as tiny as their effort was. "It was one of these rare instances in the twentieth century where an insurgency is quelled," he recalled.

The United States proved clumsier in its attempt to intervene in the region. Although Abizaid didn't realize it at the time, he and his fellow officers were in Oman that winter scouting for airfields to use in a secret mission to rescue the American hostages in Tehran. Abizaid was brought along as a translator. The operation was conducted later that spring by Delta Force—the counterterrorism unit that Casey had tried out for a year earlier—and ended in disaster when a U.S. military helicopter crashed into an Air Force C-130, killing eight commandos. The debacle made a deep impression on the U.S. Army, which was still recovering from Vietnam. Instead of surgical strikes by clandestine commandos, Pentagon generals would insist that the key to success in future operations was to overwhelm the enemy with troops and firepower.

Toward the end of his stay Abizaid decided to run the entire length of Jordan, a 270-mile journey that took him from the Iraqi border in the north to Aqaba, the port city that had been captured by Lawrence of Arabia and his Arab allies during World War I. Abizaid was trying to soak up as much of the country as he could before he left. As he jogged through the desert he was joined by Jordanian army officers, including one lieutenant who smoked cigarettes as he plodded alongside him in the searing heat. The Arabs reproached him for guzzling water, saying no Bedouin would need to drink so much. Stopping at desert encampments at night, he was served bread and tea—and called "Abu Zaid" by the nomads.

His family had grown to feel at home in the country as well. Kathy bargained with local food vendors for bruised tomatoes and taught herself how to serve Arabic coffee to their Bedouin guests, filling their shot-glass-sized cups again and again until they shook them, the signal that they were finished. She gamely put up with even the most intrusive guests. Abu Latif, a Bedouin sheikh who had played host to the Abizaids several times in the Byzantine ruin on the outskirts of Amman where his tribe lived, arrived one rainy evening in his flowing robe, accompanied by a dozen family members. "We've come to bathe," he announced in Arabic. For the next several hours they rotated through the Abizaids' bathroom, washing and raiding the medicine cabinet.

Few Army wives would ever throw themselves into a foreign culture the way Kathy did, Abizaid thought. He delighted in watching his four-year-old daughter Sherry laugh and shout with her Jordanian playmates in self-taught Arabic. And he reveled in the disorder of everyday life in Jordan: the ten o'clock news that some nights didn't start until after 10:30; the total disregard for traffic laws. "I can't think of a time when we've been happier or closer as a family," he wrote in a letter to the Olmsted Foundation. On their last night in Amman, the Abizaids hosted a small goodbye dinner, inviting their neighbor Asma Ali and several close Jordanian friends and their children. Kathy later described the gathering in a letter: "As the evening wore on, I could see that they were delaying their departure. I was sitting and watching all of our children playing and turned to ask Asma something. She was playing with the baby and crying. I found that I was crying too. In a country where families live in the same village for centuries the departure, perhaps permanent, of a friend is so much of a loss. We both felt that then."

Abizaid's two-year sojourn had caused him to fall behind his fellow West Point classmates. In his first two Army assignments with the 82nd Airborne Division and the Rangers he'd received glowing reviews. "One of the most intelligent officers I have ever known," an early battalion commander wrote in his personnel file. "Destined to become one of the truly great leaders of the U.S. military," another boss said. Now the Pentagon officer charged with placing him in his next assignment warned him in letters typed on Department of the Army stationery that he needed to get back to leading troops "as soon as possible." He briefly considered switching from infantry officer to foreign area officer so that he could remain in the

Middle East, which he and Kathy had grown to love. "Arabist or infantryman?" he asked in one letter home. The more he thought about it, the clearer the answer became. Ever since hearing his father's stories from World War II as a teenager, Abizaid had longed to lead soldiers. He chose infantryman, confident that growing unrest in the Islamic world would draw him back one day.

CHAPTER THREE

The New Centurions

Fort Stewart, Georgia
1979

Colonel James Shelton had never seen anything like it. The letter from a captain named David Petraeus went on for two pages, ticking off all the honors and achievements he had accumulated in his short career—Star Man at West Point, promoted early to captain, master parachutist badge, top of his class at Ranger School, exemplary fitness reports. Shelton and Petraeus had met each other exactly once. A few years earlier they had shared a tent one night during a NATO exercise in eastern Turkey. Petraeus had cracked up when Shelton pulled a bottle of scotch from a spare boot in his rucksack, and the two soldiers had shared a drink. Now it was Shelton's turn to chuckle. This brash captain was lobbying for command of a rifle company in his brigade. He passed the letter around his headquarters, and everyone got a kick out of it. "What do you want to do with Superman here?" the brigade's personnel officer asked. "Let's give him a shot," Shelton replied. He had only taken over command a few months earlier and already had bawled out several shoddy junior officers. If Petraeus was half as good as he claimed, he would be an improvement.

Petraeus and his wife, Holly, pulled into Fort Stewart in their yellow Corvette a few weeks later, newly assigned to Shelton's brigade in the 24th Infantry Division. Everything moved at a languid pace in rural Georgia, they found. Holly could speak French fluently, but she had a harder time with southern drawls. When, shortly after arriving, she heard a radio commercial referring to "Vince's Dawgs," she had no idea it was a reference to the University of Georgia Bulldogs football team and its coach, Vince Dooley. The 24th Division headquarters was in a creaky white clapboard building built in the early months of World War II. Beyond the main post lay the vast training grounds, nearly 300,000 acres of dense scrub pine and swamp. But training wasn't much of a priority. The commanding general spent long hours on his boat, which he kept moored near Savannah, twenty-five miles away. Days at a time would go by without him saying a word to his staff. "You're in command," he told his deputy. "Just tell me if something goes wrong." A lot was going wrong. The year Petraeus arrived, the 24th was rated "not combat ready" in the Army's internal unit assessments.

He and Holly had spent the previous four years at the U.S. base in Vicenza in a parachute infantry brigade. They had loved life in Italy, or he had anyway. The only work Holly could find as the wife of an officer was tutoring soldiers seeking their high school GEDs. Petraeus, however, spent weeks at a time traveling around Europe on joint exercises with parachute units from other NATO countries. In 1976, he and a couple of dozen soldiers from his unit went to France to train with its paratroopers. After ten days, they ended up in the Pyrenees Mountains, executing a tricky drop onto a hilltop. From there the Americans and their hosts marched several miles to a rustic château, where they were served a memorable meal by black-coated waiters. A picture snapped that evening by one of his men shows a youthful Petraeus standing outside the farmhouse in his paratrooper beret, looking deeply happy.

On the trip Petraeus noticed a larger-than-life portrait of a French officer displayed in the regimental mess and asked about it. The painting was of Marcel Bigeard, his hosts told him, a revered French general. He had fought in Vietnam in the 1940s and 1950s, was taken prisoner during the siege of Dien Bien Phu, and later forged the counterinsurgency tactics that

French units used in their war in Algeria. After returning to Vicenza, an intrigued Petraeus began reading about Bigeard, poring over a copy of *Hell in a Very Small Place*, Bernard Fall's classic account of the French war in Indochina, and a translation of the *The Centurions*, Jean Lartéguy's novel whose hero, Raspeguy, was loosely modeled on Bigeard.

Petraeus became a fervent admirer of the combat-hardened paratrooper who had helped revive the French spirit after its crushing defeat in Vietnam, a decade before the United States sent troops there. *The Centurions* quickly became one of his favorite books. The novel recounts how Raspeguy and his tight-knit band of men returned from the war to an indifferent France and re-formed their unit to fight in Algeria, this time more effectively battling Arab guerrillas on their own ground. One of Petraeus's prized possessions was an autographed picture of Bigeard, given to him as a Christmas present in 1976 by Holly's father, General Knowlton, who had left West Point for an assignment at NATO. Petraeus would hang the picture on his office wall for decades afterward. He would read and reread sections of *The Centurions*, too. Thirty years later, Petraeus would pull a copy of the novel off his bookshelf at Fort Leavenworth in Kansas and lecture a visitor on what it taught about small-unit infantry tactics.

Petraeus wasn't planning on staying long in the plodding 24th Infantry Division. Although he hadn't mentioned it to Shelton, he had lobbied to come to Fort Stewart for one main reason—there was also a Ranger battalion headquartered there that he badly wanted to join. His career plan in many ways resembled the plot of *The Centurions*. After the U.S. pullout from Vietnam, the Army had chosen the Ranger battalions to function as a nucleus of competence in an otherwise deeply dysfunctional service. They got the best equipment, the toughest soldiers, and the most realistic training. Over time, the theory went, this brotherhood of warriors would repopulate the rest of the Army, saving the institution, much as Raspeguy (and Bigeard) had done, until sold out by politicians. After doing his stint in Shelton's brigade, Petraeus planned to shift over to the elite unit that represented everything he loved about the Army. The Rangers were selective, but Petraeus wasn't worried about making the cut.

✳ ✳ ✳ ✳

Petraeus had arrived at Fort Stewart at a time of growing alarm about the Middle East. In 1979, massive protests toppled the shah of Iran. Later in the year, the Soviet Union invaded Afghanistan. Unlike in Europe, the United States had no ground forces in the Middle East and little ability to move troops rapidly to the region.

The most troubling scenario for Pentagon strategists was a thrust south into Iran by the Soviet Union, potentially interrupting the flow of oil from the Persian Gulf. To a lesser extent, Army planners worried they might be asked to prop up Saudi Arabia or another ally threatened by a hostile neighbor or Islamic radicals. In a nationwide address in early October, President Jimmy Carter announced the creation of the Rapid Deployment Force, an armada of ground, naval, and air units trained and equipped to deploy to the Middle East in a crisis. The 24th Division, where Petraeus had landed, was designated as a key part of the force.

For its new mission, the division was converted from light infantry into a mechanized division, which meant that hundreds of new tanks, armored personnel carriers, and trucks poured into Fort Stewart. Keeping the vehicles repaired suddenly became the company commanders' responsibility, one unfamiliar to Petraeus, who had spent the first part of his career in an airborne unit. So he began spending one day a week in the motor pool, overseeing his mechanics. He donned a pair of pressed coveralls and sat with a megaphone and a maintenance manual open in front of him, reciting step-by-step instructions for greasing an axle or changing an oil filter. Accustomed to being left alone, many of the mechanics grumbled that they could handle the job themselves. But with Petraeus riding herd, the amount of time the company's vehicles spent undergoing repairs declined. "If you want to show seriousness of purpose, you personally commit to it," Petraeus explained later, admitting, "We probably committed a little bit more to it than some."

Few officers spent as much time thinking about the details of their job. When a fellow captain had to deliver a eulogy for a decidedly average soldier who had been killed in a car accident, Petraeus asked him for his notes, filing them away to consult in case he was ever called upon to give similar remarks. Most mornings he would sprint the two miles from his house to Fort Stewart, and then lead the company on its early-morning run, followed by calisthenics. He was always smiling and pleasant, but there wasn't a tougher competitor on the base. After reading in the post newspaper one day about three Rangers who claimed to have set a new record running from Savannah to Fort Stewart, he handpicked a team of hardened athletes like himself and they blew the Ranger time away, with Petraeus handling the anchor leg.

While coaching his men in the post basketball league, he promised he would make sure a four-star general turned up to watch if the team made it to the championship game. He was one of the few captains who could actually deliver on such a pledge, however uninspirational it might have been to his soldiers. When the team made the finals a few months later, he hurriedly called General Knowlton, who happened to be in Washington for meetings, and he agreed to fly down to see his daughter and to sit in the stands for the evening game. Petraeus's squad won, of course.

There was another reason for Knowlton to make a special trip to Fort Stewart. The next morning, he stood beside Colonel Shelton on the Fort Stewart parade grounds for a special ceremony. His son-in-law's company had won an award for having 65 percent of its nearly 100 soldiers qualify for the Expert Infantry Badge, which required mastering more than a dozen soldiering skills. Most officers didn't know or care about the award. But Petraeus had made winning the EIB unit citation his obsession, devising a grueling training regime that included twelve-mile road marches in less than three hours wearing full rucksacks, long hours on the rifle range, and tromping around the woods with maps and compasses. "We just drilled and drilled and drilled," he remembered. On the day of the ceremony, he was standing at attention, with his men behind him in formation, as Knowlton presented him a blue unit streamer to be flown on Alpha Company's guidon, the swallow-tailed flag carried next to the commanding officer during parades and formations.

His success in the EIB competition "put Petraeus on the map," his battalion commander later recalled. But it also rubbed some peers the wrong way—he was too ambitious, too competitive, and too perfect. Petraeus didn't seem to be bothered by the sniping, and it was impossible to dispute the results. "Some guys didn't like him because they thought he was a show-off," Shelton said. "I thought he was the most amazing young officer I had."

After a job as the battalion operations officer came open, Shelton decided to promote his hardest-working captain, even though it was a major's billet and Petraeus was only ten months into his company command. A week later, Shelton got a rare call from the often-absent division commander, Major General James Cochran, who had just learned about the promotion. "I thought I was running this division," Cochran fumed. "We've got three or four majors who have been waiting for a job like that." Shelton fired back: "We thought he was the best guy for the job." Cochran backed down, and Petraeus vaulted over his fellow officers into a plum position.

The operations shop hummed under its new captain. He could write a military plan and the standard five-paragraph operations order faster than anyone Shelton had ever seen. Training exercises were bigger and more realistic than had been done for years. In one case, three companies, joined by tanks and helicopters, conducted a simulated attack using live ammunition that went on for more than hour. It was like the Fourth of July, only with real rockets. Families invited to observe from nearby bleachers broke into cheers at the cacophony of rifle fire and explosions. Once it was over, Petraeus rushed up to the battalion executive officer, Major Marty Gendron. "Wasn't that great?" he gushed. "Yeah, Dave," replied a nonplussed Gendron, who worried the exuberant captain had just expended much of the year's ammunition budget.

Better training was badly needed—and not just in the sleepy 24th. In November 1979, while Petraeus was commanding his company at Fort Stewart, General Edward "Shy" Meyer, the Army chief of staff who had once worked for George Casey's father in Vietnam, gathered with the other Joint Chiefs at Camp David to brief President Carter on the following year's defense budget. The foreign policy crises bedeviling the administration had worsened as the months passed, especially in the Middle East. In Tehran, radical students who had stormed the U.S. embassy were holding sixty-six hostages. Carter warned Iran's new leaders that he might take military action if the hostages were harmed. But could he? Meyer had come to Camp David with a distressing message. "Mr. President," he said when it was his turn to speak, "basically what we have is a hollow Army." It was an Army that couldn't fight, and not just in the Middle East.

Pentagon war plans called for rushing ten divisions to Europe in two weeks if the Soviets invaded, but most of the active-duty divisions in the United States were like the 24th—undermanned and poorly equipped, incapable of picking up and moving on short notice. Even if they could deploy, Meyer said, there weren't enough ships and transport planes to move them, or the logistics to sustain them for more than a couple of weeks. The Rapid Deployment Force, which Carter had announced in a nationally televised address months earlier, existed mainly on paper. When a *New York Times* reporter showed up at Fort Stewart to investigate the Army's ability to fight in the Middle East, Shelton was pessimistic. "My brigade's ready to fight," he said. "But as for the big picture, who knows? We'd probably be stretched very thin very soon. We'd give a good account of ourselves at the start, but I'd hate to say how long we'd survive."

Now that Petraeus was on the battalion staff, other officers who once saw him as merely amusing or annoying had to operate at his relentless pace, and some rebelled. Captain Dan Grigson was summoned one day to battalion headquarters and told by Petraeus that he was being "counseled" for not keeping up with his paperwork and ignoring tasks assigned to him by the operations shop. "If I ask anybody else to do something, they do it. With you, it's always a fight," he said. Grigson reminded him that his boss was the battalion commander, not the operations officer. "The difference between you and me, Dave," Grigson later remembered remarking, "is that you want to be chief of staff of the Army someday and I don't."

The truth was Petraeus wasn't thinking much beyond his immediate goal of transferring into the Ranger battalion. That changed in May 1981, when the 24th Division got a new commander, Major General John Galvin, who was returning to the United States from a job in Germany. Galvin's assignment was a sign that the Army was taking the once-sleepy 24th more seriously. The new tanks, armored troop carriers, and trucks were, on Galvin's orders, being repainted in a shade of tan, to blend in better in Middle Eastern deserts.

Before Galvin arrived, he had heard about the superstar captain on the battalion staff. He needed a personal aide and decided to give Petraeus the job on a temporary basis. If they meshed, he promised, he'd make the assignment permanent. Galvin didn't expect his aide to stay at his side every minute. "I don't want you to click your heels and keep my cigarettes," he told Petraeus. He wanted Petraeus to be his eyes and ears, to carry out sensitive assignments, and to be a confidential advisor—an aide-de-camp the way the term had been understood in Napoleon's army. Most important, he wanted criticism. "It's my job to run the division, and it's your job to critique me," he insisted. "I want you to give me a report card every month on how I'm doing."

Petraeus was immediately drawn to his new boss. Bookish, with a streak of Yankee stubbornness, Jack Galvin started as an enlisted man in the Massachusetts National Guard before attending West Point and being sent to Vietnam. He had been relieved from his first assignment in Vietnam after refusing his commander's order to inflate a Viet Cong body count after a battle. Exiled to a public affairs job, he was close to leaving the Army, but stayed in after he was assigned to help write a classified history of Vietnam that became known as the Pentagon Papers. The experience gave him a behind-the-scenes look at the blunders that had led the country into a losing war. Returning to Vietnam for a second tour, he was assigned to the 1st Air Cavalry, working under George Casey Sr. Later, he attended Columbia University for a master's degree in English, and taught literature at West Point. In his spare time, he wrote books of popular history and articles about strategy for military journals. He carried around a Spanish-English dictionary to teach himself the language. He was a soldier-scholar, like Petraeus's father-in-law in many ways, but more of an iconoclast, someone who had struggled to make general, was often at odds with the Army, and had emerged with contrarian self-confidence. Petraeus was the straightest arrow around and had never been crosswise with the Army brass, but he had a curious mind and loved history. For those reasons alone, he knew he would enjoy his new boss.

Galvin liked his new aide, too. A few weeks after arriving, he told Petraeus he was serious about wanting regular criticism. "I don't want to grade you, sir," Petraeus protested. But Galvin insisted, so Petraeus began leaving the reports in the commander's in-basket every month. "Sir, your

April evaluation," read the cover sheet on one of his early efforts. Galvin scrawled "OK!" on top after reading it.

One of his peeves was that Galvin wasn't in shape. Petraeus prided himself on physical toughness, a trait that he thought won him respect in enlisted men's eyes, and he tended to rate other officers by their ability to keep up with him on a run. He thought a commander should be up front, leading by example. Galvin, who was often huffing and puffing midway through a three-mile jog, liked to run in the back of the pack. "You learn more in the rear," he said. Petraeus knew he would never turn his boss into a jock, so he hid his boss's candy bars and came up with other ways of buffing up Galvin's image. After a long run with troops, while everyone else was doubled over gasping, the general and his aide would jog off, as if barely winded, saying they had to get back to headquarters. Once out of sight, they hopped in a vehicle stashed nearby and drove to the office.

Galvin had plenty of advice for Petraeus, too. He urged him not to focus narrowly on his job as an infantry officer. Success was not only a matter of being in great shape or getting top marks on evaluation reports. Think beyond the foxhole, about history and strategy, about relations between the military and their civilian bosses in Washington, about the next war, he urged. It amused him that someone with as supple a mind as Petraeus had would never admit a mistake. He needed to loosen up a little, Galvin thought. Consider going to graduate school, where he would meet civilians with different experiences and ideas. "I used to say you can't get too smart to be an infantryman," he recalled.

Petraeus soon became Galvin's alter ego, responsible for balancing his schedule, drafting his speeches, and issuing orders in his name. Their close relationship did not always go over well with the division senior staff, who thought the confident captain sometimes overstepped his bounds. Colonel Pete Taylor, the chief of staff, chewed out Petraeus several times for presuming to direct the division staff, which was his job. He found it especially annoying when Petraeus would walk into Galvin's office and close the glass door behind him, shutting out the rest of the staff. "I made it very clear to Dave that if I caught him doing it again, I would have the post engineers come over and take the door off its hinges," he said.

Being a general's aide was a double-edged sword. It was an opportunity to latch on to a powerful mentor and get a glimpse into the inner workings of the Army. But it had its downsides. It could mark an officer as a bit too eager to please and at worst as a self-serving sycophant. Most of Petraeus's peers had read or at least heard of *Once an Eagle,* Anton Myrer's 1968 novel that follows the lives of two officers from World War I through the early years of the Cold War. The protagonist, Sam Damon, is a battle-tested hero who marries the French-speaking daughter of a general and puts his soldiers' interests ahead of his career. A stoic warrior, he dies on a mission attempting to keep the United States out of war in Southeast Asia. His rival, Courtney Massengale, disdains the rank-and-file soldiers under his command and attaches himself to generals, eventually rising to four stars himself. The thick novel and its simple parable about duty and sacrifice resonated with generations of officers, including those at Fort Stewart in the early 1980s. Martin Rollinson, a captain in the 24th Infantry when Petraeus was there, remembered talking with other officers about whether Galvin's aide was like the selfless Damon or the conniving Massengale. "Some people compared Petraeus to Massengale," Rollinson recalled. "It wasn't fair, but he was so good he made people feel inferior."

There was a passage in the novel describing Massengale that captured the Army's scorn for officers who rose by using their connections rather than by leading men in battle: "He will go far, she thought, watching the proud, ascetic discipline in his face, the strange amber eyes. He will become Chief of Staff, if events follow a logical course; or even if they don't. Yet—her eyes rested for the briefest second on his ribbons—he had no combat decorations."

Petraeus knew that real combat leaders were supposed to be out in the field getting dirty with soldiers, not working as a general's aide. He hadn't given up on his goal of joining the Rangers, and asked about a transfer to the Ranger battalion at Fort Stewart, which would have established his credentials as a warrior. Galvin frowned on the idea and suggested he consider graduate school instead. Soon the issue became moot. Petraeus had been chosen to attend the Command and General Staff College at Fort Leavenworth in Kansas, where the Army sends the top 50 percent of its officers for advanced training. Although the school is usually reserved for majors, Petraeus was one of only a few officers selected to go early as a captain. He had to report in twelve months. When he asked the Rangers about joining the battalion for a short tour, he was told that it was impossible.

Shortly before Petraeus left Fort Stewart, Galvin's division faced its first big test at the National Training Center, an area in the Mojave Desert that the Army had opened in the early 1980s to practice tank warfare on a vast scale. The Pentagon expected that a conflict in the Middle East, where the 24th Division was supposed to fight, would be nothing like Vietnam, a war that most officers were eager to forget. In the Middle East the likely adversary was the Soviet Union or one of its proxies. Generals assumed the battles there would be very similar to the 1973 Yom Kippur War, in which Egypt launched a surprise attack against Israeli positions in the Sinai, followed by Syrian assaults in the Golan Heights. Despite horrendous losses, Israel counterattacked, using its air force and American-designed tanks to knock out the Arabs' air defense, then break through their ground formations and destroy them. This was the kind of war that Galvin's division was preparing to fight.

But in the desert of California Galvin's troops were regularly outmaneuvered by the more experienced Soviet-style opposition force, played by American soldiers. For two weeks, he and Petraeus crisscrossed the battlefield in their jeep, studying the 24th Division as it fought. The situation got so bad that Galvin ordered his chief of staff, who had stayed home at Fort Stewart, to fly out to the desert so that he could see firsthand the drubbing they were taking. After returning home, Galvin ordered large tracts of forest cleared to replicate the conditions in the desert. Day after day, soldiers were in the field conducting maneuvers. Over the next year, units from the 24th returned to the California desert four more times, with better results each time. The same lessons were being learned all across the Army. Everywhere units were training for the big battles between armored formations that the Pentagon had decided were the future of warfare. The buildup was fueled by massive Reagan administration defense spending, which was buying thousands of new tanks, personnel carriers, and helicopters.

But Petraeus's career was taking a new direction. After his year at Command and General Staff College, he planned to attend graduate school at Princeton University and then return to West Point as an instructor. As Galvin had urged, he was beginning to think deeply about his profession and the wars to come. For the first time since he joined the service, the conclusions Petraeus came to would put him at odds with the prevailing view of warfare in the Army. Other young officers were reaching the same point, only by less conventional paths.

*   *   *   *

Naqoura, Lebanon
Summer, 1985

As Major John Abizaid had predicted when he left Jordan, war had brought him back to the Middle East. He had taken a yearlong assignment as a member of the United Nations observer force in southern Lebanon, where Israel was bogged down in a bloody hit-and-run conflict that looked nothing like the big tank battles that Petraeus and Galvin were preparing for in the Mojave Desert.

He had been on the ground for a week when he saw the remains of his first suicide bomber. He and his partner, a Swedish officer, heard the boom and took off in their white jeep, zipping around dun-colored hills on serpentine roads until they reached the blast site, a smoking, black gash that cut through the middle of the road. Abizaid was surprised at how little of the bomber was left—a few shreds of clothing, a couple of body parts, and some blood. From the bits that remained, he guessed that the only casualty had been the bomber himself. He probably had been on his way to a nearby Israeli checkpoint when the explosives he was carrying detonated prematurely. Abizaid scribbled some notes and snapped a couple of photographs for his report on the incident, the first of dozens he would submit over the next year.

The Israelis had portrayed their incursion into Lebanon three years earlier as a limited action aimed at driving out Palestinian Liberation Organization fighters, who for years had attacked northern Israel with rockets and terror attacks. Once across the border, the Israeli army drove north to Beirut, surrounding and laying siege to the city. The assault crippled the PLO and led to the departure of its leadership to Tunisia. But instead of withdrawing, the Israelis stayed. Like the United States two decades later in Iraq, Prime Minister Menachem Begin and Defense Minister Ariel Sharon were determined to install a friendly government as part of its grander ambition to remake the Middle East. Up to that point, Israel's fight had been with the Palestinians. Once they became an occupying power, the Israelis found themselves battling a new enemy—Shiite Muslims, who had originally welcomed their offensive against the PLO but now turned hostile.

By mid-1985, when Abizaid arrived in Lebanon, the Israel Defense Forces had withdrawn from all but a narrow strip of territory along the southern border, which they had declared a security zone vital for protecting northern Israel. The zone itself was far from secure. Israel found itself attacked by fighters from numerous Shiite factions and the remnants of the PLO, all of which competed to be seen as most dedicated to forcing out the occupiers. It was a sectarian stew. Both Hezbollah, the militant Shiite group, and Amal, its more secular Shiite rival, turned to suicide car bombs, mines, booby traps, and ambushes against Israeli soldiers and the South Lebanon Army, an Israeli-backed militia composed largely of Christians.

On March 10, 1985, a suicide bomber drove a car packed with explosives into an Israeli convoy at a border crossing, near the Israeli town of Metulla. Twelve Israelis were killed and fourteen wounded. The Israelis responded with the "Iron Fist" policy that included artillery barrages on Muslim villages and reprisal raids that rounded up hundreds of Shiites at a time. Still the attacks continued. Dispirited Israeli troops castigated Abizaid and his fellow UN observers as the "United Nothing," because they did nothing to stop the increasingly powerful and frightening bombs.

By this point in his career Abizaid had experienced combat firsthand. After returning from Jordan he had spent a year at Harvard, where he earned a degree in Middle Eastern studies, and then taken command of a 120-soldier Ranger company at Fort Stewart. In 1983 he and his men parachuted onto the Caribbean island of Grenada, as part of an invasion to restore the island's pro-Western government to power following a coup. They had only been on the ground a short time when a bullet from a Cuban machine-gun position sliced through the neck of one of Abizaid's soldiers, killing him. With enemy fire snapping over his head, Abizaid ordered a sergeant to hot-wire a bulldozer that had been abandoned nearby and charge at the Cubans with the blade raised as he and his fellow Rangers advanced behind it. Abizaid and his troops soon overwhelmed the Communist troops. The bulldozer assault, which was re-created in the Clint Eastwood movie *Heartbreak Ridge,* later made Abizaid a celebrity within the Army—one of the few genuine combat heroes to emerge in the decade following Vietnam. But real combat was nothing like the Hollywood adaptation. A few hours after the airport skirmish, another four soldiers from Abizaid's company were gunned down after straying into an ambush.

After Grenada, he spent a year in the Pentagon assigned to a twelve-person study team that worked for General Max Thurman, the Army's iconoclastic vice chief of staff. Although the mainstream Army was heavily focused on preparing to fight the Soviets, Thurman believed that the United States was far more likely to be drawn into a war in the developing world. If he was right, the service needed a cadre of leaders who not only knew combat but also had a deep understanding of the Third World backwaters where they might be asked to fight—the Middle East, Asia, and Latin America. Abizaid became his model officer. Speaking to newly promoted majors at Fort Leavenworth, Thurman told his audience that if they wanted to become generals, they should imitate Abizaid's career. It wasn't enough to learn tactics and leadership. They needed to know languages and foreign cultures, to spend time abroad away from the day-to-day Army, as Abizaid had done. Eager to tap Abizaid's knowledge of the Middle East, Thurman assigned him to a group examining the Israeli incursion into Lebanon. The study focused on the technology and tactics the Israelis had used during their lightning push to Beirut, but it ignored the bloody and largely unsuccessful occupation of the country. The oversight wasn't surprising; ever since Vietnam, the Army had decided it could simply choose not to fight messy guerrilla wars. It instead planned on using overwhelming firepower and superior technology to defeat foes in short, sharp battles. The study was completed just before Abizaid headed out for Lebanon, where an entirely different kind of war was being waged.

He and the four dozen or so other United Nations observers—Argentines, Canadians, Swedes, and fellow Americans—lived and patrolled unarmed out of a main base in the small city of Naqoura and from a half-dozen smaller cinder-block outposts perched along winding roads and barren hills.

Though the UN was officially neutral, Abizaid's time in the country summoned up a stew of conflicting emotions. More than once, he found himself watching from a distance as Shiite fighters set up launchers to fire Katyusha rockets into northern Israel, where his wife and children were living. He was appalled by the brutality of the Israelis' allies, often hearing screams of tortured prisoners emanating from an old French fort used by the South Lebanon Army as an interrogation center. But he also came to understand the debilitating effect a long and unsuccessful occupation has on an army, even one as disciplined as the Israel Defense Forces. "War in southern Lebanon is difficult to imagine by common standards of reference," he wrote in a report after completing his tour. "It was neither guerrilla war of the Vietnam style nor was it the urban battle of Beirut. It was low-intensity conflict where UN sources routinely recorded over 100 violent incidents per month, ranging from ambushes to kidnappings to suicide car bombs."

After one ambush, the Israelis and their allies emptied a Shiite village of its 2,000 residents at gunpoint. As Abizaid and his fellow observers watched from a nearby hill, the soldiers set fire to the town. UN observers couldn't intervene to stop the destruction. Abizaid consoled himself with the thought that the forced evacuation might have degenerated into a massacre if he and his fellow observers hadn't been there.

Since Abizaid was one of the few UN soldiers who spoke fluent Arabic, he was made the observer force's director of operations, overseeing the outposts and patrols. He and the unit's commander, an American lieutenant colonel, regularly loaded their jeep with cartons of cigarettes to bribe the locals, removed the American flags from their uniforms, and ventured out into the Lebanese countryside. It was a rugged area with deep wadis and small villages inhabited mostly by poor farmers. Shopkeepers and mosques peddled martyr videotapes and posters, lionizing local suicide bombers who had killed Israelis. "There was no shortage of willing martyrs," Abizaid later wrote. "The martyrs who volunteered to undertake the attacks became instant celebrities, invariably leaving behind a videotape describing why they felt it necessary to sacrifice themselves. As one might imagine, these videos were given prominent display on the various militia-controlled television stations."

Town elders would scream at the UN officers that the Israelis and their Christian allies were killing civilians and preventing basic necessities from reaching their villages. The central government in Beirut was absent in southern Lebanon, and with the PLO also gone, Hezbollah and other Shiite militias filled the void, sweeping streets, fixing homes, and ferrying the elderly to medical appointments. With help from Tehran and Damascus, the militias learned how to meld violence, propaganda, and social aid programs to bring supporters to their side.

Five years earlier, Abizaid had watched as the Iranian revolution had energized his fellow students at the University of Jordan. In Lebanon, the Iranians were working through Hezbollah and other Shiite Muslim militias. Once an underground organization, Hezbollah leaders now spouted Iranian dogma and handed out Iranian funds to rebuild homes damaged by the Israelis and the South Lebanon Army. Tehran also provided powerful and sophisticated roadside bombs that terrorized Israeli convoys.

Hezbollah soon displaced Amal as the leader of the anti-Israeli resistance. "Moderates in Amal, unable to deliver on promises to force an Israeli withdrawal, lost ground to more radical Shia," Abizaid recounted. In that way, occupation of the security zone "actually worked contrary to the long-term interests of Israel by weakening the forces of moderation in southern Lebanon to the benefit of the radicals dedicated to the destruction of the Jewish state."

Abizaid could sense a feeling of doom spread through the dwindling Christian community, too. He dined with Christian village elders, greeting the men with a traditional kiss on each cheek and choking down *kibbeh nayye,* a dish made of raw minced lamb. "We are fighting against Islamic extremism," they told him, hoping that the young American officer could rally his country or the UN. There was little Abizaid could do. Stopping the suicide bombs was impossible for the Israeli soldiers, as it was for the UN. The only way to stop it was for Israel to withdraw, but that would only embolden the Shiite militants and their Iranian patrons. "There is going to be a lot more of this," Abizaid announced to his fellow observers at one point. "What's preventing Iran from doing the same thing some-place else?"

✶   ✶   ✶   ✶

Two years later Abizaid was serving at the U.S. base in Vicenza, Italy, when the telephone rang late one evening at his house. It was General Thurman, the vice chief of staff who remembered Abizaid from his time at the Pentagon several years earlier. "I'm going to take a trip to the Middle East and I want you to go with me," he barked. It was typical Thurman. Known as the "Maxatollah" for his abrasive manner and monastic dedication to the Army, he expected his protégés to drop everything when he called. The general himself had never married, giving his life to the Army.

A few days later Abizaid met Thurman in Cairo. From there they traveled to Israel, where they met with the prime minister and toured the Golan Heights and the Lebanon border. The Israeli occupation, now in its sixth year, was grinding down its soldiers and sapping morale. As they stared out into the occupation zone, the Israelis insisted that they had to remain in southern Lebanon to protect their farms and cities from rocket attacks and terror attacks. Back at their hotel that evening, Thurman asked Abizaid for his view. To Abizaid the answer was obvious. The heavy-handed Israeli presence was radicalizing Shiites, strengthening Iran and Hezbollah. It wasn't making anyone more secure. He told Thurman so.

Shortly after he returned, Thurman marched down one of the Pentagon's corridors in search of a personnel officer. He didn't even pause to say hello. "Where is Abizaid going on his next assignment?" the half-deaf, bespectacled Thurman shouted. "Who is Abizaid?" replied Colonel John Miller, who was unaccustomed to having four-star generals suddenly appear in his windowless Pentagon office bellowing questions about low-ranking officers. "Major John Abizaid," Thurman snapped. "I need you to find out and let me know."

Abizaid's career was now being guided and nurtured at the Army's highest levels.

CHAPTER FOUR

The Department

We followed a policy of unabashed elitism.
—Colonel Lee Donne Olvey

Fort Lewis, Washington
1976

Beth Chiarelli was just about to tee off under the lush pines lining the first hole at the Fort Lewis golf course when she was beckoned back to the clubhouse for a telephone call. Her husband, Pete, had tracked her down with the news she had been waiting to hear. "Honey, I just turned in the papers. We're out," he said. The young couple had been talking about getting out of the Army for a couple of years, and now that he had submitted his official papers Beth felt relieved. With a newborn infant and another baby planned, it irked her that Pete was always away on training exercises, sometimes for weeks at a time, and that he could never spend summers along the Oregon coast, as her family had done for years. Unlike Pete, Beth had no special ties to the military, and she had never planned on becoming a military spouse. She constantly mangled the acronym-laden military-speak tossed around by everyone on Army bases, including the other wives. Pete teasingly referred to her as the "demilitarized zone."

Beth had not issued ultimatums. She knew Pete loved the military. It had been part of his life since his childhood in Seattle, when his parents had played bingo at the Fort Lewis officers' club, a short drive from their house in the hilly neighborhood of Magnolia. But she had made it clear to him that she yearned for a more settled life, and Pete had come around to her way of thinking. With his four-year ROTC commitment nearly up, he talked more and more about attending graduate school and already had a job offer from a steel company in Portland, where Beth's dad was an executive. Now it was done. His resignation papers were filed. In thirty days their life after the Army would begin. Her biggest concern as she walked back to the 332-yard first hole was whether they could afford to buy Pete a few suits now that he was a civilian.

An hour later, at the seventh hole, Beth was summoned to the telephone for another call from her husband, and this time he sounded a little sheepish. After learning that Chiarelli planned to get out, Major Ron Adams, the executive officer in his unit, had made a few hurried calls and an hour later had come back with a counteroffer, Pete told her. If he would withdraw his retirement, the Army would send him to graduate school, all expenses paid, and then to West Point to teach cadets as an instructor in the Department of Social Sciences. "It's going to be fully funded and I'll get paid the whole time. What do you think?" he asked. It was so sudden that Beth didn't know what to think, except that her hopes for a simpler life in her hometown and summers along the coast were slipping away. That evening, Pete invited Adams over for Chinese takeout, and they talked over the Army offer. Pete could go to school full-time at the University of Washington while Beth got her wish to stay home with their growing family, they told her. At least they could stay in the Northwest near her family for two years. If they still wanted out of the Army later, he would have the advantage of experience teaching at the United States Military Academy. Finally it was agreed: he would stay in.

As a ROTC graduate, Chiarelli knew little about West Point and next to nothing about the Department of Social Sciences, where he would be teaching after completing graduate school. He had no idea he was entering an elite and somewhat secretive tribe. The Army, lumbering and homogeneous to outsiders, was actually a collection of these tribes. The largest are built around weapons systems. Officers in the armor branch spent their careers thinking about tank warfare. Artillery officers swore allegiance to their fearsome cannons, which they referred to as the "King of Battle." Then there were the Special Forces, which trained foreign armies and the special ops units that ran missions so secret they could not even be discussed.

When he was assigned to the Department of Social Sciences, Chiarelli was moving into one of the few tribes not built around some aspect of warfare, one so exclusive that many officers didn't even know it existed. For decades "Sosh," as it was known inside West Point's granite walls, recruited some of the best minds in the officer corps to join its rotating faculty of several dozen instructors. These young captains and majors taught economics, government, and international relations to cadets, and also formed a wellspring of unconventional thinking in a service not known for openness to new ideas. Sosh instructors were literally the longhairs—the guys whose haircuts tended to be a little less military and who called each other by first names. They saw themselves as intellectuals, or as close as you could get in a service with a deep anti-intellectual bent. It was the Army's bias for action over argument and debate that made Sosh a dangerous place for officers. Stay too long in Sosh or appear to enjoy your time there too much and you ran the risk of being branded an elitist or an egghead, in either case not the right type to lead men in combat. For that reason, those inside the fraternity didn't talk much to outsiders about the department, but to the initiated it was a special place.

For most of Sosh's history, it had drawn two types of soldiers—generals-in-waiting and dissidents. In the first category were officers who came to Sosh in the midst of stellar careers, for whom a few years in the department was another box to be checked on their way up the chain of command. In 2009, one-quarter of the Army's four-star generals had taught in the Sosh department. In the second group were the officers who were too outspoken or just too different to ascend to the top of an organization that rewarded teamwork and fitting in above all. They wanted to puncture the Army's conventional wisdom, its priorities, and its myths. Frequently they pushed their more career-oriented counterparts in the department to sharpen their ideas and take more daring positions.

Chiarelli's four years at Sosh were the defining time of his early career, turning him into an officer who decades later, when he made general, was willing to question almost everything about the way his Army was fighting in Iraq. A year after Chiarelli departed, David Petraeus arrived and had a similar experience.

＊　＊　＊　＊

United States Military Academy
West Point, New York
June 1980

When Pete and Beth Chiarelli arrived at West Point, it dawned on them almost immediately that they were joining a high-powered crowd. The department head, Colonel Lee Donne Olvey, stressed to every incoming instructor that they were the best minds the Army had to offer, and they were expected to show it during their three years there. Sosh had a mystique that Olvey was determined to preserve. "We followed a policy of unabashed elitism," he recalled.

The new crop of instructors arrived in June for a mandatory orientation session that began with a reception at Olvey's elegant Tudor-style quarters. Built in 1908, it boasted dark wood-paneled walls and a stirring view of the Hudson River below. As they mingled, Chiarelli realized that he knew none of his fellow instructors and those he met seemed far more cultivated and accomplished than he was. Many were West Point graduates who had attended Princeton, Yale, Harvard, or other fancy East Coast schools. Another new arrival, Jeff McKitrick, who became one of Chiarelli's closest friends, had spent two years working at the Pentagon and attending the School of Advanced International Studies at Johns Hopkins. Olvey himself had graduated at the top of his West Point class in 1955, gone on to Oxford as a Rhodes scholar, and then earned a doctorate from Harvard. He was married to a fetching and sophisticated Brazilian who greeted the newcomers with him at the door.

Once everyone was settled Olvey, speaking in his soft Georgia drawl, reminded the officers they were there because they were among the smartest and most capable in the Army. "You are the crème de la crème," he said. The barely concealed intellectual snobbery bothered Beth. "I can't imagine working with a bunch of men who have been told their whole lives that they are the cream of the crop," she told Pete as they drove home that evening. "It's like *Lord of the Flies* or something."

Chiarelli *was* a little intimidated. Asked to fill out a questionnaire during orientation week, he had felt a twinge of embarrassment about leaving blank a section asking him to list the scholarly articles and books he had published. His middling grades at Seattle University and a poor score on the admission test had caused him to abandon plans for law school. Studying relentlessly in graduate school, he had earned a master's degree in political science with honors and completed all the course work necessary for a doctorate. But "U-Dub," as Chiarelli called the University of Washington, wasn't Princeton or Yale. His master's thesis on the CIA-backed 1953 coup in Iran had never been published. Nor had he ever stood in front of a classroom and lectured on the intricacies of American government. Beth, Pete, and their two young children were assigned run-down World War II–era family housing at Stewart Airfield, fifteen miles away from campus. More-senior instructors received swanky quarters on the West Point grounds.

Thayer Hall, where Sosh was located, had once housed the indoor riding ring in the era when cadets were taught horsemanship. The basement had long since been subdivided into classrooms and windowless offices for junior faculty. On each desk in the morning was a fresh copy of that day's *New York Times*. For the first time in his Army career, Chiarelli was expected to know what was happening in the wider world, not just in the narrow confines of whatever Army base he happened to be assigned to at the time. Used to peppering his conversations with "sir" and "ma'am," he had to remind himself that the custom at Sosh was to use first names.

Weekday mornings at six-thirty, Chiarelli and two fellow instructors living at Stewart carpooled over to campus. Chiarelli grabbed a cup of coffee and thumbed through the paper in the faculty lounge before heading off to teach his first section of the day. Often he'd find himself embroiled in a coffeepot debate on some aspect of national security that would continue until he had to leave for class. He'd come back hours later to find a new crop of officers chewing over another topic. Officers met over lunch to vet papers they were preparing for political science conventions or discuss their doctoral research. Gradually Chiarelli's nerves settled down, and he began to actually enjoy standing in front of a room of cadets. He taught a course on government and politics of the Soviet Union; his booming voice echoed down hallways and into adjacent classrooms, becoming background music in the department.

Throwing together freethinkers and ambitious young officers in one place had been the Sosh way for decades, thanks largely to George "Abe" Lincoln, the founder of the modern-day Social Sciences Department. Lincoln was a legend in the history of the Army and of West Point. Graduating from the military academy in 1929, Lincoln had won a Rhodes scholarship to study at Oxford University before beginning his glittering Army career. In the middle of World War II, while serving in London as a planner for the Normandy invasion, Lincoln was transferred to the Pentagon, where he became deeply involved in the most sensitive debates of the war, including the decision to drop two atomic bombs on Japan. Promoted to brigadier general at age thirty-eight, he stayed in Washington until 1947, when he accepted a job as the deputy head of West Point's Department of Economics, Government, and History, shortly to be renamed the Department of Social Sciences. On his departure, General Dwight Eisenhower, then Army chief of staff, wrote him a note that read: "I attribute in very great part to you a noticeable growth in the soundness and clarity of military policy. . . . I personally have leaned heavily on your advice." Returning to West Point meant accepting a two-rank demotion to colonel, but there were compensations. He was going to be reunited with one of his mentors, Herman Beukema, the department head, and together they would work to redefine the role of the modern officer.

The Army that had entered World War II had been, in General George Marshall's words, that of a "third-rate power." West Point wasn't much better. For years it had staffed its teaching posts with recent academy graduates who sometimes had only passing familiarity with the subjects they were teaching. After World War II Lincoln and Marshall believed that the Army had to change if it was going to meet its obligations as a global power. To keep the peace in this era dominated by atomic

weapons, Lincoln envisioned a new breed of officer, schooled in disci-
plines beyond just blunt killing. They needed to understand politics, economics, and international relations. To staff his department he demanded
the brightest captains and majors he could get, men (they were all men
then) who could get into and excel in top civilian national security studies programs at places such as Harvard and Princeton and then take on
teaching assignments at Sosh that would convert the department into an
intellectual powerhouse.

Sosh, unlike some other departments at West Point, wanted its instructors to be provocative and versed in the latest scholarship. Not only
cadets would benefit, argued Lincoln, the department's founder. The chosen officers would mature as much as or more than their students by taking
a break from the regimented life of a soldier and spending a few years in an
academic environment where they would be encouraged to think broadly
and publish scholarly articles before heading back to combat units. In
short, Lincoln had in mind an elite corps of officers whose talents and
schooling would prepare them for major roles in the postwar Army.

As he began his teaching duties, Chiarelli discovered his University of
Washington education was not as much of a handicap as he had imagined.
He had read William Appleman Williams and other revisionist historians
who argued that the United States deserved more blame for starting the
Cold War than the Soviet Union. Assigning readings from Williams kin-
dled lively debate in a class of patriotic cadets. Pacing back and forth with
arms waving, Chiarelli enthusiastically held forth on how the Japanese attack on Pearl Harbor had been a justifiable response to the encirclement it
was facing in Asia from the United States. "I thought all this stuff was absolutely ludicrous," Chiarelli said, "but I loved walking into a classroom
and pretending like I believed it."

Chiarelli began to think that he might want to spend the rest of his career teaching at Sosh. Most instructors spent three years in the department
before returning to the regular Army, but he decided to stay a fourth year to
help edit a book on reforming the Defense Department that had grown out
of the department's annual summer national security conference. He also
hoped that staying the extra year would help him win one of the half-dozen
permanent teaching positions there—a job that would have meant an end

to leading soldiers. The teaching job, however, went to another officer who had already finished his doctorate, had authored a well-received book on Lebanon, and wrote pieces for the *New York Times* and *Los Angeles Times* critiquing U.S. foreign policy. Chiarelli's gamble put him in a hole. After two years at graduate school and four years in Sosh, he had been away from the regular Army a long time. The armor branch personnel managers responsible for Chiarelli's next assignment had all but given up on him. In their eyes, going to Sosh was, at best, a dilettantish diversion from real soldiering. "I am going to take your file and I am going to keep it upside down so I won't see your name. And when this is all over with, your career is finished," Chiarelli remembered his personnel officer saying.

In reality, getting promoted depended at least as much on having good connections, which Sosh had. When he took over as head of the department in 1954, Lincoln began identifying bright young cadets who one day might make good Sosh professors. If they expressed interest in returning to teach, he tracked their early Army careers. Every year, after winnowing down the list to the most promising candidates, he sent a dozen or so names to the Army personnel office, asking them to be assigned to his department. After three years of teaching, Lincoln used his connections to place them throughout the Army. Over time they started thinking of themselves as members of a special group of thinkers and achievers, and others did, too. Often they were drafted by the Army's senior generals to deal with Congress, the White House, and other Washington types. Sosh officers served as trusted aides, speechwriters, and senior strategists. At least to each other, these officers began referring to their tight little fraternity as the "Lincoln Brigade."

Olvey, who carried on Lincoln's traditions, told his instructors when they returned to the regular Army: "A member of the department is *always* a member of the department." In other words, there would be someone looking out for them. He lobbied Sosh department alumni to get Chiarelli a job at a tank unit in Germany that would put him back in the running for command of a battalion, the next step on the career ladder. Jeff McKitrick, his close friend in the department, bucked up his spirits, predicting he'd be a three-star general someday.

"Why not a four-star?" Chiarelli's wife, Beth, interjected.

"Pete's not political enough," McKitrick replied.

Chiarelli was amused by the conversation. If he couldn't be one of the Sosh department's provocateurs, maybe he could be a general. But before that could happen, he knew, he had to prove himself as a conventional Cold Warrior to the Army's armor branch, his once and future tribe.

* * * *

When Donne Olvey offered to send Dave Petraeus to graduate school in return for three years at Sosh, Petraeus had misgivings. At the time he was a student at Command and General Staff College at Fort Leavenworth, where the Army schools its top officers on strategy and doctrine. He was on his way to finishing first in his class, ahead of more than a thousand other officers, most of them already majors. The program at Leavenworth ate up a year. If he took two years more in graduate school and then went to Sosh, it would mean being away from the real Army for six years, a risky proposition for any officer, but especially for one with Petraeus's intense ambition. But General Jack Galvin, Petraeus's most influential mentor, urged him to take the detour, telling him that if he wanted to rise to the top of his profession, he needed to broaden himself. Galvin could be stiff and even a bit awkward around soldiers, but he also had a reputation as one of the Army's sharpest minds. Petraeus, who admired him immensely, decided to take the gamble.

In the fall of 1984, Petraeus entered Princeton University, joining the master's program at the Woodrow Wilson School of Public and International Affairs. He and Holly and their young daughter lived in a small townhouse not far from campus. She had been hopeful for a relaxed break from Army life, but Petraeus had planned out his two years at Princeton as if it were a military campaign. Every morning, he made the drive to campus and spent most of the day in class or in the library. He discovered it was just possible to cram the coursework for both a master's degree and a doctorate into his two years, though it meant taking on a punishing academic load. With his usual gusto, he convinced John Duffield, a former Peace Corps volunteer also in the master's program, to go for a Ph.D. as well. Sitting in adjoining carrels at the library, Petraeus and Duffield studied in the mornings, then took grueling runs around the Princeton campus before returning to their books for a few more hours of work.

His foray into civilian graduate school had its humbling moments. Used to top grades and glowing reviews, Petraeus received a D on his first exam in advanced microeconomics. A seminar paper in his second semester came back marked with a B. "Though the paper is reasonably well-written and has some merit, it is relatively simplistic and I am left feeling that the whole is less than the sum of the parts," his professor, Dr. Richard Ullman, had written on the cover sheet. Petraeus had worked hard on the paper, and Ullman's blasé reaction had taken him down a peg. "I had been the number one guy in my class at Leavenworth and a few other things over the years. I wanted to prove to myself that I could really measure up," he recalled. A chastened Petraeus asked if he could take a shot at writing a new seminar paper that looked at how the Vietnam War influenced the Nixon, Ford, and Carter administrations' calculus on using military force. He threw himself into the project, even volunteering to shuttle Zbigniew Brzezinski, who had been national security advisor during the Carter administration, back to Washington following a speaking engagement at Princeton so that he could interview him during the four-hour drive. Ullman gave the paper an A, and Petraeus decided to write his doctoral thesis on Vietnam's impact on the American military. He crammed in as much research as he could before leaving Princeton, and then wrote his dissertation while teaching at Sosh.

It was an unexpectedly rich time to revisit Vietnam—especially in the intellectual hothouse of the Sosh department. The war was a painful subject that held little interest for most Army officers. Sosh instructors, however, debated it incessantly. In June 1985 the department hosted an academic conference on the tenth anniversary of the end of the Vietnam War. Olvey assigned William Taylor, a fiery infantry officer with a Ph.D. who had served in Vietnam, to help Petraeus expand his Princeton paper and present it at the conference.

When Taylor arrived at West Point in the 1970s there were no courses on Vietnam. At the Army's Command and General Staff College, counterinsurgency and guerrilla war were almost entirely absent from the curriculum. To Taylor it seemed as if the Army was trying to blot out the memory of the painful war, and he made it a personal crusade to force it to confront its failures. Taylor wore thick horn-rimmed glasses that gave him a professorial air and was so skinny he looked almost frail, but when he started talking about Vietnam his face reddened and his voice thundered. He had spent a long year leading patrols through rice paddies and small hamlets in the Mekong Delta, but those forays had accomplished little. Even when his unit could find the enemy, which wasn't often, they returned to their base at night, turning the villages they had just fought and bled for back over to the Viet Cong. "Anything you could do wrong, we did it," he often shouted. Taylor's anger spread like a virus through the restless minds in Sosh. "Bill would go into a rant and absolutely make your brain itch," said Asa Clark, another Vietnam vet who arrived at Sosh in the late 1970s. By the time he and Petraeus teamed up on their Vietnam paper, Taylor had left the Army and was working at a policy think tank in Washington.

The conference, held in early summer in a large auditorium on the West Point campus, attracted a diverse crowd of military officers, academics, and Pentagon officials. Though Petraeus had done most of the actual writing, the better-known Taylor gave the public presentation on the paper, which argued somewhat prosaically that Vietnam had made the U.S. military and its political leadership reluctant to use force. Afterward, Petraeus settled into a folding chair in the back of the auditorium for the conference's main attraction. Major Andy Krepinevich, a Sosh professor with a doctorate from Harvard, had written a sweeping history of Vietnam that painstakingly catalogued the mistakes of the war and punctured the Army's conventional wisdom on why it had lost. Writing during his three years at Sosh, Krepinevich was able to feed off the frustration that had taken root in the department. His work came to be passed around like a seditious tract, the sort of unauthorized thinking that resonated with some and exasperated others, not least because of his Harvard pedigree and lack of Vietnam service.

After the war, the Army had blamed its defeat on a fickle American public and meddling political leaders who prohibited the military from launching a conventional assault on North Vietnam and its military. Attacks in the north had largely been confined to bombing, and even those had been continually modulated in hopes of drawing the Communist leaders into a negotiated settlement. In the South the Army chased after Viet Cong guerrillas who senior officers later insisted were merely a distraction. This argument, advanced by Army War College professor Harry Summers and others, appealed to a demoralized force that was looking for an excuse to forget Vietnam, abandon guerrilla warfare, and focus on fighting familiar types of wars. Krepinevich, by contrast, insisted that the Army had lost in Vietnam not because of meddling civilians but because of its own incompetence. Its search-and-destroy tactics had alienated the very people it was supposed to be protecting. "The Army ended up trying to fight the kind of conventional war that it was trained, organized and prepared (and that it *wanted*) to fight instead of the counterinsurgency war that it was sent to fight," he argued. To make matters worse, the 1980s Army was compounding its error by focusing almost exclusively on conventional combat, giving little thought to how it might fight future guerrilla wars, which seemed "the most likely area of future conflict for the Army," he concluded.

Other officers with less fortitude than Krepinevich might have toned down their dissertation or quietly let it slip into academic obscurity, but he had ambitions to hold a mirror up to the Army's flaws. Petraeus, listening in the audience as he outlined his arguments, was impressed. After Krepinevich finished his remarks, he introduced himself and asked if he could get a copy of the dissertation.

The two officers long had been on parallel intellectual paths. Krepinevich graduated three years before Petraeus at West Point and had gone into the artillery branch, where he was plucked from the regular Army by Olvey and sent to Harvard. There he decided on an impulse to conduct his doctoral research on Vietnam. "I always wondered, how in the hell did we lose that war?" recalled Krepinevich. He turned his dissertation into a book, *The Army and Vietnam,* that was published in 1986 to widespread praise in the *New York Times* and other mainstream publications. "From the Army perspective, the account is certainly accurate, and devastating," wrote William Colby, the former director of the Central Intelligence Agency (though he chided Krepinevich for giving short shrift to the CIA's counterinsurgency efforts in Vietnam, which he had directed). It also drew praise from Sosh's longtime Asia expert, George Osborn, who wrote in the book's foreword that Krepinevich's dogged work had revealed the "doctrinal rigidity at all levels of the U.S. Army."

The acclaim from outsiders made the Army even more defensive. In what amounted to the official response, retired General Bruce Palmer, a commander in Vietnam who had penned his own lengthy history of the conflict, wrote a review for the Army War College's journal blasting the book for its "crippling naiveté" and an overall "lack of historical breadth and objectivity." Taking a job at the Pentagon after leaving Sosh, Krepinevich received a call one day from the West Point superintendent's office asking if he was the officer who wrote "that book about Vietnam." After Krepinevich confirmed that he was, the caller hung up without explanation. Only later did he learn from a friend on the faculty that the superintendent had banned him from speaking on campus. Most important forums where he might have spread his message within the Army ignored him. He retired a few years later as a lieutenant colonel, his book all but forgotten until the Army found itself fighting another intractable insurgency in Iraq.

Petraeus later referred to Krepinevich's treatment as "unsettling" and "enough to make any internal critic think twice" about challenging Army orthodoxy too openly. But in a less confrontational way, that was exactly what Petraeus himself was doing. He had been thinking about Vietnam since the 1970s, when his ten-day sojourn to France piqued his interest in Bigeard and the French experience in Indochina. He also talked for hours about the conflict with his father-in-law, General William Knowlton, who as a young officer attached to Westmoreland's staff in Saigon had helped run a rural development program aimed at winning over Vietnamese peasants. Later, at Fort Leavenworth, Petraeus and five other students had studied the largest helicopter assault of the war, Operation Junction City, in 1967. They concluded that such search-and-destroy missions were ineffective against the Viet Cong, who simply melted away rather than fight. "Large unit tactics do not appear to have been appropriate for what was primarily a political war and an insurgency," they wrote.

Once he reached West Point, Petraeus labored in the basement of

Thayer Hall for the next two years on his own Vietnam dissertation, typing on a clunky desktop computer while also teaching classes to cadets. In the summer, between his first and second years at Sosh, he traveled to the Panama Canal Zone, the headquarters of the United States Southern Command, where Jack Galvin, his mentor from the 24th, was now in command. With leftist guerrillas fighting the U.S.-backed right-wing government in El Salvador, Galvin was overseeing the military's first counterinsurgency operation since Vietnam. The two wars were nothing alike, though. Congress, eager to stave off another overseas commitment, had with the quiet support of the Pentagon put strict limits on the effort. A few dozen American Special Forces soldiers were involved in training the Salvadoran military, trying to rein in death squads, and extending the government's control to areas cleared of guerrillas. The Americans were barred from combat.

Petraeus attached himself to Galvin for the next six weeks, living again, if only temporarily, the glamorous life of an American officer abroad. They celebrated on the Fourth of July at Galvin's porticoed residence overlooking the canal, drinking champagne sent over by Panamanian strongman Manuel Noriega. They made trips to Peru, Colombia, and El Salvador, all of which were fighting insurgencies of varying intensity. It was a heady experience. In a stopover in the Salvadoran capital, Petraeus strode into President José Napoleón Duarte's office with a loaded submachine gun tucked underneath his arm. A *Wall Street Journal* reporter who ran into the exuberant young major that summer quoted him on the newspaper's front page as saying counterinsurgency was becoming a "growth industry." Yet Petraeus was also struck by how oblivious most of his own Army was to what was happening in El Salvador. Here was a small war the Army was actually involved in, he recalled thinking, but outside of Galvin's staff virtually all of the Army's energy and thought were focused elsewhere.

Galvin, in his usual provocative way, wanted to spread the word about what was happening in his vast domain. He told Petraeus to ghostwrite an essay using a speech that Galvin had delivered in London on counterinsurgency and to get it published in a military journal. The article, entitled "Uncomfortable Wars," sounded many of the same warnings as Krepinevich had: "There are many indicators that we are moving into a world in which subversive activities, civil disturbances, guerilla warfare, and low-level violence will grow and multiply," it argued.

After returning to West Point, Petraeus finished his dissertation, writing a prescient final chapter that criticized the Pentagon view that the U.S. military should only be committed to wars in which it could use overwhelming force to achieve clear objectives. This preference for short, firepower-intensive battles would soon be dubbed the Powell Doctrine, named for its most prominent adherent, General Colin Powell. Such an all-or-nothing approach to war was "unrealistic," chided Petraeus, who had never been in combat. The Army might prefer only rapid, conventional wars with broad popular support. But sooner or later it would be sent by the country's political leaders into a protracted conflict in which its foes would try to blend in with the populace, as the Viet Cong had done. In this environment, he argued, the United States would have to limit its use of firepower and try to win over the population through political and economic measures. In short, the Army would have to apply the sort of classic counterinsurgency strategy that its generals were explicitly rejecting. He concluded by calling for the United States to rebuild its counterinsurgency forces and expertise.

Unlike Krepinevich, Petraeus never published his dissertation's controversial conclusions. Like many high achievers who pass through Sosh, he was more interested in rising through the Army than in provoking its top brass. Nor did he remain the normal three years in the department. In the spring of his second year, he left to go work as a speechwriter and advisor to Galvin, who had been appointed supreme allied commander of NATO in Europe. Petraeus's last-minute departure rankled some of his colleagues who wondered why he got to play by different rules. The truth was that even in a department that practiced unabashed elitism, he stood out as special.

To fill his teaching slot, Olvey had to pull another officer out of graduate school early. The unlucky officer was a captain named William Sutey, who arrived from Syracuse University as Petraeus was leaving. At a reception for incoming Sosh faculty members that summer, Petraeus introduced himself to Sutey and asked where he had gone to school and what he had studied. "You are going to finish your Ph.D., right?" he inquired.

Sutey explained that he had not been able to finish the required courses. He didn't mention that it was Petraeus's exit that had interrupted his studies (or that he already had a second master's degree, earned before he joined the Army). A wan smile came across Petraeus's face. Here was somebody who didn't measure up, who lacked drive or intellect—or at least that was how Sutey interpreted the bland look. In a few seconds their conversation ended awkwardly. Petraeus spun on his heel and walked away.

CHAPTER FIVE

The Trophy

Grafenwöhr, West Germany
June 1987

L ieutenant Ed Massar poked his helmet out of the turret as his M1 Abrams tank rumbled to the starting line and halted, its main gun raised to fire. Three more sixty-ton M1s drove up and took positions on his flanks as the soundtrack to *Top Gun*, Hollywood's unabashed celebration of American military prowess, blared over loudspeakers. In a nearby observation area, Major Peter Chiarelli watched anxiously through binoculars as the four tanks of Delta Company's 1st Platoon prepared to move out. Chiarelli had spent eleven months training for this moment, the last run on the last day of NATO's prestigious tank gunnery competition. Unfortunately, nothing was going according to plan. Just a few minutes earlier, the electronic gun sight in one of the tanks had failed, forcing Chiarelli to rush one of the four-man crews into a replacement tank. Freak weather on a previous run had left the U.S. in third place. Now as he watched and waited, Chiarelli silently prayed nothing else went wrong.

Spread out below him was the gently sloping countryside of Range 301 at Grafenwöhr, a vast training area near the Czech border that once had been used by the Nazis and now was a main training range for NATO. The competition had been under way for four days, and multiple teams from Britain, Belgium, Canada, the Netherlands, and West Germany had already motored through the range, blasting their main guns at the pop-up plywood targets as though it was a carnival shooting arcade. Chiarelli knew that 1st Platoon needed a flawless run to have any chance of beating the Germans, who days before had hit all thirty-two targets without a miss.

The winner would take home the sterling silver Canadian Army Trophy (CAT) as NATO's best tank platoon. Chiarelli and the two- and three-star generals watching in the reviewing stand weren't the only Americans desperate to claim the prize. Interest stretched all the way back to the Pentagon and the White House, where Colin Powell, national security advisor to President Ronald Reagan, was awaiting the results. The United States had never won the competition, an embarrassing record of futility by the alliance's most powerful member. Even after Congress appropriated billions of dollars to build the new M1 tank, the Germans had dominated the contest, winning six out of the last eight times in their Leopard tanks. "If Military Contests Were Real War, U.S. Might Be in a Pickle," read the headline on a front-page *Wall Street Journal* story about the 1985 competition, where the United States had eked out second place. This year no effort had been spared to bring home the trophy. Massar and his men were in an improved M1, rushed to Europe for the competition. When several of the main guns were found to be slightly warped, every tank was outfitted with a brand-new one, hand-selected for straightness as they came off the assembly line. Over the previous eleven months, Chiarelli's team had trained nonstop in the field and on simulators that re-created the terrain on Range 301. Hundreds of Thanksgiving dinners had been sent by helicopter to the men at Grafenwöhr, rather than letting them spend the holiday with their families. The Army even had dispatched a sports psychologist from West Point to tutor the tank crews in relaxation techniques. It was time to show Congress a return on its money, and the pressure fell on Pete Chiarelli's battalion.

He had been training the three American platoons from the 3rd Armored Division since joining the unit the previous summer. Delta Company's other two platoons had made their runs on Tuesday and Thursday and had come up short. Now the Americans were down to their last chance. That morning, a senior officer from the 3rd Armored Division staff had pulled Chiarelli aside and said he had learned the pattern of pop-up targets that Massar's platoon would see on their final run. Knowing where the targets would appear on the range and in what order was like getting the answer sheet the night before a big exam. Chiarelli copied down the information into a notebook. The division officer told him to brief 1st Platoon before they made their run. Chiarelli knew what this meant and it shocked him. His Army was determined to win the trophy, even if it had to cheat.

$$\star \quad \star \quad \star \quad \star$$

Chiarelli had arrived at Frankfurt Airport a year earlier with Beth, eleven-year-old Peter, and seven-year-old Erin. He was assigned as a staff officer in a tank battalion in the 3rd Armored Division. His first overseas tour did not start auspiciously. Before leaving Seattle, Chiarelli had sliced his right hand working in the yard with a hedge trimmer. After doctors initially told Beth they would have to amputate three fingertips, they had been able to reattach them with only a small loss of feeling. But as he walked down the ramp, Chiarelli's left hand was still heavily bandaged. He was in a foul mood. His stitches had begun bleeding during the six-hour plane ride. There to greet them was Captain Joe Schmalzel, an officer on the staff of his new battalion, with more bad news: the family quarters that had been promised to them not far from Coleman Barracks, their new post on a hillside outside the town of Gelnhausen, had been given away to another officer. The Chiarellis would have to find rental housing off-post.

Nothing in the Army ever came smoothly for Pete Chiarelli, it seemed. Returning to a combat unit after a seven-year academic sojourn, he had to prove himself all over again. Sosh had a track record of getting its people good assignments back in the regular Army, but plenty of them still saw their once-glittering careers plateau. They had stayed away from real soldiering too long and seen their less academically inclined peers bypass them on the path to colonel and general. Eventually the up-or-out rules forced them into retirement. General Barry McCaffrey, who had taught in the department in the early 1970s, joked that teaching at Sosh was the "best way to become a general and the worst way to become a lieutenant colonel." Chiarelli was in danger of proving the punch line. He had saved himself, not for the last time, with help from Olvey, the head of Sosh, who had called his contacts to secure Chiarelli this job in Germany. Olvey had sent him off with assurances that he was certain to make general one day. Maybe so, or maybe Olvey was just letting him down gently after not choosing him for the permanent faculty at Sosh. Either way, Chiarelli needed to prove he could do things his service valued and do them well. By coincidence, a month after he arrived, Colin Powell had taken over as commander of the Army's V Corps in Germany, giving him overall responsibility for two divisions and 75,000 American troops. Always attentive to the political currents in Washington, Powell informed his officers that winning the Canadian Army Trophy would be one of his goals. Word soon reached Gelnhausen, a forty-five-minute drive from Frankfurt. As the operations officer, Chiarelli got the job of training the battalion's Delta Company for the contest.

The assignment came as the Chiarellis were still settling into their new life. For the first few months, as they searched for off-post housing, the family crammed into the unused attic in the officers' quarters at Coleman. There was no bathroom, so they had to walk a few doors down to Joe Schmalzel's place to use his. When the attic finally became intolerable, they moved to a nearby hotel before finally finding a charming house for rent in a small farming village. The locals were used to the Americans after forty years of living side-by-side with the U.S. soldiers, and the kids went to the post's Gelnhausen Elementary School with other American kids. Officers and their wives socialized on Friday nights at the officers' club. Beth's biggest complaint was the same one she always had with the Army—Pete was always working. It got so bad that when their son Patrick was born, she rearranged his sleeping schedule just so he would be awake when her husband arrived home in the evening, usually sometime after 10 p.m.

There was no mistaking the importance the brass attached to winning the trophy. A few weeks after taking command, Powell came to Gelnhausen, ostensibly for a get-acquainted dinner at the officers' club. One of his motives was to make clear that anything less than first place was unacceptable. The post held special memories for Powell. His first assignment as a

twenty-one-year-old second lieutenant was as commander of an infantry
platoon at Coleman Barracks. Then as now, such dinners were boisterous
affairs with thick steaks and plentiful German beer. Colonel Stan Luallin,
the commander at Coleman, escorted Powell and his wife, Alma, into the
club a little after seven in the evening for cocktails. Chiarelli had not been
able to attend the dinner, but Schmalzel and a few other junior officers
watched the youthful-looking general circulate around the wood-paneled
room in his sharp blue dress uniform. Powell shook hands and made small
talk with his new subordinates, eventually making his way around to the
CAT team. He said he expected them to bring home the trophy that year.
"Well, we'll either win or we won't," a nervous Schmalzel replied with a
cartoonish chuckle. Powell fixed the twenty-seven-year-old captain with
a stare. "I don't joke with company-grade officers," he said, abruptly moving on.

   He loosened up a little after dinner, recalling that in his day young lieutenants and captains after a night of drinking in the very same officers' club
used to climb out onto a small second-floor balcony and leap off in a show
of toughness. "I came to understand GIs during my tour at Gelnhausen. I
learned what made them tick," Powell later wrote in his autobiography.
"American soldiers love to win" and "they respect a leader who holds them
to high standards." Neither victories nor high standards had been common
early in Powell's career. After Germany, he had done two tours in Vietnam
and soldiered through the 1970s. He and other officers of his generation
had emerged from those traumatic times vowing to resist being drawn ever
again into an insurgent war where they were prevented from using the full
might of the U.S. armed forces, as many felt they had been barred from
doing in Vietnam. "Many of my generation . . . vowed that when our turn
came to call the shots, we would not quietly acquiesce in half-hearted warfare for half-baked reasons that the American people could not understand
or support," Powell wrote.

   The lessons of Vietnam may have been all the rage in Sosh and at
Southern Command. But most of the Army wanted nothing to do with
training to fight limited wars. It had spent much of the last two decades trying to restore the fighting prowess it had lost in Vietnam. By the second
half of the 1980s, the Reagan-era military buildup was beginning to pay off.

New advanced equipment was pouring into Army units. Along with the bruising M1 tank, there were the Apache and Black Hawk helicopters, the Bradley troop-carrying vehicle, and the Patriot antimissile defense system—all of them expressly designed for fighting the mechanized armies of the Soviet Union or its proxies. After years of tight budgets, money was plentiful for better soldier pay and training. American officers were being schooled in an aggressive new conventional fighting doctrine called "Air-Land Battle," which preached the importance of precision strikes on the enemy and swift maneuvers by large armored formations. Now it was time to show off the new American capabilities. Short of war itself, nothing would demonstrate more clearly to enemies and allies that the U.S. Army was back than a victory at CAT.

There was a satisfying continuity to his new assignment, Chiarelli thought. Once his father had stood in the turret of his Sherman tank as it motored into the Nazi heartland. Now he was in Germany, too, still dreaming, as he had as a kid, of one day commanding hundreds of tanks in wartime. There were many times when he felt in over his head. He was an armor officer but had never commanded a tank company and, after nearly a decade out of a frontline unit, had only a rudimentary understanding of the new technology in the M1 tank. But in a volunteer army that increasingly saw itself as separate from the larger American society it protected, Chiarelli was a throwback to the citizen soldiers of the draft era. There was something about him that soldiers responded to. Anybody who spent more than five minutes with him could see it. He could be demanding and intense, but people liked him and worked hard for him. When Powell traveled to Grafenwöhr to observe the battalion during maneuvers that fall, he noticed it, too. A lieutenant colonel was nominally in command, but the men looked to Chiarelli to make all the decisions. "You have a problem," he warned Luallin, the commander at Coleman. "That Major Chiarelli is running the battalion." Luallin assured him they had the situation under control.

Chiarelli soon began remastering the intricacies of tank gunnery. Several of the Army's best tank gunners from Fort Knox were brought over to Germany to tutor the teams. One of the reasons the United States was continuing to lose at CAT, Chiarelli learned, was that its gunners weren't taking full advantage of the tanks' revolutionary technology. Under the competition rules, each tank team training for the competition was permitted to fire a total of only 134 live rounds in the twelve months before CAT. The idea was to replicate the amount of training a normal tank crew might receive, to stop teams from skewing the competition by spending day after day at the gunnery range. Chiarelli ordered his gunners to expend precious ammunition zeroing their guns, a process that often took as many as five or six rounds for each tank. If his men learned to calibrate their weapons precisely, he reasoned, the payoff in accuracy would be much greater than if they simply did more target practice. A properly zeroed gun could repeatedly hit an eight-inch-wide bull's-eye at a distance of 2,000 meters. Whatever rounds were left could then be used for target practice. "We were going to give these guys confidence that this tank really worked," Chiarelli recalled.

He was in the observation tower at Grafenwöhr one day after losing yet again, watching his tanks drive off the range. Lieutenant Colonel John Abrams, an officer from division who was overseeing the training, stood next to him. One of the M1s suddenly started belching plumes of smoke before clanking to a halt. Abrams was the son of Creighton Abrams, the legendary general for whom the M1 tank was named. Enraged, the younger Abrams summoned Lieutenant Joe Weiss, the maintenance officer. "What the hell happened?" he demanded. As Weiss tried to explain that a part had failed, Abrams cut him off. "You guys don't get it!" he yelled. "You'll never win this thing. What we need is excellence. Do you understand?" Chiarelli, standing nearby, was incensed that Abrams was bellowing at his soldier. "Don't talk that way to a member of my team again," he said icily.

But Chiarelli was worried. A month before the competition, Delta Company's tanks were consistently hitting only twenty-six of thirty-two targets, which was not enough to win the trophy, if past competitions were any guide. In May, Chiarelli's parents visited from Seattle. It was their first chance to see their new grandson, Patrick, who was turning one year old, and Pete took some time off to spend with his father, who was back in Europe for the first time since World War II. A few days after arriving, his father complained that he wasn't feeling well and checked into the U.S. Army hospital in Frankfurt. He had suffered a heart attack a few years earlier, and the long plane ride from Seattle had left him fatigued. He returned to his son's house some days later with doctor's orders to rest, but his condition soon deteriorated. Rushed one night to a nearby German hospital, he died on May 7. The Chiarellis flew home to Seattle for the funeral.

Two weeks later Chiarelli, still grieving, was back in Germany for the start of the CAT competition. He had started smoking again and looked haggard. But Schmalzel greeted him with some welcome news for a change: the three platoons had fired the last of their 134 rounds the previous week and scored their best results so far. Not only had they hit most of the targets but, after a year of training, the crews had cut the amount of time it took them to reload and fire a round to just seconds.

It was overcast and raining lightly the first morning of the competition when Chiarelli's best platoon, commanded by Lieutenant John Menard, rolled onto Range 301. With a booming shot from its main gun, the lead tank fired at the first target, putting a hole right in the center. Turrets swiveling, the M1s advanced down the sloped range, four abreast. Each pop-up target, a plywood silhouette of an enemy tank, appeared for forty seconds. Menard's men hit the first twenty-eight pop-up targets without a miss. But fifteen minutes into their run, the downpour intensified. It was so severe that Menard could barely see five feet in any direction. Four final targets appeared over the next forty seconds, but Menard's men, unable to make out any of them, didn't fire another shot. They finished with twenty-eight hits out of thirty-two targets, a decent showing but not good enough for first place even on the first day of competition. Chiarelli demanded the chance to rerun the course but was rebuffed. At the end of the first day, the Dutch were in the lead, having missed only two targets in their first run. The next American platoon, competing on Wednesday, had clear weather and earned a better score, hitting thirty of thirty-two targets. But Thursday afternoon, the Germans' 124th Panzer Battalion completed a perfect run, a feat that had only been accomplished one other time.

Going into the final day, the Americans' last chance rested with Massar's platoon, the weakest of the three. Even if the Americans matched the Germans' perfect score, they could only win outright—and claim the trophy as the best tank unit in NATO—by finishing their round in a faster time, giving them a higher overall score. The night before, to get fired up, they had watched a rerun of the U.S. hockey team's improbable victory over the Soviets at the 1980 Winter Olympics. Massar's platoon made the second run of the day, in the afternoon, after the British finished on the course. By then, it had been several hours since Chiarelli had received the sequence of targets the Americans would face. Chiarelli had gone to his boss, Luallin, and told him he wasn't going to pass along the information. It would only confuse them, he told his superior, insisting that they were ready. As Chiarelli watched the four tanks roar onto the range, he knew he was taking an extravagant risk. Another loss at CAT would only intensify questioning in Washington about whether the Abrams tank was worth the money.

As the four tanks of 1st Platoon started onto the range, the thumping *Top Gun* theme song was playing at top volume over the loudspeaker until a gruff voice rang out from grandstand, "Turn that goddamn music off!" The recording cut off abruptly. The order came from General Glenn Otis, the top U.S. Army commander in Europe, one of several three- and four-star generals in the VIP grandstand. As the M1s began moving four abreast down the range, the two tanks on the right side of the formation fired almost at once, the explosions from their main guns sending tongues of flame ripping toward the targets. For the next twenty minutes, Chiarelli got reports from his observers as 1st Platoon tanks tore around Range 301, hitting target after target. They completed the course without a miss.

The two dozen teams stood in formation as the judges tallied the final scores. A few minutes later, the announcement came over the loudspeaker: "The high-scoring platoon was 1st Platoon, Delta Company!" The American troops erupted in raucous cheers, embraces, and backslaps. The U.S. and German teams had both hit all the targets, but the final result was a blowout. Massar's men had taken an average of a full second less than every other competitor to fire, reload, and fire again. The U.S. team ended with a total score of 20,490, a comfortable 800 points ahead of the 124th Panzer Battalion.

Walking up to Chiarelli afterward, the division officer who had slipped Chiarelli the target sequence said, "Well, congratulations, but you had some pretty good intel, didn't you?"

"Yes I did, but I didn't tell them a goddamn thing," Chiarelli fired back.

"You took a hell of a chance," the officer said finally.

Driving back to the barracks to celebrate over a beer with his men, Chiarelli found a pay phone and called his mother in Seattle. His father would have been so proud, his mother told him as they both cried. Chiarelli had worked hard. He had come back from near-irrelevancy in an Army that only a year before had been ready to cast him aside. Maybe for the first time he could be confident there was a future for him in the military. Word of the victory was quickly relayed back to Colin Powell at the White House. He had lasted only five months in Germany before being summoned to Washington to be national security advisor in the waning days of the Reagan administration. But Powell allowed himself the general's prerogative of claiming credit. "Two initiatives that I had set in motion paid off soon after I left," he wrote in his memoirs, referring to the victory at CAT and another NATO competition that the United States had won around the same time. "These competitions may mean little to the layperson, but in NATO this was the equivalent of winning the World Series and the Super Bowl in one season."

The victory party continued when Chiarelli's men arrived back at Gelnhausen by rail car. For the first time anyone could remember, they were allowed to drive their massive M1s through the front gate, pulling up in formation to cheers from the soldiers and families who had assembled to welcome them home. The division band played the theme to the movie *Patton* as generals made speeches and handed out medals to every member of the platoon. Originally, the Army brass had wanted to decorate only Massar's men. But Chiarelli had insisted on medals for the other two platoons, too. This was a team, he declared, and they had trained just as hard. He got his way. He was still just a major, but for the moment he might as well have been Patton himself.

* * * *

A few months after the CAT competition, a Pentagon study examining the U.S. victory began with an unusually worded introduction addressed to the Soviet Red Army and its allies. "Warning to the Warsaw Pact," it read.

"If you make the decision to attack NATO ground forces in Western Europe, the most highly-skilled, best equipped and supported armored forces in the world will cut you to ribbons. . . . We, the American victors in the 1987 Canadian Army Trophy competition, issue this warning on behalf of our allies and from a position of strength."

The next war came not against the Warsaw Pact but in the Middle East after Saddam Hussein invaded Kuwait. Iraq's army had been equipped by the Soviet Union and was familiar to the vast U.S. force sent to eject them from Kuwait. There was another fortunate coincidence about the 1991 Gulf War: Saddam and his generals decided to fight a conventional war in the open desert. The big tank battle that the Army had been preparing for at Grafenwöhr in Germany and in the Mojave Desert of California actually came to pass. Chiarelli was certain he was going to be sent to the fight. He was back at Fort Lewis, near Seattle, commanding a motorized infantry battalion. At a Christmas party in December his boss, who was a bit tipsy, had even broken the news to his wife, Beth. "Don't tell anybody, but by February fifteenth you guys will be out of here," he whispered to her. The Chiarellis drove down to the Rose Bowl to watch their beloved Washington Huskies beat Iowa and made a quick stop at Disneyland with their three kids. Chiarelli and Beth were on edge the entire trip. Finally, in early February, he was told to have his men ready to go to the Middle East in six days. A week passed and the orders to move never came. Then they were told that they were going in two days. Again nothing.

Dave Petraeus also wanted to go to war, maybe worse than Chiarelli. He had packed his desert uniforms, taken his shots for the Middle East, and even updated his will. But he was trapped in the Pentagon, working as the personal aide to General Carl Vuono, the Army's four-star chief of staff. At least once a week, he would ask Vuono to release him and assign him to a combat slot—or any job close to the action. Although Vuono had laid down strict orders that the officers working for him were going to stay put, Petraeus had spent his career defying the rules set for lesser officers. So he lobbied, schemed, and begged. One week he'd try the "selfless service" angle. The next week he'd rattle off the names of other officers who had been allowed to leave their Pentagon posts. When that didn't work, he asked the Army's vice chief of staff to intercede with the chief. Nothing worked, and it was driving Petraeus crazy.

Vuono had come to rely so heavily on Petraeus that he couldn't imagine doing without him. Each day before dawn Petraeus arrived at Quarters One, the chief's residence on the edge of Arlington Cemetery, and drove with him to the Pentagon. In the evening, almost always after seven o'clock, they would return home together. Petraeus edited his speeches and helped draft his congressional testimony. On Saturdays he sat with Vuono in his study, dialing commanders all over the world to check on their war preparations. Sundays were the day they watched football games and read through binders full of newspaper articles, think tank papers, and internal Army studies. Petraeus's talents were working against him: he'd become Vuono's primary sounding board.

George Casey was also stuck in the Pentagon, working for Vuono. It was the first decent job that he had been able to land since arriving in Washington four years earlier. Unfortunately, it looked as if it had come too late to save his career. Casey had spent most of the late 1970s and early 1980s at Fort Carson, Colorado, a base whose units were at the very bottom of the Army's Master Priority List, meaning that they were the least likely to deploy and the last to get new equipment. Returning to the sleepy post after turning down a spot in Delta Force had been a big letdown. In 1978, bored with the Army, he briefly broke away to study for a master's degree in international relations at the University of Denver. He earned mostly A's but realized that the academic life wasn't for him.

He volunteered for a yearlong tour as a United Nations observer in the Sinai, where he and a group of Russian officers would share a tiny outpost on the Suez Canal for two weeks each month. In February 1982, Casey said goodbye to Sheila and his two sons at the Colorado Springs airport. "It's the only time I have ever seen my dad cry," recalled his son Sean, who was ten years old at the time. Casey wasn't going to be in any danger, but saying goodbye had dredged up his own memories of seeing off his father as he deployed to Korea and Vietnam. After a few months, Sheila decided to leave her job as an accountant and moved with their two boys to Cairo, where they rented a small apartment. Many Army families would have been put off by the chaos of the Middle East. The Caseys used Cairo as a base to tour Damascus, Jerusalem, and the ruins at Petra in Jordan.

By 1982, he was back at Fort Carson, which, thanks to the Reagan-era defense buildup, was bustling with activity. Casey rarely questioned the direction the Army was headed, as Abizaid or Petraeus did. He didn't write scholarly articles on defense policy, like Chiarelli. But he had other talents that the 1980s Army, which was remaking itself to fight the Soviets, valued immensely. He knew how to motivate and train soldiers. His troops referred to him admiringly as "George the Animal" for his energy, work ethic, and enthusiasm. And he had learned how to fight. In the absence of a real war, the National Training Center in the Mojave Desert was the place where officers proved themselves in battles against the Soviet-style opposition. As Chiarelli was preparing for the CAT competition in Germany, Casey's 700-soldier battalion got its shot in the California desert. His commander at the time was Colonel Wesley Clark, a hypercompetitive Rhodes scholar and Sosh alum. Clark nervously confided to his wife that the soft-spoken Casey didn't seem particularly driven. "I worry he's not committed to winning," Clark fretted.

Casey was more driven than he appeared. He spent hours drafting forty-page playbooks that his troops could stuff into a pocket of their cargo pants and were expected to memorize prior to their training center battles. On predawn bus rides to Fort Carson's training range, he stood at the front of the rolling bus and crammed in an hourlong lecture on Soviet tactics. He also spent weeks puzzling over the best way to surprise the enemy forces. His innovation was simple but effective. Most commanders at the National Training Center never employed their antitank missile weapons in the fight. Mounted atop 1960s-era armored vehicles, the launchers typically were trapped behind faster-moving tanks. Casey snuck his antitank weapons out onto the flanks of his battalion, where they pounded away at the unsuspecting enemy.

Two decades after the mock battle in the Mojave Desert, his former troops still marveled at their success. A few kept framed Polaroid snapshots of a 1980s computer screen showing the battalion's kills that day. "Never underestimate the killing power of a few well-positioned antitank missiles," Casey had written on one such photo, which in 2008 hung in the Pentagon office of one of his former lieutenants.

Although his family connections would have made it easy for him to land a job as a general's aide, Casey had spent most of his career seeking out positions that allowed him to roll up his sleeves with sergeants in the motor pool. He embraced the Army ideal of the hardworking commander who focused on training men for war and left the bigger strategic questions to politicians and academics. And the Army had rewarded him by promoting him earlier to major and lieutenant colonel.

It wasn't until he arrived in Washington that he realized that he hadn't made the kinds of connections that he'd need to rise to the military's top ranks. He did a one-year fellowship at the Atlantic Council, a Washington, D.C., think tank devoted to NATO issues. Afterward the best job he could find was in the Army's congressional liaison office, housed in a windowless Pentagon office known as the "hog pen." There he spent eighteen months answering arcane questions from congressional staffers about the defense budget.

Eventually, one of his former commanders from Fort Carson helped him land a better job working on Vuono's staff, helping the chief push the glacial Pentagon bureaucracy to implement his priorities. As other officers scrambled to get to the Gulf War in the winter of 1991, Casey focused on his duties. Like Petraeus, he longed to prove himself in combat and confessed to Sheila that he badly wanted to go. But he could never quite bring himself to ask for special favors. He told himself that if the Army really needed him, it would reassign him to a combat unit. He was the kind of officer who believed that the system would work.

✶　✶　✶　✶

In February 1991, after a lengthy bombing campaign, the United States and its allies pushed Saddam's army out of Kuwait in a stunning 100-hour thrashing. Petraeus and Casey watched from the Pentagon, where they were working for Vuono. At Fort Lewis, Chiarelli did his best to mask his disappointment when he learned his unit would be staying put. Standing in front of his battalion, he told his troops that they were going to get their chance, and quoted Plato: "Only the dead have seen the end of war." Privately he thought he had missed the last great tank battle. Abizaid, who was commanding a battalion in Europe, didn't make it to Iraq for the fighting either. He deployed two months after the end of the combat on a military-humanitarian mission to protect northern Iraq's Kurds, who had risen up against Saddam Hussein, prompting the dictator to launch a cruel assault on them. To Abizaid it became clear that the war the United States thought it had won was far from over.

That, of course, wasn't the lesson being drawn at the White House and Pentagon, where the triumph in the Middle East was regarded as vindication of the lessons that the American military had taken from Vietnam. "The specter of Vietnam has been buried forever in the desert sands of the Arabian Peninsula," a delighted President George H. W. Bush boasted days after the cease-fire between U.S. and Iraqi troops had been signed. "By God, we've kicked the Vietnam syndrome once and for all."

★　★　★　★

In June 1991, four months after the war ended, Vuono announced that he was retiring from the Army. Most of his staff headed on to other jobs. Petraeus moved on to command an infantry battalion in the 101st Airborne Division. Casey had nothing lined up and assumed his career was over. The phone lines in his office were disconnected and the nameplate pried off the door. For several weeks he came into work to read the *Washington Post* before heading over to the Pentagon gym.

Eventually he got a job for himself evaluating arms control agreements. Casey knew that back-to-back Pentagon assignments were an absolute career killer for an Army colonel, so he applied to George Washington University's business school, figuring that an MBA would help him land a better civilian position when he retired.

Without Casey knowing, Vuono was quietly working to get his career back on track. A couple of weeks before he officially retired, the Army chief called the commander of the 1st Cavalry Division, the unit Casey's father had commanded in Vietnam. The division needed a new chief of staff, a coveted assignment usually reserved for a colonel who has already commanded a brigade. Casey's name had been left off the last two brigade command lists. "Could you help this guy Casey out?" Vuono asked. Major General John Tilelli, the division commander, saw that Casey had been a successful battalion commander at Fort Carson. Tilelli, who had served two tours in Vietnam and had just led his division in the Gulf War, also liked the idea of bringing Casey back to the division his father had been commanding when he was killed.

Casey arrived at Fort Hood in August, a sprawling post in central Texas where the base library was named in honor of his deceased father. The base was crammed with the latest tanks, helicopters, and armored personnel carriers just back from Kuwait. Soldiers with the yellow 1st Cav combat patches, indicating that they had fought in the Gulf War, strutted across its training ranges. The division had played a comparatively minor role in the fighting, but it didn't matter. Anyone who was in the combat zone got to wear the patch on his right sleeve.

Casey had always told himself that if his father hadn't been killed, he would have left the Army after two years. He couldn't stand the idea of living in his dad's shadow. But the 1st Cavalry Division he was joining at Fort Hood wasn't anything like the exhausted force that his father had been commanding in Vietnam when he was killed. The place was full of energy, and Casey felt a surprising surge of pride as he stepped onto the base. This was the Army he had helped rebuild. Although he was one of the few senior officers not wearing the coveted patch, Casey felt at home.

CHAPTER SIX

No Job for Amateurs

If the Army continues to resist, organizing training and equipping itself to fight and win the "wars" it is currently being asked to fight, it may no longer have a sufficiently professional officer corps when the next big war occurs.
—MAJOR JOHN NAGL, INSTRUCTOR,
WEST POINT DEPARTMENT OF SOCIAL SCIENCES, 1999

Vicenza, Italy
April 1991

The shooting war had been over for two months when John Abizaid's battalion was ordered to Iraq. There was something deflating at being sent in for the Gulf War's messy aftermath. He and his men weren't even going to the desert, where the fighting had occurred, but to Iraq's mountainous north as part of a humanitarian operation to protect Kurdish refugees. Pentagon planners hadn't given much thought to the Kurds until a few days before. But in a way it was another example of Abizaid's talent for being in the right place. Although few realized it then, the deployment offered an important glimpse into the Army's future and its post-Vietnam failings.

At first the Pentagon treated the operation like a reinvasion, ordering a massive parachute drop to intimidate the Iraqi troops in the area. Flown to a NATO air base in southern Turkey, Abizaid and his 1,400 soldiers had already begun loading aircraft when word came around 2:00 a.m. that plans had changed. Worried that the airborne assault would be misinterpreted as a resumption of hostilities, the Pentagon devised a new mode of entry—so Abizaid and his men loaded onto rattletrap Turkish buses and drove across the rugged border, like tourists on a cut-rate excursion.

Their objective was Zakho, a border town ringed by snowcapped mountains. Making camp with a contingent of Marines, they found an almost apocalyptic scene—abandoned houses, overturned cars, and boarded-up shops. As the sun set that first night, the Americans saw hundreds of flickering campfires in the surrounding peaks, where the townspeople had fled. Prior to the ground war, President George H. W. Bush had urged Iraqis to rise up against Saddam Hussein. Kurdish fighters, badly miscalculating the dictator's weakness and the willingness of the United States to help them, had gone on the attack. To hold on to power, Hussein launched a brutal offensive against the Kurds. Now half a million refugees were huddled in the makeshift mountain camps, often without shelter or food. With winter bearing down and disease rampant, as many as a thousand Kurds were dying every day.

Once the scale of the calamity became clear, U.S. and European governments rushed in forces, including Abizaid's battalion, to face down Hussein's troops and coax the Kurds home. How to accomplish this was murky. Abizaid had little to guide him other than a few out-of-date maps and orders torn from a field notebook that read: "Mission: Conduct security operations in sector to protect displaced civilians. Be prepared to provide rapid reaction force to respond to requirements by headquarters."

On one point his superiors had been adamant: worried about restarting a war they had just won, they barred Abizaid from using force unless his men were attacked. For the moment things were quiet. Iraqi units had moved a few dozen miles south and dug in. But it was a volatile situation, with the potential for shooting to erupt unexpectedly, especially early in the operation. Perhaps their biggest advantage was that the Iraqis didn't know the Americans were barred from attacking unless threatened. "I know you understand the rules of engagement," Abizaid told his young commanders, referring to the guidelines for firing their guns. "Your responsibility is to accomplish your mission and protect your force. I trust your judgment and I trust you."

Abizaid's years in the Middle East, his fluent Arabic, and his talent for improvisation made him a logical choice for this undefined mission. Most of the other military men involved had barely heard of the Kurds' long struggle to carve out their own independent homeland from parts of Iraq, Turkey, and Iran. "We all took our cues from John," recalled General John Shalikashvili, a future chairman of the Joint Chiefs, who oversaw the operation from neighboring Turkey.

Abizaid's experience in the Middle East gave him a view different from the one held by most of his peers, the colonels and majors who had just fought and won the Gulf War. They returned home certain that Iraq could not withstand the awesome might of the American military. Abizaid in many ways drew the opposite conclusion. His four-month mission exposed him to the barely suppressed hatreds of Iraq, a place where countrymen fought and killed each other with stunning viciousness. He emerged from the mission even more skeptical of the ability of his soldiers or any occupiers to impose their will on the country. A decade later, neoconservatives in the Bush administration, such as Deputy Defense Secretary Paul Wolfowitz, insisted that if Saddam Hussein were forced from power, democracy would quickly flower, just as it had in the Kurdish enclave. Abizaid never believed that. A foreign force like his could stop the worst of the killing and, with civilian government agencies and aid groups, carve out small enclaves of relative peace and prosperity. Sooner or later, though, an occupying army, even one with the purest of motives, would find itself hated and attacked.

✳   ✳   ✳   ✳

Abizaid's biggest worry was what would happen when the Kurds finally came down from the mountains. If the refugees pushed south to their homes, the Iraqi troops might resume their massacre. If the Iraqis retreated, Abizaid feared, the Kurdish rebels would slaughter the stragglers. To prevent either scenario, he planned to use his soldiers as a buffer, positioning them between the returning Kurds and the Iraqi troops. His troops had to move much sooner than he expected. A few days after Abizaid's battalion arrived, Kurdish guerrillas, known as Peshmerga, began racing down from the mountains in white Toyota pickup trucks, clearly intent on revenge. At 7:00 a.m., in the midst of a heavy rainstorm, he ordered his battalion to move. They headed south, not knowing what lay ahead.

Forty kilometers into the bone-chilling drive, worried inquiries from headquarters started coming over Abizaid's radio. "Where are you?" his higher headquarters asked. His troops had outrun the protective umbrella of U.S. artillery. Soon he was being told to stop. Abizaid continued south, passing a column of Saddam Hussein's tanks fleeing the advancing Kurds. It was like a scene from the movie *Mad Max*. One tank was missing its treads and was spewing sparks as the bare wheels scraped over the blacktop, the driver too scared or indifferent to stop. When the Americans ran into an Iraqi army roadblock at the only mountain passes leading into the provincial capital of Dahuk, Abizaid's lead company commander tied a white rag to a spare antenna and moved forward tentatively, waving his arms. The Iraqis didn't budge.

Driving up a few minutes later, Abizaid radioed two Air Force jets in the vicinity and told them to make low, thundering passes over their location. When the Iraqi commander still refused to move, Abizaid had his troops dig in as if preparing to fight. The bluff worked. The soldiers sullenly moved south. Abizaid pressed on as well. Encountering another Iraqi unit outside Dahuk, he charged up to the commander and demanded that he withdraw or face destruction. Uncertain what to do, the Iraqi colonel excused himself to answer a ringing phone. "The Americans are here," Abizaid heard the flustered officer say into the phone. He paused to listen and then repeated himself. "No, you don't understand! I'm telling you the commander is standing right here in my office," he said, handing over the phone to Abizaid, who told the officer on the line that they had twenty-four hours to withdraw. Eventually they left as well.

When Major General Jay Garner, who was overseeing the relief effort, flew in a few days later, he headed straight for Abizaid. "John Abizaid, that was one of the greatest examples of military skill that I have ever seen," he said, sticking out his hand.

During their four months in Iraq, Abizaid and his troops lived in crumbling buildings without electricity or running water and washed in streams and lakes. Without firing a shot, they slowly pushed the Iraqis south. They blasted them with loud music, buzzed their living quarters at 2:00 a.m. with Apache helicopters, and fired illumination rounds— artillery shells that light up the night sky—at their positions. As a final resort, they blocked mountain passes to prevent Baghdad from ferrying in reinforcements.

Abizaid had little sympathy for the Iraqi soldiers, who had salted Kurdish fields and gassed Kurdish women and children several years earlier. But he soon realized that the Kurds, motivated by decades of persecution and massacres, could be just as brutal. It made for a dauntingly complex battlefield. Sometimes the Americans found themselves mediating between warring Kurdish factions; other times bedraggled Iraqi soldiers ran to U.S. checkpoints seeking protection. The viciousness seemed to dwarf even what he had seen in Lebanon. A few weeks before he was scheduled to depart, Abizaid was walking on a craggy ridgeline with a Peshmerga commander when he noticed three Iraqi corpses, their bodies covered with burn marks and their eyes gouged out.

"Why do you torture everybody?" he asked. "Why not just kill them?"

"Nobody fears death," replied the commander, his rifle slung over his shoulder and a scarf wrapped around his head. The survivors, he explained, needed to see the mutilated bodies of their fellow soldiers so that they understood what could happen to them if they fought the Kurds. The conversation stuck with Abizaid for years, along with other memories of brutality from his previous tours of the Middle East. The region's combustible mix of tribes, repressive regimes, and culture of revenge seemed to breed violence that swelled at times to all-out war before settling back into hit-and-run ambushes, revenge attacks, and terrorism. None of it truly threatened an army as powerful as the United States'. But Abizaid also recognized that his military couldn't stop it, either. It was especially foolish to expect short, swift victories of the sort the American people had come to demand in the wake of Vietnam.

The battalion's withdrawal in midsummer was a fittingly surreal end to its mission. They were the rear guard—the last to leave Iraqi soil across a single bridge spanning the river that formed the Iraqi-Turkish border. "This is the single most important place that has to be protected," Abizaid told Captain Sean Callahan, his best company commander. "Don't let yourself get closed in around the bridge." The first two companies from Abizaid's battalion crossed the bridge early on July 13 and began to pack up their weapons. A few minutes later, hundreds of Kurds, worried that they were being abandoned by their American protectors, surged toward Callahan's troops, forcing his men into a tight knot right in front of the bridge.

The demonstrating Kurds carried banners that read "We Love You America" and "Your Job Is Halve Done." When it became clear the Americans were leaving for good, the hysterical crowd began to hit the soldiers with their signs. A mother carrying a young child threw herself into the razor wire strung across the border, slicing her hands and face; another woman bit the battalion sergeant major on the arm. On the Turkish side of the bridge the local commander scrambled his soldiers, who looked as if they were preparing to open fire.

A furious Abizaid, his uniform drenched in sweat, rushed to find Callahan, whose men had fixed bayonets and were trying to hold their ground. "Do not allow anyone to set foot on this bridge!" Abizaid yelled as he called the rest of the battalion back across the border to augment his force. Standing on the hood of a Humvee, he assured the crowd that the United States would continue to protect them with planes and helicopters based in Turkey. As the temperatures rose, the exhausted and angry Kurds, held back by bayonets and razor wire, slowly drifted away.

Abizaid doubted the tenuous peace his soldiers left behind in northern Iraq would hold. His troops were replaced by jet fighters that patrolled in the skies over northern Iraq, ready to strike if Saddam Hussein tried to attack again. Surprisingly, a relatively prosperous enclave emerged, aided by ample international aid. But, as with most conflicts in the Middle East, it wasn't clear how long the calm would last.

After Iraq, Abizaid spent a year at Stanford University as a military fellow, reflecting on his experiences and writing about the need to prepare for guerrilla conflicts and peacekeeping missions. He visited Somalia, where the Bush administration in its waning months had sent troops as part of a UN effort to secure a cease-fire between the country's warring militias and feed its starving population. General Colin Powell, now chairman of the Joint Chiefs, supported the intervention, with the proviso that the U.S. force would be massive and would remain only a couple of months. By the time Abizaid got there, most of the U.S. soldiers had been replaced by poorly equipped UN troops from countries like Pakistan. President

Clinton had taken over in the White House, and the mission had expanded from feeding starving Somalis to stabilizing the country's government and arresting troublesome warlords.

The warlords fought back. First they attacked the poorly armed Pakistanis and then the remaining Americans. Four U.S. soldiers were killed when their unarmored Humvee drove over a hidden bomb. On his visit, Abizaid met with soldiers from the 10th Mountain Division who were trying to separate warring clans south of the Somali capital of Mogadishu. A few months after he departed, a team of Rangers and Delta Force commandos was sent to capture Somali warlord Mohammed Farah Aidid. The mission triggered a bloody and unexpected battle in which untrained fighters, armed with only AK-47s and grenade launchers, downed two Black Hawk helicopters and killed eighteen U.S. troops. Americans reacted with outrage to the horrific television footage from the battle. "I can't believe we're being pushed around by these two-bit pricks," Clinton screamed at his aides as they watched images of howling Somalis dragging the body of a dead U.S. pilot through the streets.

Unable to justify a humanitarian mission that had suddenly turned into a war, the White House ordered a withdrawal, abandoning Mogadishu to its warring clans. Many military officers blamed Clinton for the disaster, insisting that it was a mistake to commit the U.S. military to such ill-defined and unwinnable missions. General Powell had retired from active service a few days before the Mogadishu disaster. "We can't make a country out of that place," he later recounted warning Clinton on his last day in uniform.

Abizaid didn't disagree with Powell. No one could reasonably expect the military to forge a country out of a collection of warring tribes. But he didn't think the Army could completely avoid future Somalias, either. The military's instinct—to go in big and get out fast—was not acceptable. Its focus on large-scale combat and quick wars after Vietnam had left it unprepared for a whole series of smaller, messier threats that only the military could handle. "We must recognize that peacekeeping is no job for amateurs," he wrote in *Military Review*, an Army journal, during his Stanford fellowship. "It is dangerous, stressful duty that requires highly disciplined, well educated soldiers who understand the nature of the peacekeeping beast. As we get ready to fight the next war, let us also keep thinking about how we might have to keep the peace in some far off corner of the world."

It was a plea to study the operations in northern Iraq and Somalia and not dismiss them as aberrations. Abizaid believed deeply that the military didn't get to choose the kinds of wars that it would fight, and that it was likely the Clinton administration or its successors would send U.S. troops on similar peacekeeping missions in the future, probably without fully thinking through what they were taking on. He was right, just as Petraeus had been a few years earlier when he had argued the same point in his Princeton dissertation. Less than a decade passed before the U.S. Army found itself again battling lightly armed fighters who relied on stealth and hit-and-run attacks to nullify America's overwhelming might—this time in Iraq.

✵ ✵ ✵ ✵

Fort Campbell, Kentucky
September 1991

After two years as a general's aide in the Pentagon, Dave Petraeus was finally back in a combat unit. He was taking over one of the 101st Airborne Division's most storied units. His battalion was one of three that traced its lineage back to the 187th Parachute Infantry Regiment, which had been activated during World War II to fight in the Pacific. The Japanese had dubbed the parachutists *Rakkasans,* a term meaning "falling-down umbrella men," and the name stuck, even after the battalion converted into a helicopter assault force. The Rakkasans later fought in Korea, Vietnam, and, only a few months before Petraeus took command, in Iraq, where the battalion moved hundreds of miles behind enemy lines as part of a massive helicopter assault to cut off Republican Guard units fleeing Kuwait.

Most of the captains and majors now working for him had been to war; he hadn't. But he had been prepping for the day when he would take over command since arriving in Vicenza sixteen years earlier as a green second lieutenant, vacuuming up ideas and depositing them in a folder marked "First Day of Command." Now he began putting his ideas into practice.

He wanted to foster a culture of competitiveness, he told his officers. Always an exercise fanatic, he instituted a demanding physical fitness test with standards far tougher than the Army required of even its youngest soldiers. Petraeus goaded his men into taking it and then stood over them at the track counting off push-ups, sit-ups, and dips one by one. He dubbed the winners "Iron Rakkasans" and engraved their names on a plaque at the battalion headquarters. Everything was a competition for Petraeus, and every competition was a way to prove the superiority of his unit. Even a chili cook-off in the town outside Fort Campbell was treated like a major operation, with soldiers dispatched a day ahead of time to secure a space near the judges' table and scout out the competition. Some officers loved Petraeus's gung-ho spirit; others thought he was trying too hard. It was as if he believed you could become a great commander the same way he had become a West Point Star Man—by breaking the assignment into all of its thousands of components and then studying them harder than anyone else for the big test. The reality was tougher. There was much more to command than knowing small-unit tactics or winning a chili cook-off. A good officer had to convince soldiers to follow him, sometimes to their deaths. A few, like Abizaid, were naturals. Petraeus wasn't. He had moved so quickly through his relatively few rotations with frontline combat units and spent so much time at the hip of senior generals that he hadn't learned how to seem natural in front of regular troops.

He used Boy Scout language like "gosh" and "golly." He frowned on officers who chewed tobacco. He mangled words that every infantryman was supposed to know—even "hooah," the all-purpose Army reply. Every soldier learned in basic training that it was uttered in a throaty roar, meant to signal you were up for anything. Petraeus's "hooah" sounded flat and unconvincing, causing his officers to cringe inside. Several put together a list of soldier slang terms and gave it to their new boss so that he would come off better when addressing his troops. He accepted it good-naturedly. On the wall of his new office he hung his prized photo of Marcel Bigeard, the French paratrooper and guerrilla war expert, right above the framed French paratrooper certificate he had earned in 1976. Petraeus liked to quiz visitors on the identity of the foreign-looking officer in the photo; no one at Fort Campbell had ever heard of Bigeard. Choosing a French general as a role model marked him as unusual in the American Army. It made it seem like he had developed his ideas about how to be a soldier from history books and going to seminars—or, worse yet, in the salons of Paris. His men started calling their Ph.D.-degreed commander "Doc," which summed up his intellect and their misgivings about his street smarts.

Shortly after arriving, he and six of his officers found themselves camping out near a runway at a small air base in rural Tennessee. The soldiers and their new commander talked into the evening about their lives, families, and careers. Eventually the question went around the circle: Which of them had spent a night in jail? Everyone had except Petraeus. That summed up their new commander: physically tough and smart but lacking in real-world experience.

Fred Johnson, one of his company commanders, noticed that Petraeus didn't wear a "high and tight," a military haircut that was closely shaven on the sides and back. Many infantrymen at Fort Campbell believed the shorter-than-regulation trim made them look like warriors, ready to deploy at a moment's notice. It set them apart from the rest of the peacetime Army. When Johnson raised the subject, Petraeus explained that Holly didn't like his hair that short. Some of the men, Johnson replied, had commented on it. It wasn't true—nobody had mentioned it—but he wanted Petraeus to succeed, and in a unit full of combat veterans, the commander couldn't afford to appear less than warriorlike. The next day, he recalled, Petraeus walked into the battalion headquarters sporting a high and tight and promptly issued a new directive: from then on, the standard haircut for Iron Rakkasans was a high and tight.

The 1990s were known as the era of the "zero-defect Army," a time when a single mistake by an officer—or even his troops—could doom his chances for advancement. With the end of the Cold War, the Army was shrinking, and a below-average fitness report was usually enough to convince a promotion board to pass over an otherwise exemplary soldier. Petraeus exemplified this mania for detail, though his goal was not to weed out the unfit but to bind his soldiers together. Shortly after arriving, he published a booklet that laid out page after page of detailed instructions about how the battalion should look, act, and think. There were instructions on everything imaginable, and some that defied easy explanation.

Every Rakkasan was required to fasten the top button of his combat fatigues, the one right under the chin, ostensibly so uncamouflaged necks wouldn't show. Some U.S. soldiers in the 101st thought all that Petraeus's "battle button" did was make them look stupid. Actually, that was his intention. "It made others joke about us, which pulled us together," Petraeus later explained. He had borrowed the idea from *The Centurions,* the novel he had first read in 1976 that was loosely based on Marcel Bigeard's experiences fighting insurgents in Vietnam and Algeria. The hero of the book and his paratroopers wear distinctive floppy hats known as "lizard caps" that are mocked by other French troops but bind the unit together.

He also had elaborate rules for attaching equipment to the load-bearing web belts, known as LBEs, worn by every soldier in the field. During inspections, he made a point of examining the belts to make sure his troops had tied the knots just right and that they had burned off the ends of the parachute cord to prevent fraying. His own LBE was outfitted flawlessly. It had taken him hours to get it just right.

His other priority after taking command was training—often with live ammunition. One Saturday morning a month after assuming command, Petraeus and the assistant commander of the 101st, Brigadier General Jack Keane, were watching a company of soldiers practice clearing a bunker. Ahead of them, Specialist Terrence Jones tossed a training grenade through the doorway, flattened himself against a wall, and waited for the dull thud. Then he began running to rejoin his squad. Jones could hear the popping of automatic weapons and the whiz of real bullets as he lumbered over twenty yards of open ground. Reaching his squad's position, he threw himself down on the ground, using the butt of his SAW machine gun to break his fall. As he landed, his finger inadvertently squeezed the trigger. Thirty yards away, Petraeus grunted in pain and dropped to his knees. The bullet from Jones's weapon had hit him in the chest, right over the *A* in his uniform name tag.

He wasn't sure what had happened. The pain was in his back, and his first thought was that he had been struck from behind by a grenade. He tried to steady himself, but then his head started to swirl and pain enveloped his torso. He felt like he was staring down a long tunnel. Keane, who had been standing nearby, eased him down to the ground and opened his camouflage uniform. "Dave, you've been shot. You know what we're going to do here. We're going to stop the bleeding," he said in his booming voice. From the front, the wound didn't look so bad. Blood was trickling from a small hole over his right nipple. But Petraeus couldn't see the exit wound, where the bullet had come out. A four-inch chunk of his back was torn away and oozing blood. Smoke was still wafting out of the hole. Keane bellowed for a medevac helicopter and then turned back to Petraeus. Two Army medics rushed up and began cutting open his fatigues. Petraeus in his fog worried about all the work he had put in getting his knots correct. "Don't cut my LBE," he muttered. "I just got it to standard." They ignored him, swiftly cutting off his web gear and pressing gauze bandages on the wounds. "Dave, I want you to stay with us," Keane said. "Yes, sir," Petraeus replied.

As the minutes passed, Keane kept up a steady chatter, all but commanding him not to slip into unconsciousness. Petraeus was speaking less and less. Soon he started going blank, his eyes wide but unresponsive. His face was turning ashen. He vomited greenish fluid and a chunk of something. Finally the *thump-thump* of an arriving helicopter was heard in the distance. Keane announced he was going with Petraeus to the base hospital. "We all know what happened here. A soldier accidentally shot his commanding officer. Pull that unit together and get them back on the range," he bellowed. The Army Black Hawk set down twenty yards away, and Petraeus was rushed aboard on a stretcher with Keane at his side.

Petraeus went directly into the operating room at the Fort Campbell hospital. When the chief surgeon emerged he marveled at Petraeus's toughness, telling Keane that he had shoved a tube into the bullet hole in Petraeus's chest to prevent infection—a procedure done without anesthetic that normally causes patients to cry out from the intense pain. Petraeus had only grunted. The bleeding was under control, but he needed more surgery as soon as possible by a specialist, the doctor said, suggesting Vanderbilt Medical Center in Nashville. Since it was a weekend, Keane called ahead and insisted on the best surgeon on the staff to do the operation.

When the helicopter landed at Vanderbilt, tubes were protruding from Petraeus's chest, draining blood so he wouldn't suffocate. The hospital's emergency staff was waiting, along with a tallish doctor dressed like he had come from the golf course. After Keane's call, the Vanderbilt staff hunted down the hospital's chief of thoracic surgery, Dr. Bill Frist, a future senator from Tennessee. Frist did an initial examination and returned to speak to Keane, shocked at the grapefruit-sized exit wound. Used to treating hunting injuries, he had never encountered the trauma that the high-velocity rounds used by the military could cause. Rather than wait for Petraeus to stabilize, he was going directly into surgery. "Obviously, you know we have a very serious injury here," Frist told Keane.

The surgery took nearly six hours. The bullet had severed an artery and damaged his right lung, part of which had to be removed. When it was over, Petraeus was resting, still sedated, in a recovery room. He was on a respirator as a precaution, but the worst danger had passed. Frist told Keane and Holly, who had arrived by then from Fort Campbell, that the prognosis was good but recovery would take at least ten weeks. That was too long for Petraeus. His battalion's first big field test was approaching, and Petraeus didn't want to miss it, even with a gaping scar on his torso. A few days after his operation, he requested a transfer back to the Fort Campbell hospital.

Soon he began pestering his doctors and nurses. He was feeling fine and should be released, he said. His demands eventually became so bothersome that the hospital commander, Colonel Steve Xenakis, came to Petraeus's room to order him to quiet down. "Everybody recovers and heals differently," Petraeus told him. "I'm ready to go home." With Xenakis's help, he removed the intravenous tubes from his arm, got down on the floor, and started doing push-ups in his flimsy hospital gown. Running out of strength at fifty, Petraeus stood up. "Well?" he said. Xenakis said he could leave in a few days, but made him promise not to rush back to work or resume exercising anytime soon.

He broke his promise. Petraeus worried that losing part of his lung would leave him unable to match the blistering running pace he had turned in before the shooting. Being one of the fittest soldiers in the Army was part of the superhuman persona that Petraeus had strived for since he was at West Point. His stamina was part of what, many years later, he would call the "Petraeus brand," the carefully crafted identity that protected him, in his own mind anyway, from those officers who wanted to lump him with other brainy officers who were unable to handle the physical rigors of leading men in combat. A few days after he came home, Petraeus went to the Fort Campbell gym, planning for an easy workout. He started off on an exercise bike, pedaling gently. Feeling okay, he moved on to light jogging around the track. When that brought only mild discomfort, he decided to time himself in a 440-yard sprint. He dashed two times around the track and was reasonably pleased with his time, given the rolls of tape wrapped around his torso. Although he didn't realize it, the exertion had caused his lung to bleed again. His doctors warned him that if he did it again, he might need emergency surgery. "They read him the riot act, and he backed off for a while," Holly Petraeus recalled. But not for long. In less than a month, he was back with his battalion when it went to the field for their first big training exercise. His only concession to medical necessity was carrying a lighter-than-usual rucksack to avoid aggravating his incision.

Over the years, he shaped the shooting into a tale of toughness and resilience. He retold it often, joking that he had arranged to get himself shot to erase the stigma of missing the Gulf War. Admirers and journalists cited his escape from death as evidence he was destined for great achievement. Rather than degrading the Petraeus brand, the accident ended up adding to its aura.

✱   ✱   ✱   ✱

Petraeus's plan after completing his battalion command at Fort Campbell was to spend the 1994–95 academic year on a fellowship at Georgetown University. There were clear giveaways that he had no intention of spending the year in quiet academic retreat. His choice of Georgetown meant that Petraeus was in Washington, where the action was. His research topic was the crisis in Haiti, which was still unfolding. The Clinton administration had spent more than a year readying a plan to restore to power Haiti's democratically elected president, who had been toppled by a military junta. With memories of Somalia still fresh, the White House readily acceded to the Pentagon's insistence that it deploy a massive force to the country and severely limit the overall goals for the operation. President Clinton promised there would be no long-term U.S. occupation or attempt to remake Haiti's shattered economy or government. The 20,000 American troops were supposed to move in, restore security, and after a few months turn the operation over to a United Nations force.

Several months after arriving at Georgetown, Petraeus used his Sosh connections to secure an interview with Deputy Secretary of State Strobe Talbott, who was deeply involved in the U.S. effort to return Jean-Bertrand Aristide to power. Impressed by Petraeus's questions, Talbott invited him to an upcoming White House meeting on Haiti for a glimpse into the workings of the government at the highest level. Wearing his best suit, Petraeus walked into the White House Situation Room, the wood-paneled nerve center in the basement of the West Wing, and took a seat along the wall. "Who are you?" Sandy Berger, Clinton's deputy national security advisor, barked at him, noticing an unfamiliar face. Petraeus uneasily explained he was there at Talbott's invitation. Off the hook, he listened quietly as senior officials from the White House, Pentagon, State Department, and Justice Department debated the pros and cons of a plan for a new Haitian police force.

Several weeks later, Petraeus ran into Colonel Bob Killebrew, a fellow alumnus of Vuono's staff, in the Pentagon. Killebrew was assembling the headquarters for the 6,000-soldier UN peacekeeping force that was taking over from the United States in Haiti. It included 2,500 American troops along with soldiers from Pakistan, Bangladesh, Nepal, India, and seventeen other countries. He needed a handful of U.S. officers to oversee the effort and asked Petraeus if he was interested. Absolutely, he replied. He just needed to get out of his Georgetown fellowship.

Killebrew was pleased. Top-notch officers weren't exactly crawling over each other to go to Haiti and work for the UN. Petraeus, however, had long been interested in peacekeeping. He also knew that the only deficiency in his otherwise golden resume was a lack of field experience. He needed his ticket punched in a war zone, or as close to one as he could get. He flew into Port-au-Prince in February of 1995, a few weeks ahead of the U.S. handover to the United Nations. The Americans had achieved their modest goals: Aristide was in office, violence had been reduced, and the tide of refugees heading for Florida on rickety boats had stopped. There had been only one U.S. combat death—a Special Forces sergeant shot and killed at a checkpoint.

Still, Haiti was a mess. The government ruled in name only. A hastily recruited police force was incapable of even basic law enforcement. Vigilante killings and political reprisals were common. There were more than a hundred murders throughout the tiny country the month the UN arrived, including forty-five classified as assassinations. These were now problems for the UN, which at first was a tiny operation. "There were just a handful of us, literally less than the fingers on one hand, pulling this thing together in Haiti," Petraeus recalled.

With little help, Petraeus churned out detailed plans and orders covering every conceivable facet of the upcoming operations. There was Operational Plan 95-1, a comprehensive blueprint for the UN military mission, followed by a 159-page manual of standard operating procedures that covered topics as broad as "the practice of peacekeeping" and as basic as "two-way radio communications." In early March, with the 170-man headquarters staff finally nearing full strength, he ran a weeklong officer training course at the makeshift UN headquarters, an abandoned industrial park that had been converted into a sandbagged fortress. The wide variations in training and experience made it important to build cohesion in the motley force. He arranged for detailed briefings on when UN soldiers could fire their weapons, the basics of peacekeeping, working with humanitarian groups, and Haiti's unusual history and Creole culture. The training ended with a two-day war game, meant to prepare the headquarters staff for a Black Hawk Down–like crisis.

In Haiti Petraeus was exposed in depth to the problems of reconstructing a society whose government and economy had all but ceased to function. There was no insurgency of the sort he'd face later in Iraq, but many of the problems were similar. In both places, the U.S. military's plan assumed that civilians from the UN or other entities could quickly restore a working government, electricity, and other essential services. It was a wildly optimistic assumption.

So Petraeus improvised. He worked closely with aid workers and humanitarian groups, scheduling helicopter flights to move them around the country and providing Army engineers to help with quick construction projects. He brought in noncommissioned officers to train the new Haitian police force. He coordinated raids to arrest the fugitive leaders of the paramilitary groups who had gone underground. The UN had not reserved any money for the military to do its own projects, opting to funnel reconstruction through civilian groups. But Petraeus and his boss, Major General Joe Kinzer, sidestepped the restrictions, spending U.S. funds to repave roads and build police stations when it became clear the normal UN process would take months. They gave a French-speaking U.S. lieutenant colonel the job of getting the lights back on in Port-au-Prince. Without any money, the staff officer went door-to-door to embassies asking for contributions and managed to raise $250,000, which was spent on generators. UN officers remember Petraeus constantly on the phone late at night with Washington, briefing officials at the White House or lobbying the Pentagon's Joint Staff for more cash.

He believed that he was creating a blueprint for a new kind of military operation, and he wanted his peers to know it. Shortly after returning home, Petraeus and Killebrew penned a military journal article that was triumphantly titled "Winning the Peace." They argued that "in detail of planning and degree of coordination the effort to stand Haiti back up after taking it down broke new ground. . . . An environment conducive to political, social and economic development has been created in Haiti." It was exuberant overstatement. His three-month tour was not enough time to make any lasting improvements, and when the last U.S. troops left the island a year after Petraeus, conditions rapidly deteriorated.

The military wasn't quite sure what to make of the new operations it faced in places such as northern Iraq, Somalia, and Haiti. As the 1990s progressed, it began referring to them as "peace operations," and later, when that came to seem too narrow, as "military operations other than war," or MOOTW (pronounced "mootwah"). These clunky terms reflected confused thinking. Every conceivable military operation other than conventional Gulf War–style battles was crammed under this ever-broadening rubric. The list included combating terrorism, providing humanitarian assistance, protecting shipping lanes, interdicting narcotics, enforcing arms control agreements, and ten other unrelated missions. Also buried on the list was helping foreign governments fight insurgencies, a task the United States would eventually take on in Iraq.

Though these jobs required new skills, the Army and the Marines did very little to prepare for them. Too much time spent on peacekeeping would dull the Army's combat edge, generals reasoned. The conventionally trained military could always adjust on the fly. It was an idea Abizaid and Petraeus explicitly rejected. As Abizaid had noted in his military journal article, published when Petraeus was in Haiti, the Army still lacked the training, equipment, and specialized personnel for these demanding new missions. "Doctrinal voids exist at every level," Abizaid warned. "We should avoid the notion that combat-ready troops are ready for peacekeeping."

In Haiti, Petraeus had picked up lessons that would prove valuable a decade later in Iraq. Near the end of his three-month rotation, he pinned on the silver eagles of a full colonel at a small headquarters ceremony. On June 9, he flew home, heading for Fort Bragg, North Carolina, and his next plum assignment. He was taking command of the 82nd Airborne Division's 1st Brigade—John Abizaid's brigade.

On the morning of the change-of-command ceremony, Abizaid walked into his office and noticed Petraeus's possessions stacked on his gray desk and peeling linoleum floor. There's a rigid protocol surrounding changes of command, and one of the rules is that the old commander is entitled to keep his office until the swallow-tailed unit streamer changes hands at the official parade ground ceremony. Overcome by eagerness and an ambition that was always propelling him forward, Petraeus had broken it. When Abizaid saw Petraeus's boxes piled in his office, he was annoyed. "Who does this guy think he is?" he barked to his executive officer.

"On that day I think the two of them really didn't like each other," the executive officer recalled. The two men had radically different command styles. Within hours of taking over, Petraeus had already pulled a young soldier out of formation and made him produce his dog tags. "The old commander would have never done that," Frank Helmick, a battalion commander in the unit, thought. Abizaid trusted his sergeants to check such details. He was loose, funny, and even a bit sarcastic. Soldiers who wandered into his office were always struck that his desk and file cabinets were virtually empty. He seemed to run the entire 3,000-soldier brigade out of the notebook stuffed in his cargo pants. Petraeus, meanwhile, maintained binders full of rules and regulations. There was even a rule for labeling the binders, complained his officers, who were accustomed to Abizaid's more laid-back approach.

Despite those outward differences, the two men shared a remarkably similar view of their Army's future. The U.S. military's massive technological and firepower edge made it unlikely that anyone would challenge it to a tank-on-tank fight. Instead, they believed, civilian political leaders were far more likely to send soldiers to deal with murky ethnic conflicts, humanitarian crises, and internal civil wars. Only the U.S. Army could get manpower and supplies to such backwaters. Only the military was capable of interceding between these warring parties. To perform these missions well, the Army had to change, they insisted. Theirs was a view that was decidedly out of step with most mainstream military thinking at the time.

✳   ✳   ✳   ✳

Dugi Dio, Bosnia
October 10, 1996

It was late afternoon and already growing dark when Brigadier General George Casey and a force of twenty soldiers drove into the tiny mountain village of Dugi Dio. Normally, one-star generals don't lead patrols. Casey, the assistant commander of the U.S. peacekeeping force in northwest Bosnia, was there because of elderly peasants who had trudged through the mud with their belongings in bundles and on oxcarts, heading home.

The refugees were Muslims who had once lived in Dugi Dio and in nearby Jusici. They had been driven out years before in one of the first Serbian offensives of the war. Now that the fighting was over and the U.S.-led peacekeeping force had arrived, they were going back to their destroyed houses, which currently happened to be in Serb territory. Accompanying the elderly villagers were young, hard-looking men armed with guns to defend them from their former Serb neighbors who were now their enemies.

Their arrival sparked a tense standoff, with Serb police threatening to arrest the Muslim returnees. The refugees, in turn, vowed to defend themselves, by force if necessary. Casey and several UN officials had spent three weeks negotiating an agreement that allowed the returnees to remain, provided they met two conditions: they had to prove their claims to own property, and they had to promise to get rid of all weapons.

The U.S. Army had crossed the Sava River into Bosnia a year earlier to enforce a peace agreement that ended more than three years of horrific killing among Bosnia's Muslims, Croats, and Serbs. The force was gigantic, with 20,000 U.S. troops and 40,000 more soldiers from European countries, including Russia. The U.S. military was supposed to stay for only one year (a deadline that was repeatedly extended) and its mission was tightly constrained to exclude anything that smacked of nation building or put soldiers at risk. "The U.S. and NATO are *not* going to Bosnia to fight a war. They are *not* going to Bosnia to rebuild the nation, resettle refugees, and oversee elections," Defense Secretary William Perry told reporters. "The tasks of our soldiers are clear and limited . . . They will enforce the cessation of hostilities."

In theory the job of forging Bosnia into a functioning, multiethnic state was supposed to be handled by the UN-led civilian administration and the Bosnians themselves. As in Haiti, the civilians were quickly overwhelmed, and there was pressure on the military to expand its role—to fill the massive civilian gaps, to arrest war criminals, and to protect refugees who wanted to return home. When officers such as George Casey did try to undertake these tasks, they found out how difficult they could be. Casey had spent four years after the Gulf War with the First Cavalry Division at Fort Hood, Texas, overseeing the division staff and then commanding a 4,000-soldier brigade from 1993 to 1995. He readied his troops to deploy to Saudi Arabia or Kuwait in case Saddam Hussein decided to try to reinvade, and fought big mock-tank battles at the National Training Center against the same Soviet-style enemy that U.S. forces had battled for much of the Cold War. It was demanding work that required smarts and an obsessive attention to detail. Casey had performed well.

Little in his career, however, had prepared him to mediate ethnic civil wars or rebuild broken societies, like Bosnia. In the gathering darkness Casey waited as the last of the Muslim returnees' homes were searched to make sure that they had abided by their promise to get rid of all of their weapons. Standing alongside Casey were several Serb officials and the town's former deputy mayor, a Muslim who had come back with the other returnees. The Muslims warily eyed the Serbian observers. Their presence was a bit like "having Darth Vader in your house," Casey recalled. An hour passed. Nothing was uncovered in any of the nearly three dozen houses searched, until only the residence where Casey was waiting remained. He began to think he had pulled it off, the peaceful return of refugees to their communities, a small but unmistakable success on his first foray into real peacemaking. Then a Serb policeman found two AK-47s, two hand grenades, and a bag full of ammunition in the very last house—the one where Casey was standing. The weapons belonged to the Muslim deputy mayor. Casey was staggered. The agreement that he'd spent weeks negotiating between the Muslims and Serbs was off. "I'm looking at this guy going, 'What the fuck were you thinking?' " he recalled.

A standoff ensued. When the Serb police tried to arrest the deputy mayor, dozens of Muslim women lay down outside the house, blocking their departure. Trapped in a surrounded Muslim home as night fell, the Serb police were growing noticeably nervous. Fearing the situation could escalate into violence, Casey took custody of the deputy mayor and left the village. Crestfallen, he returned to the U.S. camp and told Lieutenant General Bill Nash, the cigar-chomping commander of the multinational force, about the collapsed deal.

"George, never forget it's their country," Nash told him. It was Nash's way of saying that even a force as powerful as the U.S. Army couldn't resolve centuries-old sectarian and ethnic hatreds and shouldn't try. U.S. troops could separate the Serbs and Muslims and provide basic security, but they should leave the lengthy job of building a functioning country to the civilian experts or the Bosnians themselves. No one could force these people to get along, certainly not the U.S. military. It was a lesson Casey never forgot, and one the entire Army would take with it to Iraq.

A few months later General John Shalikashvili, the chairman of the Joint Chiefs, came through Bosnia. He noticed that Nash was talking at length with John Abizaid, who was Shalikashvili's executive officer, about the situation on the ground. Before Shalikashvili left to return to the Pentagon, he pulled Nash aside.

"You want Abizaid?" he asked. Nash had worked with Abizaid several years earlier and knew his reputation as one of the Army's brightest minds. He immediately said yes. When Abizaid arrived a month later, Nash gave him Casey's job overseeing daily military operations. A crestfallen Casey was shifted to a less prestigious position as the assistant division commander overseeing logistics and supply issues.

Many officers in Casey's position would have felt threatened by the high-flying Abizaid, who at the time was the youngest general in the Army. Casey chose to embrace the newcomer, who exuded the confidence and street smarts that he lacked. Prior to Bosnia, Casey had long believed that the best Army officers focused on tough field training, taking care of their soldiers and maintaining their equipment. This muddy-boots mentality had helped the service recover from its nadir after Vietnam and had proved its value in the Gulf War. Abizaid was a different kind of officer who sought answers to problems that most officers didn't see. Instead of focusing downward on his troops, he thought about how forces such as radical Islam were transforming the Middle East and could create new problems for the United States. He was comfortable working with foreign militaries. Where Casey had struggled to win the trust of the Russian officers in Bosnia, Abizaid seemed instinctively to know how to make former Soviet officers, who bristled at their second-tier status, feel valued.

Working together in Bosnia turned Casey and Abizaid into close friends. Both were outwardly easygoing and unflappable. Over the next decade, their careers would move in parallel. Casey, in particular, seemed to study his younger friend's progress through the Army and emulate it. He would follow Abizaid in a series of increasingly important jobs at the Pentagon over the next five years.

☆　☆　☆　☆

Casteau, Belgium
June 11, 1999

After seventy-eight days of bombing, the Kosovo war was over and Brigadier General Pete Chiarelli thought he could finally relax a little. Chiarelli was working for General Wes Clark, the NATO commander running the war. Clark typically arrived at his headquarters around 7:00 a.m., so Chiarelli made it a point to get into the office by five-thirty. That way he'd have an hour to sort through the overnight traffic and pull out key pieces of intelligence that Clark needed to see first thing in the morning. Usually he didn't make it home until 11:00 p.m. It was like that seven days a week.

The Clinton administration started the war in an attempt to thwart Serbian leader Slobodan Milosevic's ruthless assault on ethnic Albanians living in the Serb province of Kosovo. The thinking was that Milosevic would buckle in a few days, but he had held on far longer than expected. Finally he'd agreed to withdraw his troops from the tiny province and allow in a peacekeeping force. That morning, Chiarelli updated Clark on the timetable for sending in the troops and then returned to his desk just outside the NATO commander's door.

Then the telephone rang. On the other end was an Army major with an urgent report: hundreds of Russian troops stationed in Bosnia were heading for Kosovo, several hours' drive away. The Russians, who had ties to the Serbs, had been insisting for weeks that they wanted to control their own sector of the province. The Clinton administration and Clark were deeply opposed to it. Chiarelli rushed back into Clark's book-lined office. "Sir, the Russians are moving forces," he warned. The two officers dashed out of the office to a videoconference on the crisis.

George Casey, who had left Bosnia for a high-profile job as the deputy director for political military affairs on the Joint Staff in the Pentagon, was also at the center of the action. He'd spent weeks shuttling back and forth between Washington and Moscow with Deputy Secretary of State Strobe Talbott negotiating the terms of the Russians' participation in the Kosovo peacekeeping force. Landing the important job had been especially satisfying. A decade earlier when Casey had tried to find a slot in the office he was now running, he had been summarily dismissed. "No, no, no. He's never been in the Pentagon. We can't use him," he'd heard someone yelling in the background when he called to ask about the job. But his Bosnia tour had given him on-the-ground experience in the region that many senior officers lacked.

Around 6:00 p.m. Clark was still trying to get a fix on what the Russians were doing when he broke away to take a call from Casey, who was in Moscow a day earlier. The head of the Russian military had threatened to seize a sector in Kosovo as soon as NATO troops deployed. The Foreign Ministry, meanwhile, was taking a softer line. Casey told Clark that he didn't think the Russians could move that quickly.

Clark disagreed. In fact, reports from the ground in Bosnia suggested that several hundred Russians were already moving. Across the border in Kosovo, Serbs who had learned of the deployment were getting set to welcome them. The key decisions were being made not in Moscow but rather on the ground in Bosnia and Kosovo. For both Casey and Chiarelli, the aftermath of the Kosovo war was an introduction to political and military crisis solving at the highest levels, and their involvement pushed them ahead of many of their Army peers in the endless competition for the next job.

Casey spent the next several weeks shuttling from the Pentagon to the Kremlin and Macedonia as part of a team hammering out the broad outlines of a deal that would place the Russian peacekeepers under NATO control but also salvage some measure of Russian pride. Chiarelli also found himself busier in the weeks after the end of the conflict than he had been during the bombing campaign. More tense issues would arise, including the return of hundreds of thousands of refugees and the disarming of Kosovar Muslims on whose behalf the war had been fought.

Chiarelli owed his career to Clark. A few years earlier he had been finishing a year at the National War College in Washington and had no job lined up. He sat in his basement in suburban Virginia and typed out letters on his Commodore 64 home computer to every division commander in the Army, asking for a job as an operations officer, or G3 in Army parlance. Landing such a position was essential if he was ever going to be promoted again. "This may not be the normal way of doing business," he wrote. "However, I would like your help as I look for a division G3 job." Only Clark, who was the commander of the 1st Cavalry Division, invited him for an interview. Although they had never met, Clark had been an instructor in the West Point Social Sciences Department in the early 1970s after returning from Vietnam. He hired him after a twenty-minute interview. Chiarelli never knew why. The best theory he could come up with was that the Sosh connections had saved him again. When Clark was named NATO commander he hired Chiarelli as his executive officer, essentially his senior aide.

Chiarelli learned a lot from Clark. Clark was an activist general who was comfortable using military power to prevent humanitarian disasters and stabilize failing states. As NATO commander he quietly encouraged U.S. troops in Bosnia to arrest mafia-like criminals and strengthen the country's moderate political opposition, knowing such moves would draw the ire of his more conservative Pentagon bosses who were opposed to anything that smacked of nation building. "You have to push the envelope," he told his soldiers. "If you put this strategy down [on paper] and circulate it, it's dead."

Chiarelli also learned a good deal about how *not* to handle himself from Clark, a brusque, highly intelligent man who had made lots of enemies during his long Army career. He never cared how hard he drove his subordinates. He wasn't deferential to his superiors, and his unrivaled ambition left him with few allies in the Army or the Pentagon. Six weeks after the Kosovo war ended, Clark got a call from Joint Chiefs chairman General Hugh Shelton, who told him that he would be replaced the following April as NATO commander. Clark, who was in Lithuania at the time, couldn't believe what he was hearing. Normally it was a three-year job, often extended to four. He had just finished his second year and had fought and won the first war in NATO's fifty-year history. "I stood there stunned. Was I being relieved of duty?" he wrote in his memoirs.

It was 3:00 a.m. back in Belgium when Chiarelli was awoken at home by a call from his apoplectic boss. They were firing him, Clark said. Not only that, Clark railed, but within minutes of hanging up with Shelton he had gotten a call from a *Washington Post* reporter who already knew he had been dismissed. The Pentagon had leaked the news to make it impossible for him to lobby the White House to reverse it. "He was definitely upset, and rightfully so," Chiarelli recalled. "This guy had just won a war and here he was being shown the door."

In Kosovo, Clark's Pentagon bosses resented his demands for more forces, especially a request for two dozen Apache helicopters. Clark wanted to use the low-flying helicopters to destroy Serbian military forces at close range, but Defense Secretary William Cohen was deeply opposed to the plan. The helicopters were too vulnerable to ground fire and might lead to U.S. casualties. In a war fought primarily for humanitarian reasons, he believed, there was no compelling reason to put U.S. troops' lives at risk. Cohen also suspected that Clark was using his back-channel contacts with the White House and State Department to reverse Pentagon decisions that he opposed.

Although Clark had the backing of the White House and the State Department on many of his initiatives in Kosovo, he had alienated his most important boss: the defense secretary. His high-profile dismissal wasn't soon forgotten in the Army. "The lesson I took from it is that your chain of command is your chain of command and that you are obligated to do your best to work within it to the extent that you can," recalled Abizaid.

In 2001, Defense Secretary Donald Rumsfeld arrived in the Pentagon deeply opposed to using the military for nation-building ventures. Within weeks of taking office he asked the Joint Staff to draw up plans for pulling American troops out of the Balkans, insisting that such missions should be handled by the same civilian agencies that had repeatedly proven themselves incapable in Haiti, Somalia, Bosnia, and Kosovo. Rumsfeld also was convinced that activist commanders, such as Clark, had been given too much latitude by the Clinton administration to use military power to help stabilize weak or failing states. He wanted to rein in the generals.

CHAPTER SEVEN

Sheikh of Sheikhs

Out of the French army's soul-destroying trial by fire in Algeria there has so far emerged one superlatively good combat commander, a 42-year-old ex–bank clerk from Toul named Marcel Bigeard. So notable is Colonel Bigeard's tactical genius and so successful his Spartan training methods that for three years, whenever French troops scored one of their rare clearcut victories over the Algerian rebels, French newspaper readers automatically looked for the name of his 3rd Colonial Paratroop Regiment.

—*Time* MAGAZINE, AUGUST 1958

Camp Asaliyah, Qatar
March 26, 2003

On the sixth day of the invasion of Iraq, Lieutenant General John Abizaid sat in for General Tommy Franks, the top commander in the Middle East, at the daily war update conducted by video with the top brass back at the Pentagon. It was midmorning in Washington. Defense Secretary Donald Rumsfeld and General Richard Myers, the chairman of the Joint Chiefs, greeted Abizaid, who appeared on-screen wearing desert fatigues. A handful of officers from Kuwait also were on the call. They wore bulky chemical protection suits, minus only the airtight headgear. Three Iraqi missiles had fallen nearby less than an hour earlier, and one of the colonels in Kuwait noted that he might have to break away if they got word a chemical attack was under way.

The Washington team nodded, but their relaxed mood was palpably different from the atmosphere of gathering dangers facing the Army in the field. A sandstorm blowing from the south had grounded helicopters and slowed the advance on Baghdad to a crawl. Attacks by Saddam Hussein's Fedayeen, the fanatical fighters in civilian clothes who prefigured the com-

ing insurgency, were escalating, especially on military supply lines that
snaked to the Kuwaiti border. Some units were down to only a few days of
fuel and ammunition.

Three months earlier, when General Franks had suggested that he
might need a deputy to help manage the war, Abizaid had jumped at the
chance. He was working for the Joint Staff in the Pentagon, far from the action. When he told Kathy, she knew it wasn't even worth trying to talk him
out of it. Now here he was on an unmarked base in Qatar, a small Persian
Gulf kingdom where Central Command kept its forward headquarters—
still not exactly the front lines. His windowless office sat inside a big sand-
colored tent. Like a Russian nesting doll, the tent was further encased by an
even larger prefabricated metal building. Outside, the desert temperatures
often soared past 110 degrees. Inside, the air-conditioning blew so cold
that soldiers often found they had to wrap themselves in fleece jackets. On
computer screens in his office, Abizaid could track minute-by-minute
movements of ground units and aircraft throughout the Middle East. He
spoke daily with senior Pentagon leaders on video teleconferences. Hundreds of officers scrambled around the headquarters cranking out Power-
Point slides by the thousands. It was a strange way to fight a war.

But it wasn't really the war that troubled Abizaid. He had no doubt that
U.S. troops would drive Saddam from power. What concerned him was
what would come after the dictator fell. Dave Petraeus, who was leading
the 101st Airborne Division through a brutal sandstorm as it drove toward
Baghdad, had the same worry. Rumsfeld and Franks's war plan assumed
that a lightning assault would quickly topple Saddam's regime. Once the
dictator was gone, they expected, Iraqis and the relatively small team of
civilians and retired generals that the Pentagon had assembled would handle delivery of humanitarian aid and any other problems that arose until a
new government could be established.

Both Abizaid and Petraeus had heard such promises about civilians
taking over the postwar reconstruction from the military in the 1990s. And
both expected that, just as in the nineties, the military would have to fill the
void when the civilian teams were overwhelmed by the chaos that followed
combat. The 9/11 terrorist attacks demonstrated the danger that could
emerge from chaotic, ungoverned places, like Afghanistan. But the Bush

administration wanted no part of nation building there or anyplace else. They hadn't absorbed the lessons of the 1990s about the military's unavoidable postconflict role. After the 2001 terrorist attacks, a small force made up of U.S. special operations troops invaded Afghanistan and, with precision bombing and local allies, quickly toppled the Taliban. The Bush administration left about 10,000 troops to hunt down the remnants of Al Qaeda. Then it turned its focus to Iraq, and to toppling Saddam and transforming Iraq into a model democracy for the Middle East. Ordered to prepare for an invasion of Iraq, the military was quite happy not to be saddled with rebuilding Afghanistan. The same attitude pervaded the early stages of the Iraq war, to Abizaid's and Petraeus's frustration. As the U.S. force pushed north, they were among the few who worried about what would happen after Baghdad fell.

Abizaid's and Petraeus's views on Iraq differed in other key respects, however. Petraeus had high hopes for the postinvasion period. "Wouldn't it be wonderful if this place turns out to be something?" he said to a reporter a few weeks into the war. "There's no reason why it couldn't be. They have lots of money, unless some petty despot takes over." Abizaid had a darker view. He knew how deep the ethnic and sectarian hatreds ran in the country and how quickly they could explode. He also recalled his time in Lebanon, when the Israelis had attempted to occupy an Arab land. Prior to the invasion, he had e-mailed his staff an academic study on the occupation. He hoped his troops would take two lessons from Israel's failure: occupation duty is hard even for the best-trained military, and the longer you stay the harder it gets.

These were the sorts of issues that Abizaid wanted to raise with Rumsfeld and other senior Pentagon officials during the video teleconference. The March 26 briefing began with the weather—a sandstorm blanketing much of the region had slowed the push north—and a discussion of that day's fighting. With the ground troops stalled, Air Force jets were doing most of the fighting that day, pounding Republican Guard units on the outskirts of Baghdad. After fifteen minutes, Rumsfeld departed, signing off with a wave. "We are glad you are so focused," he breezily announced to Abizaid, and turned the discussion over to his close aide Douglas Feith, the

Pentagon's undersecretary for policy, who suggested they talk about the postwar period.

As the discussion meandered along, Abizaid became more and more irritated. He had been warning for months that stabilizing the country after an invasion was going to be perilously hard. "The response I got was that you don't know what you are talking about," he recalled. Now, with the fall of Baghdad only days away, they were stuck debating about minor issues. Abizaid punched the white button on his console and a red border formed around his screen image in the Pentagon, Qatar, and Kuwait, indicating that he had the microphone. He suggested that the group spend a few minutes talking about how to handle members of Saddam's government.

"Senior-level Baathists with money will flee the country. They will become a problem for Interpol," he predicted. "Senior Baathists without money will be killed or will turn themselves in to us and try to trade information for clemency. Then there are the middle and lower tiers that run the country. We want them to come back to their jobs and work with us." It was these party members, the roughly 30,000 to 50,000 bureaucrats, teachers, police officers, and engineers, who did the day-to-day business of the government. Many had joined the Baath Party because Saddam Hussein's Iraq had offered no alternative. Even if their loyalties were suspect, they needed to be kept in their jobs to prevent a total breakdown in authority, he argued.

From Washington, Feith cut Abizaid off. "The policy of the United States government is de-Baathification," he said. As he spoke, Feith drew out the syllables in a way that seemed intended to shut off further discussion. Abizaid had grown to despise the word, which he thought echoed *de-Nazification* and only served to feed a fantasy that had taken hold at the highest levels of the Pentagon that the Iraq war was going to proceed like the liberation of France and Germany at the end of World War II. Occupying a Muslim country with its almost impenetrable tribal and ethnic politics and whose minority groups had a long history of killing each other was nothing like running Germany after World War II.

Abizaid pressed the white button, claiming the microphone. "You shouldn't even use the term *de-Baathification*," he told Feith. His voice had grown clipped and angry. "This is not Nazi Germany and what's needed is not de-Nazification. You have to hold this place together and if you don't keep the government together in some form, it won't hold."

Feith fired back, emphasizing that the decision came from the civilian officials who gave the military its orders. "Let me repeat to you what the policy of the U.S. government is: de-Baathification."

★   ★   ★   ★

Outside Najaf, Iraq
March 26, 2003

Major General David Petraeus couldn't afford to think about what was going to happen after Saddam fell. For the first time in his thirty-year career he was leading troops in combat. After crossing the Kuwait border and moving north hundreds of miles in only a few days, the leading edge of Petraeus's 101st Airborne Division was hunkered down outside Najaf, a city of more than 500,000 people about 160 miles south of Baghdad. Because of the whipping sandstorm, mud and sand coated Petraeus's face and reddened his blue eyes as he considered the division's next move. His orders called for stopping the Fedayeen fighters in white pickups who were mounting suicidal assaults on U.S. tanks and supply trucks. Intelligence reports estimated that there could be more than 1,000 fighters inside Najaf. Petraeus told Colonel Ben Hodges, whose brigade was awaiting orders to attack, that there was no reason to rush headlong into a potential ambush. "We're in a long war here. I want to keep our guys from getting killed in large numbers," he said.

Tanks might be able to charge into a city, but a light infantry unit like the 101st was far more vulnerable. At the moment Petraeus's division was strung out all the way to the Kuwaiti border. Supplies were running short. His helicopters were grounded. All were reasons to postpone the assault into Najaf until his division had time to consolidate its position. He told Hodges to dig in and defend the highway that skirted Najaf, which the Army needed to move supplies north. It was Petraeus's first combat experience, but he wasn't going to charge into the city when his orders were to move north fast.

It had been more than a decade since Petraeus had been shot in the chest in the Fort Campbell training accident. In 1999, he had broken his pelvis while skydiving during his free time near Fort Bragg, North Carolina. Although the painful accident required months of therapy, he liked to tell colleagues that it made him faster. He had his scores on the Army's physical fitness test to prove it. The fifty-year-old general, at five foot nine and 150 pounds, was still in better shape than the vast majority of his much younger soldiers. Few could match his toughness or his drive.

Still, he had his doubters. The long stretches Petraeus had spent at the elbow of senior generals had caused him to miss all of the nation's previous wars, big and small, over his thirty-year career—Grenada, Panama, the Gulf War, and Afghanistan. Some of his subordinates thought his lack of combat experience had made him too cautious. They wanted to charge into Najaf.

Brigadier General Benjamin Freakley, one of his two assistant division commanders, held an impromptu meeting in the command post with two other senior officers: Brigadier General E. J. Sinclair and Colonel Thomas Schoenbeck. Freakley, a Gulf War veteran, dominated the gathering, leaning in close as he spoke. The best way to protect the highway was to attack into the city, he maintained. If Fedayeen troops were fighting for their lives, they wouldn't be able to attack convoys. The other U.S. units involved in the invasion were already driving toward Baghdad. If the 101st didn't move fast, it would get left behind, he worried. The officers agreed to present a united front. Of the three, Colonel Schoenbeck, an easygoing officer who years before had played wide receiver for the University of Florida, was closest to Petraeus. "Tom, you need to convince the boss it is going to be okay," Freakley told him. "First Brigade can take this fight by itself." Schoenbeck promised to deliver the message.

In the days that followed, two brigades from the 101st edged toward Najaf. When the enemy fighters showed themselves in the city, the Americans hit them with rockets, artillery, and machine guns. It wasn't the headlong rush that Freakley wanted but a slow, deliberate attack. "We were all trying to understand, 'Who is it that's fighting?' " Petraeus recalled. Were the forces in the city Fedayeen, foreign fighters, Republican Guard or a mix of all three? Would they fight block by block or fall back? After a few days Petraeus and Hodges began getting reports that Iraqi defenses in Najaf were disintegrating. Instead of a thousand fighters, Iraqi sources were saying there were at best a few hundred left. Hodges ordered seven of his tanks to race a mile into the city and then dash back. The resistance had vanished. The siege that Petraeus had worried might take weeks had ended in a few days.

"The good news is that we now own Najaf," he told Hodges later that day. "And the bad news is that we now own Najaf." He asked for planes full of food and water for the locals, but the disorganized humanitarian relief effort in Kuwait couldn't produce them. Most of the 101st, meanwhile, pushed north toward Baghdad behind other Army and Marine units.

On April 11, the last of the resistance collapsed, setting off days of looting throughout the country. Abizaid, back in Qatar, began receiving reports that Kurdish fighters who had fought with the United States during the invasion were streaming into the northern city of Mosul. A few days later, a contingent of ninety Marines at the Mosul city hall opened fire on a crowd protesting the lack of electricity. The outnumbered Marines retreated to the airport on the edge of the city of 2 million residents and hunkered down. "You've got to get a force in here and give them some tanks," the Marine commander told Abizaid. "They've got to see we're serious about this."

Abizaid knew from his time in northern Iraq in 1991 that the pent-up hostility between Arabs and Kurds could turn explosive. He needed to lock down the city before things got worse. The best bet was the 101st Airborne Division, which had taken up a position in southern Baghdad. On April 18, Petraeus got orders to move his 20,000 soldiers to Mosul as quickly as possible. His division had performed respectably but had been only a secondary player in the invasion. Mosul was going to be different.

★   ★   ★   ★

Mosul, Iraq
April 2003

The Black Hawk helicopter made a couple of lazy circles around the walled city. From the air Petraeus could see that, except for a few checkpoints manned by ragged fighters, the streets were empty. Plumes of oily smoke from blazing ammunition dumps spiraled skyward. He ordered his pilot to land at the airport and went into the main terminal building. A layer of chalky dust coated the floors and the smell of urine hung in the air. Soldiers and Marines were trying to grab a few hours of sleep on one of the baggage carousels.

Petraeus took a seat in a passenger lounge where a couple of lieutenant colonels gave him an update. There was skirmishing in Arab neighborhoods on the city's west side. The city jail had been looted and all of the police cars had been stolen or destroyed. Electricity had been out for two weeks, the hospitals were all closed, and government workers and the police were afraid to return to their jobs.

Over the next few days, about 5,000 soldiers, an advance guard from the 101st, poured into Mosul in a massive show of force. Dozens of Apache attack helicopters buzzed overhead. "We had, in a real sense, almost a degree of omnipotence, and you had to exploit that," Petraeus recalled. He set up a temporary command post in the airport terminal and began to scratch out the closest thing that anyone had to a postwar plan. He didn't know anything about Mosul. The division didn't even have maps of the area. He was working mostly on instincts honed during his years in Haiti and a tour in Bosnia. At a minimum he decided that he needed money to pay civil service workers, buy police uniforms, and repair medical clinics, the radio station, the city jail, the bank, and the court system. He also wanted to hold elections quickly to choose a new Iraqi government for the north. Whoever was selected could at least help him figure out the basics: how to fix the power, the water, and the telephones.

He wasn't waiting for instructions or permission—or, at this early stage, help. Before the invasion, he and his fellow division commanders had been promised that the Pentagon-funded Office of Reconstruction and

Humanitarian Assistance (ORHA) would handle rebuilding the country. "Just get us to Baghdad and we'll take care of it," the head of the organization promised. In reality, ORHA was a joke. Its office in northern Iraq consisted of six civilians, one satellite phone that was incapable of receiving calls, and a Hotmail account that no one checked. Less than a week after arriving Petraeus stood in a former Baath Party reception hall, in front of a gaggle of tribal sheikhs in gold-fringed robes, ethnic Kurds in baggy pants, former generals, and businessmen in shiny suits. Behind them were the smaller tribes and ethnic groups—Turkmen and wispy-bearded Yezidis and Shabaks from outside the city. Petraeus had organized a meeting of about two dozen Iraqis to hammer out an agreement on holding elections.

His team, which consisted of the division lawyer and a lieutenant who had worked for him in Bosnia, had trouble keeping track of the constantly expanding cast of characters. The roster from the April 30 meeting listed some of the members simply as "Iraqi expatriate from Jabouri tribe," "Unidentified engineer," "Yusef judge?" and "General D?" There had been lots of fighting about who would get chairs at the main table and who would sit in the lesser seats along the wall. The bickering, which the Iraqis resolved among themselves, proved to be an unexpected blessing. It was the only way Petraeus had to figure out who was really important.

No one was quite sure how to run the gatherings, so Petraeus presided as if he were leading a staff meeting at Fort Campbell. His lieutenant passed out an agenda. The first item was always "old business." The night before the meeting there had been a hail of celebratory fire commemorating Saddam Hussein's birthday. Some of the demonstrators shot at U.S. troops, who returned fire, killing three Iraqis. Petraeus said he hoped the killings would send "a clear message" to those who were trying to disrupt their efforts to build a new Mosul. He then laid out what the group had agreed to during a marathon session a day earlier: a caucus of 213 delegates representing the region's tribes, ethnic groups, and political parties would select a provincial council and a governor, with each group allotted representatives based on their approximate population.

Almost immediately the arguments began. The Kurds and Arab tribes both insisted that they hadn't been given enough delegates. One participant argued that the entire process was invalid. Before the 101st arrived,

4,000 prominent locals in Mosul had held their own election and picked fifty delegates who deserved seats in any new government. "We voted in this very building," he shouted, and threatened to leave. Others maintained that Petraeus was allowing too many former Baath Party members who had supported Saddam Hussein to dominate the negotiations. "Any election held at this time will only benefit the old regime," a Kurdish leader insisted.

In earlier meetings Petraeus had tried to calm arguments with lectures on the democratic process. "The beauty of this system is that everyone is entitled to their own opinion," he told them. Now he was sick of the interminable debates and recriminations. If the Iraqis believed that they could roll over him and renegotiate every decision, they would never get anywhere. "Stop!" he yelled. "We are not going to begin each morning by renegotiating what we agreed to the night before. This will not happen, and if it does I will leave this room right now and we will cease this entire process." He gathered up his papers as if preparing to storm out. Iraqis rushed over to him, promising not to revisit the previous day's disputes. The proceedings still lasted six hours.

"An incredibly fascinating day," Colonel Richard Hatch, the division lawyer, wrote that evening in the journal he kept on his laptop. He'd wedged his cot in the airport bathroom, which reeked of urine but was at least quiet. Petraeus was relying on Hatch's legal training to help broker agreements between the feuding tribes. It was heady stuff for Hatch, who in his role as a military attorney was accustomed to playing second fiddle to swaggering combat officers. Still, he wondered if Petraeus's energy and determination would be enough to keep the power-sharing deals from exploding on them. "The irony of us dictating to a group what they will do to achieve a democratic government was not lost on me," he wrote.

The negotiations over the elections continued for nearly a week. Removed from the debates in Baghdad and Washington over which Baath Party members should be barred from the new government, Petraeus set his own policy. "Frankly, I would like to see discussion here of individuals rather than whole levels being excluded or included," he told the Kurds who wanted to ban all Baathists. "If we draw the line too low, there will be nothing left in government." More sheikhs trickled in and new arguments erupted. "Since nobody emerged completely happy we probably got it pretty close to fair," Colonel Hatch wrote in his journal on May 3.

Two days later the delegates gathered in the former Baath Party reception hall to elect a new government. A schedule guided the proceedings down to the minute, mystifying the more laissez-faire Iraqis. At 9:59 a.m. Petraeus stood on a plywood stage at the front of the reception hall. "By being here today you are participating in the birth of the democratic process in Iraq," he told the group. "This is a historic occasion and an important step forward for Mosul and Iraq." A Saddam-era judge who was there to certify the results read a script explaining the caucus procedures. He was followed by a bearded imam who offered a blessing. Then Petraeus took the microphone.

"At this time would the Shabaks please move to their delegation room," he announced, his voice echoing over the sound system. "At this time would the Yezidis please move to their delegation room. . . . At this time would the Turkmen please move to their delegation room; Turkmen only."

After caucusing, delegates dropped their ballots in plywood boxes built by Petraeus's engineers. The new council had been selected by noon. By 3:00 p.m. there was a governor: Ghanim al-Basso, a retired major general, who stood next to Petraeus on the wooden stage behind the ballot boxes, an Iraqi flag, and a spray of purple plastic flowers. He was a thin man with sagging eyes, rosy cheeks, and a gray mustache. During the Iran-Iraq War, Basso had been celebrated for his battlefield heroism, but he had fallen out of favor with the regime in 1993 after his brother was accused of backing a failed coup. His brother was killed, and Basso was forced into retirement. Now back in power, the new governor raised his hands over his head and in a short speech promised to be a "soldier for all of Mosul." Some delegates feared that Basso had remained a Baathist even after he left the military and had continued to profit from his ties to Saddam. He was an unacceptable candidate who would have to be replaced, they vowed. But for now at least the choice stood.

Petraeus spoke last and garnered the loudest applause. "Having walked the streets of this city, the second largest in Iraq, and having gotten to know the friendly nature of its citizens, I am beginning to feel like a

Moslawi," he proclaimed. Some in the audience were no doubt grateful to him for pulling off the first free elections in their city in decades, maybe ever. Others realized that despite the day's events this American officer was in charge and would be for several more months, maybe years. He had money, attack helicopters, and big guns. They didn't want to get on his bad side.

"Have you done anything like this before?" a CNN reporter asked Petraeus as the new council posed for a group picture.

"No. Never," he replied with an excited, almost surprised lilt to his voice.

He had been in Mosul for only two weeks, but he had created the first representative government in liberated Iraq. Was it perfect? Hardly. But it was a start.

Petraeus and Hatch assumed that at least one of the other five Army divisions in Iraq would want to conduct their own elections, so they drafted a nine-page PowerPoint briefing on how they had done it, and shared it with neighboring units. But the other divisions had other priorities. A few weeks later the Bush administration barred further elections in the country out of fear that fundamentalists, who were organizing through the mosques, would win. The most telling slide in the 101st's election briefing was one labeled "Commanding General Involvement." More than any other document, it captured Petraeus's philosophy in Mosul as he tried to rebuild a broken society and beat back an insurgency. "Must continuously suggest direction and priority . . . patience & repetition . . . Don't let up, must outlast them and outwork them."

The "them" wasn't the enemy, of course. It was the Iraqis who had agreed to cooperate with Petraeus. He sympathized with Abizaid's argument that foreign troops would produce resistance and resentment. "Try as we will to be an army of liberation, over time they will take you for granted," he liked to say. But he differed from Abizaid in that he didn't let it constrain him. He didn't just want to stabilize northern Iraq. He wanted to transform the place. "The biggest idea was that we were going to do nation building and we weren't going to hold it at arm's length. We were an occupying army, and we had enormous responsibilities for the people," he recalled.

The day after the elections President Bush named former diplomat and counterterrorism expert L. Paul Bremer III to head the Coalition Provisional Authority (CPA) in Baghdad. Bremer arrived with two orders—both hatched in the Pentagon—that upended Abizaid and Petraeus's plans. The first was a sweeping de-Baathification edict that banned as many as 50,000 former Baath party members from ever serving in government. A second decree disbanded the army.

The reaction to both was swift and violent. In June a mob of former soldiers, furious at the loss of their pensions, converged on the Mosul city hall, prompting the panicked police there to open fire. One protester was killed, and in the melee two Humvees were torched. Petraeus, who was inside the building, grabbed a bullhorn and rushed outside to calm the crowd and invite the ringleaders to meet with him and the governor. That evening he warned his superiors in Baghdad that the furious former soldiers were on the wall of the government building. "Next time they are going to be over it," he told his bosses. He and Governor Basso, who had been on the job for less than a month, quickly banned all public demonstrations in Mosul. Technically, Basso was a Baathist and should have been fired under the terms of Bremer's order. Fortunately for Petraeus, who was growing to respect the Iraqi, officials in Baghdad were preoccupied with other problems.

He was proud of his elections and the work his division was doing in Mosul. Both achievements, however, took a backseat to a prize he considered more meaningful—a combat patch on his right shoulder, signifying that he'd finally seen battle. As soon as the division got formal approval to wear them, Command Sergeant Major Marvin Hill, the division's senior enlisted soldier, snuck into Petraeus's room at the airport, grabbed three of his uniforms, and took them to a tailor he'd found in Mosul. Later that afternoon, he returned with the camouflage top, bearing a new Screaming Eagles patch. "Do you know how huge it is to have a combat patch?" Petraeus had asked weeks earlier when his troops first came under fire. Now he was speechless. He pulled on the fatigues and embraced Hill.

★   ★   ★   ★

Camp Asaliyah, Qatar
June 2003

In the first two months after the invasion, Abizaid made weekly trips to Iraq. He didn't like what he was seeing. Insurgent attacks were rising. So were checkpoint shootings in which U.S. soldiers mistakenly opened fire on drivers who ignored or misunderstood orders to halt. Whenever he returned to Qatar from one of his Iraq trips, Abizaid would sit down with his chief planner, Colonel Mike Fitzgerald, and a few other officers to brainstorm. Usually the meetings came at the end of the day, after the larger staff updates and video briefings with Bush administration officials. "We have got about a year to make a difference in Iraq and then we have got to think about getting out," he said to Fitzgerald one evening in June after returning from Iraq. After a year, he said, the United States would hit a point of diminishing returns. The population would begin to turn on them.

Fitzgerald wrote a note to himself that he'd need to move with greater urgency to rebuild the Iraqi army and police in particular. Like Abizaid, he wasn't sure how to do it without running afoul of Bremer and Pentagon policy makers.

Fitzgerald and his fellow planners could see Abizaid's frustration building with each passing day. The CPA order disbanding the army and purging Baath Party members from the government had infuriated him. He'd slashed through both with a red pen and scribbled in the margins. "By the time Abizaid was finished, they looked as though someone had spilled a can of tomato soup on them," Fitzgerald recalled. He had passed them on to General Franks, the head of Central Command, who was the top commander in the Middle East and the senior officer overseeing the war effort. Abizaid was Franks's three-star deputy and didn't have a direct line to Rumsfeld or President Bush. There was little he could do beyond register his disapproval and move on.

Although Franks was set to retire and his job was coming open, it wasn't clear that Abizaid would be staying in the Middle East. Rumsfeld had wanted to make him Army chief of staff. Even though the job would mean a fourth star, Abizaid wasn't interested. He couldn't stand the thought of being stuck in the Pentagon fighting over the defense budget while real wars were going on in Iraq and Afghanistan. He'd never particularly liked serving in Washington.

Before he turned down the chief of staff job, he called his friend Major General Karl Eikenberry, who was running the training mission in Afghanistan. Eikenberry and Abizaid had been roommates at West Point, trading assignments with other cadets so they could stay together. After West Point the two officers had led remarkably similar careers, alternating assignments in the Rangers with sojourns that took them far away from the military mainstream. While Abizaid was studying at the University of Jordan, Eikenberry had mastered Mandarin Chinese at Nanjing University. In the mid-1980s they overlapped at Harvard. If anyone would understand his desire to stay in the Middle East, it would be Eikenberry.

Over a static-filled satellite phone line, Abizaid said he was struggling to figure out where he could have the most impact. Eikenberry advised taking the chief of staff job. Iraq had become so politicized that it would be almost impossible for him to succeed. "Tommy Franks got to host the banquet in Iraq, and you are going to be the one who is going to have to clean it up," he said. "It is going to be messy and you are going to get an enormous amount of unwanted help. Knowing the personalities in Washington, wouldn't you be better off as chief of staff?"

Abizaid had always had deep doubts about invading Iraq. The first time he had heard a senior Bush administration official raise the possibility was the day after the September 11 terrorist attacks. He was flying back from Europe with Doug Feith, the senior policy official in the Pentagon. Abizaid, a general on the Pentagon's Joint Staff at the time, had been visiting his counterparts in Ukraine. Feith and a handful of other senior Bush administration officials were returning from Russia. With U.S. airspace still closed to commercial traffic, the head of European Command had arranged for them to fly back in a KC-135 Air Force tanker.

In the hour or so before boarding the plane, Abizaid had made repeated calls to Washington to check on Eikenberry, whose office was in the section of the Pentagon that had been struck by the hijacked passenger jet. The last word he got as he took off was that his best friend was still missing.

Huddling in the tanker's dimly lit cargo area, the group of senior officers and Defense Department officials began discussing the response to the attacks. There was agreement on the need to strike hard where Al Qaeda had been able to establish nodes or safe havens. The discussion then turned to other targets, and Feith raised the possibility of toppling Saddam Hussein, a course he and his fellow neoconservatives had been advocating for years. Abizaid cut him off. "Not Iraq. There is not a connection with Al Qaeda," he said. Feith refused to let it go. Abizaid wouldn't back down, either. "I never thought Iraq was at the center of the problem. I didn't see it as a threat to the vital security of the United States," he said later.

As the six-hour flight dragged on, Abizaid sat by himself and started composing the eulogy he planned to deliver for Eikenberry. The plane flew over the remains of the World Trade Center towers on its way to Washington, and Abizaid lay on his stomach looking out a small window in the tail at the smoking ruins. As soon as the plane had landed, he called the Pentagon to ask about his friend and was told Eikenberry had narrowly escaped. He tore up the unfinished eulogy.

Back in the Pentagon he was shocked at how quickly the administration shifted from Afghanistan to the invasion of Iraq. "I thought there would be a lot more debate about it. All the reasons that we didn't go into Iraq in 1991 still prevailed," he recalled. But almost no one discussed them. In the fall of 2002 Abizaid pushed to assign a separate military headquarters staff, augmented by large numbers of State Department experts, to focus exclusively on planning the occupation of Iraq, which he warned was going to be a mess. "Iraq has three very distinct minority groups that will be at each other's throats immediately," he told Deputy Defense Secretary Paul Wolfowitz and Feith. Abizaid had seen the country's problems up close just ten years earlier in northern Iraq. The response he got from senior Bush administration officials was that the postwar planning was under control. There was a group of exiles ready to parachute into a liberated Iraq and run the country, and there was going to be no long-term occupation. Abizaid was incensed. "I have had enough of Washington," he complained to a former officer involved in the postwar planning weeks before the war started. "They have no idea what they are doing. I may just pack it in."

He didn't want to be Army chief. With General Franks set to retire, there was only one job left in the military that Abizaid coveted: the head of Central Command, overseeing the Middle East and the wars in Iraq and Afghanistan. Abizaid sent word to Rumsfeld that he would retire if he didn't get the job; Rumsfeld eventually agreed to give him the position. "It was one of the few times in my career that I really fought for a job," he recalled.

On July 7, 2003, Abizaid pinned on his fourth star and took over Central Command from Franks at a ceremony held in Tampa's largest indoor sports arena, home of the National Hockey League's Lightning franchise. Franks's send-off was the sort befitting a conquering hero. Crooner Wayne Newton stopped by en route to Las Vegas. So too did a tuxedo-clad Robert De Niro and country music performer Neal McCoy, who serenaded the general with the song "I'm Your Biggest Fan."

Franks, a lanky jug-eared general from west Texas, had enlisted in 1967 when his poor grades forced him to leave the University of Texas. After earning a commission through Officer Candidate School, he spent a year in Vietnam, earned his college degree, and then rose quickly in the 1980s and 1990s. He was a savvy technician whose expertise at melding airpower, artillery, and tanks on the battlefield had vaulted him to the top of his profession. In Iraq, he told himself, it was his job to destroy Saddam Hussein's military and topple his regime. What came afterward wasn't his problem. In that regard, he was a perfect match for Rumsfeld, who also had little interest in postwar reconstruction.

Before he bade farewell, Franks practically dared the growing resistance in Iraq and Afghanistan to take its best shot. "Twenty-two months ago the United States of America, in fact the free world, looked into the face of evil," Franks said in his west Texas twang. "We came on that day to recognize our vulnerability. And the world came to recognize America with attitude. As President Bush said recently, 'Bring it on!' " He had no idea his great military victory was coming apart.

Among those in the crowd was Michael Krause, Abizaid's old history professor from West Point. As a cadet, Abizaid had been deeply impressed with Krause, who spoke fluent French and German. Krause had nominated

Abizaid for the scholarship program that sent him to Jordan. Though they hadn't seen each other in years, he had come to Tampa for the ceremony at Abizaid's invitation.

Abizaid's new job running Central Command was the most coveted in the military. He was technically one of five American commanders who divided up responsibility for the entire globe, but as the general in charge of the greater Middle East, Abizaid was by far the most important. His turbulent area encompassed two dozen countries, including Iraq and Afghanistan, where American troops were fighting. It wasn't his job to direct those wars, but he stood watch over the commanders who did. The job came with every imaginable amenity, including a Boeing jet to take him anywhere at a moment's notice. A CIA analyst traveled with him for updates each morning on the latest intelligence. An ambassador from the State Department was on his staff to advise him on regional politics. All told, Abizaid was in charge of more than 200,000 troops. When Krause caught up with his former student in a small room inside the arena, he congratulated Abizaid on his new position. Abizaid smiled and shrugged. "Boy, what a mess I have gotten myself into," he replied.

A few days later Abizaid addressed the media for the first time as the top commander in the Middle East, and immediately made clear he would be a different commander from the uncurious and smug Franks. "So what's the situation in Iraq?" he asked rhetorically. The enemy had organized itself into cells and was "conducting a classical guerrilla-type campaign," he said. The phrase captivated the reporters sitting in front of him, because it directly contradicted Rumsfeld, who only a couple of weeks earlier had proclaimed, "I guess I don't use the phrase 'guerrilla war' because there isn't one." As Abizaid left the briefing room, the head of Army public affairs, who also happened to be an old friend from his days in the Rangers, pulled him aside. "You are really in for it now. This briefing room hasn't seen that kind of candor in a long time," he told him.

Soon Abizaid was receiving rambling memos from the defense secretary telling him to keep quiet. One memo, which drew guffaws from the Central Command staff, arrived with an underlined excerpt from Che Guevara's biography, intended by Rumsfeld to prove that the violence in Iraq wasn't a guerrilla war. "It was unbelievable. It was painful," Abizaid re-called. "But it didn't change my mind." The internal debate, consisting of back-and-forth memos from D.C. to Qatar, continued for several more weeks. Publicly, the general's short statement settled it. The conflict be-came an insurgency. The exchange showed the influence Abizaid wielded as a four-star commander and acknowledged expert on the Arab world. He'd be very careful about how he used it.

His biggest problem in his new job was the command arrangement in Iraq. Shortly before he retired, Franks handed responsibility for military operations in the country to the Army's V Corps, which was led by Lieu-tenant General Ricardo Sanchez. The move had shocked Abizaid. Sanchez, a newly promoted three-star, had been given command of the corps only a few days earlier. He'd come to Iraq thinking that he was going to be one of a half-dozen division commanders in the country. Now he was in charge of the entire military effort in the country. "The burden I felt was unimaginable," he wrote in his 2008 autobiography. Abizaid told Franks the move didn't make any sense. "That's the decision," Franks replied.

It soon became clear Sanchez and his small staff, which was desper-ately short of intelligence specialists, logisticians, and strategists, couldn't handle the job. In early July, Abizaid got a call from General Jack Keane, the acting chief of staff of the Army. He had just returned from a visit to Baghdad and was deeply concerned about Sanchez's ability to handle the war effort. "Listen, this thing is over his head," he told Abizaid.

"Who do you think should take his place?" Abizaid asked. Keane sug-gested Petraeus. He had first met Petraeus when he was an assistant divi-sion commander in the 101st Airborne Division and Petraeus was one of his battalion commanders. When Petraeus was shot, Keane had helped control the bleeding and flew with him to the hospital. In the years since the shooting Keane, a garrulous New Yorker, had become an avid sup-porter and mentor, filling the role played previously by Galvin and Vuono. "We can find another division commander. Petraeus is the best guy we got," Keane insisted. Abizaid asked for time to think it over. Sanchez had served under him in Kosovo in the late 1990s, and Abizaid trusted and liked him. Franks had put Sanchez in a grossly unfair position, and Abizaid didn't want to fire him. He believed that he could help Sanchez get the specialists that he needed to succeed from the Army staff in the Pentagon, and that in the interim his Central Command staff could fill in the holes. He called Keane a few days later and said he was going to stick with his friend.

For most of his tenure, Sanchez had only about half of the staff that he needed. Some of the blame for this failure lay with senior officials in the Pentagon who were slow to fill slots because they assumed the war was over and that U.S. troops would soon be coming home. Abizaid, however, also bore some responsibility. He saw himself as a grand strategist whose job was to help shape the military's overall approach to Iraq, Afghanistan, and the broader Middle East, and he often ignored thankless but critical tasks such as pounding away at the Pentagon bureaucracy to cough up more personnel to help his overwhelmed commander.

✻ ✻ ✻ ✻

In the summer of 2003, the 101st Airborne Division stood out as the rare American success in Iraq. Congressional delegations, eager for good news, flocked to Mosul. And Petraeus didn't disappoint. He bombarded them with PowerPoint slides cataloging the division's accomplishments: the police force was growing, roads were being paved, the telephones worked, wheat was being harvested, and insurgents were being arrested. The VIPs stayed in the Ninewah Hotel, a formerly state-owned business that Petraeus had badgered the reluctant provincial governing council into privatizing. They met with Governor Basso.

Before leaving, they sat through a crisply produced twelve-minute video showing 101st soldiers arresting insurgents and fixing up Mosul. It ended with a bagpiper playing "Amazing Grace" and Petraeus's voice from a 101st Airborne Division memorial ceremony. "There is nothing tougher than the loss of a brother in arms," he intoned. "We want to find meaning and purpose in such a loss. Above all we want to answer the question: What good will come from this?" As if to answer the question, a World War II black-and-white photo of exhausted 101st soldiers holding a Nazi flag morphed into a shot of three soldiers clutching an Iraqi flag in a bombed-out building. The final image was, of course, Petraeus's idea, a way of harking back to the days of glory when the 101st had parachuted into the Normandy invasion and fought its way into Germany.

Petraeus believed in mythmaking. His peers referred to him somewhat derisively as "King David." Even Petraeus would admit the nickname carried a grain of truth. "I don't know where the King David thing actually came from, but you had to play that role a little bit," he conceded. Iraqis craved strong leadership far more than abstract concepts such as democracy, and he was more than happy to provide it.

He had put his headquarters in Saddam's northernmost palace, a fortresslike complex surrounded by man-made lakes and decorated with murals celebrating Mesopotamian warriors. He received visitors in his second-floor office, a large room with marble floors, a view of the Tigris River, and a latticework ceiling made to look like the drooping folds of a Bedouin sheikh's tent. His days began at 5:15 a.m. with twenty minutes of answering e-mails. By six o'clock he and his aide had begun a blistering five-mile dash around the palace complex that took him past the Freedom Barbershop, the Freedom Shopette, and the Freedom Laundry Service. Then he took his morning briefing in a cavernous room with tiered stadium seating for his staff and two projection screens. The briefings always began the same way: "This is Eagle Six," Petraeus would say, using his 101st Airborne Division call sign. "It's another beautiful morning in the Tigris River Valley."

He didn't worry so much about what his brigade commanders were doing as long as they were spending money, which he used as the best measure of whether they were winning over Iraqis. "I noticed Third Brigade is ahead on projects this month. First and Second brigades, do you need some suggestions or some help keeping up?" he'd ask on the morning calls. Worried that the flood of reconstruction money would spur inflation, he decided to open the border to trade with Syria. Boosting the supply of goods, Petraeus reasoned, would offset the increased demand from the extra cash and keep prices low. One evening around eleven he told Colonel Hatch, his division lawyer, to draft the order and have it in his in-box by the next morning. Hatch wasn't sure that he had the authority to open the border, so he crafted a vaguely worded "emergency" measure that would remain in effect "until revoked by a higher authority." To justify it, he cited a speech from General Franks declaring an end to illegal roadblocks and checkpoints. "It was kind of a stretch," he admitted later.

A couple of days later Petraeus and Basso flew to Rabiya, a dusty town on the Syrian border, to sign the order and declare the crossing open. He loved to fly; the altitude gave him a perfect perch from which to inventory the 101st's accomplishments for the *Washington Post* reporter traveling with him. He pointed out a caravan of fuel tankers ferrying gasoline into Mosul from Turkey. He and the military attaché in Ankara had worked with the Turks to make sure the fuel kept flowing. Mosul's Olympic-sized swimming pool gleamed in the sun. Soldiers from the 101st had fixed it just a week earlier. A bit farther out combines harvested wheat. Petraeus set the prices over the objections of the CPA, which had initially demanded a free-market approach. He wanted to make sure farmers got at least 10 percent more for their crop than Saddam paid.

His helicopter landed at the border, kicking up a giant plume of sand, and hundreds of tribal dignitaries in robelike dishdashas rushed out to greet him. He gave a short speech on the benefits of trade with Syria and then, in accordance with local custom, sat down to consume a massive feast of goat and rice with his hands. Long after he was full, the grateful sheikhs continued to pile food on his plate. The CPA prohibited the Iraqis from levying tariffs at the crossing, but Petraeus arranged an "administrative fee" of $10 for a small truck and $20 for a big truck. Some of the money went to repair the border facilities and the rest went to enrich the tribes in the area. This was how business had been done for centuries, even under Saddam.

As he lifted off in his Black Hawk, Petraeus looked down on the throng of sheikhs below waving and cheering next to brightly colored tents. A bit farther out a long ribbon of trucks was streaming across the border. "Amazing, isn't it?" he told the reporter with him. "It's a combination of being the President and the Pope." He caught a lot of flak for the quote from fellow officers who had long believed that the general's ego and ambition were out of control. Years later he would still wish he had never said it. The truth was it captured a bit of how he felt.

Exasperated CPA officials complained that Petraeus's quick elections had empowered too many Baathists and religious zealots. There were at least three or four provincial council members, including Governor Basso, who the CPA representative in Mosul said should be fired. Petraeus ignored her, maneuvering around Bremer's de-Baathification decree wherever possible. At Mosul University the edict would have forced him to relieve most of the school's faculty. He handed the problem to Hatch, who unearthed a provision in the Geneva Conventions that required occupying powers to ensure the "proper working of all institutions devoted to the care and education of children." Petraeus forwarded Hatch's brief to Baghdad, arguing that he couldn't sack the professors without violating the conventions. Bremer agreed to let him fire and then temporarily rehire teachers through the end of the school year.

"Petraeus was very clever but extremely egotistical," said Dick Nabb, the senior CPA official in the Kurdish-dominated northern territories. "He wanted everyone to know there was a new king in the area." Petraeus insisted that the Kurds fly the official Iraqi flag along with the Kurdish flag over their government buildings. It was his way of making clear that they were now part of the new Iraq, though it infuriated the Kurds, who had operated their own autonomous region for more than a decade. "What you are doing is like asking the Jews in Germany to serve under the swastika," Nabb objected. The Kurds humored Petraeus, flying the Iraqi colors when he visited and promptly taking it down as soon as he left. "You need to remind him that we are not your enemies," Massoud Barzani, who led one of the Kurds' two major political parties, implored Nabb after Petraeus's initial visit.

A man whose talents and energy had sometimes seemed too big for the Army now had a vast canvas on which to paint. Critics had to concede that he got things done. He dealt with Iraq's chronic electricity shortages by cutting a deal with a rotund Turkish millionaire to ship heavy oil across the border in return for electric power from his privately owned plants. Neither Petraeus nor anyone on his staff knew the first thing about trading oil for kilowatts. So Petraeus gathered together a few officers and the former head of northern Iraq's state-owned oil company. "You need to know enough so we don't get swindled," he instructed.

A few weeks later his oil task force began negotiating a similar deal with surly Syrian oil officials who had flown from the border to Mosul on one of his Black Hawks. The Syrians refused to even address their Iraqi counterparts. "You have been conquered and are in a subjugated state," they insisted. So Petraeus's team handled the deliberations. By day seven they thought they were close to signing a deal, and the two delegations moved to a restaurant on the Tigris River. Several hours later Petraeus radioed Brigadier General Frank Helmick, who was leading the 101st team, to find out what was happening. "Well, we think we got it, but it's not quite there," Helmick told him.

Around 3:00 p.m. he radioed again. The Syrians were refusing to sign anything until they returned to Damascus and received formal government approval. "Don't let them leave," Petraeus ordered. When he arrived at the restaurant the delegations had retreated to separate rooms. Petraeus pulled aside the lone CPA representative on the U.S. team; the 101st had flown him up from Baghdad a few days earlier to help with the deal. "Can I just fly out to the border and throw open the valve without signing a formal contract?" Petraeus asked. Once the oil and the electricity were flowing, he figured, it would be too hard for the Syrians or the civilians in Baghdad to stop. The CPA representative, an Army lieutenant colonel, said okay. He wasn't going to tell a two-star general no. Next Petraeus sat down with the Syrians. "Okay, it is now or never," he finally said. They could open the valve that afternoon and sign the formal agreement sometime later or just forget about the deal.

The Syrians agreed to open it and the two delegations quickly hustled onto five helicopters. As the sun set, the Black Hawks touched down at a cluster of cinder-block and mud shacks a few miles from the border. A small band, hastily assembled for the ceremony, played an Iraqi tune. Petraeus, the senior Syrian official, and the former head of the northern Iraqi oil office turned the valve, sending oil flowing west. The Iraqis then pulled out a knife and slit the throat of a lamb, which gurgled and thrashed. Petraeus, the Syrians, and the Iraqis dipped their hands in the oozing blood and laid them on the pipeline.

The deal surprised Secretary of State Colin Powell, who was trying to freeze out Damascus, but no one countermanded it, and the oil continued to flow. The joke in the 101st was that Petraeus now ran the only division in the Army with its own foreign policy.

$$\star \quad \star \quad \star \quad \star$$

In August 2003 Abizaid arrived in Mosul, where Petraeus presented him with a list of everything he couldn't get from Baghdad. The biggest shortfall was money; the division had reconstruction projects costing tens of millions of dollars that it wanted to do and a microloan initiative that needed funds as well. Petraeus also wanted more latitude to work with former Baathists. Too many of these people were being frozen out.

Abizaid agreed to help. But he had different reasons for coming to Mosul. He wanted to see the city and walk a patrol. He trusted his sense of the Arab world more than any intelligence report. Petraeus, meanwhile, was determined to make sure nothing happened to his four-star boss, and organized a massive security detail to go out with him. U.S. troops stood guard on almost every block and Apache helicopters cut tight circles overhead. As Abizaid's convoy snaked through the city, hundreds of young men, drawn by the hubbub, rushed out of their homes to see what was happening. "Did you see the look on their faces?" Abizaid asked Brigadier General John Custer, his top intelligence officer, after returning to the palace. He was referring to young Arab men they had seen on the patrol. "A lot of those guys were wearing military uniforms a few months ago. They don't see us as their liberators or their friends."

Instead of the 101st Airborne acting as an all-powerful occupation force, what were needed were Muslim troops who could patrol alongside American soldiers and blunt the extremists' message that the troops were anti-Islam, Abizaid insisted. A few weeks earlier he put together a list of potential allies he thought could help: Morocco, Oman, Pakistan, Tunisia, Malaysia, and Indonesia. His best bet was to bring in the Turks. Before arriving in Mosul, he'd been in Ankara, where Turkish officials offered to send several thousand soldiers. Abizaid thought they should go to turbulent Anbar Province in western Iraq. The biggest hitch was the Kurds, who had their own centuries-old feud with Turkey and were likely to fight the deployment. Abizaid and Petraeus received the leaders of the two main Kurdish political parties, Massoud Barzani and Jalal Talabani, in Petraeus's second-floor office. Abizaid knew both men from his 1992 relief mission in northern Iraq. Together he and Talabani had tried to calm the crowd that blocked his battalion from leaving.

Carrying themselves like Ottoman pashas, the Kurdish leaders took seats on the overstuffed chairs in Petraeus's office. "If the Turks move into Anbar, will you let them establish routes through your territory to supply their troops?" Abizaid asked. The Kurds grudgingly agreed to give the Turks safe passage.

Two days later Bremer called Abizaid and told him the Kurds had scuttled the deal for Turkish troops. Abizaid was incredulous. "I just talked to them. Did the Kurds veto it or did you veto it?" he demanded.

"Well, it's not a smart thing to bring in neighbors, because once you bring in one neighbor, you have to bring in the other neighbors," Bremer replied. In his 2006 autobiography Bremer wrote that there was widespread opposition among both Kurds and the majority Shiite Muslims to Turkish peacekeepers. Abizaid's plan, he insisted, never would have worked.

Abizaid ordered his aide to check Bremer's daily schedule. There were no meetings with the Kurdish leaders shown. He was convinced that Bremer didn't want the Turks or any other Muslim forces because they'd complicate the Bush administration's plans to remake Iraq—plans he thought were unrealistic. "What it all meant to me was that they didn't want forces that they didn't think were controllable," he said. "The whole idea was they wanted control. The policy makers wanted control through American forces." In the fall, he got a memo from Rumsfeld suggesting another Muslim partner. Conditions were improving in Afghanistan, and Rumsfeld opined that the Afghan warlords might send forces to Iraq. Sending ill-disciplined Afghans, scarred by decades of civil war, to a country in the midst of its own ethno-sectarian conflict was the worst idea Abizaid could imagine. The ignorance about the region back in Washington could be astounding.

It wasn't much better among some American officers in Iraq. Abizaid was getting mostly good news from his division commanders throughout the summer and fall of 2003. With each passing month they insisted they were getting more tips and a better handle on the enemy. "Over the last two weeks we've hit the weapons caches and we've really hit the money," Major General Ray Odierno told him on a visit to Tikrit in late July. In September General Sanchez and his division commanders all told him they were on the verge of breaking the resistance. Abizaid had his doubts. The de-Baathification policy was alienating tens of thousands of Sunnis. Efforts to rebuild the army and police were a mess. To prevent a future military coup, the Bush administration had capped the size of the Iraqi army at 45,000 soldiers and insisted that they be used only to defend Iraq against an invasion from outside countries such as Iran or Syria. Driving through Cairo, Abizaid pointed out the large number of Egyptian soldiers standing guard on the sooty streets. In the Arab world, big armies kept young men out of trouble and held fractious societies together. "There is no Arab army on earth that's less than 300,000 in a country the size of Iraq," he railed to his staff.

But he never said it that strongly to Bush or Rumsfeld. He wasn't afraid to disagree with his civilian bosses, particularly on military matters; his first Pentagon press conference proved it. But he didn't believe it was his job to argue with them once a decision had been made. The civilians set the policy and it was the military's job to execute it. Every senior commander struggled with how far to go in offering advice on policy issues, but in Iraq, where bad policy decisions were driving the insurgency, finding the right balance was especially tough. Should he emphasize the positive assessments coming from his subordinate commanders? Or should he focus on the deep policy disagreements he and his commanders had with Bremer and others in the administration? Was that really his job? There were no clear answers.

After one meeting in which he gave Rumsfeld a positive assessment of the security situation in Iraq, he turned to his immediate staff and asked how they thought he had done. "I felt like I might have been overly optimistic," he said. "Sir, you were overly optimistic. I don't think you really believed half of what you said," said Major General George Trautman, a Marine who was Abizaid's deputy chief for strategy.

Throughout the latter half of 2003 Abizaid debated going to Baghdad and taking command. Sanchez, whose staff had been thrown together in May, was chronically short of people in key areas such as intelligence. He was also overwhelmed by the job. His relationship with Bremer had grown so bad that the two men barely talked.

In Iraq Abizaid reasoned that he might be able to take some of the pressure off Sanchez, reach out to former Iraqi army officers, and press Bremer to rethink de-Baathification and other decisions that were causing so much unrest. "I think we should just go," he'd tell senior aide Colonel Joe Reynes. He was already spending as much as a week there every month, meeting with commanders and sheikhs. When he wasn't in Iraq or Afghanistan he was in Saudi Arabia, Kuwait, Bahrain, Jordan, or Egypt. The meetings were always the same. He'd ask for names of Sunni sheikhs in Iraq with whom he could meet on his next trip, and the Arab leaders would pass on a list and some advice. "You have to address the honor of the tribes. Pay the families when you kill one of their men; pay the sheikhs," the crown prince of Bahrain counseled in late October. Abizaid would make a fruitless pitch for them to send Arab peacekeeping troops. At some point they'd tell him what a huge mistake the invasion had been.

As soon as Abizaid seemed settled on moving to Iraq, he'd launch into an argument for staying. There were too many other problems in the region: the Afghan war, an increasingly aggressive Iran, and Al Qaeda's efforts to establish a presence in Saudi Arabia or Pakistan. If he were in Baghdad, he couldn't give much attention to these problems, which he believed posed a greater long-term threat. Eventually Abizaid decided not to move his headquarters to Iraq; he would try to help Sanchez manage the war through his frequent visits.

Abizaid's long stretches in the Middle East allowed him to see more clearly than just about any other officer the drawbacks of a long-term occupation of Iraq. He believed that as time passed, Iraqi resentment over the occupation would grow and the effectiveness of the military would be diminished. He recognized that until warring religious and ethnic groups were willing to share power, the fighting would grind on indefinitely.

In a tragic way, though, his deep knowledge of the Arabic world also constrained him. He commanded a massive military force but worried that if it tried to do too much, it would only make the situation worse. Instead of pushing for a strategy that recognized the central role that U.S. troops would have to play in stopping the violence, he often seemed to be casting about for a quick fix to Iraq's problems.

In the fall of 2003 Petraeus secured the surrender of Sultan Hashem Ahmed, Iraq's former defense minister and number twenty-seven on the

United States' most-wanted list. "You have my word that you'll be treated with the utmost dignity and respect . . . in my custody," Petraeus wrote in a letter sent through tribal intermediaries to Hashem. A few weeks later Hashem returned to Mosul, had a final breakfast with his family, and turned himself in to Petraeus. The two men talked in an airplane hangar in Mosul, and Petraeus found that the former general's assessment of some of northern Iraq's key political figures matched his own.

Abizaid knew Hashem's reputation well. The rotund former general had been a hero of the Iran-Iraq War. Despite his high position in Saddam's government, he was never considered part of the dictator's inner circle. "This guy could be what we've been looking for," Abizaid suggested to Sanchez. Maybe he could serve as defense minister? Hashem had blood on his hands from his days as an Iraqi general, but so did everybody in the country, Abizaid reasoned. There was an air of desperation to the inquiry. Bremer had no interest in resurrecting former generals in any capacity; nor did the Shiites and Kurds who had been tortured by Saddam's regime. Hashem was sent to prison and four years later sentenced to death by an Iraqi court for his role in the gassing of the Kurds.

★　★　★　★

Mosul
November 7, 2003

Abizaid sat across from Petraeus in his second-floor palace office with its view of the Tigris River, a ribbon of greenish blue stretching to the horizon. He'd come to get Petraeus's thoughts on replacing his 22,000-soldier airborne division with a much smaller force of about 8,000 troops. Abizaid and Petraeus had never had a particularly warm relationship. As they shot up through the ranks ahead of their peers, they'd always been rivals more than friends. Still, Abizaid respected the work Petraeus had done in Mosul, and told him as much. No one had done a better job winning over Sunni Arabs or working around the CPA's disastrous decision to ban former Baathists and military officers from taking part in the government. "We are in a race to win over the Iraqi people. What have you and your element done today?" was the mantra plastered on the wall of every 101st Airborne

Division command post. Petraeus had created a sense of hope in the north that didn't exist elsewhere.

Abizaid's worry was whether it could last. He doubted that any American could ever really penetrate the tribal, sectarian, and ethnic politics. He was right about Iraq's overwhelming complexity. Even Petraeus didn't fully grasp the political undercurrents that the insurgency would exploit to undo his achievements and gain a foothold in northern Iraq after the 101st departed. But Abizaid underestimated the role that aggressive commanders such as Petraeus were playing in stabilizing the fractious country, at least temporarily. Without Saddam and his henchmen around anymore, only the U.S. military had the capacity to fill the vacuum.

The news of the planned cuts didn't come as a surprise to Petraeus. Cutting so dramatically was high-risk, he warned Abizaid. But he said he thought it could work. His division had already trained 20,000 Iraqi police and military troops, who had held their own so far. As long as his successor had enough money to keep his massive reconstruction program going, Mosul could get by with fewer Americans, he said.

Shortly after their meeting, attacks spiked throughout Petraeus's sector. The 101st suffered more deaths in November and December than any other division in Iraq. Petraeus thought he knew what was causing the unrest. Part of the problem was that his reconstruction money was running out. He'd spent $34 million in both captured enemy money and whatever funds he could harass out of Baghdad. Now the cash was gone and new funds from Washington were slow in coming. At his morning battle update briefings in the marble-floored palace auditorium, he tracked the division's spending obsessively, reviewing upward of seventy slides each day. They all sent the same message: the manic pace of the division's first months in Mosul was ebbing.

"Why aren't we digging more wells?" Petraeus asked.

"Because we're out of money," his briefer replied.

"Dig," Petraeus said. He'd take a risk and bet the money would eventually come.

The other big stumbling block was the CPA's de-Baathification policy, which was finally catching up with him. Earlier in the summer Bremer had permitted him to fire and then temporarily rehire teachers through final exams. After the exams Petraeus assembled a team of Iraqis to evaluate the former Baathists for permanent positions and was delighted when it gave 66 percent of them a reprieve. He sent their voluminous findings to Baghdad on two cargo helicopters, but the CPA reconciliation committee, run by Pentagon favorite Ahmed Chalabi, never gave permission to rehire them. In late November Chalabi visited Petraeus at his stone palace in Mosul, and Petraeus pleaded with him for relief: "I am not saying that all these people should be kept, but if you are going to tell people that they're never going to work again, you might as well throw them in jail."

"At least they can eat there," a less-than-sympathetic Chalabi replied.

A few weeks later, a colleague who worked for Pentagon deputy Paul Wolfowitz visited Petraeus in Mosul and warned him to watch his back on the de-Baathification issue. "The policy Nazis in the defense secretary's office are keeping their eye on you," he said.

By boosting the number of raids and capturing several insurgent leaders, the 101st was able to drive the attack rates back down. Petraeus also worked hard to give former military officers and Baathists who had been blackballed by Baghdad a sense that they were going to have a future in the new Iraq. One way he did it was by staging periodic Baath Party renunciation ceremonies. On a drizzly winter day in December a line of about 2,200 former military officers snaked down a hill in front of the Mosul Police Academy. When he first saw the huge turnout from his helicopter, Petraeus was stunned and delighted. At best, he had expected a crowd of a couple of hundred.

Most in the crowd had fought in Iraq's bloody war with Iran during the 1980s. They felt as though they had served their country bravely. Now they were standing in the rain begging forgiveness for sins they didn't believe they had committed. "I am here for my kids and nothing else," one of the officers angrily told an American reporter. Petraeus couldn't give the men their old jobs back. All he could offer was a piece of cake, a soda, and a little bit of hope for the future. He pressed his soldiers to treat the Iraqis with dignity, and warned them not to run out of renunciation certificates. Petraeus wasn't naive; he knew the ceremony wasn't going to win anybody over. Years later he'd refer to the event as a "wild scheme." But maybe it could buy him some time with the fence-sitters before they slipped over to the side of the resistance. The penitents were searched for weapons and brought into the police academy building in groups of 100. Petraeus addressed them from a plywood riser.

"The individuals gathered here have assembled voluntarily," he said by way of welcoming. "Their only benefit will be the sense of personal closure that comes from disavowing links with the former regime and supporting those who are building the new Iraq." The Iraqis solemnly, and in many cases sullenly, raised their hands and vowed to embrace the new Iraq. Then they signed a renunciation pledge, were handed a certificate, and were encouraged to visit the "veterans' employment office" that had been set up by Petraeus's artillery unit.

Before he left Iraq, Petraeus also tried to shore up Basso's hold on his office. The governor's detractors had unearthed a tape of him giving a pro-Saddam speech prior to the invasion and broadcast it on Mosul television. Once again, council members began to complain that he was a Baathist and needed to go. Petraeus met with the two top Kurdish leaders, Talabani and Barzani, and received commitments from them that they would support the governor. He thought Basso was fine.

Although he didn't realize it, Petraeus was holding Mosul together with the force of his personality and his 22,000 troops. Neither was sustainable over the long term. As soon as he left, the political compromises that he had imposed on the Iraqis—in many cases for their own good— would start to unravel. The provincial council, which rarely made a decision on anything without Petraeus pushing, forced Basso to resign less than a week after the 101st left Iraq. The reconstruction effort slowed as well. Without Petraeus's hectoring, Mosul would get less money from CPA and Baghdad. The city was headed for problems.

As the 101st prepared to head home, Petraeus and Sergeant Major Marvin Hill, the division's senior enlisted soldier, spent a Sunday afternoon walking the palace grounds, which they had dubbed "Camp Freedom." "We were looking at all the things that had changed and remembering all the division had accomplished," recalled Hill. He'd been warned prior to going to work for Petraeus that the general was a noncommissioned officer's nightmare—a real micromanager. But Hill liked the general's energy and was proud of what the division had accomplished.

After an hour, they walked back to Petraeus's office in the palace and talked about their next jobs in the Army. Petraeus told Hill that he'd be an ideal candidate to take over the Sergeants Major Academy at Fort Bliss. His Iraq experience would be a huge boon there and the job would give him time to see his family.

Petraeus had been hoping that the Army would reward his success in Mosul by promoting him to three stars and giving him command of 18th Airborne Corps, one of the top combat commands. He'd learned a few days earlier that he wasn't going to get it, and when he told Hill his disappointment was unmistakable. Hill said the Pentagon almost certainly had other plans for him. Petraeus agreed. The decision, however, seemed to send a signal: success in Mosul was not what the Army most valued.

CHAPTER EIGHT

"We Didn't Know"

Camp Victory
March 2004

It was his first day in Iraq and Major General Pete Chiarelli was going downtown. He had arrived the night before and slept a few hours at the airport camp where the Army had its main headquarters. Now he was headed to an appointment in the Green Zone, the walled enclave in the city center where L. Paul Bremer III and his Coalition Provisional Authority were installed. It was no more than a twenty-minute drive, but the road linking the airport and the Green Zone was hazardous, so generals usually flew. As his helicopter lifted off the pad with its side doors open, he looked out on the capital. It was a teeming city of tightly packed concrete houses and neighborhood shops that stretched mile after mile into the distance. The only skyline was formed by towering mosques, a few hotels and apartment complexes, and battle-damaged ministries. Even the patches of eucalyptus and date palms were coated in a yellow-brown dust. The roads were almost deserted at that early hour. Things looked peaceful, at least to a newcomer skimming above the rooftops.

This was Chiarelli's new domain. He was the commander of the 1st

Cavalry Division, just beginning a yearlong deployment in Baghdad. His was the only division assigned to the capital and had probably the most critical mission in Iraq. The other five major military headquarters, commanded by one-star or two-star generals, were scattered throughout the country. All the commanders, including Chiarelli, reported to General Sanchez, who oversaw all military forces in Iraq. Sanchez, in turn, reported to Abizaid, who was constantly crisscrossing the region.

Chiarelli and his 20,000-soldier division were taking over from the 1st Armored Division, which was finishing its tour and going home to its base in Germany. The formal handover wasn't scheduled for a few weeks, and many of the soldiers under Chiarelli's command were still arriving, driving up from Kuwait in long convoys through the desert. Reaching Baghdad, they funneled into a half-dozen forward operating bases around different sections of the city. Chiarelli would oversee them from the division headquarters, which at least for the time being was a large green tent on the north end of the airport base, known as Camp Victory.

For decades, he had dreamed of taking command during wartime, never sure his chance would come; now it had, finally. His division, the same one that George Casey's father had led in Vietnam, had a history that reached back into the frontier wars of the nineteenth century and reflected the constant evolution of the American way of war. Once its troopers had moved on horseback wearing Stetsons and yellow kerchiefs. In Vietnam, the division had been known as the 1st Air Cav and was equipped with hundreds of helicopters to seek out the Viet Cong on search-and-destroy missions. Later, as the Army erased the memory of that conflict, the 1st Cav converted into a heavy division, equipped with the latest tanks and precision-guided weapons. In his imagination Chiarelli had once seen himself directing its armored columns on a vast open plain, the Army's vision of modern warfare. His year in Iraq was going to look nothing like that. This was occupation duty in a crowded city of 8 million people, with car bomb attacks, rampant crime, and only a few hours of power a day.

When Chiarelli pressed the Army staff in the Pentagon to let him bring his division's full complement of hundreds of Abrams tanks and personnel carriers, he was told the heavy armor was unnecessary for his mission. His troops were supposed to be manning checkpoints and patrolling in

Humvees. Inside their tanks and Bradley Fighting Vehicles, they wouldn't be able to interact with civilians. One other big concern was that the tanks and Brads sent the wrong signal to the Iraqis and the rest of the Arab world. Their presence on the streets made it appear as if the liberated capital was under siege.

"Why not let me leave the armor over there and park it if it's not needed?" Chiarelli had asked his superiors in Baghdad and Washington. Eventually General Sanchez told him he could bring over about a third of his armored vehicles—less than he'd wanted but better than nothing.

Before leaving Fort Hood in Texas, he had drilled into the nearly 20,000 soldiers under his command that their primary mission would be not fighting but improving daily life for ordinary Iraqis. He sent his officers to the Texas capital, Austin, to spend several days observing a big city's sewage, trash collection, and power systems. He flew them to London for briefings on the British counterinsurgency operations in Northern Ireland, and later to Jordan for a weeklong course on Arab society and culture.

He had turned fifty-four a few days earlier. In his middle age, he was beefy and imposing, no longer the slightly plump and easily awed officer he had once been. Along with his desert fatigues and body armor, he wore the wraparound sunglasses and high suede boots favored by tankers. In his battle garb he resembled a stiff-gaited robot warrior, as most soldiers did, but in fact he was the most compassionate of generals, always struggling to control his overflowing emotions. In his journal a few weeks earlier Chiarelli had recorded his feelings about leaving his wife, Beth, at Fort Hood. By the time he came home, Patrick, the youngest of his three children, would be in college, out of the house for good. "Day 1," he wrote on the day he departed for Iraq. "Got out of own bed for the last time in a year at 0600, very difficult . . . Toughest thing I have ever done . . . Knowing I will never live in the house again with Pat makes me tear up . . . I will never forget Beth whispering in my ear through tears that she was afraid to be alone."

As difficult as leaving had been, Chiarelli didn't view the coming year, as many in the military did, as something to be endured. He was fascinated by the Middle East, and there was no way he would hold himself aloof. "Drank camel's milk and ate dates with a Kuwaiti in the desert today.

Carpet on the desert and all, it was an experience," he wrote in a journal entry from Kuwait, the division's last stop before Iraq.

Now that he was on the ground, he was plunging ahead. His first appointment after the short flight to the Green Zone that morning was in the Republican Palace, where the CPA had its headquarters, with James Stephenson, the head of the U.S. Agency for International Development's mission in Iraq. For weeks, Chiarelli's aides had been sending Stephenson e-mails telling him that the commander of the 1st Cavalry Division wanted to see him as soon as he arrived. A craggy-faced veteran aid worker who went by the nickname "Spike," Stephenson couldn't imagine why. His job was to rebuild Iraq, or, more accurately, to keep tabs on the big U.S. engineering firms that had won USAID contracts to undertake mammoth infrastructure projects. The Army officers he had encountered defined their job as capturing or killing shadowy insurgents, and he expected that Chiarelli would be little different. When this imposing general walked into his ground-floor office in body armor and goggles, with a Kevlar helmet under his arm, Stephenson was pretty sure they didn't have a lot to discuss.

Chiarelli removed his gear and the two men sat in frayed chairs facing each other. "What can I do for you?" Stephenson inquired. Chiarelli launched into a ten-minute description of the problems in Baghdad and what he thought needed to be done. The way to tamp down the violence in the capital, he said, was to deliver as quickly as possible more hours of electricity, cleaner streets, running water, and, if possible, jobs. Iraqis had to see their lives getting better. "USAID is critical for what I want to do because the expertise resides with you," he said. As the division commander, he had millions of dollars at his disposal but was limited, in most cases, to expending no more than $10,000 at a time. To do what he had in mind, he needed help from USAID, which had more money, as well as expertise in writing big contracts and planning construction projects. It wasn't the first time a military officer had proposed to work together, but Chiarelli was the first who actually seemed to understand what USAID did. Still, Stephenson could tell Chiarelli didn't understand how things worked in the Green Zone. The general acted like there was a big pot of money that he could tap for new sewage lines, power stations, health clinics, and other projects around the city. It wasn't that simple. Congress had approved $18.6 billion the previous fall to help rebuild Iraq's shattered infrastructure, and Stephenson's portion of that was more than $2 billion. But most of that money had already been earmarked for just one company, Bechtel Corporation, which had won contracts to do a few large projects that would take years to finish. The projects were generating few jobs for average Iraqis and would do little anytime soon to change the crushing realities of life in Baghdad. Stephenson didn't like the approach, but those decisions had been made in Washington. After Stephenson explained this, they parted, promising to talk again. But Stephenson was being polite. There were too many obstacles to the kind of joint venture Chiarelli had in mind. "I thought he had the right ideas. I just couldn't see how I could help him," he recalled.

Charging through the halls of the palace, Chiarelli told his aides that every time he visited the Green Zone he wanted to see Stephenson. There was a pure optimism about Chiarelli, a fundamental faith in everybody's motives until he had evidence to the contrary. For years Beth, his wife, would teasingly call him "Skippy," the straightforward American soldier who always tried to do the right thing and thought most everyone else did, too. Most Iraqis, he believed, were not that different from Americans. They wanted peaceful, normal lives, with schools and doctors for their families, and they would stop fighting each other if their basic needs were met. These convictions sprang from growing up in Seattle, with grandparents who were Italian immigrants and wanted better lives for their children. His ideas could seem at times wildly at odds with the realities of the Middle East. Abizaid, for one, thought Chiarelli didn't appreciate the tribal, sectarian, and ethnic antagonisms that were a major source of Iraq's violence. When Chiarelli briefed him on his plans for a massive public works program in Baghdad, Abizaid showed little interest. "It was really hard for me to understand whether Abizaid thought what I was doing was right or wrong," he later admitted.

In some ways it was the breadth of Chiarelli's ambitions that made him unusual. Anyone with any experience in Iraq knew it was prudent to think small—to "stay in your lane," as the phrase went. But Chiarelli never did. He had read as many books as he could find about counterinsurgency, talked at length with the commander of the outgoing division

about Baghdad, and carefully studied what Dave Petraeus had done in
Mosul. Petraeus's model was a starting point. But Baghdad had more than
three times as many people as Mosul and was more violent. Fixing the
capital's problems, Chiarelli believed, demanded far-reaching changes not
just from the military but also from the civilians running the reconstruction effort. During his time in the Social Sciences Department at West
Point he'd acquired a trait common to many Sosh alums: he thought that
he could parachute into a place, identify an intractable problem that was
well above his rank, and then articulate a solution so perfect that everyone
would rush to embrace it. In Iraq his goal was to "totally reprioritize what
we were doing," he recalled.

He'd spent only three days in country, but he was already convinced
most of the civilians in the Green Zone were fooling themselves about what
it was really like outside the walls: "Bremer is a mini-Rumsfeld. He is quot-
ing statistics, as he nears the end of his stay, that make him look good and
are not based in reality—'unemployment in Baghdad is 11 percent.' Give
me a break," he jotted in his journal. "CPA is more than dysfunctional,
enough said." He noted as well that Bremer had ordered the closing of *Al
Hawza,* a newspaper published by supporters of Muqtada al-Sadr, a fiery
anti-U.S. cleric. The paper had recently published an editorial with the
headline "Bremer Follows the Steps of Saddam." Within hours of the closure, hundreds of Sadr's followers were protesting in the streets near the
newspaper's offices. "The decision to shut down the *Al H* newspaper will
prove to be a big mistake," Chiarelli predicted. His instincts about the
mood in the capital were right.

★ ★ ★ ★

Baghdad
April 4, 2004

The first reports came in a little before seven o'clock in the evening. An
American patrol escorting sewage trucks in the Baghdad slum of Sadr City
had been ambushed. The patrol consisted of nineteen men, along with a
translator, in four Humvees. Two of their vehicles already had been

knocked out by the enemy gunfire. The embattled platoon had sought refuge in a house down a side street and was still taking fire. Chiarelli was at the division headquarters near the Baghdad airport when he got word of the attack. "Sir, there's at least one kid in bad shape, and his platoon is still pinned down," Colonel Robert Abrams reported over the radio. Abrams was already on his way to Forward Operating Base War Eagle, the American outpost on the outskirts of Sadr City.

It had only been a few days since Bremer had shuttered *Al Hawza,* the tiny Baghdad newspaper loyal to Muqtada al-Sadr. The United States followed that move by arresting one of the firebrand cleric's top deputies. Most commanders considered Sadr, the son of a martyred Shiite cleric, to be little more than a street thug who had used his father's name to build a following in east Baghdad's slums. His impoverished supporters weren't willing to die for him in large numbers, U.S. intelligence reports insisted. The reports were wrong.

"Terrorize your enemy," Sadr proclaimed following the newspaper closure and the arrest of his aide. "God will reward you well for what pleases him. It is not possible to remain silent in front of their violations." In Sadr City, hundreds of armed men, many dressed in black with green scarves wrapped around their heads, stormed police stations and piled trash at intersections to block patrols. Ragtag police and army units deserted en masse. When he heard about the spreading anarchy, Chiarelli could have jumped in his Black Hawk and flown the ten miles to the city's east side, where the firefight was unfolding. But he stifled the urge. From everything he could tell, Lieutenant Colonel Gary Volesky, the battalion commander at War Eagle, was on top of it. He didn't need a two-star general showing up to interfere. Nor was Chiarelli in a position to start issuing orders anyway. His soldiers were deployed all over Baghdad, but he wasn't scheduled to take formal command for another two weeks. Until then, the 1st Cav reported to the outgoing commander, Major General Marty Dempsey of the 1st Armored Division. The temporary arrangement meant that Chiarelli's soldiers, the troopers he had spent months training, were fighting for their lives only a few miles away, but he could only monitor the battles over the radio.

So he sat or paced in his headquarters, a tangle of nerves. The incoming reports provided only sketchy information. When the radio went quiet, Chiarelli left his air-conditioned tent to grab a quick smoke, a habit he had reacquired since arriving in Iraq. He knew that his staff was taking its cues from him, and tried to keep his composure. He told them not to keep pestering the battalion for updates; the battalion didn't need headquarters making their lives more difficult. Walking outside, Chiarelli called Dempsey by cell phone. "I know my guys are in good hands with you, Marty," he said.

But in Sadr City the rescue was failing. Minutes after the first call for help, three convoys of Humvees and trucks sped out of War Eagle. As soon as they entered Sadr City black-clad fighters crouched on rooftops unleashed a torrent of fire that tore through their unarmored vehicles, forcing them all to turn back. In one instance sixteen soldiers traveling in an open-bed truck had been cut to ribbons. One was dead and all the rest were wounded. Colonel Abrams called Chiarelli from War Eagle and gave him a preliminary casualty count, warning that the numbers were going to rise. Start sending dustoff helicopters for the wounded, the colonel advised, and keep them coming. At War Eagle's makeshift aid station casualties were everywhere, some on stretchers and some on bare ground.

Out in the city a rescue effort consisting of seven tanks broke through to the stranded soldiers. Of the original nineteen soldiers who had been ambushed, seven were wounded and one was dead. Seven rescuers were killed and more than sixty were wounded, most by shrapnel and bullets that tore through their vehicles. About 500 Sadr supporters died during the two-hour fight.

That night, as the casualty toll was still climbing, Chiarelli stepped outside his headquarters tent, his eyes welling in the dark. He thought about the families who would shortly be notified that their sons and husbands were dead. He thought about Beth, who, as the wife of the division commander, had the difficult job of doing what she could to ease the pain of those families. And he thought about his mission. No one had imagined his men would be in full-scale battles on the streets of Baghdad. There had been only one major attack on U.S. troops in Sadr City the previous year.

What was happening? "You didn't expect to be in that kind of fight," he recalled.

He went back inside and placed a call to General Eric Shinseki, the retired former chief of the Army who had been belittled by Bush administration officials for suggesting that it would take several hundred thousand troops to stabilize Iraq. Shinseki had been one of Chiarelli's mentors and as much as anybody was responsible for his rise to command of the 1st Cavalry Division. No one was at Shinseki's home back in the States, so he left a message, his voice choking up on the answering machine. "Sir, I just wanted to tell you we got into a really hard fight. I wanted you to hear it from me."

At seven the next morning Chiarelli choppered out with Dempsey to War Eagle. He stopped in first to see Volesky. "We'll make it through," Chiarelli said, embracing his battalion commander. Then he headed off alone to the aid station. Mounds of bloodied uniforms and boots were still piled outside. The badly wounded had been evacuated hours earlier, but dozens more with less serious injuries were still laid out on stretchers. The sight of bloodied soldiers was not something Chiarelli had ever experienced before. He walked down the rows of prostrate men, telling them they had performed heroically and handing out coins with the 1st Cav insignia on them. He didn't want to be the general who flew in after the action and gave out trinkets, but there was not much more he could do. One of the wounded, a young enlisted soldier, looked up at Chiarelli. "Sir, why didn't we bring our tanks?" he asked. Chiarelli had no answer that would suffice. He wanted to tell the soldier that he had fought with the Army to bring some armored vehicles. But even those few tanks were still in transit, not scheduled to arrive in Baghdad for a couple of more weeks. "We didn't know," he finally told the soldier. "We didn't know."

He didn't get around to recording his thoughts about the battle until four days later: "Rough couple of days. Sunday night we lost 7 soldiers (+1 from 1AD)," he wrote, using an abbreviation for the 1st Armored Division. In his leather-bound notebook, he copied out the names of the dead soldiers.

The memories of the April 4 battle stayed with him—the powerless feeling as he sat in his headquarters while his men fought and bled on the streets, the inevitable second-guessing about whether he had done everything he should have to prepare them. "1AD was in command," he wrote in his diary. "Nevertheless, I would not have done anything different." There was one thing, though: a day after the battle, Chiarelli drafted a sharp request to bring over the rest of his armor from Texas. When the Pentagon failed to respond, he kept pestering his superiors. "Our request for additional tanks and Bradley's is not going over well. No one will call me," he wrote in an e-mail at one point. "What I find concerning is the number of people outside Iraq who are arguing against our request without giving us the benefit of the doubt."

Sometimes it seemed as if the whole of the U.S. military had decided the war was over, while his men were fighting block-by-block battles. Every day helicopters marked with red crosses would land at the Combat Support Hospital in the Green Zone, carrying the wounded. Around this time, in a move to reduce personnel, the Army medical team had been cut in half in Baghdad. That meant fewer doctors to treat wounded 1st Cav soldiers. At the Green Zone hospital, he jotted bitterly in his journal, "they have 21 beds and of those 17 are filled by Iraqi prisoners."

In the late afternoons he often walked over to the hospital to visit his soldiers in the recovery wards. He began carrying index cards in his breast pocket with the names, hometowns, and parents' names of every soldier in his division killed in action, a stack that grew and grew during his year in Iraq, eventually numbering 168. He went to all of their memorial services, and when he had a spare few minutes, he'd study the cards.

The fighting, which began in early March in Sadr City, quickly spread across a wide arc south and west of Baghdad. Needing more troops to handle the uprising, General Sanchez, the top commander in Iraq, canceled the departure of the 1st Armored Division and wheeled its troops south of Baghdad to reclaim the Shiite-dominated towns where Sadr's supporters had seized police stations and government buildings. Meanwhile, an even bloodier battle was going on with Sunni insurgents in Fallujah, where the Bush administration had ordered the Marines to storm the city in response to the brutal murder of four American contractors there. Abizaid had argued for postponing the moves against Sadr until after the Fallujah attack.

"I am not sure we should be going on two different fronts in this environment," he told Sanchez, who disagreed. In a decision that proved disastrous, Abizaid backed his field commander.

Only days into the Fallujah assault President Bush suspended it after Sunnis in the fledgling governing council threatened to quit. Abizaid, who was in Baghdad at the time, disagreed with the decision, arguing that it would embolden Muslim extremists. But it wasn't his call. He told Bremer and Sanchez that he would deliver the president's order in person.

On April 9 his helicopter touched down amid an insurgent mortar barrage at the U.S. base on the outskirts of Fallujah. Inside the headquarters building, the Marines launched into an update that lasted only a few seconds before Abizaid stopped it, telling them that a decision had been made to halt operations. One seat in the room, reserved for the division commander leading the attack, was empty. Major General James Mattis, a smart and fierce officer who went by the radio call sign "Chaos," had been out visiting his troops when his convoy was ambushed. He strode into the headquarters about thirty minutes late, his pants spattered with the blood of his wounded driver. When Abizaid delivered the bad news he exploded. Mattis had been reluctant to launch the assault initially, asking for more time to pick off the enemy with snipers and build contacts in the city, but had been overruled. Now he believed his Marines were only days from taking the city. "If you are going to take Vienna, take fucking Vienna," he snarled at Abizaid, updating a famous quote from Napoleon Bonaparte.

Abizaid knew what it was like to be in a firefight and lose troops, and he'd expected that Mattis would be upset. But the Marine's fury caught him off guard. Part of him wanted to tell Mattis that he'd argued strongly for giving the Marines time to finish the assault and that the president had overruled him. He resisted the urge. He listened to his subordinate general yell, then nodded and walked away without a word. Once the civilians had made their decision, Abizaid believed it was his job to execute it as if it were his own.

At Sanchez's headquarters the mood was grim. "We had accomplished the seemingly impossible task of uniting everybody in the country against us," recalled Colonel Casey Haskins, a member of Sanchez's staff. Mortar attacks into the Green Zone suddenly came in daily barrages, and attacks on supply convoys headed north from Kuwait soared. One day in early April, eighty trucks were lost. In the dining halls, the once-plentiful array of choices dwindled. By mid-April, the hot breakfast entrée was sliced hot dogs. Lunch consisted of Meals Ready-to-Eat, the packaged rations issued to soldiers in combat. Hoping to quash rumors about possible evacuations, Bremer had an aide reassure the CPA staff that plenty of supplies had been stockpiled. But the briefing only stoked rumors of a possible evacuation. A worried Spike Stephenson quietly began putting together a contingency plan for getting his staff out of the country.

Chiarelli worried, too. On April 13 he noted in his diary: "We have lost an additional 6 soldiers, including an Apache and crew. Things remain tense." In long talks every night, his field commanders in the 1st Cavalry Division reported killing dozens of insurgents, losses so severe that any ordinary foe would have surrendered. Volesky, whose battalion had suffered so many casualties on April 4, had devised a crude but effective tactic for rooting out the enemy. He would dispatch several tanks to Sadr City after nightfall, knowing the sound of the rumbling engines would bring the insurgents running with their AK-47s and grenade launchers. As the Iraqis drew near, American infantrymen, hidden on nearby rooftops and equipped with night-vision goggles, opened fire—a bloody payback for the mauling that had been inflicted on Volesky's men. Sadr's men kept fighting into May. A year after the United States had deposed Saddam Hussein, raw sewage still flowed down streets, unemployment was off the charts, and electricity was intermittent at best. There was a seemingly endless pool of men and boys willing to battle the Americans. When they weren't fighting, Sadr's operatives could flood the streets with thousands of demonstrators.

"Do these people even want us here?" a frazzled Bush asked Abizaid in a mid-April videoconference. "Can you find anybody to thank us for giving them democracy and freedom?"

"Part of the problem is that there is no strong Iraqi leadership," Abizaid replied. Iraqi soldiers and police officers weren't going to fight for American commanders, he insisted. They needed to establish a legitimate government as quickly as possible.

Chiarelli didn't have as much experience with the Middle East as

A five-year-old George Casey and his sister, Joan, play with their father on the beach near their summer home in Scituate, Massachusetts. In Korea, his father commanded an infantry company, earning a battlefield promotion to captain at Heartbreak Ridge and the Silver Star, the Army's third-highest honor.
Casey Family Photo

Major General George W. Casey Sr., a few weeks before his death in Vietnam in 1970. As the commander of the Army's 1st Air Cavalry Division, he oversaw the U.S. incursion into Cambodia. Casey seemed sure to ascend to four stars, as his West Point classmates had foreseen in 1945 when they predicted, "He will be the Army's best."
Casey Family Photo

George and Sheila Casey on their wedding day, June 27, 1970. His father could not attend the ceremony because he was in Vietnam. On July 7, 1970, the elder Casey's helicopter crashed in bad weather as he was on his way to visit wounded soldiers. George had promised his new wife that he'd go to law school, but his father's death caused him to change course.
Casey Family Photo

Petraeus graduated near the top of his class from West Point. Here he receives his commission as a second lieutenant. A few weeks later, he married Holly Knowlton in the West Point chapel. *Petraeus Family Photo*

Petraeus joined the elite 509th Parachute Infantry Battalion in Vicenza, Italy, shortly after Casey left the unit. In 1976, Petraeus became fascinated with General Marcel Bigeard, a renowned French paratrooper who helped forge the counterinsurgency tactics used in Algeria. He would exchange letters with Bigeard over the next three decades. *Petraeus Family Photo*

Abizaid in 1985 with two Lebanese fighters during his one-year tour as a United Nations observer in southern Lebanon. He wrote that "War in southern Lebanon is difficult to imagine . . . neither guerrilla war of the Vietnam-style, nor the urban battle of Beirut." *Abizaid Family Photo*

Chiarelli (second from right) stands with one of the tank crews preparing for the 1987 Canadian Army Trophy competition, held in Germany. Nothing demonstrated more clearly to enemies and allies alike that the U.S. Army had recovered from Vietnam than a victory in the tank competition. *Chiarelli Family Photo*

Abizaid (far right) and senior commanders cross from Iraq into Turkey after a four-month humanitarian operation in 1991 that exposed him to Iraq's combustible mix of tribal, religious, and ethnic groups. His experience gave him a view of Iraq different from that of most of his peers, who had just fought and won the Gulf War. *Abizaid Family Photo*

Casey meets with Turkish troops in Bosnia in 1996. Little in his career had prepared him to mediate ethnic civil wars or rebuild broken societies, like Bosnia, and he learned that even a force as powerful as the U.S. Army couldn't resolve centuries-old sectarian and ethnic hatreds. *Photo by Gene Sizemore, U.S. Army*

Abizaid, in full combat gear, confers with General Gordon Sullivan, the Army chief of staff, at Fort Polk, Louisiana, where Abizaid's brigade was fighting a mock battle in the swampy woods. The innovative and aggressive tactics that he used to defeat the opposing force were recalled for years. A few months later, he turned over command of the brigade to David Petraeus. *Abizaid Family Photo*

The U.S. military made the Al Faw Palace complex its main headquarters in Iraq in 2003 and renamed it Camp Victory. The base violated just about every rule of counterinsurgency operations, which preached the importance of small groups of soldiers living among the people. *Photo by Staff Sgt. Stacy Pearsall, U.S. Air Force*

Chiarelli awards the Purple Heart to soldiers wounded in fierce battles with Muqtada Sadr's militia in 2004. Chiarelli's field commanders reported killing dozens of insurgents, losses so severe that any ordinary foe would have surrendered. *Photo by Staff Sgt. Rebekah-mae Bruns, U.S. Army*

In June 2005, Casey flew back to Washington to get President Bush's approval for his new strategy of focusing on the training of Iraqis to take over the fighting from U.S. troops. During the meeting, Bush asked Casey to extend his command for at least six more months. Casey had a fleeting feeling that, like his father, he might not come home. *White House Photo*

John Abizaid testifies with Defense Secretary Donald Rumsfeld before the Senate Armed Services Committee in 2005. Abizaid had been deeply frustrated by the Rumsfeld-led Pentagon's failure to prepare for the aftermath of the U.S. invasion of Iraq. *Photo by Staff Sgt. Myles Cullen, Department of Defense*

Casey was beginning to feel the strain after two years in command. The seating of a new government in May 2006 hadn't reduced violence, as he'd hoped. But he was determined to stick with his strategy. "I firmly believe that the longer [the Iraqis] feel they can rely on us, the longer it is going to take them to find the political will to reconcile . . . something they are not ready to do." *Photo by Capt. Amy Bishop, U.S. Army*

Chiarelli accepts the Multi-National Corps–Iraq flag from Casey in January 2006, starting a new assignment as Casey's second in command. At a time when there was little good news from Iraq, Chiarelli was one senior officer who exuded confidence and new ideas. *U.S. Army Photo by Pfc. Sean C. Finch*

John Abizaid and George Casey greet Defense Secretary Robert Gates in December 2006. A few months earlier, Abizaid had warned his close friend Casey that "sectarian violence in Baghdad could be fatal. We've got to reverse the obvious trends soon." Shortly after his arrival in Baghdad, Gates told Casey he was being replaced and asked if he would be interested in taking over as Army chief of staff. *Photo by Cherie A. Thurlby, Department of Defense*

George Casey gives up command to David Petraeus in a February 2007 ceremony at Al Faw Palace. His final days in Baghdad were full of ceremonies and reminders that he was not leaving in triumph. "Sir, your relief is here. You're supposed to be smiling," Petraeus said at one point. "I am smiling on the inside, Dave," Casey replied. *U.S. Army Photo by Sgt. Curt Cashour*

Petraeus answered questions from the press after meeting with Defense Secretary Robert Gates at a Marine base in Fallujah in 2007. He had begun as a skinny, hyperambitious lieutenant and had grown into a general who, though still demanding, was far more comfortable with uncertainty and experimentation. *Photo by Staff Sgt. Myles Cullen, Department of Defense*

General David Petraeus shares a glass of tea with an Iraqi man during a patrol of a downtown Baghdad book market in June 2007 at the height of the U.S.-led offensive in Baghdad. Despite rising violence and record U.S. deaths that summer, Petraeus highlighted the few pockets of normalcy in the Iraqi capital to counter the growing doubts about his strategy back home. *Photo by Staff Sgt. Lorie Jewel, U.S. Army*

General David Petraeus, standing in the rotunda of Al Faw Palace, administers the reenlistment oath in July 2008 to 1,215 soldiers, extending their service in the Army. *U.S. Army Photo*

Petraeus gives Barack Obama a helicopter tour of Baghdad in July 2008. Petraeus's success in Iraq had made him the most influential officer of his generation, and his ideas about warfare were avidly sought by leaders of both political parties. *Staff Sgt. Lorie Jewel*

Beth Chiarelli pins a fourth star on her husband, Pete Chiarelli, in August 2008, thirty-four years after he first entered the United States Army. Defense Secretary Robert Gates and Chiarelli's mother, Theresa, look on. "I can think of no one more deserving of a fourth star," Gates said in his remarks that day. *U.S. Army Photo*

Chiarelli walks to a Black Hawk helicopter at an Army base in Indiana in 2009. He'd badly wanted to return to Iraq but instead was promoted to vice chief of staff of the Army, serving under Casey. He saw his job as making sure that the military's penchant for order and discipline didn't cut off debate about what the Army had undergone in Iraq. *Photo by D. Myles Cullen, U.S. Army*

Abizaid did, but he grasped what was happening. The most important battle was not over who would control the streets; it was over who would win
the allegiance of the people living there. And as lopsided in the Americans'
favor as the street skirmishes were, Chiarelli feared he was losing the bigger
battle.

In mid-April, he went one evening with Colonel Kendall Cox, his chief
engineer, to the walled compound in the Green Zone that served as Bechtel's headquarters in Iraq. Chiarelli had wanted to meet with Bechtel since
learning from Spike Stephenson that the San Francisco–based engineering
firm controlled nearly $2 billion in USAID reconstruction projects. He
was ushered into the company's dining facility, an air-conditioned double-
wide trailer. A white bedsheet had been thrown over a large table at the rear
of the trailer and set with real silverware and china in his honor. Around
the table were places for Chiarelli and Cox, a handful of Bechtel executives,
and Stephenson. After dinner, Cliff Mumm, a grizzled Bechtel engineer
who had spent decades in the field, laid out the company's plans for rebuilding Iraq's main power plants, sewage-treatment facilities, and large
bridges. Most of the American-run projects he was describing had stalled
because Bechtel had been forced to send its workers out of the country
until security conditions improved. Mumm argued for using U.S. troops to
guard Bechtel's work sites.

"Stop, just stop!" Chiarelli bellowed. "I know you are a good company
and you are doing wonderful things. But none of this—nothing—is going
to get built unless I get the sewage off the streets of Sadr City. If I don't
clean up the streets, I'm going to get run out of Baghdad, and you are going
to be right ahead of me!" In the days leading up to the meeting, he and Cox
had painstakingly compiled a list of all of Bechtel's and the other big contractors' projects by going from office to office at the CPA. The effort was a
mess. In late 2003 the Bush administration told the CPA that it had three
weeks to put together a plan to spend $18.4 billion in reconstruction
money. Short on time, the CPA funneled most of the money into a small
number of expensive infrastructure projects. One of Bechtel's biggest was
the overhaul of sewage-treatment plants that served Baghdad. CPA didn't
set aside any money to connect the plants or most of the other big water
and power projects up to actual houses. Instead it assumed that foreign

donors would come up with $2 billion to $3 billion to cover those bills. By the spring it was clear to Chiarelli that the foreign money wasn't ever going to arrive.

Having cut off the Bechtel executive, Chiarelli hijacked the rest of the dinner with his own PowerPoint briefing. His main slide consisted of stick-figure Iraqis standing between crudely drawn houses and big squares representing sewage-treatment plants and power stations. The pipes and the power lines emanating from the plants stopped before they reached the homes.

"Rather than spending money to build a sewage-treatment plant, let's start at the other end," Chiarelli said. "Let's start in the guy's front yard and improve his life, and if that means we continue to dump raw sewage in the Tigris River, so be it. It's been dumped in there forever; the Iraqis aren't upset about it. What they are upset about is the sewage in their front yard."

He suggested using the money that had been set aside for mammoth infrastructure projects to lay cheap sewage pipe, repair pumps, buy generators, and rehabilitate electrical substations. At least those kinds of projects would make life more bearable, and they could be done with local contractors, which would create jobs for Iraqis. He had already divided up his engineering brigade into five battalions that lived at each of the forward operating bases around Baghdad and could help with the smaller projects. But to really have an impact he needed more money and more engineering expertise. There was little that Bechtel, which was committed to the CPA's list of fanciful projects, could do to help him.

A few weeks later he and Spike Stephenson from USAID got fifteen minutes with Bremer to make a similar pitch. The occupation chief wore his customary white button-down shirt with rolled-up sleeves, khakis, and combat boots. On his desk was a wooden plaque bearing the message "Success Has a Thousand Fathers." Early in the occupation when visitors noted that he'd left off the other half of the aphorism—"But Failure Is an Orphan"—Bremer confidently replied, "Failure is not an option." Ever since the April uprisings, failure had become a grim reality. He blamed the collapse on Rumsfeld, Abizaid, Sanchez, and the rest of the military, who he thought hadn't committed enough troops to contain the spiraling violence. Knowing that Bremer's time for them was short, Chiarelli and Stephenson hurriedly explained that they had devised an initial list of projects in the Sadr City neighborhood that they could accomplish for about $162 million. They planned to spend the money on small-scale projects that created jobs and were actually visible to people. These were the kind of projects that could turn the tide in the violent slum.

"I'll give you money when you get the place secure," Bremer curtly told him.

"Sir, I can't get it secure until you give me some money so that I can get people to work," Chiarelli replied. His troops were spread too thin across Baghdad to lock down the capital. In Sadr City, for example, there were about 2.5 million people packed into a slum that had been built for about 300,000. He was trying to control the place with a 600-soldier battalion. There was no way he could fight 2 million people, he said. He needed to win their allegiance or at least their tolerance with some small, visible successes.

"Do you agree with this?" Bremer asked Stephenson, who said he thought the plan was worth a try. Bremer was just weeks from leaving the country and had nothing to lose. He gave them enough money to get started on their project list.

A few days later, a dozen of Stephenson's USAID staffers clambered onto Black Hawks at the Green Zone landing pad and flew to 1st Cav headquarters near the airport. Most had never been in a military helicopter before and fumbled with shoulder and lap belts before takeoff. It was a field trip of sorts, organized by Chiarelli to introduce them to his brigade commanders and vice versa. The two groups gathered outside under a canopy, the scruffy aid workers in cargo pants and hiking boots next to the Army officers in their tan uniforms and short haircuts. "We didn't give a shit about the war," recalled Kirkpatrick Day, one of the USAID staffers who attended. But conditions in Baghdad and elsewhere had gotten so bad that it had become almost impossible for Day and his fellow aid workers to leave the Green Zone and do the humanitarian work that had brought them to Baghdad.

Chiarelli stood in front of the group, welcomed them, and told the story of the April 4 battle in Sadr City and the casualties his men had suffered in the days since the fight. "He's tearing up and his voice is cracking as he's talking about what his men had been through and what needed to be done," Day recalled. The son of a Navy pilot, Day had grown up in military bases around the world and had spent the previous few years doing postconflict reconstruction work in Kosovo and East Timor. He was unflappable and experienced at operating in chaotic foreign cultures in a way that the 1st Cav officers weren't. In Baghdad, he headed the Office of Transition Initiatives, a small arm of USAID whose mission was to do quick projects. In forty-eight hours he could write a contract for millions of dollars and, working with a cell phone and a list of contacts, put more than a thousand men to work. It was just what Chiarelli had in mind. The jobs program, which began in Sadr City in mid-June, paid workers $4 or $5 a day for picking up trash, cleaning out clogged sewers, or some other project from the list that Chiarelli's and Stephenson's staffs had put together. Soon there were thousands of men working across Baghdad.

Chiarelli, who was hearing from his battalion commanders that attacks were dropping steeply in areas where they were spending money, had his staff sort through daily situation reports from the field and prepare charts that proved the program was suppressing violence. When Deputy Defense Secretary Paul Wolfowitz came through Baghdad that summer to meet with the division commanders, Chiarelli spent an hour showing him that data, and made sure Day was on hand at his headquarters. "That young man, sir—Kirk Day—is a goddamned hero," he told Wolfowitz as the scruffy Day slumped in his chair. Wolfowitz in turn convinced Congress to put up an additional $200 million for the jobs program. Day, however, had his doubts about what he and Chiarelli were really accomplishing. "These are not real jobs," he reminded him. Maybe the temporary work kept some of the men from joining the insurgency, but those gains could be as fleeting as the work unless a real economy replaced the taxpayer-funded illusion they were creating.

It *was* an illusion—and Chiarelli, despite his enthusiasm for the program, knew it. His goal to "totally reprioritize" the U.S. effort demanded that he take on the contractors, the embassy, and the fledgling ministries.

Soon he was summoning representatives from all three groups to his headquarters for weekly meetings, where he and Colonel Cox, his engineer, would harangue contractors who were falling behind schedule on big projects in the capital. When he learned that several ventures had been delayed for months because contractors were required to abide by peacetime federal contracting rules and were making Iraqi subcontractors follow Occupational Safety and Health Administration standards, he was irate. "What I'm getting is not what I require," he bellowed at representatives of Black and Veatch, an engineering firm that was responsible for repair and cleaning of the main sewage line running south through Sadr City. "And we're paying the price in soldiers."

On July 23, he poured out his frustrations at a meeting in the Republican Palace with Ronald Neumann, a senior diplomat. "We are blowing our window of opportunity," he insisted. Other than Day's modest program, the reconstruction effort was failing. A recent bidders' conference, where the contractors solicited bids on upcoming projects from local firms, had been a "total disaster," Chiarelli complained. The projects had been posted in English on a U.S. government website, completely ignoring the fact that Iraqis spoke Arabic and rarely had Internet access, even if they were lucky enough to have electricity to run a personal computer, he said. Neumann, who had once served as ambassador to Algeria, replied that he'd had similar problems with Bechtel there, and he recommended calling the CEO if Chiarelli wanted quick action. But Chiarelli had something else in mind: why not cut out the big contractors entirely and route reconstruction money directly through his division? "I can go from identifying a project to breaking ground in less than a month, working with Iraqi contractors," he declared. "It takes the big contractors six months."

He didn't even need Bechtel's engineering expertise, he boasted. His men had found a group of engineers at Baghdad University who had trained in Europe, spoke decent English, and didn't require any security to move around the capital. He'd also stumbled upon a plan for revitalizing infrastructure that the city government had drafted in the late 1970s just prior to the Iran-Iraq War. Most of the projects had never been completed. He'd only been in Iraq for five months, but Chiarelli was sure that he and his battalion commanders, who lived on small bases scattered throughout the city, knew what Iraqis wanted far better than the embassy or the contractors stuck in the Green Zone. The U.S. government, for example, liked building schools in Iraq, but Chiarelli insisted that they were a waste of money. "You know, when a guy is unemployed sitting at his house surrounded by sewage, no water and no electricity, it might make him feel good for a couple of days to walk his kid to school, but sooner or later he's going to get tired of that," he said.

Could he absorb $100 million? Neumann asked. "Easily," Chiarelli replied. To do what he wanted actually required about $500 million, but $100 million was a start. In his frustration he was, in effect, proposing to unite the civilian and military efforts in Baghdad. Not only would his division fight the insurgency, it would control the reconstruction budget, an approach that had been tried in the latter years of Vietnam. General Creighton Abrams had dubbed it the "one war" strategy. The meeting ended with the diplomats promising Chiarelli they would raise the issue with Ambassador John Negroponte, who had served in Vietnam as a young foreign service officer and had taken over from Bremer a couple of weeks earlier.

On August 3 Chiarelli had perhaps his best day in Iraq. He and Kirk Day put 18,000 people to work in Sadr City building a landfill and laying PVC pipe to begin removing the ankle-deep sewage that usually collected in the sprawling neighborhood's streets. Five months had passed since his troops fought the pitched battle with Sadr's militia. Now the slum was quiet. A jubilant Chiarelli toured the area and talked with the laborers who filled street after street. "I have these pictures of 18,000 people at work," he'd recall years later. "Sadr City was moving in our direction." For at least that one day he was sure he was winning the war.

CHAPTER NINE

All Glory Is Fleeting

Al Faw Palace, Camp Victory
July 1, 2004

O kay, who's my counterinsurgency expert?" asked General George Casey, sounding impatient. It was his first day in command and his first meeting with the staff he had inherited from General Sanchez, who had left Iraq for good that morning. A dozen Army, Navy, Air Force, and Marine officers sent to Iraq from posts around the world stared at him, stumped by his question. Finally Air Force Major General Steve Sargeant spoke up. He had spent his career flying jets, an experience that was largely irrelevant to a fight against low-tech Iraqi guerrillas. "I guess that must be me, sir," said the general, who was in charge of strategic plans at headquarters. The Air Force officer's hesitant answer drove home to Casey how little progress the military had made during its first year in coming to grips with the kind of war it was fighting.

In the four years prior to his arrival in Iraq, Casey had held some of the most critical jobs in the U.S. military, overseeing U.S. Army forces in Kosovo in 2000 and serving on the Pentagon's Joint Staff after the 9/11 terrorist attacks. He had managed to be well liked by Clinton administration officials and by Defense Secretary Donald Rumsfeld. In many ways, Casey was the model Pentagon general: steady, apolitical, and hardworking. He didn't make bold decisions or draw attention to himself. He was an efficient manager who knew how to make big bureaucracies run and how to anticipate problems.

He'd been only occasionally involved in the Iraq war before arriving in Baghdad. In the lead-up to the invasion, Rumsfeld's insistence that the Iraqis would have to take charge of rebuilding their country had stifled most serious postwar reconstruction planning. From his position on the Joint Staff, Casey sensed that there was going to be a need for the U.S. military to oversee the rebuilding effort. Just three months before the invasion he assembled a small group of active and retired officers that was rushed to the Middle East to deal with electricity generation, clean water, and other expected postwar problems. The small pickup team consisted of only fifty-eight people and was better suited to a relatively peaceful mission than to the chaos in Iraq. But with Rumsfeld's aversion to nation building, it was probably the best anyone could do.

After the 2003 invasion, Rumsfeld selected Casey to be the Army's vice chief of staff, a job that came with a promotion to four stars. He sat through hundreds of hours of meetings focused on troop rotation schedules for Iraq, plans to start bringing soldiers home, and the hurried push to buy more armor for the thin-skinned Humvees that were being shredded by insurgents' bombs. To Casey initially the occupation didn't seem all that different from the 1990s peacekeeping operations. The two missions had much in common. But in the Balkans the military had pressed the Clinton administration to ensure that its aims in the war-torn country were limited. Its job was to enforce a peace agreement between warring parties. In Iraq the task was far tougher. The military was essentially being asked to rebuild a society and defeat a ruthless armed resistance.

It wasn't until he arrived in Iraq that Casey started to understand the huge challenge he faced. Casey's headquarters at Al Faw Palace were located on the western outskirts of Baghdad. On the morning he took command, his palace office was mostly empty except for a few pictures of his wife, sons, and grandchildren. Video screens, flags, and maps covered the walls. A chandelier dangled from the elaborately carved, pastel-colored woodwork on the ceiling.

Saddam Hussein had built the palace in 1992 as a present to himself following the 1991 Gulf War. When Baghdad fell a dozen years later, the U.S. military moved into the sprawling building and its surrounding grounds. The hulking stone structure sat in the middle of a weed-choked lake. The only approach to its heavy wooden doors was a two-lane bridge. In the first year of the war the Army had remade the complex into a version of the military bases it had left behind in the United States. To house the 50,000 soldiers who lived and worked at Victory, it bought thousands of small trailers, which the Army called "containerized housing units," and arranged them in neat rows. Troops dined on leathery steaks and Baskin-Robbins sundaes in dining halls the size of airplane hangars, each decorated with sports memorabilia shipped from back home. They could shop in large post exchanges, stocked with luxuries such as flat-screen television sets, DVD players, and the latest video games.

Inside the palace, staff officers worked in modular cubicles in marble ballrooms and former bedroom suites. Fluorescent lights were nailed to the walls to augment the glow from crystal chandeliers. Outside the palace the smell of fuel and raw sewage hung in the air. Generators droned, tank and Humvee engines roared, and helicopters thumped. The massive base violated just about every rule of counterinsurgency strategy, which preaches the importance of small groups of soldiers living among the people and providing security. But the Army didn't know much about counterinsurgency when it built Victory Base Complex in 2003. It built what it knew.

On his way into Iraq, Casey had been told by officers in Kuwait that if he wanted to understand the enemy he needed to seek out a colonel in the palace named Derek Harvey. Harvey was a forty-nine-year-old intelligence officer who spoke Arabic and had an advanced degree in Islamic political thought. For months he'd been interviewing prisoners, poring over interrogation transcripts, and meeting with Sunni tribal leaders. Almost no one seemed interested in his work when Sanchez was in charge, which the short-tempered Harvey considered astounding. A couple of days after Casey arrived in Baghdad, he invited Harvey to step outside on one of the balconies at his new palace headquarters. "Do you smoke?" Casey asked, holding up two cigars. Harvey nodded, and they walked out onto a stone balcony overlooking the palace's man-made lakes.

Harvey gave his new commander a tutorial on the insurgency, interrupted only by the drone of helicopters and the lapping of greenish water against the palace walls. The insurgency was being led by former Saddam loyalists who were well organized and had access to lots of money and ammunition. Their forces were being augmented by foreign jihadists whose numbers were on the rise following the Abu Ghraib prisoner abuse scandal and the failed Fallujah assault. To win, the United States had to kill former Saddamists. But it also had to co-opt more moderate Baathists and win over the Sunni tribal leaders whom Saddam had pacified with bribes.

They talked for almost three hours. Casey peppered him with questions about the Sunni-Shiite split and the relationships between the foreign fighters and the Sunni tribes. Before parting, Harvey told Casey that the war was very different from the peacekeeping missions that Casey had overseen in the 1990s. "We don't understand the fight we're in," he warned his new boss.

The enormous mess he'd inherited didn't fully hit Casey until he started to read some of the awards for valor given to soldiers and Marines who had fought in the spring battles in Sadr City, Fallujah, and Najaf. In the Pentagon he had pored over the classified accounts of the uprisings. But the dry reports didn't capture how close some units, such as the soldiers from Chiarelli's 1st Cav Division, had come to being overrun. Casey was a fifty-six-year-old general who had never been in combat, taking command of a foundering war effort. He knew he'd have to learn fast.

☆   ☆   ☆   ☆

He had not planned on going to Iraq. Six months earlier, on Christmas Eve 2003, he and his thirty-one-year-old son, Ryan, had rushed out to do some last-minute Christmas shopping at the Pentagon City shopping mall, just across the river from the White House. Casey's relentless work ethic had helped him vault ahead of other Pentagon generals. Like most Washington workaholics, he typically put off his Christmas shopping to the last possible minute. As he wandered through Ann Taylor, sorting through the racks of women's sweaters, he spotted General Richard Myers, the chairman of the Joint Chiefs of Staff, who waved him over. Myers mentioned a new idea to deal with the worsening situation in Iraq. Abizaid had cornered him on a recent trip to Iraq and suggested putting a four-star general in Baghdad to command the overall military effort. "We really need it. We just can't be cheap here," Abizaid insisted. The new four-star wouldn't replace the overwhelmed Sanchez, who was a three-star. Instead he and his staff would focus on crafting a long-term counterinsurgency strategy and working with political leaders. Beneath him, Sanchez's headquarters would handle the day-to-day military operations and troop movements.

Ryan stood just out of earshot as Casey talked to Myers, who was surrounded by the chairman's plainclothes bodyguards. When they were finished Casey mentioned to his son that they were looking to send a new general to Iraq. "Are you interested?" Ryan asked him.

"I already have a job," he replied wistfully. He'd just been sworn in as vice chief a few months earlier, but Ryan could tell that his father would much rather be leading troops than overseeing bureaucracies and waging budget wars. "That's the difference between you and Wes Clark," he said, referring to the hyperambitious former general who had been an early mentor to Casey and was now weighing a run for president. "Clark would say he wanted the job and push for it. You would just wait for someone to offer it to you." They quickly dropped the conversation and went back to the sweater racks.

A couple of months later Casey was told to put together a short list of candidates for the Iraq job. On a warm spring evening he went over to Quarters One and handed the names to General Peter Schoomaker, the Army chief. They sat on the veranda in rocking chairs, with the Washington Monument and Lincoln Memorial in view.

"Your name's not on here," Schoomaker said after a moment.

"I thought you wanted me to stay here," Casey replied.

"This may be more important," the chief said. "Could you do it?"

"Yeah, absolutely."

Casey's name went on the list. Rumsfeld initially wanted his military aide for the job. But with the Abu Ghraib scandal in all the newspapers, anyone who was that close to the defense secretary had little chance of

Senate confirmation. Abizaid also had considered taking the job himself. When he learned that Casey was in the mix, he quickly latched on to him as the best choice.

Since their time together in Bosnia, Abizaid and Casey had remained close. They both commanded 15,000-soldier divisions in Germany in 2000. When Abizaid's unit was deployed in Kosovo, Casey called him from the bleachers at Fenway Park. "Hey, John, guess what I'm doing right now?" he said, holding the phone up so Abizaid could hear the crowd noise. A few months later, when Casey's troops were in Kosovo, Abizaid made sure to phone Casey from the stands of the brand-new ballpark in San Francisco, where he was watching his beloved Giants. In 2001 and 2003, when Abizaid twice left positions on the Pentagon's Joint Staff, Casey was selected as his replacement both times. Although Casey was a few years older than Abizaid, he looked to his friend almost as a mentor. Abizaid was smart and witty and had a reputation as a big strategic thinker. A part of Casey wanted to be seen by his Army peers in the same light.

Rumsfeld had dealt with Casey on the Joint Staff and liked him. Bush went along with the consensus, and Abizaid quickly called Casey with the good news.

When he arrived home at eight-thirty that evening, Sheila was on the third floor, unpacking boxes at their home at Fort McNair. Although he had been in the vice chief job for several months, the Caseys' move into the stately, century-old residence that came with the job had been delayed by renovations to the house. "Honey, we need to talk," he said, motioning her toward a chair. He hadn't even told his wife that he was being considered for the position. Not sure how to break the news, he blurted it out: "I'm going to Iraq." He might be leaving in only a few days. Sheila burst into tears. Why hadn't he told her he was up for the job? she asked as they embraced. "It happened pretty quickly," he explained.

"I don't have a good feeling about this, George. It brings back memories of your dad," she told him.

"I know."

His father's death was not something Casey talked much about, even with his wife. After the Vietnam Veterans Memorial opened on the National Mall, it had taken Casey some time before he felt ready to see it. When they found his father's name, George had been overcome, unable to speak more than a few words until he and Sheila returned to the car. As they drove home, he told Sheila that visiting the wall had been the most emotionally wrenching moment of his life.

Several years later, when he was promoted to four-star general, Casey's family gathered at Fort Myer, where he was living at the time, for his promotion ceremony. After the party, his brother and sisters all walked down to their father's grave, retracing the steps they had taken on the day he was buried thirty-three years earlier. George and his mother held back. The next morning they made their own quiet pilgrimage to the grave site. They could only imagine how overjoyed the elder Casey would have been to see his son rise to four-star rank.

Now George was off to war. Sheila could have told him no and, despite how badly he wanted the job, he would have turned it down. He had walked away from Delta Force without bitterness, and he had always promised Sheila that anytime she wanted to leave the Army all she had to do was tell him and they would be out. But she didn't. This was the life they had made for themselves, and she knew the assignment was one he had yearned for all these years. Soon they moved to the kitchen and talked for hours, not about whether he would go but about everything that needed to be done beforehand. One of the first things, she reminded him, was to telephone their two grown sons. Sheila didn't want them hearing about it on the nightly news. And, she reminded him, he had to talk to his mom, knowing that telling her was the kind of difficult conversation her taciturn husband might avoid.

"Did you call your mom?" she asked the next day.

Yes, but there had been no answer, Casey replied, so he had left a vague message on her answering machine.

"George, you have to tell her it's important or she'll never call!" Sheila chided.

When his mother did finally telephone from her house in Massachusetts, it was Sheila who answered. George was out. "I might as well tell you," she said. "George is going to Iraq."

"Okay," his mother replied, with no trace of emotion in her voice. She rushed down that weekend to see him off. Later Casey found out he wouldn't be leaving until July. There was too much preparation to do, and the Senate wasn't going to vote on his new assignment for several weeks.

Unexpected as it all was, Casey wasn't daunted by the new assignment. He wasn't an Arabist who had prepared his whole career for a job in the Middle East, but Abizaid was, and he would help. Casey had never been in combat, but he did have experience running big organizations and was confident that he could come up with a winning war strategy. He told himself he had more experience with the political and military problems of re-constructing war-ravaged countries than most Army officers. In Kosovo he'd even dealt with a tiny insurgent uprising in which some of the Kosovar Albanian rebels in the Presevo Valley region of the province launched a se-ries of covert attacks on the Serbian police. He had dealt with it by sealing off the valley and negotiating with the local mullahs, who helped him se-cure the surrender of the head of the Albanian rebel group.

He hadn't interviewed with either Rumsfeld or Bush before being cho-sen. No one asked him for his ideas about what needed to be done, and he hadn't thought about it very much. Schoomaker had given him a book en-titled *Learning to Eat Soup with a Knife: Counterinsurgency Lessons from Malaya and Vietnam* that had been written by a young officer from the Sosh department. It was the first book Casey had read on guerrilla war. His new assignment required Senate confirmation, but he was uncontroversial, the compromise choice everyone could support. Senator Hillary Clinton pronounced him boring. "Boring is good, General Casey, and I applaud you on that," she told him. "Clearly, you're a master at it. And it goes to the heart of your success."

"I'm going to have to think about that for a minute," he replied, draw-ing chuckles from the half-empty hearing room. The only nervous moment came when Casey was asked how long it would be until the 140,000 Amer-ican troops were home. The Army was proceeding on the assumption that it could be in Iraq another three years, until early 2007, he said in an answer that he had prepared ahead of time, but he stressed that was only an estimate, not a prediction. There was no real way of knowing how much longer the war would last. It was a safe response, and the lawmakers moved on to other topics. That evening, the Senate voted unanimously to con-firm him.

His sole meeting with Rumsfeld before leaving lasted just twenty minutes. The seventy-one-year-old defense secretary greeted Casey warmly and offered him a seat at the small round table in his third-floor Pentagon office. A military aide served coffee in white and gold Pentagon china. Although President Bush was still giving triumphal speeches about bringing democracy to the Muslim world, Rumsfeld made it clear he wasn't particularly interested in remaking Iraq. Like the senators from the confirmation hearing, he wanted Casey to figure out a way to bring American troops home soon. Take a few weeks to assess the situation before reporting back, he told Casey. But there was one parting order he did want to pass along: to resist the temptation to do too much. Military officers thought they could fix everything, Rumsfeld warned, and the more the United States tried to do for the Iraqis, the less they would do for themselves and the longer U.S. forces would be stuck there.

"I understand, Mr. Secretary," Casey replied. He told the story of his attempt to arrange the return of Muslim refugees to the villages of Dugi Dio and Jusici while serving in Bosnia, a six-week experiment that collapsed when weapons were found in the homes of the deputy mayor. The experience had taught him that can-do Americans can't want peace more than the people they are trying to help. Rumsfeld seemed satisfied that they understood each other. Casey thought so, too, but he didn't want to forget their conversation. He jotted the word *attitude* in the green notebook he carried. It was a small reminder not to disregard what he had learned in Bosnia—not to fall into the trap of thinking he could fix everything wrong with Iraq.

He departed from Andrews Air Force Base a few days later, without talking to Bush. Casey and Sheila had gone to the White House for a private dinner with the president and Laura Bush, but that had been a social occasion, with no real discussion of Iraq. Bush had told himself he would not micromanage his generals, the way Lyndon Johnson had done. Just as some parts of the Army had vowed never to refight Vietnam, so too had the president. But Bush took his own maxim to the extreme, leaving his commanders without any real instructions except for the advice they got from Rumsfeld. While the president was insisting that the United States was in a life-or-death struggle to change the Middle East, Rumsfeld was essentially telling his top commander that he shouldn't try too hard.

✶   ✶   ✶   ✶

Baghdad
August 2, 2004

When Casey sat down to compose a quick e-mail to Abizaid after his first month in command, much seemed possible. "There is a strategic opportunity for success," he wrote in early August 2004. No one had given him a mission statement, so he and John Negroponte, the new ambassador, had composed one in Casey's Pentagon office before they left. The goal was to leave behind an "Iraq built on the principles of representative government, respectful of the rights of its citizens and the rule of law, able to maintain order at home, defend its borders, and establish peaceful relations with its neighbors." To get there Casey and Negroponte spent their first month sketching out a campaign plan that had been decided on quickly, without exploring a lot of alternatives. Classic counterinsurgency theory held that to defeat insurgents, military forces had to win the trust and support of the people. "I came at it a little differently," Casey recalled. "I said, 'Yeah, it's the people, but the way we're going to get to the people is through a legitimate Iraqi government.' " And the key to producing a legitimate government, he assumed, was the national elections scheduled for January. The voting would channel the insurgents into politics; every effort should be made to ensure they happened on time, he insisted. The assumption that fair elections would blunt the insurgency was widely held among senior U.S. officials at the time. Unfortunately, it was completely wrong.

There was a bit of the Jesuit in Casey, probably the product of his Catholic education at Boston College High School and Georgetown. He enjoyed hashing out ideas and turning them over in his mind—or, even better, puzzling out his thoughts on paper. He'd set glasses on top of his head, pull out a red pen, and revise documents word by word for hours. "I can't help myself," he muttered when at the end of a long day one of his subordinates suggested that a general must have better things to do than editing a PowerPoint slide.

Rumsfeld's parting instructions had been to take a few weeks to study the situation, but after only seven days in Iraq, he was in his first video session with the defense secretary, who directed him to begin a major assessment of the effort to rebuild the Iraqi police and army. Four days later they spoke by phone, followed by another videoconference and another phone call several days after that. In all, Casey participated in twenty-three phone conversations or video meetings with Rumsfeld during his first two months, an average of one every three days. Rumsfeld was a stickler for chain of command. When Casey was scheduled to update Bush, Rumsfeld required a prebrief so that he could approve any information that went to the president. Sometimes it seemed Casey's staff was doing little more than churning out briefing slides for Washington.

After one videoconference, Casey's senior aide, Colonel Jim Barclay, got a call from General Peter Pace, the vice chairman of the Joint Chiefs. "The secretary liked the briefing," he said, referring to Rumsfeld. "But he wants Casey to stop saying *um* so much when he's talking."

"Sir, I can't tell him that," Barclay protested. "But hold on. He's right here."

He transferred the call into Casey's Green Zone office, and Pace told Casey himself. After hanging up, Casey and Barclay shook their heads. Like everyone else who worked with Rumsfeld, Casey received periodic one- or two-sentence notes—known as "snowflakes"—on issues that caught the defense secretary's attention. Sometimes Rumsfeld would wonder why it seemed to take so long to plan a raid and arrest a particular insurgent target. Casey rarely worried about individual raids and was puzzled how such picayune details were bubbling up to the secretary's level. One of the first snowflakes asked that Casey start training Iraqis to replace the relatively small number of U.S. special operations troops acting as bodyguards for senior ministers, who were prime assassination targets. The lesson was unmistakable: no part of the U.S. effort was too small to escape Rumsfeld's green-eyeshade mentality on troops.

Beneath Casey were two deputy commanders. One was Lieutenant General Tom Metz, who oversaw daily military operations. Shortly after Casey took command, he had identified sixteen key cities that U.S. troops had to clear of insurgents prior to the January elections. Metz's job was to direct those battles, while Casey crafted the overall strategy and made sure the newly sovereign interim government didn't interfere. The two men had been close friends since they were twenty-two-year-old lieutenants in Germany.

The other was Petraeus. Casey's relationship with him was more complicated. The same week Casey arrived, *Newsweek* featured Petraeus on the cover in full battle gear underneath a headline that asked "Can This Man Save Iraq?" Only a couple of months after he had returned home from Mosul, Petraeus had been promoted and sent back to Iraq to oversee the training and equipping of the army and police. "General Petraeus . . . is the closest thing to an exit strategy the United States now has," the *Newsweek* article enthused. Casey was annoyed, though not surprised. Rumsfeld was angry. During a stopover in Ireland shortly after the article appeared, his top aide stuffed the offending *Newsweek* behind other magazines in the airport gift shop so that the secretary wouldn't see them again. Casey quickly got orders to shut down the Petraeus publicity machine. "From now on, I'm your PAO," he told Petraeus, using the military acronym for public affairs officer.

For several months their relationship remained strained. Their leadership styles were completely different. Casey was cautious, often to the point of inaction. "Almost nothing has to be done right now," he counseled subordinates. "When you are talking about a major policy initiative, it needs to be thoughtful and deliberate. Hasty decisions in this type of environment will generally be wrong." In contrast, Petraeus believed that the United States had a narrow window of opportunity that was rapidly closing. It was better to take risks than do nothing.

Casey typically attended meetings with senior Iraqi officials alone or with one aide. Petraeus went everywhere with an entourage of smart young officers that included two Rhodes scholars and a Columbia University Ph.D. His energy, knowledge, and eagerness to fix Iraq shone through in just about every meeting. "Sir, if I could," he'd often interject before launching into a discourse on the problem of the day. It was hard for the new Iraqi leaders to tell whether Casey or Petraeus was in charge.

At an early Iraqi national security council meeting, Petraeus grabbed a seat at the main table with Casey, the prime minister, the minister of defense, the interior minister, and other senior Iraqi officials. "We're fine here at the head table," Casey told him, directing him to a seat against the wall with the other second-tier staffers.

Despite the tension, Casey badly needed Petraeus to succeed. He wanted the troops Petraeus was cranking out to fight alongside U.S. units as they cleared insurgent strongholds prior to the elections, putting an Iraqi face on what were essentially American assaults. By January, Casey hoped, there would be enough police and army units to guard polling stations during the election and allow for cuts in U.S. forces in 2005.

In early August, Petraeus's forces were tested for the first time since the April battles in Sadr City and Fallujah. A U.S. Marine patrol in Najaf, about 100 miles south of Baghdad, unknowingly strayed too close to a house where Muqtada al-Sadr was hiding, provoking a lengthy firefight. After the battle, Sadr's militia fighters quickly seized police stations and government buildings throughout the city. "I was looking for the opportunity for the new Iraqi government to have a success and demonstrate that it could function," Casey recalled. This was it. He ordered two U.S. Army battalions and three of Petraeus's new Iraqi battalions to help the Marines retake the city from Sadr's forces.

The U.S. troops, backed by helicopters and fighter jets, did most of the heavy fighting in the labyrinthlike cemetery around the Imam Ali shrine. The Iraqis were asked to play a supporting role. Still Petraeus was nervous. The troops had walked patrols in Baghdad, but this was the first time that they were being pressed into battle against their Iraqi brethren. A day after they arrived, Petraeus began fielding frantic calls from the Iraqi units' U.S. advisors, reporting that the troops were desperately short of ammunition and rifles. As night fell, he and his small command gathered up all the bullets, mortar rounds, and guns they could find in storage depots and heaved the weapons onto the back of Chinook cargo helicopters.

Seeking refuge from the U.S.-led assault, Sadr and his militia forces retreated inside the Imam Ali shrine, one of the holiest sites in Shiite Islam. Casey met with the new prime minister, Iyad Allawi, in a small garden outside his residence in the Green Zone. The CIA had sources inside the shrine who were updating them on Sadr's location, and Allawi wanted the troops to attack the mosque and capture or kill Sadr.

General Metz, who had raced down to Najaf to monitor the fighting, warned that the Iraqis needed at least twenty-four hours to come up with a plan. The delay gave Sadr time to negotiate a cease-fire and escape. "It got played as a victory for Sadr much like that stuff does, but it was good," Casey recalled. The Iraqi army forces hadn't crumbled under fire as they had in April. He and Allawi also grew closer during the crisis. "Frankly I didn't expect such a key success so early," Casey wrote in a note to Abizaid after the fight. "Muqtada Sadr gave the interim government its first real test and he lost." He was so hopeful that he suggested to Abizaid that he might be able to reduce the number of U.S. troops in early 2005, after the scheduled January 30 elections.

Not all of Casey's subordinate commanders were as convinced that the United States was on the right track. On August 14, as the Najaf battle was drawing to a close, Casey convened a meeting with his top commanders at Al Faw Palace. Around the table were Metz, Petraeus, Chiarelli, and several other senior officers. The new U.S. ambassador John Negroponte was sitting next to Casey, his position meant to signal that the civilian and military efforts were finally united. Casey started by laying out his plan for the next six months. "We have two priority efforts—training Iraqi security forces and the elections," he told his commanders.

Marine Lieutenant General James Conway, who was responsible for Fallujah and surrounding Anbar Province, complained that Sunni tribes in his province had been given no voice in the new government and saw it as illegitimate. Allawi's ministers, meanwhile, ignored the area. "The silence is deafening," he complained.

Chiarelli was upset as well. Less than two weeks earlier he'd turned out 18,000 people to work in Sadr City laying sewer pipe, wiring houses for electricity, and picking up trash. He saw the turnout as a major victory that he hoped would spur more funding for similar projects throughout Baghdad and the rest of the country. Casey and Negroponte, however, were moving in a different direction. As part of their strategy they shifted $2 billion out of the reconstruction projects that Chiarelli was championing to pay for more equipment for Iraqi army and police forces.

As he headed into the palace meeting Negroponte knew he was going to get an earful on the subject from Chiarelli. Although he'd been in Iraq only six weeks, the ambassador had already grown tired of hearing about Chiarelli's bold plans to fix the embassy-led reconstruction effort by cutting out U.S. contractors and focusing on smaller projects and jobs for Iraqis. "I am not going to listen to Chiarelli . . . bitch about the State Department," he told Casey. Negroponte didn't have a choice, though. Chiarelli was incensed and let it show more than usual. He didn't deny the need for more army and police forces, but he didn't think the money to pay for them should come out of the reconstruction effort, which was already wasting too much money on big-ticket ventures that offered little immediate payoff in Baghdad's neighborhoods. He wondered in conversations with diplomats in the Green Zone whether the United States was pursuing a "bankrupt strategy" by ignoring the crumbling infrastructure and its crippling unemployment. These were driving the insurgency, he insisted.

Chiarelli never got a chance to prove his approach could work. The flare-up in Najaf triggered a new eruption of violence in Sadr City, and his soldiers spent much of the next ten weeks fighting over the same ground they had fought for in April. In the earlier battle Sadr's militia had fought with rifles and rocket-propelled grenades. Now they were using more-deadly roadside bombs. It seemed as if the cleric could turn up the violence at will. Once calm was restored, Chiarelli restarted his reconstruction program for two months before turning Baghdad over to a new division with different priorities. He returned to the United States convinced that he had been on the right track and penned a long article in *Military Review,* an Army journal, laying out his theories. "Will Sadr or his lieutenants attack again? Probably. But support for the attacks will not last if infrastructure improvements continue," he wrote. His article also took a swipe at Casey and Negroponte's strategy, which made training a higher priority than reconstruction. "If there is nothing else done other than kill bad guys and train others to kill bad guys, the only thing accomplished is moving more people from the fence to the insurgent category," he wrote.

★   ★   ★   ★

Chiarelli's loss in the summer of 2004 had been Petraeus's gain. Most of the $2 billion taken out of the reconstruction budget went directly to his new command overseeing Iraqi army and police development. He felt good, and it wasn't just because of the money. In Najaf his Iraqi units had held together, which was an improvement over the disasters that preceded his arrival. In late September Petraeus put down his thoughts in an op-ed in the *Washington Post*. His article began with a series of caveats. Training and equipping a quarter million Iraqis was a "daunting task." Insurgent violence made it even harder. "Nonetheless, there are reasons for optimism," he wrote. "Today approximately 164,000 Iraqi police and soldiers . . . are performing a wide variety of security missions. Equipment is being delivered. Training is on track and increasing in capacity. Infrastructure is being repaired."

Soon after the op-ed appeared, Petraeus's forces suffered a series of humiliating setbacks. In early October the newly formed 7th Iraqi Battalion was rushed to Samarra, a Sunni insurgent haven north of Baghdad, on seventy-two hours' notice to fight in an American-led operation to take control of the city. On the way there, it was hit by a car bomb that killed one Iraqi soldier and wounded seven. As the injured were being treated, the commander and several of his aides quit, triggering an exodus of hundreds of rank-and-file troops from the 800-man unit. "They just walked out the gate and didn't come back," said Major Robert Dixon, an American advisor attached to the unit. Other disasters followed. In late October, Petraeus flew his Black Hawk to the Kirkush Military Training Base on the Iranian border to oversee the graduation ceremony for the 17th Iraqi Battalion. A band played as the new troops in their crisp tan-and-black uniforms marched past a reviewing stand. Petraeus gave a short speech. Immediately following the parade the troops were loaded onto buses, trucks, and minivans for two weeks of vacation. Petraeus hopped on his helicopter bound for the Green Zone. The helicopter flew fast and low over the dreary parched landscape, rising and falling to avoid electrical power lines that crisscrossed the desert. Hot autumn air whipped at his face. He felt good; he had produced yet another battalion.

A few hours later, his executive officer rushed into his Green Zone office. Three of the minivans carrying forty-nine of the new recruits had been stopped at a fake checkpoint. The soldiers were ordered out of the vans, forced to lie facedown in the sand, and executed with a bullet to the back of the head. "It was just a horrible experience," Petraeus recalled. "We felt like they were our guys. These weren't just some Iraqis. These were our troopers. I'd seen them graduate. I'd been out there." A few days later he got another grim report from Mosul: dozens of soldiers, also going home on leave, were found headless on the side of the road. Many of the officers on Petraeus's staff blamed themselves for the deaths. They should have realized that troops, who were required to turn in their rifles before they went home on leave, were easy targets.

Assassinations weren't Petraeus's only problem. He depended on un-armed civilian contractors to ferry new AK-47s, body armor, and helmets to Iraqi bases. Soon insurgents were targeting them, too. "It was just a battle. Everything was a flat-out fight. Every single logistical convoy and delivery of equipment," he recalled. When he commanded the 101st in Mosul, Pe-traeus had a massive staff made up of topflight officers. His new training command was an undermanned pickup team that had been thrown together without vital equipment such as armored Humvees or sufficient radios.

In November, as U.S. soldiers and Marines gathered on the outskirts of Fallujah, Petraeus's units were once again thrust into the fight. In the months since the Marines' aborted April assault, Fallujah had become a car bomb factory under the control of radical fighters. Casey was determined to seize it from the insurgents prior to the January elections and believed that Petraeus's troops had to play a role in the attack to blunt the inevitable claim in the Middle East that U.S. troops and warplanes were destroying a Muslim city.

As the Iraqi units prepared to move to Fallujah, hundreds of terrified soldiers deserted. Major Matt Jones, who worked as an advisor, recalled that 200 soldiers in his Iraqi battalion quit before they even left their base. One of the deserters was the battalion commander. "He stole his pistol and his staff car—a Chevy Lumina—and an AK-47. We never saw him again. That wasn't exactly a good day for morale," Jones said.

Many of the units that made it to Fallujah were nowhere near ready to fight. General Conway, the Marine officer leading the attack, was dumb-founded when he saw the Iraqi troops, and immediately called Petraeus. "Why did you send me all these guys without any boots and kit?"

"What are you talking about?" Petraeus replied. "We issued all that stuff to them."

"Well, you may have. But they don't have it. What you got is a bunch of guys running around in flip-flops and running shoes."

Petraeus raced out to Fallujah with one of his Iraqi generals to try to figure out what had happened. The Iraqi soldiers he found looked miserable, hungry, and cold. "Didn't we issue you this stuff?" he demanded. "Where is it?" When they'd gone home on leave they gave the equipment to their younger brothers and sisters, the Iraqis explained. "Our families needed the blankets," one of the recruits told him.

Back in Baghdad, Petraeus comforted himself by reading *Seven Pillars of Wisdom*, T. E. Lawrence's account of the Arab revolt during World War I. Lawrence had dealt with many of the same problems—poor leadership, desertions, and shortages of equipment. He found himself drawn to one scene in which Lawrence emerges from his tent to find that his Arab allies, whom he had been fighting with for months, are gone. They'd gone to visit their families, leaving him alone in the desert. "That just resonated with me," Petraeus recalled.

The Iraqis' failures were frustrating to Casey, who felt that Petraeus's briefings to Bush and Rumsfeld in the summer and early fall had overstated the progress that he was making. "Look, you have got to be very careful when you are talking to civilian leaders," he snapped after one video teleconference with the president, who had dialed in from his Crawford, Texas, ranch. "Don't be so optimistic." Frustrated with the setbacks, Rumsfeld began demanding more-frequent updates. Casey and his staff, in turn, began demanding more and more data as well. Petraeus never complained, but his staff bristled at the second-guessing.

In June Abizaid had assured Petraeus that he would get whatever he needed for the new training command. Yet it had taken months to get him the U.S. staff he'd been promised. His initial staffing request sat for almost two months in Baghdad before it was forwarded to the Pentagon. It took another two months to find the soldiers to fill it. In October the Army began sending over soldiers from the 98th Division, a reserve unit based in upstate New York. Petraeus placed some of the new arrivals in his headquarters and made the others combat advisors. The critically needed advisors were supposed to toughen up the Iraqi formations.

The reservists, however, were ill prepared to lead foreign forces in combat. Most were drill sergeants who spent two weeks each summer on active duty, putting American teenagers through basic training. Many of these part-time soldiers had joined the 98th because they thought the unit would never deploy overseas. Now they were being asked to fight alongside inexperienced Iraqi units and live on Spartan bases—a mission typically handled by elite Special Forces teams.

Petraeus's staff knew they had a problem when the soldiers started unpacking shipping crates filled with their broad-brimmed drill sergeant hats, easel boards, flip charts, and urinal disinfectant cakes. They had assumed they were going to run basic training, teaching Iraqis how to shoot, march, and care for their equipment—not be pressed into battle with them. In late 2004, Brigadier General James Schwitters, Petraeus's deputy in charge of the Iraqi army training effort, told Petraeus that only about a third of them were effective in their jobs. Most of the advisors didn't even know how to operate an AK-47, the rifle of choice for the Iraqi military. Schwitters was one of the Army's most experienced, unflappable professionals. He had commanded Delta Force, where his troops gave him the radio call sign "Flatliner," a reference to a dead person's electrocardiogram reading. Nothing seemed to unhinge him. His assessment of the American soldiers advising the Iraqi army battalions was blunt but accurate.

Outwardly and with Casey, Petraeus adopted a can-do attitude. He was going to figure out how to make it work with the soldiers that he had been given. He and Schwitters created a training academy north of Baghdad to teach the advisors the basics of fighting with foreign troops. Both men knew, though, that the solution was far from ideal, and not the proper way to conduct a mission that Bush and Rumsfeld were saying was the most important in Iraq. In truth, the Pentagon and Casey had no idea how difficult it was to rebuild a military in a country that was being torn apart by an insurgency. In the Balkans, where there was no fighting, the United States had handed the mission of training army and police forces off to private contractors, its NATO allies, or the relatively small Special Forces. The most relevant lessons when it came to rebuilding a foreign military were from Vietnam, but that war had been long forgotten.

Petraeus's other big worry was Mosul. He had poured his heart into stabilizing the city, and still referred to himself as a Moslawi, or citizen of

Mosul. "I go back and it's like the return of the prodigal son," he told a *Newsweek* reporter in June 2004. "There's even a street in Mosul named for the 101st Airborne, and you know it's authentic because there are two misspellings in [the street sign]." In the fall of 2004 his project was coming apart. Petraeus had turned over the city in early 2004 to Brigadier General Carter Ham, who led a force about one-third the size of the 101st. Ham also received far less reconstruction money than Petraeus. "I wasn't as aggressive as I needed to be in asking for money," Ham would say years later. His other handicap was that he wasn't Petraeus. "Petraeus has this big room-filling personality," he recalled. "That just isn't me." After Petraeus had departed, the political deals that he had brokered began to unravel. He had urged Ham to make sure that the provincial governor, Ghanim al-Basso, a Sunni Arab, stayed in his job. "From day one the message from the council was that Governor Basso had to go," Ham recalled. Basso was fired a few days after Petraeus left. The next governor, who was appointed by the council, was assassinated in June 2004 after only a few months in office.

In late August 2004 Petraeus visited northern Iraq, ostensibly to inspect a new regional police training center. His real goal was to check on Mosul, and he arranged to spend two days there, visiting Ham and his former Iraqi cohorts. A few weeks earlier, a female law professor whom Petraeus helped place on the Mosul city council had been found tortured and killed in her home. Attacks were on the rise, and the police chief and new provincial governor were feuding. Petraeus visited a police station in downtown Mosul and gave a pep talk. Afterward, Mohammad Barhawi, the Mosul police chief, warned him that foreign jihadists were infiltrating the city and that he was having trouble with the governor, who was trying to drive him from his job.

Before he left, Petraeus stopped by the governor's office. "I lost fifty-three soldiers in Mosul and it pains me enormously to see you two bickering," he told him. "This is a time when all Moslawis have to pull together." As night fell he headed to his helicopter, which was waiting for him with its rotors spinning. Petraeus turned to his assistant, Sadi Othman, a skillful translator who had stayed with Petraeus for years. "You can't go home again," he said ruefully.

Three months later, insurgents attacked Mosul's police stations. Petraeus was in his Baghdad office when Barhawi called in the midst of the battle, begging for help. The Iraqi's voice, normally strong and deep, trembled with fear. There was little Petraeus could do but try to stiffen Barhawi to fight back. "You've got to hang in there," he told him. "This is your opportunity to show what you're made of." Petraeus had equipped Mosul's SWAT team with new vehicles, body armor, and heavy machine guns. It had far more firepower than the insurgents could ever muster. "Just get out there with your machine guns and your SWAT team and you can fight these guys off," he said, trying to sound as calm as possible.

Ham suspected that Barhawi had been cooperating with the insurgency for months and might have been involved in the assassination of the Mosul governor. Petraeus was more sympathetic; he believed that Barhawi, a former general in Saddam's elite Republican Guard, was a good man who was under intense pressure from the enemy to surrender or switch sides. "We knew he was a former special operations guy and all this stuff, but in the early days when Mosul had nothing he stood up and was ready to lead," he recalled. Since Barhawi had become chief, insurgents had kidnapped his sister, blown up his house, and shot him in the calf. Even after he had been wounded in the fall of 2003, he continued to run the Mosul police force from his hospital bed. But as Petraeus hung up the phone, he could tell that his friend had nothing left. Barhawi fled to Kurdistan with a sack full of cash. The police, whom Petraeus had touted as a model, collapsed as insurgents took over nearly all of the city's two dozen stations.

In the weeks after the Mosul uprising Petraeus looked tired and dispirited. He was working sixteen to eighteen hours a day and guzzling coffee to stay awake. He believed that a commander should never express doubt in front of his troops. "You might put your head down privately somewhere, but then when the door opens you've got to show determination and total commitment. You've got to be unyielding," Petraeus often said. But his slumped shoulders and bloodshot eyes betrayed him. For the first time in his accomplished career he was failing.

✳   ✳   ✳   ✳

Baghdad
November 14, 2004

Abizaid knew things weren't going well and that relations between Casey and Petraeus had been strained. He wanted to try to fix things and thought he could, if the three of them could talk it out. They were three of the most experienced generals in the Army, solid professionals and dedicated soldiers. He knew the Middle East and what it took to bring stability to its fractured societies. Petraeus had probably thought and studied more about counterinsurgency than anyone. Casey knew the Army and its capabilities like few other officers. If the three of them could think through the problems, they might be able to devise a new way forward. They met around the mahogany conference table in Casey's Al Faw Palace office. "Between the three of us we need to figure this out in a nonaccusatory manner," Abizaid said. "We are missing something philosophically. This is the only war we have got. We have to win it."

It was a meeting that could easily have happened in Saigon in 1968, the last time the United States found itself in a war against a vicious insurgency with no victory in sight. A few days earlier the Marines had taken Fallujah, flattening the Sunnis' stronghold in a block-by-block operation. The huge attack had destroyed the insurgency's primary safe haven and knocked the enemy off balance. But Abizaid took little encouragement from the victory. A year and a half after the fall of Saddam Hussein, the Iraqis were still unwilling or unable to fight for their own country. Ninety-five U.S. troops had been killed and 560 wounded in the battle. By contrast, only eleven Iraqi soldiers died in the fighting and just forty-three were wounded, he said.

"The feeling in D.C. is, 'What the fuck are the Iraqis doing?' " Abizaid said.

In a weird paradox, the more American troops fought to stabilize the country, the more resentment they generated among ordinary Iraqis, frustrated at the presence of U.S. troops in their neighborhoods. They had to do something to change the dynamic, Abizaid said. There was only one real course: they had to figure out a way to get Iraqi troops to take more responsibility for maintaining order. Abizaid was quick to reassure Petraeus that the Iraqis' failures weren't his fault. Many of the men sent to act as advisors didn't have the experience or skills to train soldiers for combat. "Dave, I think we have missed the mark," Abizaid conceded. "We didn't give you the best and the brightest. We put the third team out on the field." The key to fixing the Iraqi forces was using the best and most experienced U.S. troops as combat advisors, he argued.

As Abizaid searched for a historical parallel his mind drifted back to what he recalled from studying Vietnam. It was hardly an inspiring example, given the South Vietnamese army's collapse in 1975, but it was the last time the Army had tried to rebuild a military on anything like the scale it was doing in Iraq. In the early 1960s the Pentagon had created a special command to select, train, and oversee U.S. officers advising South Vietnamese units. Maybe it was time to build a similar advisory command in Iraq, Abizaid said. He suggested filling the advisory jobs with lieutenant colonels from the Army War College. These were officers who had promising careers ahead of them and in most cases had already done a tour in Iraq or Afghanistan. "That could be what we want," Casey agreed. They'd need to clear it with the Pentagon first.

Abizaid also was worried that the United States wasn't finding tough Iraqi leaders who were willing to stand up to the insurgents. "In the Middle East there is usually one guy who holds a unit together," he told Petraeus. He wanted to step up efforts to lure Sunnis and even some of Saddam's former military commanders back into the army. "I don't sense that we have a Sunni outreach program that isn't AC-130-based," he said, referring to the heavily armed ground attack planes that had killed hundreds of insurgents in Fallujah. Petraeus said that they were trying but were running into resistance from the predominantly Shiite interim government, which feared a Sunni coup. "They are afraid of Sunni leaders," he said. The meeting ended with more questions than answers. Everyone was coming to the conclusion that the insurgency would continue for several more years and that the Iraqi security forces would not be able to handle the fight anytime soon. "It's tough to make a nation of sheep move forward," said Abizaid. "But that is our deal; that is our challenge."

More immediate problems intervened, as they always did. Every six months Casey got an assessment of military operations in Iraq. He usually asked one of the British generals to write it, believing that a foreign officer would be more willing to give him the honest assessment he needed. The December 2004 review was brutal. There was more and more hard evidence that the strategy wasn't working, at least not on the ambitious timetable that he had laid out in August. U.S. military operations over the previous six months had eliminated insurgent safe havens in a dozen cities. The Shiite uprising in Sadr City had finally been beaten down by Chiarelli's men. Despite those military successes, conditions were worsening. Since October, more than 300 Iraqi government officials had been assassinated as part of a campaign aimed at hollowing out the ministries. Polling data showed that 40 percent of the Sunnis in Baghdad supported the armed opposition, more than supported the current interim government. If the Sunnis didn't turn out to vote in January, there was very little chance that the elections would produce a representative government that could win over insurgent sympathizers, the six-month assessment warned.

It wasn't only Casey's staff that had doubts. The CIA station in Baghdad was issuing dire warnings that the country was too unstable for elections. Even Ambassador Negroponte wondered if it wouldn't be prudent to postpone. "I think it may be too risky," he suggested one evening over dinner in Casey's residence, a small villa across the lake from Al Faw. Casey insisted that they had to go forward and asked Negroponte to sleep on it. The next morning Negroponte dropped his objections. In an effort to ease worries, Casey temporarily boosted the number of troops in the country to 150,000, the highest number since the invasion.

At 7:30 a.m. on Saturday, December 12, 2004, Casey strode into the small auditorium for his morning briefing. Behind him about thirty staffers sat in five tiers of stadium-style seating. Each morning all his major subordinate commands updated Casey on the last twenty-four hours, their presentations projected on three large flat-panel screens at the front of the room. That morning Casey received the normal update on the security situation in major cities and towns, each of which was assigned a color grade—red, orange, yellow, or green—depending on the insurgency's strength. Casey noticed that Fallujah was rated orange, which meant that the insurgent threat there was still significant. It had been nearly a month since a Marine-led force had essentially destroyed the city in ten days of brutal house-to-house fighting. Although a few holdout insurgents still took occasional potshots, the city was essentially devoid of life, insurgent or otherwise. Casey asked his staff to reassess Fallujah to determine if it still belonged in the orange category. The next day the staff upgraded it to yellow.

Did anyone have a problem with revising the assessment? Casey asked. No one in the room protested. But Major Grant Doty, a slim, bespectacled strategist who was watching the briefing by live video from his desk elsewhere in the palace, was frustrated. "This is the most fucked-up thing in the world," he thought. The staff had changed the color rating on Fallujah just to make Casey happy. He started typing an e-mail to the general, noting that he was "shocked and disappointed" by the change in the city's status. "I think this is a mistake and was in response to the false perception that this is what you wanted, and they were going to give it to you," he continued. It really didn't matter whether Fallujah was rated yellow or orange, Doty thought. But changing it because the commander suggested doing so indicated a much larger problem. It all smacked of Vietnam, when officers inflated body counts so that headquarters could feel good about how the war was going.

Casey didn't reply directly to the e-mail, but Doty noticed that in the weeks afterward he began getting invited to more meetings with the boss. When Casey would make day trips to units around the country, he started bringing along Doty, too. Doty wasn't sure if his contrarian e-mail was the reason for his new access, but he thought it might be. Unlike many senior generals, Casey was open to second-guessing from his staff, even if he didn't always act on it.

It wasn't the first time Doty had approached Casey with advice. A few weeks earlier he'd sent Casey an e-mail critiquing the boss's performance during a CNN interview. Casey needed to drive home an overall theme or message in his interviews with the national media, Doty had told him. A printout of the e-mail had come back with the words "exactly on!" written in Casey's cursive scrawl at the top.

Doty, a former instructor in West Point's Social Sciences Department with a master's degree from Yale University, had arrived in August and was assigned to Casey's "initiatives group," a small team that was supposed to come up with unconventional ideas for the commander. In twenty years in the Army, Doty had frequently felt like an outsider. He thought the war had been a mistake, but he had vowed to himself that he would do what he could to help. He resolved to make himself a bit of a pest, someone who questioned assumptions and fought bureaucratic tendencies.

Since Casey had arrived, the American officers in the palace had been telling themselves that they were figuring out how to win. They had constructed a strategy, dubbed it counterinsurgency, and thought they were on their way to victory. But Doty wasn't convinced. The United States was in a brutal fight, unlike anything it had trained for, and yet people on the staff weren't questioning and debating. The incident in the morning briefing with Fallujah proved it. He wanted Casey to be flexible and improvisational and to foster the same spirit in his officers. He advised Casey to go to the briefing early one day and ask people what they were reading. If it didn't have something to do with Iraq or Arab culture, Casey should tell them to read something that did. He suggested building a library and stocking it with classic accounts of past counterinsurgency wars. He could start with David Galula's dissection of the French army's war in Algeria against Arab guerrillas or Bernard Fall's *Street Without Joy,* which chronicled the debacle in Vietnam. Casey heard him out, but Doty left unsure what would come of his efforts. Casey was hard to decipher, and Doty hadn't said everything he really thought—that the United States was settling into a delusion that it was winning.

*　＊　＊　＊*

Casey woke on January 30, the day of the elections, a little after 3:00 A.M. He wanted to take a quick aerial tour of Baghdad and get to the Green Zone before the polls opened at 7:00 a.m. His helicopter lifted off in darkness from Al Faw Palace and made a few lazy loops over west Baghdad. It was a cold, wet morning, typical of January. He and Prime Minister Allawi had banned all vehicle traffic in Iraq's major cities in an effort to prevent car bombs and limit the enemy's movement. To keep the insurgents off balance, they had made the announcement one day prior to the balloting. Working furiously in the weeks before the election, U.S. special operations units also had captured some key insurgent leaders tied to Abu Musab al-

Zarqawi's terrorist movement. But there was no way of telling whether it would be enough.

As the sun rose over Baghdad, Casey took in the city with his aide, his executive officer, and Doty. From the air the Iraqi capital looked almost deserted—no cars, no trucks, and, unusual even for that hour, almost no people on the streets. He had spent the previous seven months preparing for this moment. Now there was nothing left for him to do. "Is anyone going to show?" he wondered.

His helicopter touched down in the Green Zone around six-thirty, and Casey moved briskly to his office and turned on the BBC's televised coverage. Around seven Ghazi al-Yawer, Iraq's portly president, strode into a polling place in his crisp white dishdasha and with a flourish dropped his ballot into a box. Casey waited anxiously for the next two hours. Small numbers of people were turning out to vote, and he worried the election would be the disaster that the CIA was predicting. At 10:00 a.m. his division commanders, who were scattered around the country, updated him via video teleconference. Most were reporting a light turnout. The best news came from Baghdad, where Chiarelli reported that hundreds of people were walking to polling sites from Abu Ghraib, a Sunni enclave just west of the capital. A few minutes later, Chiarelli excitedly interrupted the briefing. "It's not hundreds of people coming in from Abu Ghraib, it's thousands of people," he said. A cheer of joy, mixed with relief, went up from the dozens of people in the briefing room with Casey.

The U.S. command reported a record number of attacks on the day of the elections, but the vast majority of them were minor or ineffective. U.S. forces stayed largely out of sight, leaving security duties around the polling stations in Baghdad and other big cities to Iraqi army and police units. By late afternoon cable news outlets were beaming back to the United States pictures of long lines of ecstatic Iraqis holding up their purple-stained fingers to prove that they had cast votes in the country's first free election in more than three decades. Later that afternoon Casey took off in his helicopter for a two-hour tour of Baghdad and the neighboring cities. Throngs of people filled Baghdad's streets. Many of them were lined up outside polling sites, playing soccer, or celebrating. Casey asked his pilots to fly out to Fallujah. There the scene was different. The streets were mostly empty.

In all of Anbar Province, the heart of the Sunni insurgency, only about 2,000 people voted.

Around 6:00 p.m. Casey was preparing to meet with his staff when Rumsfeld called. "George, when the eyes of the world were on you, you stood and delivered," the defense secretary told him. "Thank you, Mr. Secretary," Casey replied. "I'll pass that on to everybody." Petraeus telephoned Deputy Defense Secretary Paul Wolfowitz, who had been one of the leading advocates for the invasion. More than 100,000 Iraqi soldiers and policemen had turned out to help guard polling places, he said. For the first time since the fall of Baghdad, Iraqi tanks were out on the capital city's streets. Given the past month's failures, this was great news. Wolfowitz asked Petraeus to send photos of soldiers and tanks. He wanted to show the American people that the Iraqis were finally taking responsibility for their own country.

As the day drew to a close Casey stood and addressed his staff. "What a historic day," he said as the applause welled up from his men. He then returned to his quarters and called Sheila, who was crying tears of joy and relief for him. When he hung up, Casey and his aide, Major Tony Hale, walked out onto the patio behind his quarters at Camp Victory and smoked cigars. Hale brought out a bottle of grappa, an Italian brandy, and they toasted their success. "From then on, I thought, 'This will work,' " Casey recalled years later.

The next morning Casey spoke with Abizaid by phone. The two friends chatted amiably while Casey's staff listened: "Yeah, John, I know. Great outcome, great outcome," Casey said. In the Pentagon's daily summary of U.S. press clippings there wasn't a single negative article, he noted. Doty, sitting on the black leather couch in Casey's small Green Zone office, couldn't resist puncturing the euphoria a bit. Turning to Casey, he recalled the end of the movie *Patton*. World War II is over. Patton, played by the actor George C. Scott, walks his dog. He is only a few months from his death. In the background, Scott's deep, rough voice recalls that when victorious Roman generals returned from war they were honored with a parade. The conquering general would ride in a triumphal chariot. Just behind him stood a slave who would whisper in his ear, "All glory is fleeting. All glory is fleeting."

"Maybe I should be the slave at the end of *Patton* whispering, 'All glory is fleeting,' " Doty said.

Casey shot Doty an annoyed look. He knew the elections weren't going to solve all of Iraq's problems. Only the Shiites and Kurds had really turned out to vote. Most Sunnis, who made up the bulk of the insurgency, had boycotted the elections and would almost certainly continue to fight. But after seven exhausting, frustrating months, he needed a moment to savor his victory.

CHAPTER TEN

The Bunker in Jadiriyah

Al Faw Palace, Camp Victory
March 4, 2005

Defense Secretary Donald Rumsfeld was furious. "I am not sure I am ready to move this forward to the president," he growled at Casey over the video hookup from the Pentagon. Rumsfeld was referring to Casey's strategy to accelerate the training of Iraqi army and police forces so that U.S. troops could start coming home. Casey had been briefing the defense secretary on the plan since January.

The idea was relatively straightforward. The tough fighting in the fall of 2004 had shown that Iraqi units operating with small teams of embedded U.S. advisors performed better than Iraqi units fighting alone. Casey was proposing to expand the teams to every brigade and battalion in the Iraqi army and as many police units as possible. With such close partnership, the Iraqis would progress faster and soon take over the lead in fighting the insurgency. The initial concept was from Abizaid, but he'd also warned Rumsfeld in an earlier e-mail that it would bring significant new risks: U.S. advisors would be living with Iraqi troops in "isolated and exposed places." To make it work, the teams would have to be filled with tough, resourceful soldiers.

Rumsfeld's problem wasn't with the strategy. He was angry at what he considered a grave bureaucratic sin. Casey had shared a version of his plan with the U.S. embassy in Baghdad. His instinct was to work closely with the ambassador and his staff. The ambassador, in turn, had informed the State Department, and somehow Rumsfeld had found out about it. "Please explain how this happens, that the world gets papered with a military proposal from Embassy Baghdad that hasn't been considered or approved at our level, despite the fact that the president has repeatedly said that he wanted to be involved in it," Rumsfeld had written in an e-mail to Casey and Abizaid two days before the videoconference. Whenever Casey opened his mouth Rumsfeld cut him off. "You act like the whole world started with you and Petraeus," he scolded at one point. Casey kept his cool. The best way to handle an angry Rumsfeld was to let him vent.

The defense secretary wasn't much of a counterinsurgency strategist, but he was an expert bureaucratic infighter who wanted to control the flow of information to the president. He didn't want the State Department to see the plan until it was shown to Bush. By that point, it would be too late for Condoleezza Rice and her aides to muck around with it. Working for Rumsfeld was a mixed blessing. He defended his subordinates from meddling by other agencies like an angry pit bull. He was frequently warm, charitable, and funny. But his rabid defense of his bureaucratic turf was also isolating. It would cut Casey off from the growing frustration in the White House and the State Department as violence rose and the president began to lose confidence in his leadership. It also prevented Casey from getting feedback that might have exposed the flaws in his plan.

After barking at Casey, Rumsfeld dropped his objections and arranged for him to brief the president. Casey and a few key aides sat in the secure videoconference room at Al Faw. Abizaid joined in from Qatar. Bush participated from the White House. The average counterinsurgency war lasted between nine and thirteen years, Casey explained to Bush. There was no way that U.S. forces were going to be in Iraq for that long. Therefore they had to train Iraqis to take over by increasing the number of advisory teams. As Iraqi troops took on more responsibility U.S. troops could pull back, reducing the stigma of the American occupation and bolstering the legitimacy of the government.

The president had reservations. The new approach seemed to focus more on shifting the fight to the Iraqis than on defeating the insurgency. "George, we're not playing for a tie. I want to make sure we understand this, don't we?" Bush said. He had grand visions for Iraq. He still wanted to transform it into a model democracy and, in contrast to Rumsfeld, was in no rush to hand it off to a bunch of incompetent Iraqi troops.

Bush's critique not only caught Casey by surprise but stung him. "Mr. President, we are not playing for a tie," Casey shot back with a rare edge to his voice. "I just can't accept that. We are playing to win." He was used to hostile questions from Rumsfeld. But this was different. The president was questioning his commitment. He was, in effect, suggesting that Casey was sending soldiers to their deaths for a strategy that he didn't think would actually win. After the briefing, Abizaid tried to ease the tension. "George, you shouldn't yell at the president," he said half jokingly.

In June Casey flew back to Washington with Abizaid to secure Bush's final approval for his new strategy. The war wasn't going well. Ibrahim al-Jaafari, a physician who spoke so softly that he often seemed to be whispering, had been sworn in as interim prime minister. Casey had hoped that Jaafari, a Shiite, would reach out to rival sects and ethnic groups and unite the country, but so far he was disappointed. "This guy is a political wind sock," he told Abizaid. Violence rose as Sunnis, who felt disenfranchised by the January election, turned to extremists. In May there were a record 142 car bombs. When Casey landed in Washington he was dreading his meeting with Bush. "Goddammit, I just don't feel like I am prepared," he groused to his senior aide.

The president put him at ease. "Thanks for pushing back at me. I appreciate that," Bush said, referring to the tense videoconference. He approved Casey's new strategy. Actually fielding the advisory teams at the heart of the new approach would prove tougher than Casey had anticipated, however. The Army staff in the Pentagon initially balked at finding 2,500 majors, lieutenant colonels, and senior sergeants for the teams. It didn't sound like a lot of extra manpower. But the Pentagon generals complained that to fill the request they would have to strip combat brigades of their leaders. Instead of assigning seasoned officers to the teams, as Abizaid and Casey wanted, the Army would instead rely heavily on inexperienced reservists.

At the White House that day, though, everyone was still hopeful. After the president had signed off on the strategy, Casey updated him on the plans for the latter half of 2005. They were still on track for a constitutional referendum in October 2005 followed by another national election in late December. "You know, Mr. President, George will be gone by then," Rumsfeld interjected, noting that the general's official orders were for only twelve months and expired in August.

The president thought for a minute. "Eisenhower didn't leave the war after a year."

"Eisenhower lived in London," Abizaid playfully shot back from across the table.

"I shouldn't be asking you this . . . ," Bush said. Rumsfeld rose to his feet, stood behind his Iraq commander, and began to chant enthusiastically, "Oh, yes, you should, Mr. President! Yes, you should!"

With Rumsfeld egging him on, Bush asked Casey to stay in Iraq through at least the end of 2005. Casey later got his official orders extending his time for six more months—the first of three such extensions. Three decades earlier Casey's father had been only a few months away from finishing his second tour in Vietnam when he received new orders assigning him to stay in Vietnam and take command of the 1st Cavalry Division. Shortly after he was extended, he died in the helicopter crash. As Casey studied his new orders, he thought of his dad and had a fleeting feeling that he might be killed before he made it home. He didn't mention it to anyone until he left Iraq for good.

✷　✷　✷　✷

Petraeus, meanwhile, had his own Washington problems. In early 2005 Rumsfeld had dispatched a team led by General Gary Luck, a retired former head of U.S. forces in Korea, to look into the effort to rebuild a new army and police force. They arrived in Baghdad convinced that the effort was on the verge of collapse. Petraeus did in fact need help—lots of it. His staff was made up of inexperienced National Guardsmen and whomever he could grab from Sosh and the 101st Airborne Division. His task was massive. But he bristled at the suggestion that he needed a lifeline from Washington. Petraeus had always believed that he could make up for a lack of resources with more effort. War was about will, perseverance, force of personality, and determination. No one possessed those qualities in greater abundance; he'd proven it his entire career. It wasn't in his nature to admit that he was failing. As Jack Galvin had observed twenty years earlier, he never admitted mistakes.

Petraeus led Luck's team through a three-hour briefing. It rapidly turned contentious, with Luck interrupting several times to ask him what he needed to speed the development of the Iraqi forces. Soon the exasperated general was waving his wallet at Petraeus. "Dave, here, take my wallet," he said in his southern drawl. "I am not here to criticize you. I am here to help you."

When that failed, Luck tried a new line of questioning. How many Iraqi battalions would it take to secure Iraq without the United States? The answer, Petraeus said, depended on a host of factors—the enemy's strength, politics, and the quality of the battalion and brigade commanders.

"Come on, Dave! What's the requirement?" asked Lieutenant General Raymond Odierno, another member of Luck's team. Petraeus, his voice tight and angry, repeated his earlier caveats. But Odierno wasn't going to let it go. *What is the requirement?* he demanded again.

After the meeting, Odierno spoke privately to Petraeus. The two generals had sped up the career ladder ahead of their peers and had both commanded divisions in northern Iraq in 2003. Petraeus's 101st Airborne Division was everyone's favorite success story. Odierno's 4th Infantry Division was cited as an example of the overaggressive failed tactics in the early days of the war. The criticism actually had seemed to burnish his reputation with Rumsfeld, who favored a hard-nosed approach. "Look, you need to understand that Washington is impatient," said Odierno, who stood six feet four inches tall and had the body of an offensive lineman. He towered over his much smaller colleague.

"I got it," Petraeus replied. "But there is hardly a Ministry of Defense here. There is hardly a Ministry of the Interior. There is no training and doctrine command." His biggest problem was finding Iraqi commanders who wouldn't abandon their troops in the middle of a firefight. He needed time.

"The best leaders we have found so far are from a jail alumni association," Petraeus told Odierno. He was referring to an unplanned unit that the interim interior minister had created and named the Special Police Commandos. "This is the force that will save Iraq," the minister had boasted to him in the fall of 2004. At first Petraeus had been skeptical; the Iraqis regularly made grand promises that never panned out. When he finally went to see them he'd been impressed. Several hundred commandos, clad in mismatched uniforms and led by tough sergeants, were training at a bombed-out base just beyond the western gate to the Green Zone. Iraqi units typically did a horrible job maintaining their equipment, but the commandos' weapons, scrounged from Saddam-era stockpiles, were clean and well oiled. Petraeus had been knocking his head against a wall for months trying to build a unit like the commandos, with little success. Out of nowhere a seemingly outstanding unit had appeared only a few hundred yards from his headquarters. It was almost too good to be true—a desert mirage.

"How did you pick these guys?" Petraeus asked the commander of the unit, Major General Andan Thavit, who also happened to be the interim interior minister's uncle.

"I knew them all in jail. Every one of us was arrested by Saddam," Thavit replied. He had been a two-star general in Saddam's intelligence service until an unsuccessful 1995 coup attempt landed him on death row. Before his nephew summoned him to Baghdad, the jowly sixty-three-year-old general had been sitting at home. Now he ruled his men with a mixture of fear and charisma. Thavit wore black leather jackets regardless of the weather and chain-smoked. When commandos entered his sparse office, they stamped their right boot, flashed an exaggerated salute, and stood rigidly at attention. He frequently threatened to cut off the testicles of any of his soldiers caught stealing. No one was entirely sure if he was kidding.

Petraeus supplied them with uniforms, ammunition, and a fleet of camouflage-painted Dodge Ram pickups with machine guns bolted to the back. The commandos raced off to fight insurgents. In Mosul, occupying police stations that had been overrun in the November 2004 fighting, they withstood a four-hour barrage that killed twelve commandos but didn't break the unit. Without them, Mosul never would have been able to participate in the January elections, Petraeus said.

The commandos were not perfect soldiers, by any means. They looted constantly. "Every time they'd move from one place to another they'd take a lot of stuff with them. It was just very unprofessional conduct," Petraeus recalled. In early 2005 there were persistent but unproven rumors that they were abusing prisoners. In the spring Petraeus obtained pictures of detainees who had been beaten in the commandos' custody. He was furious. "I know you guys think you know [how to handle Iraqis] better than we do and that a little abuse is accepted," he told Thavit angrily. "It is not acceptable." Thavit promised to stop immediately.

At the time Petraeus had other problems. His command was now responsible for training and equipping more than 100 battalions, the growing commando force, and more than 130,000 regular police. To meet the growing demand he figured he needed to add about 150 U.S. troops to his 550-soldier training outfit. The request, however, languished at Casey's level for months. Finally Petraeus demanded a meeting with Casey's chief of staff, Marine Corps Major General Tim Donovan, who had to sign off on the request before it could be sent to the Pentagon. For the next five hours he and his staff went through all 150 positions in the manning document with Donovan, justifying the need for each one. They jokingly dubbed the marathon session "Operation Breaking of the Will." A few days later, Donovan ran into Petraeus at Al Faw Palace and told him that he was going to have to trim the request a bit more. "Goddammit, chief, you are screwing us," Petraeus yelled, slamming his fist into the wall.

Abizaid had promised Petraeus whatever he needed, but he wasn't getting it. Petraeus didn't directly blame Casey for the struggles he was having finding troops for his staff. After a rocky start, the relationship between the two generals had warmed. Instead he guessed that both Casey and Abizaid were under pressure from Rumsfeld to bring down troop numbers. Even a request for a measly 150 soldiers was going to set off alarms in the Pentagon.

Casey *was* under pressure from Rumsfeld to cut forces, but some of the pressure was also self-generated. He firmly believed that the longer the United States stayed in Iraq, the longer radical groups such as Al Qaeda would pick away at its forces. Sooner or later the attacks would exhaust the patience of the American people. The only way to win was to pare back troop levels and make the Iraqis do more. Casey knew that his subordinate commanders, including Petraeus, weren't going to volunteer to get by with fewer soldiers. Iraq was a "troop sump," he said, meaning there was an almost endless supply of tasks to be done in the country. If he didn't set tight limits, he believed, the force would grow forever.

✷   ✷   ✷   ✷

By the summer of 2005 Iraq's "purple finger moment," in which Iraqis held up ink-stained fingers to celebrate their first election in three decades, had long passed. It was obvious to lower-ranking officers that something was badly wrong. One of the most influential young skeptics was Lieutenant Colonel John Nagl, who returned from a year of tough fighting in Iraq in the fall of 2004 and found that he was something of a celebrity. Nagl's fame came not from battlefield heroics, but from the book on counterinsurgency that he had written while teaching in the Social Sciences Department at West Point. In it, he contrasted the U.S. defeat in Vietnam with the British victory in Malaya in the 1950s against another Communist insurgency. The difference, Nagl argued, was that the British generals saw the folly of using massive force against guerrillas who were often indistinguishable from ordinary villagers. Instead they focused on building local governments, training security forces, and protecting the civilians. In Vietnam, the United States resorted largely to search-and-destroy tactics after they began funneling in large numbers of troops.

Nagl's conclusions about Vietnam were not that different from those Petraeus had reached in his own dissertation a decade earlier. "In these dirty little wars," Nagl wrote, "political and military tasks intertwine, and the objective is more often 'nation building' than the destruction of an enemy army." Nagl's work exemplified George Lincoln's original conception of Sosh as a place that should challenge the Army's conventional wisdom and prepare it intellectually for the rigors of modern warfare. In Iraq, new ideas were coming to an amazing degree from former Sosh professors, including Chiarelli, Petraeus, and Nagl.

When Casey took command in 2004, Nagl had been nine months into his yearlong deployment as the operations officer of a 700-soldier battalion in Khalidiyah, a poor Sunni city near Fallujah made up of block upon block of concrete houses surrounded by high mud walls. If Casey had asked, Nagl would have told him that his unit was losing. His men had minimal understanding of the culture and the centuries-old tribes that dominated the area. The police his battalion trained were routinely murdered, and most residents wanted nothing to do with the Iraqi or U.S. forces. "I don't think we could have picked a more foreign place on earth to fight an insurgency," he confessed.

On his way back to the United States in the fall of 2004 Nagl stopped by Al Faw Palace to see Grant Doty, a friend from Sosh who was working for Casey. He spoke briefly with Petraeus, whom he knew through Sosh connections. No one else had taken the time to talk to one of the Army's most knowledgeable counterinsurgency experts and to hear his take on the war, on what was working in the field and what wasn't. Nagl spent most of 2005 in the Pentagon, where his disillusionment grew. He railed to reporters and whoever else would listen that U.S. units were desperately short of interpreters. Often his battalion had dispatched patrols without any Arabic-speakers. "If soldiers can't interact with the population, all they are doing is trolling for IEDs," he said, using the military acronym for roadside bombs. He barraged Petraeus with e-mails complaining that the Army had no counterinsurgency doctrine and needed to ramp up an effort to write one immediately. And he worried that the military, just as in Vietnam, didn't want to learn how to fight guerrilla wars. "Beware of the majors of Desert Storm," he often said. These were officers who had fought in the 1991 tank battle and refused to believe there was any other type of war. It was the Army equivalent of "Don't trust anybody over thirty."

In northwestern Iraq, Colonel H. R. McMaster, the commander of a 3,500-soldier armored cavalry regiment, was leading his own rebellion in the summer of 2005. McMaster had long been a "water walker," pegged early in his career, like Petraeus and Abizaid, as a future general. He had earned a Silver Star for his battlefield prowess in the Persian Gulf War. The Army's official history of the conflict opened with a vivid description of his tank crew destroying a much larger Iraq formation: "McMaster spotted the tanks. 'Fire, fire sabot,' he yelled as he kicked up his tank's metal seat and dropped inside to look through his thermal imager. His clipped command was a code that automatically launched his three crew mates into a well-rehearsed sequence of individual actions."

After the 1991 war McMaster earned a doctorate in history from the University of North Carolina and wrote an acclaimed book on Vietnam. Relying on recently declassified documents, *Dereliction of Duty* built a damning case that the Vietnam-era generals had caved in to President Lyndon Johnson and Defense Secretary Robert McNamara, backing a war strategy they knew would fail. By the time McMaster was writing, Vietnam was no longer such an open wound, and General Henry Shelton, the chairman of the Joint Chiefs, invited McMaster for breakfast at the Pentagon to talk to the military's top four-stars about his research. Shelton had read the book on the recommendation of his executive officer, David Petraeus, then a colonel.

McMaster went on to work for Abizaid in Kosovo and at U.S. Central Command. Abizaid saw a little bit of himself in the young, intellectually restless officer. McMaster was emotional, stubborn, gracious, wickedly funny, full of boyish enthusiasm, and constantly questioning his commanders, especially in Iraq, where he led the 3rd Armored Cavalry Regiment. "Why did the U.S. military have to retake the same cities from insurgents again and again?" he asked. Why had there been no theater reserve force in the country that could react to a surprise enemy offensive or exploit fleeting opportunities? Why had the enemy been allowed to maintain safe havens? They were legitimate questions, but they also drove his superiors crazy.

"You need to stop thinking strategically," McMaster's brigadier general boss in Mosul warned him in the summer of 2005. It was Army-speak for "Shut the hell up, Colonel, and worry about your little piece of the war." His bosses sometimes had a point.

McMaster's piece of the war was Tal Afar, a city of about a quarter million residents set on an ancient smuggling route near the Syrian border.

Foreign fighters linked to Al Qaeda were using it as a staging area before heading off to Baghdad and Mosul. On the eve of an assault by McMaster's regiment, General Casey flew in to hear his plan for retaking the city.

It was a tense time. In the weeks leading up to the operation, McMaster had asked for an extra battalion of about 800 soldiers to help clear the city's southern district, a warren of muddy streets and alleys too narrow for the regiment's tanks. He had expected a quick answer. After all, the attack into the city was the only major operation planned during the summer of 2005, and Tal Afar was key terrain for Al Qaeda. Instead he got no response.

Now the operation was days away and McMaster knew he was going to have to get by with fewer troops. He told Casey that he was going to position his forces in a sector adjacent to the troublesome southern district and try to draw the enemy fighters out so that they could be more easily killed. He didn't mention the memos he'd written requesting the extra soldiers. It was too late to get them there before the attack was scheduled to kick off, anyway.

When the briefing was done the two officers hopped into an SUV for the short ride back to the airstrip where Casey's plane was waiting. The regimental command post on the outskirts of Tal Afar was a big plywood building that looked like a beached ark. There was an old Saddam-era airstrip and several boxy brick buildings nearby. A single ribbon of blacktop led the five miles into the city. As they bumped down the rutted road toward the airfield, Casey told McMaster that he needed another battalion for his attack. After hearing the plan, Casey had reached the same conclusion as McMaster. The extra soldiers would drive out the insurgents in the densely packed southern portion of the city that had McMaster so worried. As he spoke, McMaster realized that his memos asking for more troops had been forwarded to Baghdad but had never made it up the chain of command to Casey.

Years later Casey would concede that such incidents were fairly common, and he suggested that his subordinate generals' reluctance to ask for additional troops grew out of the Army's can-do culture. "It's our nature to get the job done with what we have," he said. "And I was up against that all the time." An extra infantry battalion was flown in to help McMaster hold the city but didn't arrive in time for the invasion.

McMaster saw a bigger problem. President Bush wanted to transform Iraq into a model democracy for the Middle East and an ally in the war on terror. Realizing those lofty goals demanded a massive commitment of troops, money, and civilian expertise. But the Pentagon was moving in a different direction. Rumsfeld was consumed by a desire to leave. In Baghdad the military's strategy was focused on handing over the fight to Iraqis.

In his mission statement for his regiment, McMaster laid out his main objective as defeating the enemy and setting "conditions for economic and political development." His superiors asked him if he was setting a higher standard for his area than he had been given. To McMaster the conclusion was inescapable: the United States was not fully committed to winning. "We're managing this war, not fighting it," he complained.

✳   ✳   ✳   ✳

In the summer of 2005, Casey summoned Colonel Bill Hix to his office. He had a special mission for Hix: take one month and visit as many U.S. brigades and battalions as possible, then write a report grading the war effort. The two had forged an unusual relationship for a colonel and a four-star general. Hix, the son of a CIA operative, had spent most of his career in the Special Forces and had advised the Philippine military in its fight against Islamic guerrillas. Among the Americans in the palace, the bald, broad-shouldered colonel was the closest thing Casey could find to a counterinsurgency expert. He acted almost as a tutor, schooling Casey on a form of warfare he didn't really understand. As Casey grew more comfortable, Hix evolved into a trusted advisor.

In Army terms, Hix was a "fireproof colonel." He'd put in enough time to earn his full retirement pension and knew he was never going to make general. He served at his own pleasure and had nothing to lose. He and Casey frequently disagreed, particularly on the question of more troops, which Hix favored. "When I think I need more troops I will ask for them," Casey would tell Hix. But Casey liked his candor.

Most of Hix's time was spent in meetings or in his cubicle, where he worked fourteen-hour days, cranking out slides and writing briefing papers for Casey and the Pentagon. Sometimes Casey brought him along when he went out to meet units. But the trips provided only fleeting glimpses of Iraq. By the summer of 2005 Hix was desperate to get out of the palace and see the real war.

To accompany Hix on his inspection tour, he drafted Kalev Sepp, a retired Special Forces officer who had fought in El Salvador, earned a history doctorate from Harvard, and taught classes in guerrilla war at the Naval Postgraduate School. Sepp had arrived a few days earlier at Hix's invitation to deliver a series of lectures to Casey's staff on counterinsurgency operations. As soon as he learned about the study, Hix had dashed back to Sepp's cubicle. His friend wasn't there, so Hix scribbled a quick message on a Post-it note. "You owe me *big*, Bill," it read.

The two visited thirty-one different units and evaluated them using a checklist of counterinsurgency best practices developed by Sepp. Successful armies isolated the civilian population from the enemy by providing security, stable government, a strong police force, and decent jobs. They built sophisticated intelligence networks, used the minimum amount of force necessary in raids, and offered amnesty and rehabilitation to former insurgents.

Hix and Sepp didn't want the units to feel as though they were being graded. So they tended to ask the field commanders open-ended questions: What were their priorities? What were their biggest concerns? What was keeping them from succeeding? Their fifteen-page report reached a dire conclusion: most of the U.S. units that they visited were ineffective. In a handful of cases brigade and battalion commanders didn't understand how to defeat an insurgency. One commander in restive Anbar Province strode into a meeting with them, lit a cigar, and propped his feet on his desk. "We got three today," he told them proudly. For him it was all about the body count.

Even if units in the field did everything right, they still didn't have the manpower they needed to win. There weren't enough U.S. and Iraqi troops in the country to drive insurgents from their safe havens and prevent them from returning, the report found, echoing McMaster's frequent complaint. The advisory teams were too small and inexperienced.

But the biggest shortcoming, the report found, was the lack of political and economic progress in the country. On those rare occasions when the government did make its presence felt outside of the Green Zone it displayed a pro-Shiite sectarian agenda that fueled the insurgency. If Casey wanted to fix the foundering war effort, he had to expand beyond training Iraqi troops and take on political and economic development in the country. Technically, the U.S. embassy was responsible for these areas. But the embassy was sorely lacking in money and manpower. Smart commanders tried to fill the gap, but they didn't have the expertise to build local governments and jump-start the economy.

Casey needed control of all aspects of the counterinsurgency campaign, Hix and Sepp argued. There was a historical precedent for the power grab. In the latter days of the Vietnam War the United States placed the economic and political development in the country under the control of General Creighton Abrams, who took over from William Westmoreland. Some historians maintained that Abrams's "one war" approach had produced positive results by the early 1970s. The shift had just taken place too late—after the American people and Congress had given up on the war.

In early September Hix and Sepp described their report's findings for Casey and his senior staff. Sepp knew that Casey's father and Creighton Abrams had been friends in Vietnam, and decided to take a chance by playing up the personal connection. "Sir, it is time to do what your father's friend Creighton Abrams did and merge the civil and military effort in Iraq under a single director, which would be you," he said. Casey set his hands on the conference table in front of him, tilted his head, and stared off into the distance. He didn't say anything.

Hix warned that the U.S. military could build Army and police forces forever, but without economic and political progress they would eventually crumble. "All these Army and police forces are going to be like Wile E. Coyote going off a cliff without an economic and political foundation underneath them," he said. Hix then turned up the pressure. He understood that governance and economics were the State Department's turf. But if the United States lost, the blame wouldn't fall on the secretary of state or the ambassador. It would fall on Casey. Only the Pentagon had the half-trillion-dollar-a-year budget and the manpower to deliver. "This is your war," he told his boss.

A few days later Casey flew with his two advisors to central command headquarters in Qatar so that they could give Abizaid and his staff the same pitch. Abizaid had just come from watching a video shot by French journalists that showed insurgents setting up a roadside bomb as bystanders and police applauded. As long as U.S. troops were in Iraqi neighborhoods, the violence would continue, he believed. He listened intently to Hix.

"So you are telling me that we have a total absence of effective government at the local level in Iraq?" Abizaid asked.

"Sir, in some cases it's worse than just an absence," Hix replied. The Shiite-dominated government was targeting Sunnis and driving them into the insurgent ranks. Fixing the problem would require about 10,000 additional troops who would report to Casey and focus solely on economic development, infrastructure repair, and local governance. In Vietnam, a slightly smaller country, Abrams had used a force of about 7,000 soldiers and aid workers.

Casey sent the report to Rumsfeld, but he and Abizaid decided that asking for control of the economic and political aspects of the war effort wasn't going to work. "I made the judgment that it was going to take an awful lot of energy to get it done and the likelihood of success was low," Casey recalled. At the time the State Department was proposing building Provincial Reconstruction Teams to conduct development projects in each of the eighteen provinces. The effort consisted of only a few hundred Foreign Service officers and lacked the money to make a real difference. Still, Casey thought that the civilian-led teams were a reasonable first step. At least the State Department was trying. The answer was to make State do more, not to do everything himself.

Casey did adopt Hix's recommendation to train incoming officers in the principles of counterinsurgency. He didn't need to fight with Washington for permission to do it and it didn't take very many extra troops. The one-week immersion course was a significant step forward for an Army that was receiving virtually no counterinsurgency training back in the United States. One officer cycling through an early class said that his unit's preparation for Iraq had consisted of "kick in the door, two in the chest," recalled Sepp. Casey's classes preached the importance of using measured force to avoid alienating the Iraqi people and stressed the importance of mentoring Iraqi forces. Soldiers also received some instruction in Iraqi culture. Ideally such training would have occurred back in the United States, where there was more time. But the institutional Army, strained by the heavy pace of deployments, was slow to adapt. "Because the Army won't change itself, I am going to change it here in Iraq," Casey had said. The first U.S. officers began passing through the school, which Casey playfully dubbed the "Hix Academy," in November 2005.

When he left Iraq, Hix went to work in the Pentagon, where his frustration grew. In Washington, the Joint Staff, the State Department, and the Bush administration were willing to do just enough to prolong the war, he believed, but not enough to prevail. Their outlook on the war was "eerily similar to the escalatory minimalist approach" that had failed so miserably in Vietnam, Hix wrote in an e-mail to Casey in early 2006. "We need to rededicate ourselves to winning the war," he added.

His critique was almost identical to McMaster's in Tal Afar. Hix, however, had played a major role in helping Casey develop his strategy for Iraq, which focused on pushing Iraqis to take the lead in the fight, and he felt a measure of responsibility for its shortcomings. In retrospect he said that he was too quick to buy into a bit of decades-old wisdom from British colonel T. E. Lawrence that became a mantra for U.S. troops throughout Iraq in 2005 and 2006. "Do not try to do too much with your own hands," Lawrence of Arabia had counseled. "Better the Arabs do it tolerably than you do it perfectly. It is their war, and you are to help them, not win it for them." By late 2005, Lawrence's maxim was plastered on the wall of command posts throughout Iraq as if it were a religious commandment.

But Lawrence had been fighting a completely different type of war than the Americans were. He and his tribal militias were trying to drive out the occupying Turkish army with hit-and-run attacks, not govern a country. "Lawrence was the insurgent," Hix concluded. "His insights are useful, but we were wrong to treat them as canon law."

✯　✯　✯　✯

Casey's small plane touched down on the narrow landing strip outside Tal Afar, where a car was waiting to ferry him the short distance to McMaster's makeshift plywood headquarters. After a year in combat, McMaster's regiment was heading home. Casey took a seat at a table piled high with muffins, coffee, and sodas while McMaster delivered what he thought was a routine briefing on his pullout plans.

"Publish the orders," Casey said suddenly as he rose to his feet. He pulled out a Bronze Star and pinned it to McMaster's tan uniform. The surprise visit was an honor he bestowed on only a handful of his best field commanders. McMaster's regiment had won praise for its successes. Like Petraeus, McMaster had had the good sense to make sure he had plenty of reporters around to document his troops' triumphs.

When his soldiers had arrived four months earlier they'd found an all-out sectarian war. Gangs of Sunni religious extremists kidnapped Shiites and left their headless corpses on the city's streets. The city's terrified police force, made up entirely of Shiites, holed up in the ruins of a sixteenth-century Ottoman castle in the city's center, sending out small teams to conduct reprisal attacks on mostly innocent Sunnis.

McMaster's first priority was to stop the killing. At a time when many commanders were pulling back from cities and handing over their sectors to Iraqi forces, he established twenty-nine small outposts in an effort to separate the feuding groups. He replaced both the city's pro-insurgent Sunni mayor and its Shiite police chief with outsiders from nearby Mosul. Lastly, he closely controlled the Iraqi army and police forces in the city. With his area on the verge of civil war, McMaster believed that only an outside force could mediate between warring Sunnis and Shiites.

Casey and Abizaid had long believed that U.S. forces in Iraqi cities fueled resentment over the occupation, and emphasized that their top priority should be to build up Iraqi forces. McMaster insisted that only American troops could stop the killing. In sharply worded assessments, he catalogued the Iraqis' flaws. Local Sunnis were terrified of the abusive Shiite police commandos sent from Baghdad. The Iraqi troops were incapable of standing up to brutal Sunni insurgents. They couldn't feed themselves without U.S. help or repair broken equipment. When one of their soldiers was killed by insurgents, the unit wasn't even able to ship the body home. Instead the battalion commander ordered his men to put the decomposing corpse in a room with the air-conditioning turned on full blast. In a scene reminiscent of a Faulkner novel, the Iraqis then passed a hat hoping to collect cab fare for the 500-mile trip to the dead soldier's family home in Basra. Eventually McMaster paid the fare.

U.S. advisors complained that McMaster didn't give their Iraqis a chance. "The Iraqi division commander in Tal Afar was really no longer the division commander," Colonel Doug Shipman told an Army historian. "He was now taking very direct orders from a colonel in the American Army." In Baghdad, the U.S. one-star in charge of the advisory program told McMaster that he didn't understand Casey's strategy, which emphasized training Iraqis and taking a step back so that they could handle the fight. McMaster testily dismissed the criticism. "It's unclear to me how a higher degree of passivity would advance our mission," he said.

After Casey pinned on McMaster's Bronze Star, the two walked down a narrow hallway and ducked into McMaster's windowless office. Casey knew there was tension between McMaster and some of the officers above him. He told McMaster that he was an extremely talented officer who had a better sense for the war's complexities than just about any other commander. But he needed to listen more and be willing to take no for an answer, especially when it came from his superiors. The two officers were polar opposites. McMaster, passionate and intense, was a risk taker who always craved a good argument. Casey tried to be a team player and searched for consensus.

By late 2005, McMaster's approach of moving U.S. troops into Iraqi cities and safeguarding citizens was starting to gain notice in Washington, where it had caught the eye of Phil Zelikow, a top advisor to Secretary of State Condoleezza Rice. To sell the strategy as a potential model for the rest of Iraq, Zelikow decided he needed to come up with a pithy phrase that described it. He settled on "clear, hold, and build," a play on General Creighton Abrams's "clear and hold" strategy in Vietnam. U.S. and Iraqi troops would clear insurgents from an area. Instead of leaving, they would stay behind, as McMaster's troops had done, establishing small outposts to protect the people. Lastly, they would rebuild the government and infrastructure.

In late October, Secretary Rice unveiled the concept in testimony to

Congress and Rumsfeld hit the roof, insisting that the term made no sense. "It is the Iraqis' country. They've got 28 million people there. They are clearing; they are holding; they are building. They're going to be the ones doing the reconstruction in that country," he railed to reporters.

Casey felt betrayed as well. When Rice next visited Iraq he pulled her aside. "Madam Secretary, what's clear, hold, and build?" he asked.

"That's your strategy, George," she said.

"Well, if it's my strategy, don't you think it would have been appropriate for someone to ask me about it?" Casey replied.

Later that day, he confronted Zelikow, whom he had hosted in Iraq a few months earlier. Casey didn't explicitly object to the "clear, hold, and build" phrase, though he agreed with Rumsfeld that the priority needed to be on building up the Iraqis to take the leading role. He was most upset that Zelikow hadn't sought him out to discuss the idea before he and Rice took it public. "This is bullshit. It is personal. You came here and I opened the books to you. I gave you free access to everything, and you don't have the courtesy to call me and tell me what you are doing," he said. In fact, Rumsfeld's insistence that the Defense Department dominate the strategy debate and his refusal to listen to outside critics had made such cooperation almost impossible.

With Iraq collapsing into civil war, President Bush cited McMaster's approach as proof that after "much trial and error" and many bloody setbacks, the United States had finally found a winning strategy. An influential *New Yorker* article described McMaster and his troops as "rebels against an incoherent strategy." By that point, McMaster's regiment was home; U.S. troop levels in Tal Afar had been cut by more than half, and the security in the city was starting to deteriorate.

$$\star \quad \star \quad \star \quad \star$$

Baghdad
November 2005

"I understand you are looking for a kidnapped boy," an Iraqi colonel whispered to Brigadier General Karl Horst as they walked out of a routine meeting inside the Interior Ministry. "You need to go to this location." He quietly pressed a piece of torn paper into the American officer's hand. Horst, one of two assistant commanders in Baghdad, had been looking for the fifteen-year-old for several days, ever since the boy's distraught parents told him that their son had been abducted by a Shiite militia with ties to the Interior Ministry. The scribbled note was his first lead.

The location listed on the colonel's note was a three-story concrete building near the Green Zone, known as the Jadiriyah bunker. When Horst arrived there, a dozen police officers in camouflage uniforms blocked the entrance. He told them to let him pass. They refused. After an extended argument and a call to the interior minister, an Iraqi general showed up and agreed to take him on a quick tour of the facility.

For the next fifteen minutes they wandered up and down the same empty halls and stairwells. Horst was furious. "I want to see the prisoners," he demanded.

"We're getting there," the general replied.

Down a dark hallway, he smelled a pungent odor coming from behind two locked double doors and ordered the jailers to open them. "The man who has the keys is gone for the day," the general replied. Horst threatened to break open the lock with a sledgehammer, and the guards quickly produced the missing key. Inside the six-foot-by-twelve-foot room were a dozen blindfolded inmates. One of the prisoners began nodding toward a second set of locked doors at the back of the small, windowless room.

As the door opened, Horst was hit by an overpowering smell of dirty bodies, urine, rotten food, and human feces that made him retch. One hundred fifty-six prisoners—all but three of them Sunnis—were sitting in lines with their legs crossed. The guards stepped outside, and the prisoners began lifting up their shirts to show bloody whip marks where they had been beaten. Many of them had been held in the building for months. At least sixteen inmates had died there.

The guards identified themselves as part of an off-the-books unit within the Interior Ministry that patrolled largely Sunni neighborhoods of western Baghdad. "They'd run missions at night, gather up Sunnis, torture and kill them," Horst recalled. Aside from a small cartoon-covered notebook with names written inside it, there were no records in the building.

None of the Sunnis in the torture facility had been charged with a crime. There was also no sign of the fifteen-year-old boy. The United States evacuated two dozen emaciated prisoners to a military hospital. Horst snapped some pictures and stuffed the worst-looking torture implements—whips, handcuffs, a bloody metal pole, and a mace—into a box as evidence. During his nine months in Baghdad, Horst had come to believe that the Shiite-dominated police were waging a coordinated campaign to clear Sunnis out of the capital's mixed neighborhoods. Now he had proof.

Petraeus had left Iraq about two months prior to the discovery of the prison bunker to take command of the Army's Combined Arms Center at Fort Leavenworth. Before he was assigned there he'd been told that the Pentagon brass were considering him for three slots: the Leavenworth position, a top slot on the Joint Chiefs staff, and an assignment as the superintendent at the U.S. Military Academy. The superintendent job was a terminal three-star position, meaning that if Petraeus was put there, he could never get promoted again. In early 2005, Army secretary Fran Harvey had casually mentioned to Colonel Mike Meese, the Sosh department head, that Petraeus might be headed to West Point. Meese, whose position in Sosh gave him more influence than the average colonel, flipped. "Sir, that is the stupidest thing I have ever heard," he said, arguing that it would take the talented general permanently out of the war.

Petraeus was given the Leavenworth slot. He'd been replaced in Iraq by Lieutenant General Martin Dempsey, a smart and affable officer who had led the U.S. division in Baghdad in 2003. Before Petraeus departed, he'd heard rumors that Shiite militias were infiltrating the Special Police Commando force that he had spotted training on the edge of the Green Zone in late 2004 and had enthusiastically backed. The first hints of a problem came when General Thavit, the hard-nosed Sunni who had founded the group, was shunted aside by the Shiite-dominated government in the spring of 2005. Over the course of the summer the commando force grew rapidly and complaints about them multiplied. In Tal Afar, McMaster's regiment snapped pictures of the police commandos' abuses and sought their permanent removal from the sector. Hix and Sepp's report to Casey in August 2005 noted that several U.S. officers had expressed concern about the Shiite force.

Petraeus successfully pushed to have one police commando commander removed and cut off U.S. support to the Interior Ministry's major
crimes unit when its troops were caught abusing prisoners. But it was
tough to get hard evidence of widely rumored atrocities because there
weren't enough advisory teams. The ten-man teams, each of which was assigned to a 500-man Iraqi unit, simply couldn't keep eyes on the Iraqis
twenty-four hours a day. "You had such limited means to put hands
on [the commandos] and the need was so urgent to get them out there,"
Petraeus recalled.

Horst had been worried about the Shiite police forces since early summer, when he had first mentioned his concerns to Casey. He thought that
sectarian violence and militia infiltration of the police were a bigger problem than Al Qaeda extremists coming into the country from Syria. "That's
not the read that I am getting from my guys, Karl," Casey had told him.
Like Petraeus, Casey had heard the rumors of Shiite militias taking over the
police but could never nail them down. "We were always trying to figure
out what the heck was really going on there," he recalled.

Horst believed the prison bunker proved that his earlier instincts had
been right. A few hours after the last Sunnis had been taken from the facility he met with Casey and gave him the photographs from the prison
bunker along with the box of torture implements. "Sir, this is a manifesta-
tion of the sectarian problem that we have been trying to describe," he said.

Casey took off his glasses and rested them on the top of his head as he
stared at Horst's pictures. He rubbed his eyes with both hands, something
he did only when he was thinking hard or worried. He'd seen this problem
coming. In an e-mail to a senior U.S. embassy official nine months earlier,
he'd outlined the potential pitfalls of his strategy to shift the fight to the security forces. One of the biggest was that the government would "politicize
the security ministries, the military and the police forces, heightening
Sunni anxieties." Now Casey was staring at a brown cardboard box of torture implements that suggested his greatest fear was being realized.

The discovery couldn't have come at a worse time. The second round
of elections was set for December 30, just five weeks away. The Sunnis had
boycotted the first vote in January 2005, and Casey was working to convince Sunni leaders to go to the polls in December. He reasoned that if the

Sunnis took part in the balloting and won a place in the new government, the fighting might die down some.

He promised Horst that he'd press Prime Minister Ibrahim al-Jaafari to investigate what had happened at the bunker. He also wanted to assign an American team to probe whether the interior minister knew about the abuse. Horst's body was coursing with adrenaline as he walked out of Casey's small Green Zone office. He found Casey hard to read and wondered if he understood the severity of the problem. The secret prison proved that the U.S. strategy wasn't working, Horst thought. The military was essentially handing power to a sectarian government and suspect militias. It was time, he believed, to try something different.

CHAPTER ELEVEN

"What Would You Do, Lieutenant?"

Green Zone, Baghdad
November 2005

Just before nine in the morning a convoy of Chevy Suburbans pulled up at the Adnan Palace, an ugly pyramid-shaped building on the western edge of the Green Zone. Casey clambered out of one vehicle along with several aides and diplomats, pushed through the towering wooden doors, and headed up the marble staircase to the second floor where Bayan Jabr, the interior minister, was waiting. A small man with a closely cropped salt-and-pepper beard who had spent years in exile during Saddam Hussein's rule, Jabr now presided over a force that included some 135,000 local police and 30,000 national police commandos. He and Casey settled into a pair of cushioned armchairs. Like other government officials, Jabr normally didn't start working until much later in the day, but Casey had wanted to see him first thing.

"This is what we found," Casey said, pointing at a cardboard box that his aide had brought to the meeting and placed on the low coffee table in front of them. It was the same container Karl Horst had shown Casey the day before, with the whips, shackles, and other torture devices that his men had removed from the Jadiriyah bunker. Sticking out of the top was a fear-some-looking barbed club. Jabr recoiled and then let out a resigned sigh. "Iraqis," he muttered, as if such behavior was a national trait. Casey handed him photographs of the emaciated, broken men who had emerged from the dank prison. He wanted no misunderstanding. The secret prison was in an Interior Ministry building less than a mile from his office and guarded by men on Jabr's payroll. The only possible conclusion, Casey said in a level but firm voice, was that Jabr himself or the people around him had known about the facility and had condoned it.

With his French-cuff shirts and passable English, Jabr was one of the smoother members of the cabinet. He knew nothing about this, he sput-tered. He was far removed from such sordid matters. Many of the guards had trained under Saddam Hussein, when all prisoners were treated this way. What did Casey expect? "We will have an investigation," he said. The meeting lasted no more than fifteen tense minutes. By the time Jabr ap-peared before the press later to announce the joint Iraqi-U.S. investigation of the prison, the minister had recovered his composure. Most of the pris-oners had been foreign terrorists, he told disbelieving Western reporters, holding up several passports. "Nobody was beheaded or killed." It had been worse under Saddam.

Casey found Jabr hard to believe, too. After returning to his office, he ordered a secret investigation to assess whether the minister had known about the prison. Though it was never acknowledged publicly, U.S. and British intelligence eavesdropped on the top levels of the government, in-tercepting their cell phones and text messages. When the secret report came back a few weeks later, there was no definitive proof linking Jabr to the torture operation. But Casey was convinced that he at least had known about it. The bunker was run, the United States believed, by a relative of Jabr's, known as Engineer Ahmed, who was often seen around Adnan Palace. The United States wanted to use the Jadiriyah incident to force per-sonnel changes at the Interior Ministry, starting with Jabr. When Casey and U.S. ambassador Zalmay Khalilzad presented Prime Minister Ibrahim al-Jaafari with the classified report a few weeks later, the subject only seemed to make him weary. "He just said, 'Okay. I'll look at this,' " Casey recalled. He and Khalilzad talked about whether they should try to force the prime minister to do something by giving him a deadline to take action or calling a press conference to further expose the abuses in the ministry. Casey decided it was the ambassador's call. "As a military guy, I didn't feel like I ought to dictate to the prime minister," he explained. Eventually the subject of Jadiriyah was dropped. No one important was fired, and Jabr remained in senior government posts.

There were more episodes like this one the longer Casey remained in command, moments that raised fundamental questions about the course the United States was embarked upon in Iraq. If the Interior Ministry had been infiltrated by Shiite militias that abused Sunnis and was headed by a minister who denied the evidence, how could the United States proceed with its plans to place it in charge of security? Wasn't that a path to failure? Casey wasn't blind to these and other contradictions. He had been in command for nearly eighteen months, longer than any other senior American, military or civilian, and knew better than most the flaws at the core of the U.S. effort. Not that Casey doubted the course he was on. He was in many ways the prototypical officer, curious and thoughtful, open to new information and ready to adjust—but usually at the margins, enough to assure himself that whatever problems existed were being addressed, if not entirely resolved. The meetings at Adnan Palace and with the prime minister were good examples. He wasn't going to let the incident pass, but he wasn't going to provoke a showdown, either. It wasn't his job. This was a sovereign country, and it was up to the ambassador to handle the prime minister and major political issues, not him. Besides, he told himself, the last round of national elections was only a few weeks away. The next government would be better.

Casey had arrived in Iraq determined to keep his goals limited, not to take on tasks beyond the military's purview and ability. It was the same mind-set that the Army had adopted during the 1990s peacekeeping missions in an attempt to avoid another Vietnam-like quagmire, which had destroyed the force. The longer he remained in Baghdad the more he became convinced of this logic. Military power could drive down the violence and buy time to build a government. But the military couldn't force the Iraqis to get along with each other; it couldn't win the war. There were big downsides to expanding the military's role. Asking the Army to do more, he believed, risked breaking the institution to which he had dedicated his life and cared for deeply.

By early 2006, however, people who mattered were beginning to doubt him and the strategy. In November, Senator John McCain went public with his criticism in a major speech at the American Enterprise Institute, a conservative think tank a few blocks from the White House. The lunchtime audience overflowed into the hallways, straining to catch every word from the former prisoner of war who would shortly announce his candidacy for the presidency. "There is an undeniable sense that things are slipping," he said, reciting the worrisome trends in Iraq. He was careful not to blame the White House or even Rumsfeld, whom he privately considered a disaster. Instead the former Navy pilot aimed his remarks at the military men in Baghdad. U.S. commanders had been slow to adopt "a true counterinsurgency strategy" that emphasized protecting the population and holding on to areas cleared of insurgents, he said. Wrongheaded plans were afoot to reduce troop levels and hand off the mission as quickly as possible to the Iraqi army and police. "Instead of drawing down, we should be ramping up," he declared, and instead of rotating its generals after one-year tours, the Pentagon should keep the best of them in Iraq, mentioning Petraeus, Chiarelli, and others. "We need these commanders and their hard-won experience to stay in place." He didn't praise or even mention Casey. That was the way a mugging was done in Washington.

★ ★ ★ ★

Petraeus was about as far from the war as a soldier could get. When he first learned that he had been chosen to head the Combined Arms Center at Fort Leavenworth, Kansas, he was disappointed. He wasn't entirely sure what his new command even did. Digging into it on the Internet, he learned that he'd have responsibility for running the Army's nationwide network of training centers and schools. He would also oversee the drafting of Army doctrine. Gradually Petraeus's enthusiasm built.

Every couple of days Petraeus would regale Colonel J. R. Martin, his former West Point classmate, with some new aspect of the job that had piqued his intellect. Martin had a more immediate worry: "I was concerned that he wouldn't be able to get promoted out of it," he recalled.

Even among Petraeus's clique of supporters, the orders sending him to the Kansas outpost were seen as a sign that the higher brass thought that the ambitious general, after almost thirty months in Iraq, needed a good rest— or that the Army needed a rest from him.

On a crisp October afternoon, Petraeus took command at Fort Leaven-worth from Lieutenant General William Wallace. When Wallace had been sent to Kansas in mid-2003, it was widely seen as punishment, meted out by Rumsfeld, after the general confessed to a reporter that the United States hadn't anticipated the waves of crazed Saddam Fedayeen guerrillas that harassed U.S. troops on their initial drive to Baghdad. "The enemy we're fighting is a bit different from the one we war-gamed against," he'd said. At Leavenworth, Wallace hadn't made big changes. Petraeus wasted no time in demonstrating that he had an altogether different approach to the job. After an honor guard fired the traditional fifteen-gun salute, a sergeant handed Petraeus a gleaming brass shell casing from the barrage. "I don't know how you got it polished up so quickly," he said, fingering the spent cartridge, "but you clearly know how I like to operate."

Far from the battlefields of Iraq—where the war was going from bad to much worse—the bright and ambitious general began plotting an insur-gency of his own, one aimed at changing his service. Like any good guer-rilla, Petraeus chose to attack a spot that was poorly defended: the Army's counterinsurgency doctrine. By 2005 the doctrine hadn't been revised in more than a quarter of a century; it was a dusty document that few even bothered to read.

A year earlier, Wallace, whose first assignment in the Army had been as an advisor to the South Vietnamese army, had assigned a lieutenant colonel who had never laid eyes on Iraq to rewrite the document. The over-whelmed officer labored in almost complete obscurity. In a matter of days, the new commanding general made rewriting the counterinsurgency doc-trine his top priority. Doctrine provides an intellectual framework for how to fight different kinds of wars. Often it is written to reflect conventional Army wisdom. In rare instances, new doctrine has driven major changes in the Army. In the early 1980s the Army unveiled the AirLand Battle Doctrine, a recipe for defeating much larger Soviet armor formations. It called on commanders to strike ninety miles behind the front lines with

helicopters and artillery, using speed, cunning, and intuition to surprise the more mechanistic Soviets. The doctrine, which drove the Army
for two decades, was an explicit rejection of Defense Secretary Robert
McNamara's rigid, measurement-focused approach to war.

Petraeus wanted his counterinsurgency doctrine to have the same impact as AirLand Battle. At the time, he had a couple of big strikes against
him. One was Fort Leavenworth itself. Even by Army standards, the base
is in the middle of nowhere. A nineteenth-century frontier fort located on
the high bluffs overlooking the Missouri River, an hour's drive from
Kansas City, it is probably best known as the site of an old limestone
prison. It doesn't get much attention from Washington except when a
high-profile inmate arrives in leg irons. Leavenworth is also home to the
Army's staff college, where young, rising officers learn to do war planning.
The post's red brick houses, lecture halls, and softball fields make it feel
more like a tweedy midwestern liberal arts campus than an Army base.
Petraeus had spent a year there in 1982—an uneventful sojourn, except
that he graduated first in his class. He hadn't been back since.

The second major handicap Petraeus faced was that doctrine is hardly
an exciting topic. He asked Conrad Crane, a classmate of his from West
Point who had written extensively about counterinsurgency and taught
history at the Army War College, to oversee a large team that was going to
rewrite the new doctrine. Petraeus enlisted a number of high-profile Washington figures, both military and civilian. Among those included was Eliot
Cohen, a Johns Hopkins professor who had been a critic of the Bush administration's handling of the war and would go on to serve in the influential position of counselor to Secretary of State Condoleezza Rice. He also
called on now Lieutenant Colonel John Nagl, the Rhodes scholar and Sosh
alum whose book on Vietnam and Malaya had made him a minor celebrity,
appearing on the cover of the *New York Times Magazine*. In early 2006,
Nagl was working in the Pentagon, where he was growing increasingly disillusioned with the war effort.

Finally Petraeus called a friend who had served in the Clinton administration, Sarah Sewall, who was running Harvard University's Carr Center
for Human Rights. He'd met her in the early 1990s when he was doing his
research project on the U.S. intervention in Haiti. The center agreed to

cosponsor a Fort Leavenworth conference to provide suggestions for improving the new doctrine's first draft. Petraeus made sure the conference received the proper attention, flying in congressional staffers, journalists, and a bevy of political scientists, human rights advocates, and military historians.

He held court before them for two days. At a dinner on the first night, he unveiled a recent article he'd written for *Military Review* on the fourteen most important things he'd learned from soldiering in Iraq. The observations weren't especially novel, but the crowd of counterinsurgency experts and Washington insiders was adoring. The next day the participants set to work on revising the first draft of the doctrine. It was pathbreaking.

For decades, the American way of war had been to bludgeon the enemy so thoroughly with heavy firepower that he would realize he had no chance and submit quickly. In this way, the Army hoped to avoid drawnout conflicts like Vietnam that sapped both the military's willingness to fight and the support of the public at home. This approach was the essence of the so-called Powell Doctrine, named after General Colin Powell when he was chairman of the Joint Chiefs during the 1991 Gulf War. As he first had done twenty years earlier in his dissertation, Petraeus took direct aim at Powell's tenet that the country could simply choose not to fight in messy guerrilla wars. "Most enemies of the United States . . . know they cannot compete with U.S. forces" in a conventional war, the 453-page manual began. "Instead they try to exhaust U.S. national will, aiming to win by undermining and outlasting public support."

The most radical aspect of the manual was its insistence that the primary focus in counterinsurgency wars should be on protecting the civilian population and not on killing the enemy. It made this point in a series of Zen-like warnings dubbed the "paradoxes of counterinsurgency."

"Sometimes, the more force is used, the less effective it is," one of the Powell Doctrine–defying precepts maintained. And so it went, point after point: "Sometimes, doing nothing is the best reaction." "Some of the best weapons for counterinsurgents do not shoot."

Petraeus's manual also attacked an idea that had become gospel in the Army during the 1990s peacekeeping missions—that protecting the force was of paramount importance in low-intensity wars. The manual insisted that in counterinsurgency wars soldiers had to assume greater risks in order to distinguish the enemy from the innocents, safeguard the population, and in the end achieve greater safety. "The more you protect the force, the less secure you may be," the doctrine warned.

The new manual received lavish press coverage engineered by Petraeus, who acted as his own publicist. Most generals keep journalists at arm's length, believing the surest way to stunt their careers is to appear to be grandstanding in the press. Petraeus was different. He courted journalists with the same intensity he brought to every task, remembering their names and returning their e-mails at all hours. Thanks to Petraeus's finely tuned public relations sense, stories about his new doctrine and the brain trust that developed it were featured on the front pages of the *Wall Street Journal,* the *New York Times,* the *Los Angeles Times,* and the *Washington Post.* The doctrine's authors even made an appearance on *Charlie Rose,* and Lieutenant Colonel Nagl had a seven-minute sit-down with comedian Jon Stewart on *The Daily Show.* In the history of Army manuals, there had been nothing like it. In its first week, the manual was downloaded more than 1.5 million times. It was later reprinted by the University of Chicago Press as a paperback, and reviewed in the *New York Times Book Review.*

The manual helped the exhausted Army feel as if it had expertise in the type of warfare it was facing in Iraq, and it positioned Petraeus as the most cogent thinker about the deepest strategic and tactical questions the country was facing. Anybody could see he wanted to get back to the war. In his second-floor office at Leavenworth, he would obsessively log on to the classified computer network used by commanders in the war, tracking operations, movements of units, and casualties as they unfolded four thousand miles away.

✳   ✳   ✳   ✳

As Petraeus plotted his return, Pete Chiarelli was already on his way back to Iraq. In December 2005, the White House had nominated him for a third star and appointed him to serve under Casey as the commander in charge of daily military operations for a force that now numbered 160,000

U.S. troops along with 23,000 more from Britain and a smattering from other countries. Chiarelli was ecstatic.

He had only been back from his first tour since March, but it had been a restless few months. After returning to Fort Hood and spending a few weeks with his family, he had headed for Washington to deliver briefings at the Pentagon, on Capitol Hill, and at some foreign policy think tanks about his year in Iraq. The road show, as he called his presentation, was a hit. What 1st Cav and USAID had accomplished in Sadr City was a blueprint, he argued, for the unconventional approach the U.S. government, both military and civilians, needed to try throughout Iraq. He talked about the April firefight in Sadr City with a passion that few other generals could duplicate. As he spoke, an aide would unveil a chart that showed attacks concentrated in areas with the worst government services. It was followed by another chart that showed violence dropping off almost entirely after the money started flowing and the jobs programs got under way.

At a time when there was little good news from Iraq, Chiarelli was one senior officer who exuded confidence. Chiarelli's ideas also had some appeal to the Bush administration. He wasn't insisting that the answer was more troops, a prerequisite for any general who hoped to earn Rumsfeld's nod.

For once his timing was perfect. Major General John Batiste, who had been chosen as Casey's deputy, suddenly retired out of frustration with Rumsfeld and the way the war was being fought. Rumsfeld needed a bright former division commander, preferably with Iraq experience, to take Batiste's place. The assignment went to Chiarelli.

The nationwide elections that month came off even better than expected. Nearly three-quarters of Iraq's registered voters cast ballots on a day that was largely free of attacks. As expected, the clear victors were the Shiite parties, known as the United Iraqi Coalition, which won 128 seats. But Sunnis, who had largely boycotted the previous votes, turned out in much higher numbers, and the four main Sunni blocs won 59 seats in the 275-member parliament, up from 17.

Ever the optimist, Chiarelli hoped Iraq had turned a corner. The victorious parties still needed to choose a prime minister and form a government, a process that would grind on for several months. But maybe,

Chiarelli told himself, the next government would be less treacherous than Jaafari's crowd. He took over as Casey's deputy on January 17, moving into his own lakeside villa at Camp Victory, two houses down from his boss's quarters. Now that he had responsibility for the entire country, Chiarelli was brimming with ideas. His new civilian aide, Celeste Ward, suggested mapping out the still-to-be-named prime minister's first 100 days in office. Maybe the new leader could visit all eighteen provinces, including Sunni-dominated Anbar Province, where voter turnout had been poor. At each stop he'd present a check for a new reconstruction project, such as a water-treatment plant or a school, as a visible sign of national reconciliation.

Once the new government was in place, Casey was eager to start reducing the size of the force to about 110,000 troops by the fall, with the first cuts coming in January. He also wanted to shrink the number of coalition bases by half, to about fifty. Fewer bases would drive home the idea that the new government was in control. Casey and Chiarelli hoped that once the new government was in place, Iraq would stabilize.

Not everyone agreed. The biggest reservations came from military intelligence officers who had been fretting over the possibility of a coming Sunni-Shiite civil war for almost a year. Colonel Marcus Kuiper, Chiarelli's senior intelligence officer, was on his first tour of Iraq and had been in the country for only a few weeks, but he'd seen analyses from his predecessors. He sensed that the elections and wrangling over the next prime minister in parliament were likely to heighten sectarian tensions. "We're going to have great difficulty making progress until the Shia feel secure and the Sunnis feel they can't overthrow the government," he told Chiarelli. The worst-case scenario was a major attack by Sunni extremists. Chiarelli listened, but Kuiper could tell his boss thought the assessment was too dire.

On February 22, Sunni religious extremists struck the Al Askaria Mosque in Samarra, one of the holiest sites in Shiite Islam, destroying its famous golden dome. By evening Casey's cell phone was ringing incessantly with calls from panicked Sunni officials. Do something fast, they pleaded. Sunni mosques were being burned to the ground by revenge-minded Shiites. The country was on the verge of a bloodbath. From his base in Tampa, Abizaid told his staff to shift surveillance drones and other intelligence-gathering equipment from Afghanistan to Iraq. "Give them all they need," he ordered. "This attack could unhinge everything." Casey and Chiarelli flooded the streets with troops, and Chiarelli caught the head of the Iraqi ground forces on his way to the airport for a trip to the United States and convinced him not to leave.

Other Iraqis weren't as helpful. Casey and Khalilzad pleaded with Jaafari, who was fighting to keep the prime minister's job, to issue a curfew and appeal publicly for calm. Jaafari hesitated. He saw the bombing as an act of treachery by the Sunni Baathists, and he knew that any Shiite politician calling for restraint risked appearing weak. He finally agreed to make the public statement but refused to impose a curfew for forty-eight hours.

Two days after the bombing, a worried Casey typed out a hasty e-mail to Chiarelli and his other commanders: "Troops, polit situation took a turn for the worse yesterday," he began, warning them not to share what followed: "Situation is as volatile as I have seen it." The curfew was in place, but Sunni sheikhs and politicians had been slow to condemn the attack and Shiite patience was "waning quickly." Iraqis had passed along intelligence that thirty car bombs were heading to Baghdad. Casey wanted his men to look for signs that militia groups were stockpiling weapons or preparing for sectarian war. He didn't know when the sectarian tension would subside, but he concluded, "It won't be soon."

After the mosque bombing, violence steadily increased. The war was changing. Shiite gunmen, many of them members of Muqtada al-Sadr's militia, known as Jaish al-Mahdi, went block by block in mixed neighborhoods forcing Sunnis from their homes and in some cases killing those who resisted. Sunnis fought back with massive car bombs in crowded markets. Between late February and early May, 3,034 bodies were found in Baghdad. In late February Casey received an intelligence report noting that most of the bodies in Baghdad were concentrated in Sadr's strongholds. Unless the violence could be contained, the report warned, there would be "intense sectarian strife across several provinces—likely resulting in civil war." In the margins of the report, Casey drew a star and jotted two words to himself: "Must act."

Sometimes he sat in his office or his quarters at night and methodically composed lists of ideas and questions to ensure he wasn't missing something: "What's going on?" he wrote one day after noticing that attacks by Al Qaeda were growing larger and more deadly. "Are Sunnis with military experience moving to AQ?"

"May need an offensive," he wrote in another list. At the same time, he mulled ways of halting the fighting. "Negotiated settlement," he jotted, wondering if there was a way to bring the warring factions into what would amount to peace talks. He wanted to change the atmosphere. Maybe, he mused, they should "level Abu Ghraib," the Saddam-era prison that, after the 2004 prisoner abuse scandal, had become a symbol to Iraqis of the hated occupation.

✳ ✳ ✳ ✳

Outside Samarra
February 2006

Chiarelli didn't need a list of new ideas. Even after the Samarra mosque bombing, he was certain he knew what needed to be done. The problem was getting others in the military to embrace his ideas. A few days after the attack, he flew to the U.S. base on the outskirts of Samarra and was ushered into a dimly lit command post. He'd come to hear what the battalion responsible for the city planned to do to bring it back under control and win over the people. Even before the mosque bombing, Samarra had been a difficult place. The United States had mounted large assaults to clear the city of insurgents three times before. Each time the enemy had returned.

As he sat on a folding chair listening, Chiarelli became annoyed. The battalion had plenty of plans for killing or capturing insurgents. Troops, operating from a small patrol base in the center of the city, went out on daily patrols and raids of insurgent safe houses. They were working on finishing a ten-foot-high sand berm around the city so that they could prevent insurgents from going in and out. But he hadn't heard any mention of plans to revive the economy, build up the local government, or bring jobs to its residents.

After listening for more than an hour, Chiarelli said he'd heard enough. "This is unacceptable. You are going to go around conducting operation after operation, but you don't give these people some reason to hope their life is going to get better," he said. Then Chiarelli stood up and stormed out. It wasn't often that a three-star general dismissed a battalion's entire plan. More confusing to the officers in the room, Chiarelli's thoughts on what was needed in Samarra were completely at odds with what their brigade commander, Colonel Michael Steele, had told them.

Steele, a barrel-chested former offensive lineman on the University of Georgia national championship football team, was sitting just a few chairs from Chiarelli. He'd led the 1993 rescue mission in Somalia made famous in the book and film *Black Hawk Down*. The experience on the chaotic streets of Mogadishu had driven home to him the importance of aggressively pursuing the enemy. Before his men left Fort Campbell in Kentucky he'd gathered them in an auditorium to tell them what he expected of them. "Anytime you fight—anytime you fight—you always kill the other son of a bitch," he said, pacing back and forth like Patton. "You are the hunter, the predator—you are looking for the prey." He had undisguised contempt for anyone, including Chiarelli, who suggested that the Army should be trying to create jobs or convince insurgents to lay down their weapons. "This is real, and the guy who is going to win is the guy who gets violent the fastest," he told his troops, some of whom began using "kill boards" to track how many Iraqis they had shot during the deployment.

Steele repeated none of this as Chiarelli was sitting across from him that day in Samarra. He was, after all, only a colonel, and Chiarelli was a three-star general. A few weeks later Chiarelli returned to Samarra for another visit, which was even more disturbing. This time his aide called Steele and told him that Chiarelli was bringing along Major General Adnan Thavit, who had led the police commandos and was a native of the city. Thavit knew all of the sheikhs in Samarra, and Chiarelli thought that he might be able to provide Steele with some insights. First Steele tried to bar the Iraqi officer from coming, arguing that he planned to discuss classified information. Chiarelli was astonished. "Thavit is on our side," he thought. "Don't they understand?" At Chiarelli's insistence he grudgingly let the Iraqi into the briefing. Later Steele refused to give Thavit a seat in the convoy of Humvees that was ferrying Chiarelli's entourage back to the helicopter pad. Major Steve Gventer, Chiarelli's aide, pointed out that the sixty-four-year-old Thavit would have to walk. "I don't fucking care," Steele yelled. Gventer hustled away and found Chiarelli, who ordered Steele to surrender his seat.

Steele's disdain for Iraqis, though extreme, was not atypical. Three years of occupation duty had left the Army tired and indifferent. Worried about suicide attacks and car bombs, convoys now routinely fired off warning shots at cars that strayed too close. The gulf between occupier and occupied had never been wider. Chiarelli was bothered by the incident with Steele's brigade but kept going back to Samarra, determined to win over at least some of his subordinates.

In Baghdad, the parliament fought over who would be the next prime minister. Months passed. Violence continued to climb. The government that was supposed to unite the country was paralyzed. Chiarelli's optimism that Iraq had turned a corner began to fade as the months without a new prime minister went on. He began looking for ways to show average Iraqis that life would improve. In April, Chiarelli's helicopter lifted off in an eddy of hot wind and turned west. Leaving the sprawl of Baghdad, it soon was speeding low over palm groves and green wheat fields, part of the country's farm belt, which is startlingly lush to anyone who thinks of Iraq as purely a desert country. The pungent smell of manure wafted up from the ground. Over the *whap-whap-whap* of the rotors, Chiarelli told the Iraqi general flying with him that he was arranging for aerial pesticide spraying of the date palm groves below. Saddam Hussein's government had done the job every year, but the groves had gone unsprayed since the American military had arrived, and the once-lucrative crop was a mess. A smaller harvest meant fewer jobs for Sunnis in western Anbar Province, fueling the insurgency in what had become one of the most violent and chaotic spots on the earth. "We're going to do it!" Chiarelli said of the spraying. "I'm following it every day." He planned to give credit for the idea to the still-to-be-decided prime minister in the hope that it would further bolster his support in the Sunni heartland. The general nodded but said nothing, seemingly puzzled by the American general's interest in dates.

Chiarelli landed at al Asad Air Base, a vast American installation in the middle of the desert. There, they were met by Colonel W. Blake Crowe, the regimental commander in far western Anbar Province. With his high and tight haircut and buff biceps, Crowe was the picture of a squared-away Marine. The Marines were under Chiarelli's command, and Crowe, the son of a former chairman of the Joint Chiefs of Staff, was keen to make a good impression. But he was also a Marine, and they tended to look upon the Army as a plodding outfit without the Corps's warrior ethos.

Ushering Chiarelli into the regimental command post in a crumbling one-story masonry building, Crowe and a half dozen of his officers launched into a detailed briefing about enemy activity in the area and the difficulty of performing the kinds of civic tasks that Chiarelli wanted. Only a few days earlier, Crowe said, a suicide car bombing just outside their front gate had killed two policemen. The only workers willing to help clear a large ammunition dump, among other Chiarelli-type projects, had to come all the way from Baghdad. But the hiring of these outside workers had angered the local sheikhs, causing still more problems and attacks. Crowe's implication was clear: the tactics preferred by Chiarelli might work in Baghdad, but in violence-ridden Anbar the Marines would have to handle things their own way, and that meant, first and foremost, killing insurgents. He didn't have enough troops to cover the vast territory he was responsible for and carry out the kinds of assistance projects Chiarelli wanted.

Chiarelli heard Crowe out. "If you're saying you've got to get an area secure before you do any reconstruction, you'll never get any reconstruction done," he said. Crowe, realizing that his presentation had gotten him nowhere (except perhaps in trouble with a general), said he was trying his best. He described how his Marines had recently tracked a suspected insurgent leader to an isolated house. A year ago, he said, they probably would have called in an air strike to kill him. Mindful of Chiarelli's directives on limiting destruction, they raided the house and captured the man alive. "You probably got more intelligence and avoided killing civilians," said Chiarelli, beaming. "That's what I'm trying to make everyone understand." The Marine evidently was off the hook.

★　★　★　★

On May 20, the new government finally formed with an obscure Shiite politician named Nouri al-Maliki as the prime minister. It was hardly the moment of reconciliation and unity that Casey and Chiarelli had hoped it would be. A few minutes into the proceedings, the main Sunni coalition stormed out. Its members were angry that the government was being formed without a decision on who would run the Interior and Defense ministries, the only two ministries left unfilled. "I call for a withdrawal!" Abdul Nasir al-Janabi, a conservative Sunni Muslim, had bellowed on his way out the door. As the national anthem, "My Homeland," played over and over, Ambassador Khalilzad worked furiously to persuade Janabi and his fellow Sunnis to return. Casey watched apprehensively from the sidelines dressed in his formal Army greens. It was the first time he'd worn the uniform in Iraq, and it reflected his fervent hope that the seating of the new government, which included more Sunnis than the previous administration, was going to be a major turning point in the war. "I wanted to show that this was a new setup, a new order for Iraq," he recalled.

Casey met with Maliki almost daily for the first few weeks. His assessment was mixed. The new prime minister seemed sharper than Jaafari, but he had two big handicaps. "One, he absolutely believes the Baathists are coming back to power. He's scared to death of them," Casey recalled telling Bush and Rumsfeld. His other weakness was that he came from the secretive Dawa Party and was surrounded by stridently anti-Sunni advisors.

Casey hoped for teams of advisors from the State Department and other agencies to help the new Maliki government, the third since Casey took over in 2004. That spring, Bush had assembled his cabinet and ordered them to find people willing to go to Iraq. Secretary of State Rice was put in charge of making sure they delivered. Six days after the Maliki government formed, Rice announced that she'd found forty-eight people who were willing to help.

"Excuse me, ma'am. Did you say forty-eight?" asked Casey, who was participating in the White House meeting by video from Al Faw Palace.

"Yes," she said.

"That's a paltry number," he replied curtly.

Rice told him that he was out of line. But Casey wasn't going to apologize. Colonel Hix, who had done a major strategy assessment for Casey months earlier, had estimated that it would take as many as 10,000 people to mount a reconstruction effort similar in scope to the one in Vietnam. Casey never expected 10,000 advisors. But he certainly had hoped for more than four dozen. The military could build up police and army units. But it desperately needed assistance developing the other parts of the government. He felt let down. Casey couldn't help wondering whether his strategy depended too much on people who couldn't deliver.

After the meeting Rumsfeld shot him a message thanking him for his patience with Rice. The defense secretary had been one of his staunchest supporters since he arrived, and Casey appreciated his strong vote of confidence. But he often felt that the defense secretary didn't understand the war, or at the very least was losing patience. A few days earlier Rumsfeld had asked for a study that explained why so many soldiers were still being killed and wounded. Casey worked on the briefing with a few close aides, ordering them not to tell his field generals why he needed the casualty data. "For me to go down to my division commanders and ask, 'Are you doing everything you can so your guys don't get killed?' It's insulting," he recalled.

The results were predictable. Most of the soldiers and Marines were dying on patrols. Rumsfeld's request, though, sent a clear message: he wanted Casey to cut the fatality rate, and he didn't want American soldiers intervening in the worsening sectarian fighting.

In mid-June Casey returned to Washington to update Bush and Rumsfeld on his plans for the rest of the year. By the fall, he said, he was on track to reduce the U.S. force to about 110,000 soldiers from the 134,000 then in the country. Before he made any further cuts he wanted to clear it with Maliki, but he thought it was doable. Despite the mosque bombing and the growing sectarian violence, Casey still believed that the new government could unite the country.

In Baghdad Chiarelli was slowly coming to the opposite conclusion. In the few weeks since Maliki's government had taken office the sectarian violence had grown far worse. Major General J. D. Thurman came to Chiarelli in late June with a chart of the capital covered with red dots showing all the bodies found the previous day. Thurman was in charge of U.S. troops in Baghdad and reported directly to Chiarelli, who oversaw daily military operations throughout the entire country. Thurman's chart was a cause for serious alarm. There were more than a hundred dots, most concentrated in west Baghdad's mixed Sunni-Shiite neighborhoods, where Shiite death squads and rogue police units were pushing out the Sunnis.

"We've got to get in to see Maliki and explain what's going on in the city," Chiarelli said. As a start, he hoped to lock down Sadr City, which had become a staging ground for the death squads.

A few hours later he and a senior British general from Casey's staff laid the chart in front of the stoic prime minister. "This is not all the bodies. These are just the bodies we're finding," Chiarelli said. The Iraqi army and police had probably picked up dozens more. Most of the victims had been bound and blindfolded before they were shot in the head, he explained.

Maliki studied it intently for several minutes but didn't seem overly alarmed. "It was much worse under Saddam," he told the stunned generals, referring to the intimidation and murder inflicted against his people— the Shiites—by the old regime. When it came to Sadr City, he would not budge: any operations in the Shiite slum had to be cleared through his office.

Chiarelli's doubts about Maliki grew more acute over the course of the summer. It was late one night when one of his staff officers stopped Chiarelli in the hallways at Al Faw Palace. There was highly classified information that he needed to share as soon as possible. "It's bad," the officer advised. The next day, Chiarelli sat in a windowless secure room on the palace's second floor reading transcripts of translated conversations involving Maliki. (The United States has never publicly acknowledged listening in on the conversations of senior officials.) There were late-night telephone calls from the prime minster to one of his aides, a woman named Bassima al-Jaidri, who had served as a civilian in Saddam's military. As they conversed, she urged Maliki to remove certain Sunni commanders in the army and replace them with Shiite officers. It was clear that Maliki was under tremendous pressure from Shiite political parties to fashion the army into a sectarian force. Chiarelli got updates every day on highly classified intelligence, but rarely was the information so revealing. When Casey read the transcripts the following day in his office, he, too, looked astounded.

It was standard practice for Casey or his staff to update the prime minister before a sensitive military operation. A few weeks later another classified intelligence report showed the cell phone and text messaging traffic from Maliki's office after he and his aides received briefings about a pending raid. Minutes after the update, people in Maliki's office were making calls to pass on key details—the intended target, where the U.S. forces were headed, which bridges and roads would be blocked. It wasn't clear who was responsible for the leaks or exactly whom they were telling, but it certainly looked as if they were tipping off potential targets. The report stung Chiarelli. He'd made it a personal policy to treat Iraqis as full partners, and here was strong proof that his assumptions about them were flawed.

The leaks from Maliki's office weren't entirely surprising. He was new and inexperienced. He had been a virtual unknown, at least to U.S. officials, when he was finally chosen after a five-month impasse. As a compromise candidate from the tiny Dawa Party, Maliki's greatest challenge in his first months in office was to hold together his shaky Shiite coalition, which included supporters in parliament who were opposed to cooperating with the Americans. In the best possible light, tipping off fellow Shiites about raids was a way for Maliki to build credibility with a powerful constituency that he needed to survive Iraq's unforgiving politics. And official American policy—reiterated by every senior official from Bush down—was to help Maliki succeed. But Casey and Chiarelli needed to do something. They couldn't confront Maliki directly without risking a major rupture with their new partner, but they couldn't let the leaks continue, either. In the future they decided to delay briefing him and his aides until minutes before a sensitive operation was planned to begin.

★ ★ ★ ★

Al Faw Palace
July 2006

Casey had been back from leave only a few hours when Chiarelli cornered him after the regular morning update. "This is the last chance to extend the Strykers, and I think we need to do it," he said. He was referring to the 172nd Stryker Brigade, named for its armored vehicles, which could survive a rocket-propelled grenade blast but were still nimble enough to negotiate most of Baghdad's streets. The brigade's soldiers and equipment were packing up to go home after a year. Chiarelli and Casey had talked about halting the unit's departure when Casey was in the United States. He had been reluctant to agree. Adding more forces might lead to a temporary reduction in violence, but more troops couldn't fix the underlying political disputes fueling the war, Casey believed. Now that they were face-to-face, he could see the fear in Chiarelli's eyes. Baghdad was falling apart.

Casey called Rumsfeld, who signed off on the extension. Later he explained his rationale in an e-mail to the defense secretary and Abizaid. "John/Mr. Secretary . . . We're in a very fluid situation here," he wrote, describing the latest wave of kidnappings, car bombs, and murders. The seating of the Maliki government hadn't reduced violence, as he had expected. In fact, it was getting worse. "We're beginning to see retaliatory efforts by Shia extremists as less tit-for-tat violence and more as a semi-organized effort to expand geographic control into Sunni areas." Then came the hard admission: "We need . . . to keep more coalition troops here than I originally intended to help the Iraqis through this."

A single additional brigade wouldn't change anything permanently. Casey wanted Rumsfeld and Abizaid to know he wasn't losing faith in the strategy all three of them had decided upon. "I firmly believe," he wrote, "that the longer [the Iraqis] feel they can rely on us, the longer it's going to take them to find the political will to reconcile—which they must do for Iraq to move forward. The extra brigade will help the security situation, but it's not likely to have a decisive effect without a commitment from the religious and political leadership of Iraq to stop the sectarian killing— something they are not ready to do."

Casey had worked himself into a corner. After insisting since his arrival that there was no military answer to the violence in Iraq, he was now admitting that a political solution wasn't likely anytime soon. He told himself that insurgencies typically take a decade to resolve and that the recent setbacks were just part of that long, slow process. The truth was that after two years in Iraq, he was running out of ideas.

Shortly after extending the 172nd Brigade, Rumsfeld rushed to Fort Wainwright, Alaska, to meet with the soldiers' spouses, who were furious and felt betrayed. About 300 soldiers in the Stryker unit had already made it home to Alaska. They had to head back immediately to Iraq. Another 300 were in Kuwait. For weeks after his decision, Casey received nightly e-mails from wives chastising him for keeping their husbands in the war zone for another four months. Reading them was painful. He knew better than most generals the helpless feeling that worried families experienced as they waited for their loved one to return from a war. He'd never forgotten what it was like standing in the passenger lounge at Baltimore-Washington International Airport as his dad disappeared down the jetway, headed back to Vietnam for his third tour. If anything, senior Bush administration officials fretted that his concern over the strain on the force had made him too reluctant to ask for additional troops.

Casey was scheduled to come home in the spring of 2007 and there were already quiet discussions about who would replace him. When Chiarelli was home on leave in August, he had stopped by the Pentagon and heard the buzz that he was likely to get the top job in Iraq. Later that day, he ran into Celeste Ward, his civilian political advisor, who was also home on leave. Summoning her into a vacant office, he told her that he might be asked to replace Casey and come back for a third tour. Would she be interested in working as his political advisor?

"I don't know," she replied. She was two-thirds of the way through her second tour and ready to put Iraq behind her. With the way things were going in Iraq, Ward was surprised Chiarelli was even interested.

"Do you really want that job?" she asked him. "Do you want to be the person who is going to preside over the final debacle?"

"I think I can make it work," he replied.

Chiarelli hadn't completely lost hope that if he could just get the economy to function, provide jobs, and build a decent government, Iraqis would put their sectarian hatreds behind them. Ward wasn't sure what to make of his optimism. In 2003 she had left her job at a foreign policy think tank when she heard the Pentagon was looking for civilians to build the new Ministry of Defense. She had been reluctant to head off to a war zone, but volunteered because she believed in the invasion and felt obligated to help. A Stanford graduate, she was smart and a little bit cynical. By 2006 she was convinced that Maliki had different goals for the country than the United States did. Increasingly it appeared to her as if the Shiite-dominated police, working with illegal militias and death squads, were determined to drive the Sunnis from Baghdad. Sunnis and Shiites weren't fighting because they lacked jobs, clean water, and electricity. It was much more complicated.

As the violence worsened over the summer, she'd join Chiarelli on the smoking patio at Al Faw Palace and gently voice her doubts. Maybe the unconditional support of Maliki and his sectarian government was driving the Sunnis into the arms of extremist groups, including Al Qaeda, that at least promised protection from the death squads. Chiarelli listened, but she could tell that he still believed the Iraqis could overcome their hatreds. "They lived for thirty years under Saddam Hussein. They just don't know how to run a government and administer a country," he replied.

On a helicopter ride over Baghdad, General Abdul Qadir Mohammed Jassim, the head of the ground forces, had told Chiarelli that for most of his life he hadn't even known whether his neighbors were Sunni or Shiite. They were all just Iraqis. Chiarelli loved the story and must have repeated it a hundred times. It proved reconciliation was possible. All they needed was a decent government to provide for them and jobs. Some days Ward thought that Chiarelli was fooling himself. Other days she had a grudging respect for his optimism.

Gradually, Chiarelli's frustrations grew over the late summer and fall. The date palm spraying effort that he had championed hadn't worked out the way he'd hoped. He'd tried to get the Ministry of Agriculture to back it, but they proved woefully incompetent or unwilling to expend effort helping the Sunnis. So he ordered his men to find a private contractor. The United States paid a firm based out of Dubai to spray the date palms and then gave credit to the Iraqis, claiming in public that they had organized and executed the first spraying since the beginning of the war. Everyone in Iraq knew it was a lie.

Chiarelli also was disgusted with Bayan Jabr, who had been the interior minister during the Jadiriyah debacle and had taken over the Finance Ministry under Maliki. He refused to spend money for infrastructure projects in Sunni areas. The government had pledged $50 million to help rebuild Tal Afar after Colonel McMaster's successful tour there, but a year later had spent only about $12 million, despite Chiarelli's protests. The city was falling back into the hands of Sunni insurgents.

Near the end of the summer, General Thurman, the commander in Baghdad, took Chiarelli on a tour of Adhamiyah, the only major Sunni enclave left on the capital's east side. He and Thurman had grown up in the military together as armor officers. Both of their fathers had been butchers, and their wives often joked that they had married SOBs—sons of butchers. Thurman wanted his friend to see up close what was happening in the once-prosperous Sunni neighborhoods. As Chiarelli walked down Adhamiyah's streets, piled with trash, a woman dragged him into her house to see her refrigerator, which was full of maggots. She had no clean water. The militia had blown through the neighborhood and shot up the electrical transformers. The area looked worse than any of the slums he'd seen in Sadr City during his first tour in 2004. "We wanted to get members of the government to come down and see what was going on," Chiarelli recalled. "We couldn't get them to leave their offices. It was so frustrating."

When U.S. troops arrested members of the swelling Shiite militias, Maliki frequently intervened. Chiarelli happened to be at Thurman's headquarters when a call came from Casey's staff ordering the release of a Shiite bomb maker who had been picked up south of Baghdad. Incensed, Thurman ripped off the Velcro patch that held his two stars and started waving them in the air. "Goddammit, I am going to just quit," he bellowed while Chiarelli stood there, sympathetic but unsure what to say. He couldn't tell his friend that it wasn't that bad, because he felt the same way. The thought of resigning had crossed his mind, too. From the moment you pinned on your first lieutenant bars, he thought, the Army drilled you to consider the moral dimensions of being an officer. He recalled seeing an old Army training film in ROTC class at Seattle University that showed a team of soldiers, clad in Vietnam-era uniforms, firing a mortar while under enemy attack. In a freak accident, the mortar tube malfunctions, injuring several soldiers. Soon after the explosion, one of the other mortar teams nearby refuses to fire, insisting they might get injured as well. At that point, Chiarelli remembered, the short film ended with a final question: "What would you do, Lieutenant?" Back then, the answer the Army wanted—the moral answer—was obvious: stand with your soldiers, share the risk, and keep firing.

But he faced a different dilemma in Iraq. How could he remain in his job if he wasn't effective? Didn't he owe it to his soldiers and his country to resign and go public with a statement explaining in terms the public could understand how and why they were failing and what they needed to do to win? His closest aides could see the frustration in Chiarelli's face. He had gained weight and was smoking far too much.

He also felt increasingly under fire from some corners of his own military. Shortly after he arrived in Iraq a reporter for *Time* magazine had shown Chiarelli a disturbing video from Haditha, west of Baghdad. Twenty-four Iraqis, including some women and children, had been killed after a bomb attack on a Marine convoy. When Chiarelli learned that the Marines hadn't investigated the incident, he ordered an inquiry, which came back later that summer. He spent the next ten days with his top staff reading every page of the foot-and-a-half-high report, which painted a disturbing picture of the Marines' actions. The investigation concluded that senior officers in the 2nd Marine Division had been negligent in failing to investigate the killings—a conclusion that Chiarelli endorsed after plowing through the voluminous report. "We had to learn from this, and one of the things we looked very hard at was whether something was missing in the training. Could this have been handled differently?" he recalled. He was particularly disturbed that the killing of that many civilians hadn't been considered significant enough to warrant any special attention at headquarters in Baghdad.

He also was dealing with allegations of misconduct by Colonel Steele, the 101st Airborne Division brigade commander with whom he had clashed in Samarra. A few months after Chiarelli's visit there, soldiers from Steele's brigade had killed four men on an island in the Tigris River. Several soldiers from the unit swore to investigators that Steele had instructed them to kill all military-age males on the island—a claim Steele denied. The investigation ultimately concluded that Steele had led his soldiers to believe that distinguishing combatants from noncombatants—a main tenet of the military's rules of engagement—wasn't necessary during the mission.

Chiarelli gave him a written reprimand, effectively ending his chances for promotion. On the day Steele arrived at Al Faw Palace for his punishment, several of Chiarelli's staff were so worried about what the volatile colonel might do that they insisted his aide, Major Gventer, stand outside his office with a round chambered in his sidearm. But there was no blowup. After receiving the news, Steele sat down on the palace's marble staircase, his head in his hands.

Chiarelli was certain he had made the right call, but his insistence on a thorough investigation of the Haditha incident and on disciplining Steele, a well-known officer, had led some in the military to question if he was being too hard on troops caught in a tough, unpredictable war.

Even one of Chiarelli's proudest achievements in 2006 had led to pointed criticism. He was convinced that the killing and wounding of Iraqis at the hundreds of checkpoints around Iraq was creating new insurgents. "If this sort of thing was happening in Texas, it wouldn't have been too long before the population was armed and taking action," he said. He wanted every casualty that occurred at a checkpoint to be reported to his headquarters and investigated. He ordered new equipment, including sirens, bullhorns, and green lasers, to help soldiers get drivers' attention without firing warning shots. The number of civilians killed by U.S. convoys or at checkpoints fell to about five a month from a high of twenty-five. Chiarelli received dozens of cards and letters from the States, accusing him of being more worried about Iraqis than about his own men. A soldier griped in the *Washington Times* that because of Chiarelli's meddling the "military had gone severely soft." He hadn't changed the rules, but as with Petraeus and his counterinsurgency doctrine, Chiarelli was challenging something more fundamental: the notion that had taken root in the 1990s that protecting soldiers' lives was more important than safeguarding civilians on the battlefield. No one would criticize him to his face, but he confided to friends that he feared he was getting a reputation as "the general who doesn't want to kill anybody." It was the sort of accusation that could end a promising career.

✶   ✶   ✶   ✶

Green Zone, Baghdad
September 3, 2006

The graying men around the conference table carried themselves with assurance and the easy affability that comes with age and accomplishment. They were the members of the Iraq Study Group, a panel of experts and former officials appointed by Congress. For most the fact-finding tour was their first trip to Iraq, and the men had shed their gray suits for khaki pants and blazers—the war zone uniform of visiting dignitaries. They were creatures of Washington, and Chiarelli recognized most of the faces. There was James Baker, the secretary of state for Bush's father, and William Perry, who had been secretary of defense under Clinton. A few chairs away was Robert Gates, the former CIA director (who two months later would replace Rumsfeld at the Pentagon), and Ed Meese, Reagan's attorney general. Chiarelli had briefly met Meese years earlier when he was teaching at West Point and acting with Beth as a faculty sponsor for Meese's son, Mike, who had been a plebe in 1978 and was now a colonel in charge of the Sosh department.

In some ways, Chiarelli felt that he was back at Sosh, a young professor wondering if he belonged. "Teaching at West Point, you had days when it worked and days when it didn't," he recalled. "That day it worked." He didn't use PowerPoint charts or read from notes. He could do this one cold.

He started with a recitation of the same points he'd been making for more than two years. Killing the enemy and training the Iraqi army and police weren't enough. To win, the U.S. government had to reorient the effort to deliver electricity, jobs, clean water, and health care. It needed to push advisory teams into the ministries to teach the Iraqis how to run a government. Chiarelli had given more than forty members of his own staff to help the ministries, but it was nowhere near enough.

Nine months earlier his critique would have focused just on his own country's shortcomings. Now Chiarelli realized the Iraqi government bore a lot of the blame for the chaos. Maliki was a Shiite pawn. The Ministry of Health was run by Sadr's operatives, and they were using access to health care as a weapon in the war against Sunnis, who worried they'd be killed if they went to the hospital. The United States had to use its leverage over Maliki to get him and his government to act in a less sectarian manner.

After the meeting, Perry, the former defense secretary, took Chiarelli aside and asked him if he needed more troops. "Could I use a few more brigades? Sure," he replied. "You can send all the force you want here, but if you don't get some sort of reconciliation started, it will still be a mess." Perry walked out of the conference room with Gates. Neither had met Chiarelli previously and both had been deeply impressed. That guy, they agreed, might end up as chairman of the Joint Chiefs someday.

The Iraq Study Group was a sign that things were changing in Washington, often to the surprise of the generals in Baghdad. With the U.S. congressional elections a few weeks away and the war going badly, President Bush's Republican allies were in danger of losing their slim majority in the Senate. After leaving Casey largely on his own for the previous two years, the White House had begun a far-reaching reexamination of the military strategy, an effort led by White House national security advisor Stephen Hadley. At the Pentagon, General Peter Pace, the chairman of the Joint Chiefs, had assembled a group of officers, including Colonel H. R. McMaster, to study options. The retired general Jack Keane, one of Petraeus's mentors, had teamed up with the American Enterprise Institute, a conservative think tank, on a plan to flood Baghdad with troops. His work had caught the attention of Vice President Dick Cheney's office. None of the reviews had yet reached Casey or Chiarelli. They had their hands full with other matters.

On October 12, seventeen Iraqi soldiers were arrested by U.S. troops in the Baghdad neighborhood of Mansour, a Sunni area that was home to Iraq's elite under Saddam Hussein. The seventeen were from a predominantly Shiite unit based in Sadr City and were detained because they were far from their assigned sector. Under questioning, they claimed that they were on a mission ordered by the prime minister's office. When word of the incident reached Casey, he demanded an immediate meeting with Maliki, bringing along Ambassador Khalilzad. The Americans had been hearing rumors of secret military operations by the prime minister's office. To Casey's surprise, Maliki admitted that he had ordered the raid, bypassing the chain of command that ran through the Ministry of Defense, where the United States had advisors, down to individual Iraqi brigades and battalions. The chain of command existed to prevent one person from using the military for personal vendettas, as Saddam Hussein had done. Casey told Maliki that it protected him from allegations that he was using his forces to further a sectarian agenda.

Maliki, however, was unapologetic. Following the standard procedures took too long, the prime minister explained. Sometimes he got information that needed to be acted upon immediately. He was the commander in chief, and he would do whatever he needed to fight terrorism. Casey fired back that his actions had been unacceptable and asked that he stop.

"Is that a threat?" Maliki replied through a translator. (The Arabic word for "ask" has the same meaning as "order.")

No, replied Casey, he was asking Maliki not to circumvent the established procedures. The Iraqi national security advisor, Mowaffak Baqer al-Rubaie, interceded to defuse the confrontation, and the meeting broke up a few minutes later, resolving nothing. "You shouldn't talk to the prime minister like that," Rubaie warned as they walked out. Afterward, Casey dashed off an e-mail to Abizaid describing the tense exchange with Maliki. "He either got the message and wouldn't acknowledge it—or he didn't get it. I think the former," Casey wrote. "We need to get this stopped."

Abizaid happened to be in Baghdad when he got Casey's note. For much of the summer and fall, he'd been consumed by growing tensions with Iran and the Israeli war in Lebanon with Hezbollah. "My number one concern right now is a strategic or tactical miscalculation with Iran," he'd told his staff a few weeks earlier. "We need to know what we are going to do in the first ten days of a war." He ordered them to lay out 10,000 potential infrastructure targets in Iran just in case the United States was forced into a conflict. Abizaid also was wrestling with his own future. The president had asked him to serve as the director of national intelligence, a new post in Washington set up to prevent another 9/11 attack, and he was leaning toward doing it.

He still made regular trips to Iraq and talked almost daily with Casey by phone, but he'd largely left the handling of the war up to his friend. His public statements on Iraq reflected his belief that the overall strategy was working. "Despite the many challenges, progress does continue to be made in Iraq," Abizaid had testified before the Senate several weeks earlier. The e-mail from Casey, however, was worrisome. His relationship with Maliki appeared to be deteriorating. With the Iraq strategy review under way in Washington, Abizaid knew, there was an appetite for major change, and he feared that if he and Casey didn't act, decisions might be forced on them. Abizaid met with both Casey and Chiarelli. He had a long discussion with Thurman, the Baghdad commander, who pulled out a city map and showed him how the Shiite offensive was driving Sunnis into only a few enclaves in west Baghdad.

He didn't want to second-guess Casey, but he decided to be frank. "Sectarian violence in Baghdad could be fatal," he warned in an e-mail to Casey on the last day of his visit. "We've got to reverse the obvious trends soon." Maybe, he told Casey, their staffs could work together on coming up with new options for restoring security. Abizaid had been particularly frustrated by the Army's inability to find capable officers to serve as army and police advisors. On one trip he'd met with an overweight, fifty-six-year-old air defense officer who was advising an infantry battalion in combat. The officer didn't know a thing about fighting insurgents or leading an infantry battalion.

In his e-mail, Abizaid didn't tell Casey what to do, but he did warn that "the dynamic needs to change." It was as far as he could go without ordering Casey to try something different. As dire as Abizaid's warning was, he closed by reassuring his friend that no one was losing faith in him. "Your personal leadership has already helped steady the ship," he wrote. "I'm so worried about the situation that I'm going on leave next week."

Casey didn't budge. "There are no short-term military fixes," he declared in a return message a few days later. The 4th Infantry Division was scheduled to leave Baghdad in a few weeks after a one-year tour. Canceling its departure, coupled with the arrival of the replacement division with nearly 20,000 troops, would have nearly doubled the U.S. forces in the capital almost overnight. But that was "a course of action I cannot recommend," Casey explained, "until I see greater commitment from the Iraqis to solve the sectarian situation in their capital." There had been 350 executions in Baghdad in the last twelve weeks, primarily by Shiites, he estimated. "While we will continue to do everything we can militarily to contain sectarian violence in Baghdad, the situation will not improve until . . . Iraq's leaders take appropriate action," Casey told Abizaid.

It was a wrenching statement for an American military commander to make. There was nothing he could do to improve the situation. The best he could promise was to try to contain the Sunni-Shiite fighting until Maliki and other leaders took steps to halt the killing, though the prospects for that looked bleak. In the same message he had noted that the prime minister was imposing even tighter restrictions on operations, which had forced several raids to be canceled.

Casey had been reading Stanley Karnow's history of Vietnam and was struck by how senior generals there also struggled with corrupt and chaotic governments. "What do you do when the president of the country you are trying to save has views that are diametrically opposed to yours?" Casey recalled thinking as he read one passage.

Since his arrival, Casey had told himself that he was responsible for overseeing the security strategy, while the embassy was in charge of governance and reconstruction. The violence, he now believed, was being fueled by political and sectarian disputes that couldn't be repaired with military power. He could see the strain on his troops. "I had watched the Fourth Infantry Division in Baghdad, who had lived through this transition to the sectarian fight, and it really took a toll on our guys," he recalled. "They didn't understand it. They'd ask themselves, 'Why are these people killing each other? We're here to help them. What's going on?' It was really draining."

As a young lieutenant in Germany, Casey had served in units ravaged by Vietnam, and the experience had made a profound impression on him. He still believed that a decent outcome was possible in Iraq and that troops should remain in the country to keep a lid on the worst violence. But he wasn't going to commit his troops fully to a fight that he believed only the Iraqis could settle. Casey was falling back on the Powell Doctrine, the post-Vietnam dictum enunciated by General Colin Powell, which held that American forces shouldn't intervene in messy, political wars that don't offer clear exit strategies or outcomes.

Over the next two months, Casey found himself increasingly out of step with his civilian bosses in Washington, a situation he had once vowed to avoid. A few days before the November congressional elections, Bush's national security advisor, Steve Hadley, made his first trip to Iraq. Hadley was weighing whether to send in more troops. He had also seen the intelligence suggesting that Maliki's government was acting on sectarian impulses to punish Sunnis. He wanted to get a read on the prime minister.

Hadley and his aides, Meghan O'Sullivan and Peter Feaver, met first with Casey, who insisted that progress was being made despite the rising violence in Baghdad and growing frustration with the war at home. Maliki's government had acted in overtly sectarian ways since taking office, but Casey wasn't convinced that the prime minister was driving the violence. In some cases, Maliki had been given bad advice by sectarian advisors or was too inexperienced and politically weak to stop the malfeasance. Maliki was also handicapped by his deep fear of a Baathist coup. On occasion he would inform Casey that he had intelligence of secret plots to spring Saddam Hussein from prison and spirit him back to Damascus. The anti-Baathist paranoia led him to distrust Sunnis, Casey explained. But he was confident that Maliki could still unite the fractured country. His government, after all, was only six months old and his military forces were growing stronger by the day. He just needed time and support.

After having breakfast with Hadley and his team, Casey handed them off to Chiarelli, who arranged for Hadley to meet several battalion and brigade commanders at Thurman's headquarters. He then left the room so that they could get an unfiltered view of what was happening on Baghdad's streets. The commanders' accounts of the Maliki government were far bleaker than Casey's, and their pessimism stunned the civilians. One officer said that in his sector police officers had recently driven through Sunni areas of Baghdad shooting up electrical substations to cut off the power there. Another commander was livid that the Ministry of Finance had closed the only bank in one of his Sunni sectors, forcing the residents there to make a deadly trip through territory controlled by Shiite militias to collect their monthly pension payments. What was the United States doing about this? Hadley asked. Very little, the officers replied.

As Hadley's team prepared to leave for the airport, Chiarelli got an unexpected phone call from Casey telling him that Maliki wanted the United States to remove a series of checkpoints that had been placed around Sadr

City following the kidnapping of an American soldier near there. In the week that the barriers had been in place, sectarian killings had fallen in Baghdad, Chiarelli recalled. Shiite death squads were having a much harder time leaving Sadr City to conduct killing sprees in Sunni neighborhoods. Casey could have refused the demand by Maliki, who was under intense political pressure from his constituents to take down the checkpoints. But Casey believed that if Maliki was going to have a chance of succeeding, he couldn't undercut him publicly.

Chiarelli felt otherwise. The order was like "a kick in the teeth," he recalled. He explained what had happened to Hadley, who was still absorbing what he'd heard from the brigade and battalion commanders. For most of the ride to the airport, no one spoke. Finally the taciturn Hadley broke the silence. "I wish I had come here more often," he said.

A few days later Hadley drafted a classified memo for Bush and his top advisors that gave the White House a picture of the depressing situation. "We returned from Iraq convinced we need to determine if Prime Minister Maliki is both willing and able to rise above the sectarian agendas being promoted by others," Hadley wrote. "Reports of nondelivery of services to Sunni areas, intervention by the prime minister's office to stop military action against Shia targets and to encourage them against Sunni ones, removal of Iraq's most effective commanders on a sectarian basis and efforts to ensure Shia majorities in all ministries—when combined with the escalation of Jaish al-Mahdi's (JAM) killings—all suggest a campaign to consolidate Shia power in Baghdad . . . [T]he reality on the streets of Baghdad suggests Maliki is either ignorant of what is going on, misrepresenting his intentions, or that his capabilities are not yet sufficient to turn his good intentions into action."

Hadley's impressions did not differ greatly from Casey's or Chiarelli's. Where they did disagree was in what to do. Casey favored strengthening Maliki and his security forces. Hadley suggested a long list of possible steps, including more troops, which Casey opposed and which Chiarelli doubted would do much good.

In early November, after the Democrats took control of the Senate in the midterm elections, Bush fired Rumsfeld. A few hours after he learned of the dismissal, Casey wrote Rumsfeld a quick note: "Thank you for your courage and support throughout this long and difficult mission. I really appreciate your leadership and I'll continue to say so publicly." Rumsfeld had not been an easy boss, but Casey had felt since their brief meeting before he took command that they saw the task in Iraq in roughly similar terms. And Rumsfeld had always stood up for him in Washington.

A few days after the midterm elections, Abizaid was summoned to testify before the Senate Armed Services Committee. Abizaid had always been able to charm lawmakers. He was eloquent, witty, and, at times, disarmingly honest with them; he had a way of always coming off as the smartest, most levelheaded guy in the room. This time, though, the lawmakers weren't interested in hearing what Abizaid had to say. They had brought the general to Washington so that they could vent their frustration. Abizaid had hoped to mollify the angry senators with a new military strategy. He'd been pressing Casey to bolster the U.S. advisory teams that were embedded in Iraqi army and police units. Abizaid believed the teams were the key to victory, and he had been frustrated that senior Army officers in the Pentagon had staffed them for years with mostly inexperienced troops. Abizaid asked Casey to triple the size of the ten- to fifteen-man teams. Instead of relying on the Pentagon to assign personnel the advisory units, he wanted to use officers who were already serving in Iraq to man them. "I believe in my heart of hearts that the Iraqis must win this battle with our help," Abizaid told the senators. Only the Iraqis could end the country's civil war, he insisted.

Abizaid tried to tout his new approach as a major change. But to the lawmakers the new plan sounded a lot like Casey's current approach. The strongest attacks came from the committee's two presidential hopefuls, John McCain and Hillary Clinton. For the first time in Abizaid's golden career, powerful people were questioning his credibility and competence in public. McCain summarily dismissed Abizaid's new plan as the "status quo." The senator's voice dripped with sarcasm and anger as he recounted for Abizaid the details of a mass kidnapping in Baghdad the day before. "Was it encouraging when in broad daylight yesterday people dressed in police uniforms were able to come in and kidnap 150 people and leave with them through Iraqi checkpoints?" McCain asked. "General, it's not encouraging to us. It's not encouraging to those of us who have heard time after time that we're making progress, because we're hearing from other sources that it's not the case."

Senator Clinton was just as searing. "Hope is not a method," she lectured. "I have heard over and over again that the Iraqi government must do this and the Iraq army must do that. Nobody disagrees. The brutal fact is that it is not happening." Abizaid testily shot back: "I would also say that despair is not a method. And when I come to Washington I feel despair. When I'm in Iraq with my commanders, when I talk to our soldiers, when I talk to the Iraqi leadership, they are not despairing."

After the hearing Abizaid was furious. Rumsfeld had always served as a lightning rod for lawmakers' fury over the foundering war effort. Now that he was gone, their anger was raining down on senior commanders, like Abizaid and Casey. "I'll never do that again," Abizaid fumed to his staff as he left the Senate hearing. "I'll never go up there again." In late October, Abizaid had accepted President Bush's offer to serve as the director of national intelligence, a civilian job overseeing the CIA and other intelligence agencies, but a few days prior to the Senate hearing, after talking it over with Kathy, he withdrew his name. He was exhausted after more than three years in command and reluctant to take a political job. He also decided the position wasn't right for him. He enjoyed thinking about issues such as the societal and political forces at work in the Middle East, and he disdained the grind of running a big bureaucracy. He had shown little success at getting the other parts of the U.S. government to support the war effort in Iraq. At times, he even had a hard time getting his Army to support his vision for fighting the war. Before Rumsfeld was fired, the defense secretary had asked Abizaid to postpone his retirement from the military to the spring of 2008, and Abizaid had reluctantly agreed. Everyone around Abizaid, especially his family, could see that he was burned out. He talked regularly about his desire to retire to the Sierra Nevada, thousands of miles from the second-guessing in Washington. "I really miss spending time with your mom," he'd say wistfully to his children.

With Rumsfeld gone, the gulf between Casey and the White House became even more apparent. Bush was planning on giving an Iraq speech before Christmas and in mid-December assembled his advisors in the wood-paneled White House Situation Room to consider options. Casey appeared by video hookup and argued for continuing with the current strategy. By the summer of 2007, he predicted, the Iraqi security forces would be capable of operating with only limited support, allowing him to begin a long-delayed drawdown in American units.

Bush wasn't convinced. "So, more of the same?" he asked Casey doubtfully.

It was obvious the president wanted to send additional brigades to Baghdad. Casey reiterated that he was opposed to such a move unless Sunni and Shiite leaders in Iraq showed a willingness to reconcile. "If the Iraqis can get political agreement, then, if asked, we can surge," he offered.

But Bush had concluded that if his administration didn't do something to arrest the decline, Congress was likely to force a withdrawal. Even staunch Republicans were losing patience with the war. "We've got to go after JAM before the summer," he argued. The discussion resumed the following day, with Bush pressing the case for more troops and Casey resisting. "We've got sufficient forces in Iraq," Casey emphasized at one point, noting that, for all the country's problems, the Iraqi army was not splintering along sectarian lines.

Abizaid, who was also present, took a middle course. "I suppose you're going to tell me you're against the surge?" Bush asked him.

"No, that's not what I'm going to tell you. I'm going to tell you the pluses and minuses of it," he replied. The extra troops would show commitment, reduce sectarian violence, and buy Maliki and other leaders time to make necessary political compromises. On the negative side, the surge would add strain to an already stretched Army, prevent the United States from addressing the deteriorating situation in Afghanistan, and constrain the president's ability to use ground forces if there was a flare-up with Iran. Abizaid also warned that unless the State Department devoted more people and money to developing Iraq's government and economy, the surge wouldn't work.

Bush had already made up his mind. A temporary increase in forces might be "a bridge to a better place," he suggested.

"Perhaps," Casey replied, giving slightly.

Bush didn't blame Casey for the failures in Iraq. "Everything he did, I approved. I am not going to make him the fall guy for my strategy," the president told his staff. Casey had inherited a mess when he arrived in Iraq more than two years earlier. The resistance had been growing and there was virtually no strategy to combat it. Neither he nor his troops had had any experience or training in fighting a counterinsurgency war. Casey had made mistakes. He'd underestimated the difficulty of building competent Iraqi security forces and had too much faith that elections would curb sectarian behavior and unite the country. But he'd also received little help or guidance from the rest of the U.S. government.

In late December, Gates arrived in Baghdad on his first overseas trip since taking over as defense secretary. He had sent word ahead of time that he needed a few minutes with Casey. When they were alone, Gates got straight to the point. The Army chief of staff job would be coming open in a few months, and Casey was the leading candidate. Was he interested? Gates asked. Casey said he was. He had been thinking about leaving Iraq for a while but wasn't sure where he would go next. The chief's job was the highest-ranking post in the Army. It was the job his father had once seemed destined to claim.

✳   ✳   ✳   ✳

Chiarelli's last day in Iraq was spent waiting for a plane. His one-year tour complete, he had handed over command to Lieutenant General Ray Odierno the day before and was due to leave that afternoon with his headquarters staff for Germany, where Beth and other families were waiting for their arrival. Everything about that year had been difficult, and leaving was no exception. The C-17 that was supposed to carry them home was late. Hour after hour he and his headquarters staff sat sprawled at the Glass House, a building away from the main Baghdad airport terminal that served as a VIP lounge. Even this long into the occupation, the place was a mess, with plywood boards covering the broken glass panels, and cheap and ripped chairs the only places to sit except for the floor. Their wait was the Air Force's revenge for all the times he'd yelled at them, Chiarelli joked with his chief of staff, Brigadier General Don Campbell. As it got late, foraging parties set off in search of food. Somebody suggested going back to Al Faw Palace for the night, but Chiarelli said no: they should sit in the terminal until the plane arrived, whenever that was.

"I just don't have the same feeling of accomplishment as I did when I left the last time," Chiarelli told Campbell, referring to his tour with 1st Cav. He looked tired. He had been smoking too much and sleeping only four or five hours a night. Even now that it was over, he couldn't stop replaying all that had gone wrong. Chiarelli was still hopeful he might be returning for a third tour in only a matter of months. He was already planning what he would do differently. "Will you come back with me?" he asked Campbell.

As his departure approached, he had written a long memo about everything that had gone wrong during the preceding year. Even the title, "What Happened During My Tenure," captured Chiarelli's shock and disillusionment. It was nearly six pages of observations, each carefully numbered, most of them about the Iraqi government's failings: "We had high hopes that [Maliki] would come in and energetically help to stabilize the situation. . . . What followed, unfortunately, was stasis and then a slow but definite growth of sectarianism on the part of the government. . . . The IPs [Iraqi police] were corrupt and often participated in sectarian violence (kidnappings, torture, executions). . . . The Prime Minister has called us off of operations against JAM numerous times. . . . We also have direct evidence that people from his office were tipping off potential targets."

Chiarelli did not spare his own government. He had been reading a book entitled *Bureaucracy Does Its Thing,* a classic study written in 1973 by Robert Komer, a former CIA official sent to Vietnam by Lyndon Johnson to lead the civilian reconstruction effort. Komer had written his penetrating indictment of the war effort upon returning to the United States, and Chiarelli found that much in the three-decade-old essay still applied to Iraq. "Robert Komer's observations," he wrote, "are frighteningly apt here. . . . 'The sheer incapacity of the regimes we backed, which largely frittered away the enormous resources we gave them, may well have been the single greatest constraint on our ability to achieve the aims we set ourselves at acceptable cost.' " He closed the memo with thoughts about how to shift course. "The good news is that we still do have tools at our disposal, and some of our tools we have failed to use to their full capacity." Chiarelli hoped he would have another chance to command.

Their plane finally arrived the next morning, and he and his staff loaded their gear into the belly of the cargo jet and flew home to Germany. They arrived a few hours later to a heroes' welcome in Heidelberg, held in the post gymnasium. Beth, his daughter, Erin, and his son, Peter, greeted him. Soon after his arrival they left on a skiing vacation in the Austrian Alps with Don Campbell and his family. Chiarelli was a nervous wreck, religiously checking his e-mail, hoping he would get a message about his next assignment. He heard nothing. At the end of their weeklong vacation, as the Chiarellis and Campbells were driving back to Heidelberg, they stopped along the highway for a snack and saw a German newspaper with a picture of Dave Petraeus on the front page. Chiarelli translated the story with his rusty German. Petraeus, it seemed to be saying, was the leading candidate to replace Casey. A few days later came the official announcement: Bush had chosen Petraeus as the next top commander in Iraq.

CHAPTER TWELVE

The Army of the Tigris

Baghdad
February 8, 2007

At 7:27 a.m. Casey took his place before a wall of video screens and waited for the first briefer to start his morning update. Instead Petraeus's image popped up on one of the screens in front of him.

"General Casey, sir, Dave Petraeus here. How are you doing this morning?" he asked, his voice echoing through the room. Petraeus had just arrived in Baghdad and was scheduled to take command from Casey in two days.

"Good morning, Dave," Casey muttered. He was running the briefing from the Green Zone and Petraeus was at Al Faw Palace a few miles away. He hadn't expected to see his replacement turn up so soon, and his weary tone made clear that he was ready to drop the pleasantries and get on with the day's business. Petraeus didn't seem to get the message, and he tried to make conversation by discussing Casey's nomination to be Army chief of staff. "Congratulations on your nomination getting through the Senate Armed Services Committee," he continued. "Let's hope for a similar result when the vote goes to the full Senate." Several officers in the room blanched. The Senate had unanimously confirmed Petraeus for his new job, and his remark inadvertently seemed to imply that Casey might have a tougher time on Capitol Hill. A handful of prominent Republicans had already indicated that they were going to vote against him. Casey said nothing.

"Sir, your relief is here. You're supposed to be smiling," Petraeus joked, trying one last time. Casey gazed up at his replacement's image on the screen in front of him. After an exhausting two and a half years in Iraq, he was ready to go home, but not on such a low note. "I am smiling on the inside, Dave," he said.

His final days in Baghdad were full of small ceremonies and reminders that he was not leaving in triumph. Two weeks before, Casey had jetted back to Washington for the hearing on his nomination. In the Senate hearing room bright television lights shone in his face as he stared up at the two dozen lawmakers in front of him. He knew many in official Washington thought that he was being given the chief's job as a consolation prize. The unspoken comparison was to General William Westmoreland, who'd presided over a losing war and returned to lead the Army. The thought burned him. Serving as Army chief shouldn't be a reward, he bluntly told the lawmakers. It was a duty. "It's about personal commitment to the men and women of the United States Army," he said.

For Casey the three-hour confirmation hearing had become an endurance test; the key to surviving it was not to let the senators get to him. "That was sealed in my mind," he recalled. The toughest moment had come early on under questioning from Senator John McCain, a prisoner of war in Vietnam who also came from a proud military family. McCain, who was readying his run for the presidency, had softened his criticism of Bush's wartime command. He now placed the blame for the failure in Iraq squarely on Casey, and his disgusted tone made it clear that he considered Casey's time in Iraq an unmitigated failure.

Sheila Casey, sitting in the front row, seethed at McCain's rough treatment of her husband. Two years earlier he'd sought her out at a Washington party to praise her husband's leadership. She couldn't fathom how his opinion of her husband could have changed so radically, except that he was now running for president. Although McCain insisted that he wasn't questioning Casey's patriotism or honor, the senator clearly was attacking Casey's intelligence and military judgment. The general's sins were denial and inaction. As sectarian violence rose, Casey had continued to offer up "unrealistically rosy" assessments of the war, McCain complained. Instead of arresting the decline by pushing more troops deep into Iraq's most violent cities, the general had stuck with his approach of building up Iraqi forces and searching for a quick exit. "We have paid a very heavy price in American blood and treasure because of what is now agreed to by literally everyone as a failed policy," McCain lectured.

Democrat Senator Carl Levin prodded more gently, suggesting that even President Bush had conceded that Iraq was "maybe a slow failure." Casey winced but refused to give an inch. "I actually don't see it as a slow failure. I actually see it as slow progress," he said softly. To Casey it seemed as if the White House and some Senate Republicans were trying to pin the failure in Iraq on him and shift the focus off the weakened president. He had been around Washington long enough to know that this was how politics worked. Still, he hated it.

In his final meeting with Maliki after returning to Iraq, Casey presented the prime minister with the 9mm pistol that he'd carried throughout his Iraq tour. Although most U.S. officials had serious doubts about Maliki, Casey still believed that he could overcome his paranoia and anti-Sunni impulses and effectively lead the country. "You are commander in chief. But soon you will have control of all of the Iraqi forces. I am giving you this as a symbol of the transfer," he said, handing over the gun.

He spent a couple of hours with Petraeus in his palace office. A month earlier President Bush had announced that he was sending five additional brigades, or about 20,000 troops, to Iraq. Bush was gambling that the extra soldiers could drive down the sectarian killing in the capital and give Sunni and Shiite leaders in the country some breathing room to reconcile. In his confirmation hearing, Petraeus said that he intended to push his troops into Baghdad's most violent neighborhoods, where they would live in small combat outposts and focus on protecting residents from the roving death squads and suicide car bombs. As they sat at the mahogany table,

Casey urged Petraeus to be clear about the change. "Don't pretend that you're still trying to put the Iraqis in the lead when you're taking over security responsibility from them," he said. "You owe it to the troops."

Casey disagreed with the new strategy and insisted that, despite the rising violence, the government and security forces were still improving. "You're in a lot better shape than people back in the U.S. think you are," he said. Petraeus listened and scribbled a few notes. He felt a twinge of sympathy mixed with disbelief. After four years of war, Casey and Petraeus shared more than they sometimes acknowledged. They had spent more time in Iraq than any other Army generals and knew better than any of their colleagues the intense pressure and loneliness of commanding. Casey had given two and a half years of his life to a strategy that was clearly failing, Petraeus thought. Now he couldn't admit he was losing.

The change-of-command ceremony took place the following day with Abizaid, who was in his final months as the head of Central Command, in charge of the proceedings. The three generals marched into the palace's cavernous rotunda, where a crowd of about 200 had assembled. Iraqi generals and cabinet ministers filled the first two rows of seats. American officers, a mix of field generals and cubicle dwellers, sat behind them. The official change of command took only a few seconds. A military band played the 101st Airborne Division song in honor of Petraeus. Then Abizaid passed the Multi-National Force–Iraq flag, a gold-fringed banner bearing the image of a winged Mesopotamian bull, to a sergeant major, who handed it to Casey. Casey presented the flag to Petraeus, who gripped it tightly with both hands and flashed the ceremony's only smile.

Abizaid stepped up to the lectern and did his best to buck up Casey. "History will smile upon your accomplishments," he intoned, his voice bouncing off the palace's marble walls. With his arms folded across his chest and his legs crossed, Casey looked as if he were trying to roll up into a ball. His eyes flitted over the rotunda's crystal chandelier and marble columns the width of redwoods. In all his years in the military he had never felt so alone.

After Abizaid spoke, Casey stood at the makeshift lectern in Al Faw Palace. In his remarks he didn't let any of his anger show. Pushing his glasses up on his nose, he praised Petraeus and in a final defense of his strategy expressed optimism that soon the country would be able to "assume responsibility for its own security." From the moment he had arrived in Iraq Casey had been determined to start bringing soldiers home. He'd constantly been casting about for the always elusive Iraq exit strategy. He wanted to win, but he also was determined to shield his Army as much as possible from the long, grinding war. "I didn't want to bring one more American soldier into Iraq than was necessary," he said repeatedly during his Senate hearing.

Now it was clear that Petraeus was going to take the war in a completely different direction. His remarks, which followed Casey's, signaled more than just the changing of the guard in Iraq. They marked the end of the post-Vietnam era for the Army. Ever since the disastrous war, senior Army leaders had tried, and ultimately failed, to keep their force from becoming too deeply embroiled in messy political wars that defied standard military solutions. It was a pattern that had repeated itself in Haiti, Somalia, the Balkans, Afghanistan, and then Iraq, where generals often focused more on exit strategies than on plans for victory. Petraeus wasn't interested in the drawdown plans often advanced by Casey. Instead he wanted to push U.S. troops into cities and leave them there. Only a heavy and sustained American presence could win the war, he believed.

He spoke first to his troops. Their job was to reduce the violence and protect the people so that the government could function and the economy might return to life. "These tasks are achievable. The mission is doable," he said, leaning forward and gripping the lectern with his left hand.

Next he spoke to the Iraqis. In his previous two tours he had sat through countless lectures from sheikhs, generals, and politicians recounting the country's history as the birthplace of learning and the cradle of civilization. Petraeus addressed them as if he were the supreme sheikh of a proud tribe, referring to their country majestically as the "land between two rivers." He had come back to help the *Sha'ab al-Iraqi*—the Iraqi people—build a new country and realize "the abundant blessings bestowed by the Almighty on Mesopotamia." His last words were in Arabic. *"Baraak Allah fee a sha'ab al-Iraqi,"* Petraeus said—may God bless the Iraqi people.

A snare drum snapped out a deliberate tempo, and the three generals marched out of the rotunda. Petraeus rushed off to meet with the staff he was inheriting from Casey and set them to work on his new strategy. Casey paused on his way out the door to shake hands, force a last smile for his staff, and pose for pictures before he boarded a cargo plane headed home. After a few minutes, he glanced up and noticed that Iraq's defense minister, interior minister, and national security advisor had all formed a tight circle around him. The middle-aged men with graying hair and mustaches looked to Casey as if they had no idea what came next. They stared at him. Casey stared back. Eventually he draped his arms over their shoulders. "You guys are going to be fine," he said. "You know what to do." He was probably the only one in the palace who believed it.

✳ ✳ ✳ ✳

While he was back in the States, Petraeus had done his best to keep up with the classified intelligence assessments produced by Casey's command, but the reports didn't fully capture how bad conditions had become. The night of the change-of-command ceremony he flew into the Green Zone for a welcome dinner at the U.S. ambassador's residence. Even before the main course had been served, Defense Minister Abdul Qadir al-Obaidi and the Speaker of the parliament, Mahmoud Mashhadani, began screaming at each other. Both men were Sunnis. The volatile Mashhadani castigated Obaidi for not doing enough to help his Sunni brothers. Rising to his feet, Obaidi shouted that he was defense minister for all Iraqis, regardless of sect or ethnicity. The only thing that was stopping the two men from throwing punches was the narrow table. The U.S. ambassador calmed the two men down, but a few minutes later the screaming erupted again. A dispirited Petraeus excused himself before dessert. "I've got to get back to Camp Victory," he lied. "We have another update tonight."

A Black Hawk ferried him back to his stone villa in the shadow of Al Faw Palace. He spent most of his time there in one room, which was furnished with a bed and a desk. The bed usually lay unmade. The desk was piled with books, a computer, a secure telephone, and a picture of his son, who was in his final year at MIT and about to become an Army lieutenant. Tucked inside one of the desk's drawers was a list of soldiers who had completed an excruciating physical fitness test that he had created in 1992.

Petraeus's bosses had frowned on the test as an unnecessary distraction. His replacements had abandoned it, reasoning that they had better things to do than hover over troops with a stopwatch counting sit-ups, pull-ups, and dips. But Petraeus loved it. It measured the qualities that he valued in an officer: will, discipline, and perseverance. These were what he would need in Iraq.

As he settled into his cot, Petraeus's mind was racing too quickly to sleep. He couldn't even concentrate enough to read. The fight between the defense minister and the Speaker had thrown him. The two Sunni politicians were supposed to be political allies. They couldn't even make it through a dinner together.

In his first days of command, he laid out his strategy in terms that even a soldier fresh out of basic training could grasp. The main mission was to make Iraq's neighborhoods safer. Instead of commuting to the battlefield from big bases—some of which boasted swimming pools, bus systems, and post exchanges the size of a Wal-Mart—he ordered troops to move into austere outposts scattered throughout Baghdad. There they could keep a closer eye on Iraqi army and police forces and stop the worst of the sectarian bloodletting. Prior to the country's descent into civil war, many of Baghdad's neighborhoods included both Shiite and Sunni families. By 2007 there were virtually no mixed enclaves left. The sectarian cleansing in the months before his arrival ironically made Petraeus's job easier. It allowed him to concentrate his troops on the fault lines between Sunni and Shiite areas where the violence was the most unrelenting.

Petraeus's other big push was reconciliation. Most insurgents and militia fighters weren't religious zealots and could be convinced to lay down their weapons. "We need to get as many people into the tent as possible," he told his generals a few days after taking command. In the final months of Casey's tenure, Sunni tribes in Anbar Province had begun switching sides to fight alongside the United States against Al Qaeda–affiliated Sunni extremists. The tribes were angry at Al Qaeda's arrogance, brutality, and efforts to replace tribal law with a draconian form of Islam that even prohibited smoking. The fledgling tribal alliance, known as the Anbar Awakening, was one of the few bright spots in Iraq in 2006, and Petraeus was determined to find and exploit similar fissures.

Lastly, he told his commanders and his staff that he expected them to demand the forces they needed to prevail. President Bush had promised about 21,500 additional troops, but Petraeus was convinced that he'd need as many as 8,000 on top of that. The Pentagon's Joint Staff usually didn't deny field commanders' requests outright. Instead it dragged its feet. Just ten days after the change-of-command ceremony Petraeus complained to his senior staff that he was "vexed" by the slow deployment of the reinforcements. The president had promised him that he would get whatever he needed for his strategy, and he intended to keep pushing until someone ordered him to stop. "We want the Joint Staff to tell us we can't have the troops," he told his generals in late February. "We are going to make them tell us no." A few days later he returned to the issue. "We aren't going to hold back on troop requests. If they tell us no, fine. I will state the risk to the mission. But they have to tell us no. We want them to tell us no." Petraeus had been so worried about the troop issue that he seriously considered making his acceptance of command contingent on the president naming his old friend Jack Keane, who was a backer of the new strategy, as the new chairman of the Joint Chiefs of Staff. Keane could fight the Pentagon wars and let Petraeus focus on the real enemy. But Petraeus discarded the idea as too presumptuous. Instead he came up with another means of holding the Pentagon's feet to the fire. Each morning he tracked his troop requests on a PowerPoint slide. If the Pentagon was withholding so much as a two-person dog handler team, he knew it and was willing to fight for it if necessary.

As Petraeus implemented his new strategy, he relied heavily on the 1st Cavalry Division, which had recently returned to Baghdad. Chiarelli had left the unit a little over a year before, but many of the officers and senior sergeants from Chiarelli's days in command remained. These soldiers had absorbed his ethos and his ideas; they also knew Baghdad. Shortly after Petraeus was chosen for the top command in Iraq, he sent an e-mail to Lieutenant Colonel Doug Ollivant, the 1st Cav's lead planner. Ollivant, who also happened to be a Sosh alum, had won a counterinsurgency essay contest that Petraeus had sponsored at Fort Leavenworth. His essay argued that 800-soldier battalions had to be the nexus for all security, reconstruction, and military training efforts in counterinsurgency wars. In his e-mail, Petraeus asked Ollivant whether he thought the ideas he'd promoted in his essay could work in Baghdad. Ollivant said he wasn't sure. In Iraq, the Maliki government was fueling the sectarian violence. U.S. commanders had to weigh their actions carefully to ensure that they weren't building a Shiite-dominated government and police force that would crush the Sunni minority in Baghdad. Petraeus encouraged Ollivant to ignore the normal chain of command and keep feeding him ideas. "You're a very bright guy and these are exceptional times. We're going to get one last shot at this and we need to make it really count," Petraeus wrote. "We're putting it all on the line and we need to be cognizant of that. It's not business as usual as I am sure you know."

✻ ✻ ✻ ✻

Al Faw Palace
February 19, 2007

The daily briefing began when Petraeus strode into the palace's first-floor amphitheater. Several dozen officers, sitting behind long tables and slender microphones, sprang to their feet.

"Good morning," Petraeus mumbled as he took his seat before the wall of screens displaying PowerPoint slides and images of colleagues connected via secure video from other spots around Baghdad. He uncoiled his microphone, and his aide rushed over with hot coffee in a black 101st Airborne Division travel mug.

"Okay, let's go, please," he said, and the briefing began.

Most generals used their morning briefing to stay abreast of the previous day's attacks, raids, arrests, and reconstruction projects. Petraeus explained that his morning update was going to be different. Part of what made commanding in Iraq so hard was that the disputes driving the killing varied from city to city and even neighborhood to neighborhood. He knew he couldn't dictate solutions to his battalion and company commanders. But he also couldn't just allow everyone to stumble across their own answers. The morning briefing, he said, was going to be his mechanism for imposing his vision on a force of 170,000 troops sprawled across more than 120 combat outposts.

The way Petraeus operated was nothing like the conventional portrait of a wartime general. It wasn't Patton, riding crop clutched tightly in his left hand, exhorting his soldiers from the top of a tank. Rather, it was the slight and scholarly Petraeus swirling his emerald-green laser pointer over pie charts and columns full of data. "I am going to manage you by slides," he told his troops.

Orchestrating the briefing was an art, Petraeus believed, one he had perfected over years of command. When he was running it, his voice deepened and his back, normally pitched slightly forward, straightened a bit. On a typical day Petraeus covered forty-five to sixty slides, each of which would first be briefed to him by a colonel or a major. Intelligence, enemy attacks, Iraq's sclerotic electricity output, and press coverage merited daily attention. Other areas of interest to Petraeus, including bridge and road reconstruction, chlorine supplies at water-treatment plants, oil exports, Iraqi politics, and even chicken embryo imports, were covered weekly. Most subjects that Petraeus added after he took over from Casey weren't military problems. They were generally considered State Department or civilian problems that senior military officers, with the exception of generals such as Chiarelli, had explicitly avoided during the first four years of the war. Petraeus was now making them military problems.

In his baritone, Petraeus regularly asked incredibly detailed questions. A report about a bank branch that Finance Minister Bayan Jabr had shuttered in a Sunni neighborhood in west Baghdad prompted queries that lasted for weeks. The closing of the bank was a small piece of a broader effort by the Shiite-dominated government to starve Sunni neighborhoods of essential services. Petraeus wanted to know: Why had the Shiite finance minister closed the bank? How quickly could the local manager reopen it? How many guards did the bank need and what was the plan to train them?

Every morning Lieutenant Colonel Charlie Miller, a longtime Petraeus acolyte and Sosh refugee, would capture the queries and send them out to various combat units around the country. For all of his power, Petraeus was rarely in a position to dictate solutions. But by asking questions he could nudge his troops to search for answers.

The broken-down electricity grid got the same treatment as the Baghdad bank. In four years the United States had pumped more than $4 billion into the electrical system, yet somehow daily output had fallen. Many Iraqis were livid. Petraeus didn't know a lot of Arabic, but the words *maku karaba,* "no electricity," were burned into his brain. In early March Petraeus latched onto a single electrical transmission tower southwest of Baghdad that was known as Tower 57. Insurgents had toppled it with a bomb more than a year earlier. Morning after morning for months Petraeus leaned into his microphone and, with all of Al Faw Palace and much of the Green Zone listening, he badgered Major General David Fastabend, the senior operations officer on his staff, about fixing Tower 57. Fastabend knew what Petraeus was doing. "It wasn't just the tower to him," Fastabend recalled. "The tower became a symbol of things that were broken in Iraq and never got fixed." It was an emblem of the Army's exhaustion and frustration.

The daily grilling about Tower 57 was humiliating for Fastabend. At times he doubted that Petraeus understood the magnitude of the electricity problem, which included a corrupt, incompetent ministry, surging demand, and regular insurgent attacks. "This is the most intractable damn thing in the world," Fastabend groused. Petraeus didn't seem to care. With Petraeus breathing down his neck, Fastabend hatched myriad schemes to fix the tower. Contractors were hired, paid, and then fired for refusing to finish the work in what was still insurgent-controlled territory. About thirty Iraqi soldiers then escorted government repairmen to the site, but the workers were spooked by snipers and fled. Finally the fed-up electricity minister refused to send another repair team until the United States guaranteed the area was secure. Petraeus sent a letter to Prime Minister Maliki complaining about the electricity minister's foot-dragging. He also harangued the U.S. Army unit responsible for the insurgent-controlled area around the tower, known as the Triangle of Death. "You need to figure out what it is going to take to get the tower fixed," Petraeus said. He didn't care if the division moved its entire headquarters to the site of the toppled tower.

The operation to fix the tower was a massive military assault. More than 400 Iraqi soldiers, four Apache helicopters, and a U.S. team equipped with special vehicles to clear roadside bombs were mustered to protect a ten-man repair crew for a week. The Iraqis took eleven casualties.

Fixing Tower 57, which was just one small piece of a dilapidated 400-kilowatt line, hardly fixed the electricity problems. In fact, engineers had already figured out a way to make do without the tower, routing power into Baghdad via another line. Nor would fixing it stop insurgents from toppling another tower elsewhere. The big steel pillars were easy pickings. Still, Petraeus believed that fixing the tower sent a message to the enemy about U.S. resolve. It also sent a message to his men. "If the commander day after day is asking about Tower 57, then you probably take a look in your own area of responsibility and ask, 'Are there other Tower 57s in our area? What are we doing about them?' " Petraeus recalled.

★ ★ ★ ★

Petraeus's first few months were brutal. As U.S. troops pushed into neighborhoods they hadn't previously occupied, Sunni and Shiite extremists counterattacked, blowing up bridges, destroying mosques, and leveling markets. The U.S. death toll was especially heavy. More soldiers and Marines died during the spring of 2007 than during any previous period of the war. Insurgent bombs were growing larger and more lethal—big enough to flip a thirty-five-ton Bradley fighting vehicle and kill the six soldiers and the interpreter inside. Attacks, such as the May kidnapping and mutilation of three U.S. soldiers just a few miles from Tower 57, had become increasingly sophisticated and grisly.

Petraeus knew that sooner or later troops would hit their limit. The fighting and casualties didn't harden soldiers. It broke them. Eventually discipline problems and suicides, which had risen with each year of the war, would spike. Reenlistments would plummet, just as they had during the latter days of the Vietnam War. "I've occasionally wondered if there's some sort of bad-news limit," Petraeus confessed in mid-May after eleven soldiers and Marines were killed in a day. "How much tragic news can you take in one lifetime?" The Army seemed well on its way to finding out.

In May 131 soldiers were killed, the second-highest total of the war. Some Republicans were openly talking about supporting legislation to change the strategy in Iraq and start bringing soldiers home. Petraeus was running out of time. On June 3 he attended the weekly meeting that Prime Minister Maliki held with his generals and senior ministers in the presiden-

tial palace in the Green Zone. The Iraqis took their seats around a conference table. Petraeus grabbed a chair away from the fray, near a massive
mural of broad-backed workers toiling in factories and on farms—a relic of
Saddam's Stalin fixation. While the Iraqis argued in Arabic, he read
through a draft of his weekly letter to Defense Secretary Robert Gates. The
letters were a Sunday afternoon ritual. Without Gates's support, Petraeus
knew, he'd have little chance of sustaining his current strategy. In contrast
to Rumsfeld, who'd deluged Casey with irrelevant snowflakes, Gates
worked to build a consensus among moderates in Congress for a long-term
commitment to Iraq. He also pushed the military to spend more money
on weapons and equipment of immediate use in Iraq and Afghanistan.
Petraeus's letters shaped the secretary's understanding of the war. He also
used them to organize his own thoughts.

"It's been a difficult week to characterize," Petraeus began in the June
3 letter, rattling off the week's death and destruction. Three mosques had
been destroyed in a mixed Sunni-Shiite neighborhood in southwest Baghdad, sectarian murders were up over the previous week, five British contractors had been kidnapped, and two helicopters had crashed. He saved
one intriguing development for the end: "For the first time we saw the
Sunni population in Baghdad start to fight back against Al Qaeda in
Ameriyah," he noted. It was too early to tell if the small group of fighters in
the west Baghdad neighborhood was connected to the tribal revolt against
Al Qaeda–affiliated groups that was sweeping through Anbar Province.
"But nonetheless it is another data point that suggests that average Iraqis
don't want what Al Qaeda is offering," Petraeus continued. "We helped
the element and we'll see how it evolves. I suspect the Iraqi government
will have significant qualms."

Petraeus didn't describe the fighting, which unfolded only a few miles
from Al Faw Palace. Days earlier Lieutenant Colonel Dale Kuehl, the battalion commander in charge of the area, had received a call from the Firdas
mosque, located in the west Baghdad neighborhood. "We are going after
Al Qaeda," Sheikh Khaled, a prominent Sunni imam, told him. "What we
want you to do is stay out of the way."

"Sheikh, I can't do that," Kuehl replied. He spent twenty minutes trying to convince Khaled to work with his troops to kill the Al Qaeda fighters.

But Khaled wouldn't budge. On May 30, mosque loudspeakers through-out Ameriyah broadcast a call to war. Dozens of young men armed with Kalashnikovs, pistols, and hand grenades swarmed into the streets and at-tacked the extremists, who launched their own brutal counterattack the next day. Khaled barricaded inside the Firdas mosque and, surrounded by dead bodies, called Kuehl again, begging for help. The forty-one-year-old commander rushed two platoons of troops in armored vehicles to drive off the enemy.

As Petraeus was writing to Gates, Kuehl was meeting for the first time with the military leader of the Ameriyah fighters, who went by the nom de guerre of Abu Abed. A short, chubby man in his late twenties with a wispy goatee, he appeared to be in charge of about a dozen men. The meeting, which took place in the battered mosque, didn't go well. Exhausted from two days of nonstop fighting, Abu Abed insisted that his men take over se-curity for all of Ameriyah. He was suspicious of U.S. forces and feared the Shiite-dominated army units in his neighborhood. Kuehl countered that he wanted the right to approve any moves by the fighters.

The two men eventually agreed to conduct a trial mission together on June 4. It was an alliance of desperation. The Americans were Abu Abed's last hope. Sunni religious extremists were determined to kill him; if they didn't succeed, Abu Abed feared, the Shiite-dominated army would arrest him for his past ties to the insurgency. Kuehl, meanwhile, was still reeling from the worst month of his tour. He had lost fourteen soldiers in the pre-vious thirty days. He was ready to take a risk.

The fledgling alliance in Ameriyah was just the sort of opportunity that Petraeus had been hoping for. His counterinsurgency manual placed a heavy emphasis on co-opting locals. "These traditional authority figures often wield enough power to single-handedly drive an insurgency," the manual states. Casey had made some effort to talk with insurgent leaders, but he had been limited by the Bush administration's reluctance to negoti-ate with the enemy. Petraeus had a freer hand, and he used it.

Although Lieutenant Colonel Kuehl didn't realize it, Petraeus's com-mand had helped spark the anti–Al Qaeda revolt in his Baghdad sector. Shortly after taking over, Petraeus had created the Force Security Engage-ment Cell, essentially a department of peace negotiations, to seek out reconcilable enemies. He had put a British general in charge. "The Brits are good at talking to unsavory actors," he reasoned, citing their experience in Northern Ireland. Several weeks earlier General Graeme Lamb, the first British general to lead the reconciliation effort, had made contact with a Sunni insurgent leader named Abu Azzam who had taken part in some of the first anti–Al Qaeda tribal uprisings in western Iraq in late 2006. By early 2007 Abu Azzam wanted help driving Al Qaeda extremists from his rural village closer to Baghdad.

Lamb, in turn, had introduced Abu Azzam to Lieutenant Colonel Kurt Pinkerton, the battalion commander in charge of the area. "See what you can do with this guy," he said. Slowly the two men formed an alliance. In early April, Pinkerton asked the Iraqi for help finding recruits for the local police force in the area around Abu Azzam's village. "A week or so later, I drove out to a school compound and there were about eight hundred to a thousand men waiting to volunteer," Pinkerton recalled. He snapped a picture of the teeming crowd that made its way up to Petraeus. As was often the case in Iraq, something big was happening and U.S. commanders were only catching fleeting glimpses.

When Abu Abed started building his fledgling force in Baghdad's Ameriyah neighborhood two months later, he borrowed some fighters from Abu Azzam's group and turned to his fellow Iraqi for advice on working with the United States. The Americans, meanwhile, were also trading information about these potential allies. Pinkerton drafted a seven-page memo outlining his alliance with Abu Azzam that was sent to commanders throughout Baghdad, including Kuehl. "If you are not a very good diplomat, start learning," Pinkerton advised in the memo. "Reconciliation isn't about any one party winning, but about all parties' willingness to compromise." He suggested a series of gestures that had helped him win Abu Azzam's trust, such as releasing low-level prisoners, giving him responsibility for security in his village, and rewarding his tribe with small reconstruction contracts.

Although Petraeus had emphasized the importance of reconciliation, the real work didn't happen at his level. The enemy was too fragmented. Instead, the reconciliation effort depended on midlevel commanders seizing the initiative and making peace with their former enemies. Throughout the summer, these officers brokered alliances with dozens of Sunni insurgents throughout Baghdad. They organized neighborhood watch groups that guarded checkpoints. Like Lieutenant Colonels Pinkerton and Kuehl, they revised the rules as they went, relying on their best instincts, informal advice from their fellow officers, and their knowledge of the local politics and personalities.

By late June Petraeus's command was getting requests from his corps headquarters, which oversees daily military operations, asking for formal guidelines on the alliances. In its four years in Iraq, the United States had issued thousands of regulations governing just about every facet of a soldier's life; the Army loved rules. Petraeus, however, resisted the urge to put anything in writing that would constrain officers' options. He wanted them to experiment.

The Sunni reconciliation program marked a huge shift in strategy. Under Casey the focus had been on building the government and bolstering Maliki. Working with the armed Sunni groups, which were outside of the Shiite-dominated government's control, undermined the central government's authority. One of Petraeus's main tasks over the summer was to convince Maliki, who saw the former insurgents as criminals, to at least tolerate the alliances.

Even before Petraeus set foot in the country for his third tour, Iraqi officials complained that he was overbearing, arrogant, and pushy. He put demands on government leaders and on rare occasions yelled at them. A regular target was Lieutenant General Ahmed Farouk, who ran Maliki's Office of the Commander in Chief, a secretive arm of the government that was responsible for firing several Sunni army and police commanders. In one meeting, Farouk announced that the prime minister's office was forming a special unit to inspect checkpoints in the capital. Petraeus erupted, dismissing the idea as nonsense. It was the equivalent of President Bush forming his own armed unit to scrutinize traffic cops in Washington, D.C. "We all know what the real problem is. It's that you don't have an NCO corps or junior officers who will enforce standards on checkpoints," Petraeus barked. He leaned across the table and stared directly into the eyes of Maliki's favorite general. "Everyone knows this. We've been talking about it for months. What are you going to do about it?" Petraeus's red-faced rant quickly outran his interpreter, who gave up translating. Petraeus kept yelling. He wanted to stop Farouk from forming the unnecessary unit. But the outburst also had a larger purpose. He wanted to discredit Farouk, whom he saw as a malign and sectarian influence on Maliki, and run him from the weekly security meeting.

In 2006 and 2007 U.S. officers talked about the Iraqis as if they were an inviolable force of nature: "We can't want it more than the Iraqis," generals would grouse. Petraeus believed he could make the Iraqis want what was best for them, though it would take time.

Petraeus never raised his voice with Maliki, but their relationship grew testy the longer it continued. He and Ambassador Ryan Crocker, a fluent Arabic-speaker, met with the prime minister on Thursdays in his office. Crocker took the chair closest to Maliki. Petraeus sat on the ambassador's right. "Where are the M-16 rifles you promised us?" Maliki would rail one day. A few days later he'd accuse Petraeus of withholding ammunition from his troops.

"With respect, Mr. Prime Minister, I am prepared to give you my side of the story if you are willing to listen," Petraeus would interrupt. To Maliki it looked as if the United States was more interested in organizing insurgents into militias than in building legitimate security forces. The prime minister's aides began complaining that the United States didn't even know how many Sunnis were participating in the neighborhood watch units.

In truth, it was hard for the Americans to keep count. The program was growing too quickly. By early fall Kuehl had 231 citizens on the U.S. payroll in Ameriyah, but there were at least 600 men in Abu Abed's neighborhood force. Every month Kuehl gave the Iraqi about $160,000, most of which Abu Abed used to pay his men and buy local support. He sat behind a desk wearing a black cavalry hat, a gift from his American benefactors, and doled out money and favors to supplicants who lined up each afternoon outside his door. "I know Abu Abed was cutting deals in Ameriyah that we never saw and didn't understand," Kuehl said. Abu Abed also undoubtedly kept some of the money for himself.

The U.S. military, with Petraeus's encouragement, had helped the anti–Al Qaeda uprising in Ameriyah take root and spread to other areas of

Baghdad, causing violence levels to drop throughout the capital. In the summer of 2007 the military didn't control these fledgling uprisings. No one did.

✷ ✷ ✷ ✷

Arlington, Virgina
May 2007

As chief of staff, George Casey lived in Quarters One, a Victorian brick mansion at Fort Myer that he'd known since childhood; as a young boy he'd once set off the outdoor sprinkler system there, disrupting a garden party that he was attending with his parents. The house sat atop a hill over-looking Washington's marble monuments and Arlington National Cemetery, where his father had been buried just weeks after he'd been commissioned as a second lieutenant.

One of George Casey's first acts after taking office was to invite the re-tired general Edward "Shy" Meyer for lunch. Meyer, a longtime family friend, had been a protégé of Casey's father. On the morning the elder Casey was killed, Meyer had tried to talk him out of flying his helicopter in bad weather. Nine years later, with the Army at its nadir, Meyer was named Army chief, the position Casey now held. He had been renowned for his bluntness in the job. In 1980 he had famously told Congress that the Army, still recovering from its defeat in Vietnam, was a "hollow force" that lacked the equipment and the motivated and educated soldiers it needed to pre-vail against the Soviets. His warning helped spur the Reagan defense buildup.

Casey and Meyer ate at a small table in his Pentagon office. Casey's main job as chief was ensuring that the Army was holding up under the strain of two wars and was ready for any future conflicts. Some senior officers were concerned that the service, consumed with occupation duty and counterinsurgency, was losing its ability to fight a conventional war. Artillery units in Iraq and Afghanistan were being used as military police. Armor officers walked foot patrols, and when they were back in the United States, they spent most of their time recovering or preparing to return to the wars. They didn't have time to practice battalion- or brigade-sized assaults in their tanks. There were troubling indicators with regard to personnel issues. Suicides were rising. The Army was having a hard time retaining enough officers to fill jobs.

Casey invited Meyer to the Pentagon because he wanted some advice. "What were the early warning signs after Vietnam that the Army was in trouble?" he asked. Had anyone seen it coming? How quickly had the force collapsed?

It had been almost impossible to pin down the breaking point, Meyer replied. For years the force was strained by Vietnam but still holding together. Then all of a sudden it just fell apart. Experienced captains and sergeants started streaming out of the service, and no matter what the brass tried it was impossible to stanch the bleeding. It took ten years to pull the Army out of the spiral—and shifting to an all-volunteer force at the same time didn't help. "There's an invisible red line out there. You won't know it until you cross it," Meyer said. "Once you cross it, it's too late."

One key to keeping the Army away from the red line was convincing battle-hardened captains to stay in the military, Casey believed. But, worn down by repeated deployments, they were leaving at a growing rate. It wasn't nearly as bad as it had been during Vietnam, but the Army had missed its goal for keeping captains two years in a row. Casey settled on the idea of a $20,000 retention bonus aimed at these officers in the Army. The Pentagon had long used cash bonuses to entice enlisted soldiers to stay in the service, but this was going to be the first time it had ever tried such a program out on officers.

Before he signed off on the bonuses, Casey asked division and brigade commanders in Iraq and Afghanistan to survey their captains and see if the cash payments would make a difference. The answer was mixed. Perhaps the most eloquent response came from Colonel J. B. Burton, who in the summer of 2007 was in charge of U.S. troops in west Baghdad and Ameriyah. "This is a very tough crowd of warriors," Burton wrote. "They have spent the past four years in a continuous cycle of fighting, training, deploying, and fighting and seen no end in sight. They have seen their closest friends killed and maimed leaving young spouses and children as widows and single parent kids. . . . It's not about the money, at least not $20,000. What these warriors really want is for their Army to invest in them personally by giving them time back to invest in themselves and their families."

The long deployments weren't the only gripe. Young officers also were frustrated that their Army hadn't changed its training, equipment, and strategy quickly enough. At lower levels, captains and majors insisted that they had had to adapt to survive on Baghdad's violent streets, but their generals were a step behind. The growing anger was captured most clearly in an essay written by Lieutenant Colonel Paul Yingling, a rising officer who was just about to take command of a 540-soldier battalion. Yingling published his critique, which was entitled "A Failure in Generalship," in the June 2007 edition of *Armed Forces Journal,* a privately owned military publication. The essay was a passionate, angry, and in part naive cry for accountability and change at the top ranks. "America's generals have been checked by a form of war that they did not prepare for and do not understand," Yingling wrote. The essay's most oft-repeated line came at the end: "As matters stand now, a private who loses a rifle suffers far greater consequences than a general who loses a war."

Yingling would admit that some senior officers had pushed for change. Both Petraeus and Chiarelli, for example, had written extensively about their experiences and the need to incorporate the lessons that young officers were learning in Iraq. To Yingling, though, the Army brass's problems extended far beyond the efforts of a few reformers. The shortcomings in the general officer corps, he maintained, grew out of a personnel system that encouraged conformity and discouraged risk takers.

Within hours of its publication, the essay was rocketing around the Army by e-mail. Yingling had credibility because he had volunteered for two tours in Iraq, the second one working for Colonel McMaster in Tal Afar. He had a sterling pedigree that included three years teaching in the Sosh department at West Point and a recent selection to command a battalion. In short, he had a lot to lose.

He had decided to write the essay after attending a Purple Heart ceremony at Fort Hood. As he watched the troops receive their awards, he grew angry at his Army's failings in Iraq. He was ashamed that he hadn't spoken out more forcefully about the failures he had witnessed. By the end of the ceremony he could barely look the wounded troops in the eye. "I can't command like this," he recalls thinking. He insisted that there wasn't a lot of original thought in the piece. Rather, the essay was a distillation of conversations with fellow soldiers on patrols, in mess halls, and on training exercises.

Casey picked up the essay on the recommendation of Lieutenant Colonel Grant Doty, a Sosh alum who had worked for him in Iraq as a major and was now his speechwriter. Doty thought that he might want to send Yingling a note thanking him for writing the controversial piece. It would send a strong message to young officers that the top brass was willing to listen.

Casey said he would. But try as he might, he couldn't get through the essay. When he reached the part that accused generals of lacking "moral courage," he stopped reading. He had made mistakes in Iraq, but so had everyone. And he resented the insinuation that he and his fellow officers had caved in to political pressure. Even the oft-repeated charge that the generals had done little during the 1990s to prepare for insurgencies such as Iraq and Afghanistan left him raw. The country's history was full of instances in which America had entered wars unprepared and made major changes. "I tried not to be pissed off about it. I did," he said. He never wrote the note.

Chiarelli was more sympathetic to Yingling's argument. If he had been a lieutenant colonel, like Yingling, looking up at the generals in their palaces, he probably would have written the same sort of thing, he told himself. Chiarelli had been deeply frustrated by his last tour and disappointed that he hadn't been chosen to command. After spending a few weeks without a job, Defense Secretary Gates asked him in early 2007 to become his senior military assistant. Gates had been impressed by Chiarelli's passionate presentation months earlier when he had been in Baghdad as a member of the Iraq Study Group. Chiarelli jumped at the chance to work with the defense secretary. It would let him stay connected to Iraq.

Chiarelli didn't agree with everything in Yingling's article, but he liked his willingness to prod his superiors to take risks. What Chiarelli didn't like was some of his fellow generals' circle-the-wagons reaction to the essay—in fact, it disgusted him. The harshest criticism came at Yingling's home base at Fort Hood, the vast post in central Texas. After the essay appeared, Major General Jeff Hammond summoned all of the captains on post to hear *his* thoughts on the officer corps. About 200 officers in their twenties and thirties, most of them Iraq and Afghanistan veterans, filled the pews and lined the walls of the base chapel. "I believe in our generals. They are dedicated, selfless servants," Hammond said. Yingling wasn't qualified to judge the Army's generals because he had never been one and probably never would be. "He has never worn the shoes of a general," Hammond told the captains and majors, many of whom found Hammond unconvincing. They didn't want to hear a defense of the generals. They wanted someone to take accountability for what had gone wrong.

The higher Chiarelli rose, the more sympathy he had for officers willing to challenge the status quo in the Army. "The most important thing right now is that we listen to these junior officers. We need to allow them to write. We need to allow them to criticize," he'd say. His vision was an Army officer corps more like the intellectually freewheeling Sosh department at West Point.

Chiarelli found that he liked working for Gates, who was pushing the military services to scale back purchases of expensive weapons systems in favor of equipment suited to Iraq and Afghanistan. He helped the defense secretary speed up the fielding of a new armored vehicle with a V-shaped hull that could withstand blasts from roadside bombs better than the Humvee. He also was happy Gates called for a bigger budget for the State Department so that it could play a greater role in reconstruction in Iraq and Afghanistan.

Chiarelli's job as the secretary's senior aide practically guaranteed that he would get a fourth star. What he really wanted was to be the top commander in Iraq. In the fall of 2007 Chiarelli traveled to the Army War College in Pennsylvania to address generals headed to Iraq and Afghanistan. The darkened room with its big video screens and amphitheater-style seating looked like a NASA command center. Chiarelli had planned his presentation to be provocative. He opened with a searing seven-minute video that had been filmed by a reporter in Ameriyah just eleven days before Lieutenant Colonel Kuehl and the former insurgent Abu Abed met in the

Firdas mosque. The lights dimmed and the face of an Army specialist appeared on the big screen. "It's a joke," the young soldier from the video said. "We will have spent fourteen months in contact. The first week we were in Baghdad we lost two guys in our battalion and it hasn't stopped since." The video shifted to a shot of one of Kuehl's Bradleys that had been struck by a massive roadside bomb in Ameriyah. Soldiers watched helplessly as six of their colleagues and an interpreter burned to death inside. A few seconds later it cut to a scene of the same troops storming into the house of an elderly woman in search of the triggerman who had killed their friends. The frail woman let out a terrified, feral wail. "God help me! God help me!" she pleaded.

The woman's screams faded and the video jumped again. Now the troops had just shot an unarmed cabdriver who had ignored their orders to stop. A few minutes later they were rushing to save an Iraqi soldier whose legs had been blown off by a roadside bomb. It ended with a close-up of another young Army specialist angry at the extension of his tour from a year to fifteen months: "We were supposed to be flying home in six days. But because we have people in Congress with the brain of a two-year-old we are stuck here. I challenge the president or whoever has us here for fifteen months to ride along with me. I'll do another fifteen months if he comes here and rides with me every day."

The lights came up and Chiarelli told the generals that he was the one who had pressed Gates to extend tours to fifteen months after the president committed to sending the additional 30,000 troops to Iraq. The alternative, meting out three-month extensions over the course of a year, would have been even more painful to soldiers and their families. "It was a necessary evil," he said. Then for the next hour he talked with the generals about his successes and his admittedly larger failings during his last tour. His biggest disappointment had been his inability to get the U.S. military more involved in the effort to build the Iraqi government. "If I got involved in Iraqi governance and economics, I got my hand slapped," he said. "It wasn't from Casey. It was from the embassy. And it frustrated the hell out of me."

He was packing up when Casey walked into the room for his presentation to the same generals. He was the senior officer in the Army and moved around with an entourage of colonels who reflected his status. "Pete, what are you doing here? I thought you were a horse holder," Casey said, using the Army slang for an aide whose main job is to shadow his more important boss, in this case Gates. Casey was only needling him, but Chiarelli looked crushed. His shoulders slumped and the blood drained from his face. It felt like a jab, reminding him that he was still the junior three-star general and not a *real* commander. Chiarelli had always seen himself as a bit of an outsider within the clubby general officer corps. He regularly boasted that in his entire Army career he'd never been tapped for an early or "below-the-zone" promotion, like most golden boys. He was one of those rare Army leaders who had plodded up the chain of command, proving wrong all those who had thought he wasn't quite good enough.

The rumor was that Petraeus was going to leave command at the end of the year, and Chiarelli had already started thinking about what he would do if he was picked for the top job. He'd push harder to reform the corrupt ministries and use the high-profile command to rally the military and the rest of the U.S. government to jump-start the economy. The job was just beyond his grasp. Chiarelli shoved his speech notes into his briefcase and quickly hustled out of the room.

✯ ✯ ✯ ✯

Green Zone, Baghdad
July 2007

Petraeus and Admiral William "Fox" Fallon boarded a Black Hawk helicopter for an aerial tour of Baghdad. Fallon had replaced Abizaid, who retired as the top commander in the Middle East a few months earlier.

Abizaid had left the Iraq war strategy largely to Petraeus during his final weeks in command. He'd signed off on all Petraeus's requests for additional troops with no argument. Fallon, by contrast, had decided to focus his attention on what he saw as the shortcomings of Petraeus's strategy, which he thought was failing. He'd crafted his own plan calling for swift cuts to U.S. troop levels and a renewed focus on shifting the fight to the Iraqis. Petraeus had invited him on the helicopter tour as a last-ditch effort to convince Fallon to ease off. The temperature had soared past 115 degrees and the hot air pouring through the helicopter's open windows felt like a hair dryer on maximum power. Soon every uniform was drenched in sweat. Petraeus's enthusiasm bordered on desperation. After a few minutes, the two officers were hovering over downtown Baghdad; Petraeus was pointing out a soccer field. "They have real games there. The teams wear uniforms. You wouldn't believe it," he said. The helicopter banked over an empty public swimming pool. "They are fixing that pool, by the way," he told Fallon. "You see that amusement park? It's empty now, but on Thursday and Friday nights it is full of people."

Fallon kept asking about the Sunni areas of the city, where trash filled the streets and stores were shuttered. Petraeus tried to direct his attention to more positive areas. After forty-five minutes in the area the two men went their separate ways. The sales pitch backfired. "He's not seeing the whole city," Fallon groused. He worried that Petraeus's preternatural enthusiasm and ego wouldn't allow him to admit that the war might not be winnable. Rumors of Fallon's contentious visit spread through the palace. In the morning update, Lieutenant General Ray Odierno, who had replaced Chiarelli as the number two commander in Iraq overseeing daily military operations, did his best to reinforce confidence in the strategy. He had played a key role in pushing for the extra surge forces and deciding where to place them. "My sense is that we are in the pursuit mode in many areas throughout Iraq," he said. "The extremists are running in Baghdad. They are running in Anbar and in Mosul. The Iraqis are starting to see the results of our offensives." Publicly Petraeus and Odierno weren't going to show a hint of doubt.

When the two generals were paired up, some in the Army buzzed with concern about how they would get along. In 2003 they both commanded divisions in northern Iraq. Petraeus easily charmed the media and visiting congressmen, his division quickly becoming everyone's favorite success story. Odierno's 4th Infantry Division was often cited as an example of overaggressiveness in its single-minded pursuit of FREs—former regime elements. The generals clashed a year later when Odierno visited Baghdad as part of a Pentagon team looking for ways to accelerate Petraeus's training of Iraqis.

In 2007, the pressure cooker of Iraq drew the two men closer. On particularly hard days Petraeus and Odierno, recalling a Civil War moment that Petraeus had read about, would quote Ulysses S. Grant's exchange with William Tecumseh Sherman after the bloody first day at the Battle of Shiloh. Unable to sleep, Grant was standing beneath a tree as rain fell on him. Sherman appeared out of the darkness. "Well, Grant," Sherman said, "we have had the devil's own day, haven't we?"

"Yup," Grant replied. "Lick 'em tomorrow, though."

The really difficult days dwindled over the summer as commanders organized former Sunni insurgents into armed neighborhood watch groups, known as the Sons of Iraq. By the fall the United States had almost 70,000 sons of Iraq on the payroll. To control Iraqi neighborhoods, U.S. commanders blocked off neighborhoods with concrete barriers that made it harder for Sunni extremist groups and Shiite death squads to come and go. In some cases the Americans used the barriers to keep Shiite-dominated national police and army forces out of Sunni areas. The idea for the walls had come from the field, not headquarters. David Kilcullen, an Australian specialist on guerrilla war whom Petraeus had recruited as his counterinsurgency advisor, referred to the walls as "urban tourniquets," a temporary measure designed to stop the bleeding so that the patient doesn't die.

In September Petraeus returned to Washington to give his first assessment to Congress on whether his strategy was producing lasting results. He and his staff went through twenty-seven different drafts of his opening statement. The final version ran a stunning forty-five minutes. The Iraq debate had become too superheated for logic. So he decided that he was going to bludgeon skeptical lawmakers with data. His testimony was going to be a war of attrition.

A few days before the hearing, the Bush administration arranged for several officials well acquainted with congressional hearings and Iraq to come to Petraeus's house at Fort Myer to fire questions at him in a mock hearing. In Washington, it was known as a "murder board." The civilians who had been sent to help him prepare told him to start slashing his statement. Petraeus began stripping out paragraphs with his executive officer, Colonel Pete Mansoor, and Captain Liz McNally, a Rhodes scholar who acted as his speechwriter.

The final presentation, which Petraeus delivered in a flat monotone, still ran a lengthy eighteen minutes. Violence levels were down in eight of the previous twelve weeks, he told the lawmakers. Civilian deaths had fallen by 45 percent. The number of weapons caches discovered was higher, suicide attacks were down, and Iraqi defense spending was increasing. "The military objectives of the surge are, in large measure, being met," he concluded. To hold on to the fragile gains, he recommended sustaining the increased troop levels and the fifteen-month tours through the summer of 2008.

A few days after he had returned to Baghdad he met with Prime Minister Maliki, who was ecstatic. "We all thank God for your successful hearings," he said. "I can now see the beginning of a victory in Iraq." Petraeus tried to tamp down his confidence. "Obviously we are going to need to see continued security improvements, but we are also going to have to show progress in other areas," he said. In particular, Petraeus was eager to see the Iraqis hold provincial elections that would allow Sunni tribal leaders who had boycotted earlier balloting to amass some political power. The Iraqis also had to settle on a formula for distributing oil revenues and develop a plan to find permanent jobs for the more than 100,000 Sunnis participating in the Sons of Iraq neighborhood watch program.

Like Casey and Chiarelli in 2006, Petraeus found it almost impossible to pin down Maliki's real intentions toward Sunnis. A few weeks after his fall testimony he and Ryan Crocker met with the president via a video teleconference link from Baghdad. Maliki had been feuding with his Sunni vice president, Tariq al-Hashimi, and Bush asked whether the prime minister disliked all Sunnis or just Hashimi. "Maliki is not viscerally anti-Sunni, but he thinks that Hashimi is out to get him and he might be right," replied Crocker, who had been working closely with the country's political leaders for almost a year. "This is not a government of national unity," the ambassador continued. "The only time the Iraqi leaders behave that way is when you hold their head under water for a while and then let them back up."

The Sunni tribal leaders' fledgling alliance with the United States, the increase in American troops, and Petraeus's counterinsurgency strategy continued to drive down violence. The United States also caught a break when radical cleric Muqtada al-Sadr, who was losing control of his militia, called for a six-month cease-fire. The sectarian and ethnic tensions that had sparked the civil war in 2006 were still strong but increasingly were being pushed below the surface.

✶ ✶ ✶ ✶

In September 2008 the last of the U.S. reinforcements started heading home. Petraeus was just a couple of weeks away from leaving as well. He'd been chosen to lead U.S. Central Command, replacing Abizaid's successor, Admiral Fallon, who resigned after a short, rocky tenure. In the United States Petraeus was being hailed as the most influential military officer of his generation. The problem, as he reminded his staff, was that the war wasn't over. Daily attacks had plummeted to levels not seen since early 2004, when the insurgency was in its infancy. But the relative quiet was still dependent on the presence of U.S. forces and the relationships that they had forged with former Sunni insurgent groups. How dependent? No one actually knew.

In an area south of Baghdad known as the Triangle of Death, the Rakkasans battalion that Petraeus had commanded in the early 1990s was going to find out. Petraeus had visited the battalion more than any other in Iraq, doling out advice on counterinsurgency and just about everything else, including what dance steps to use when the unit went home and partied. "If you want to throw a good welcome-home ball for your troops, you need to learn how to do the electric slide," Petraeus counseled the battalion commander. "Then you need to get out and do it. Everyone else will follow." It was pretty good advice if you were commanding the battalion in 1992, joked Lieutenant Colonel Andy Rohling, the current commander.

By 2008, the Rakkasans epitomized Petraeus's counterinsurgency strategy. They had been so successful that they were averaging less than one attack a day and were on the verge of turning over their sector, which only a year earlier had been one of the most violent in Iraq, to a company about one-third the battalion's size. Colonel Rohling called his company commanders together a few weeks before the handover to lay out the plan.

The battalion headquarters was in a half-finished power plant that a Russian construction company had abandoned on the eve of the 2003 invasion. Al Qaeda–affiliated fighters had occupied it for much of 2005 and

2006. American troops had seized the compound in a bloody nighttime raid the following year and had held it ever since. The partially completed steel-and-cement skeleton stood ten stories. Graffiti on its support beams praised Saddam Hussein and listed the names and dates of "martyrs" and their suicide missions. Surrounding it were green pastures, reed-choked irrigation ditches, and dirt-poor farmers.

Rohling and his company commanders crammed into the battalion's main conference room, which they had fashioned out of plywood sheets on the power plant's second floor. "This is where we've been and what we're trying to avoid," Rohling said. He flashed a slide showing Vietnamese civilians scrambling to board a helicopter perched precariously on the roof of the CIA building in Saigon. No one laughed.

Rohling's best counterinsurgent was Captain Michael Starz. He stood out for his passion, intelligence, and youthful bravado. Under Rohling's plan, Starz's ninety-man company was turning its area over to a thirty-soldier platoon. Starz, who had the look of an earnest graduate student in camouflage, had bluntly told his boss a few days earlier that he thought it was a dangerous and dumb idea. The area was too complex. The fledgling relationship he was trying to foster between the local Sunni tribes that had until recently backed the insurgency and the Iraqi army was too strained and fragile.

When Petraeus ventured out into the field—typically twice a week—he made sure that he spent at least an hour with company commanders such as Starz. He'd kick out their bosses, close the door, and ask the young officers what they thought was really happening in their sector. What had they learned? What mistakes had they made? What did they need to win? Petraeus knew that captains such as Starz had the best understanding of the politics and personalities on the ground.

Starz's sector, which included the cities of Mohmudiyah and Yusufiyah, had been among the most violent and unforgiving in Iraq. Over the years insurgents had inflicted heavy casualties on U.S. troops in the area, and in brazen attacks twice kidnapped U.S. soldiers off checkpoints, torturing and killing them. It also was the place where four angry, drunk soldiers raped a young girl and murdered her and her family. By mid-2008, several thousand of the area's young men had been organized into Sons of Iraq groups and were being paid $400 a month to guard street corners. "We pretty much employ all the extremists in my area," Starz said. He said it without pride or outrage; this was how the war was being won.

A few weeks before he turned over his sector, he grabbed a briefcase packed with crisp $100 bills and paid a visit to the Owesat tribe. The first time that Starz had driven down the dirt road that leads into the tribe's village, insurgents had seeded it with more than twenty roadside bombs, one of which killed Lieutenant Tracy Alger, a thirty-year-old officer from rural Wisconsin. "The people who killed Tracy were all from this tribe that we are going to pay," he said. "To tell you the truth, it doesn't bother me that we are paying them. I am very detached from it. I don't hold any anger in my heart." As Starz entered the village, barefoot tribal elders all rushed to greet him, and the tribe's preeminent sheikh welcomed him with kisses on each cheek. Sheikh Musahim al-Owesat led him past a cluster of boxy one-story cement houses to the tribe's diwan, a large room with benches and pillows lining the walls and a wheezing air conditioner connected to a clanking electric generator. Soon the men of the tribe were lining up to collect their $100 bills from one of Starz's lieutenants.

"How old are you?" Starz asked one boy, no more than fourteen. The United States wasn't supposed to pay anyone younger than eighteen. Before the boy could answer, the sheikh barked at him to take his money and leave. "His father was killed in the fighting and his family needs the money to survive," Sheikh Musahim explained. Starz crossed his name off the list for the next payday but let him keep the money. "I guess he'll be our target audience in a couple of years," he said philosophically. Tables full of cash were replaced by a feast of eggs, watermelon, bread, yogurt, and tomatoes. It was Ramadan, when Muslims fast during the day, but few seemed reluctant to eat. Starz was fasting to see what it was like to go without food or water in 120-degree heat. Once the meal was done, Starz said goodbye to Sheikh Musahim, who lavished him with praise. "I respect you and love you as a human," the sheikh told him.

Soon his convoy was back on the road, rumbling past new, U.S.-funded poultry farms. The area south of Baghdad had raised most of the chickens for Iraq when Saddam Hussein was in power. Now Starz's unit was trying to relaunch the industry. His brigade commander had spent about $1 million to import 95,000 chicken embryos from the Netherlands, which were of hardier stock than the scrawny, disease-prone local chickens. Petraeus loved the project and demanded regular updates on its progress in the morning briefing.

The chicken-farming initiative might have been borrowed right from one of Petraeus's favorite novels, *The Centurions,* the 1960 book that follows French paratroopers as they fight insurgencies in Vietnam and Algeria. In one of the novel's more memorable passages a French officer in Vietnam explains to another, more conventionally minded colleague how his unit had changed its approach, abandoning firepower-intensive attacks for a strategy that focused on winning over the locals and even helping them raise pigs. "We no longer wage the same war as you, Colonel," the officer says. "Nowadays it's a mixture of everything, a regular witches' brew . . . of politics and sentiment, the human soul, religion and the best way of cultivating rice, yes, everything, including even the breeding of black pigs. I knew an officer in Cochin-China who by breeding black pigs, completely restored a situation which all of us regarded as lost."

The chicken farming initiative in Starz's sector wasn't producing the same stirring results that pig farming did in Lartéguy's novel. It was turning out to be far cheaper to import whole frozen chickens from big industrial poultry farms in Brazil than it was to raise and slaughter fresh ones south of Baghdad.

Starz's most prized project was to rebuild the ancient Sayeed Abdullah shrine, which honored a Shiite saint and had been leveled by Sunnis when Iraq was melting down in a civil war. He had convinced the Iraqi commander he was partnered with to use some of his reconstruction money to contract with a local Sunni tribe to rebuild it. Whatever their sect, most people in his sector were eager to make peace with the United States. They were less willing to forgive each other, and Starz saw the contract as a step toward a sturdier peace. On his way to the shrine, he stopped by the office of Captain Mohammed Amjen, the Shiite commander of the local unit. Loose hand grenades were scattered across Amjen's desk. On the wall hung a picture of his predecessor, who had been killed four months earlier by a female suicide bomber. Amjen passed on some rumors about Al Qaeda fighters moving back into the area. A few minutes later the two officers headed out to the shrine.

There they struck up a conversation with the construction foreman, a Sunni tribesman clad in a dirty dishdasha. His face was covered by a few days' worth of stubble. "Al Qaeda destroyed everything in this area," the foreman said, shaking his head.

"Tell the truth," Amjen replied, angrily waving a finger. "Your tribe was Al Qaeda. And they didn't destroy everything. They didn't touch the Sunni mosques. They just killed the Shiites."

The foreman, not wanting to alienate his patron, quickly changed the subject. "Without Captain Starz and Captain Amjen none of this would have happened. You both are kind and generous. May God bless you and make you undefeated in all your battles."

Petraeus had pushed young officers to seek out local leaders, many of whom had supported the insurgency. His "bottom-up" reconciliation strategy required meticulous intelligence work and a deep understanding of local politics. It also demanded a mind-set shift. In Petraeus's Iraq there were very few good guys or bad guys, and certainly no "anti-Iraqi forces," the Orwellian term that Rumsfeld had once coined to describe the enemy when he decided that *insurgent* was too flattering.

Back at his base in an abandoned potato plant, Starz tried to explain how his perspective had changed during his second yearlong tour. He was less idealistic and far more practical. He'd come to realize that concepts such as democracy and loyalty to country or the central government didn't resonate. "Loyalty is constantly shifting here, and there is no moral component to it," he said. "It's so foreign to our way of thinking, and it's hard to respect. But you have to remember that it is a different way of seeing the world."

As for counterinsurgency, "it comes naturally to me," Starz said. "I like the thinking part of it." It was the somewhat hidebound pre-Iraq Army that he had joined out of West Point in 1999 that now seemed strange. As Starz prepared to leave, he resembled one of the French paratroopers in *The Centurions,* who ebulliently celebrates the changes he and his fellow officers have been able to make in battle as they cast off the rigid, bureaucratic tendencies of the French Army and adapted to the messy guerrilla war they were fighting. "I'd like two armies: one for display, with lovely guns, tanks, little soldiers, fanfares, distinguished and doddering generals . . . an Army that would be shown for a modest fee on every camp fairground," the French officer says. "The other would be the real one, composed entirely of young enthusiasts in camouflage who would not be put on display but from whom all sorts of tricks would be taught. That's the Army in which I should like to fight."

It was the Army that Petraeus had forged in Iraq.

Big Green

First to fight for the right,
And to build the nation's might,
And the Army goes rolling along
Proud of all we have done,
Fighting till the battle's won,
And the Army goes rolling along.
—"THE ARMY SONG"

Fort Monroe, Old Point Comfort, Virginia
December 8, 2008

The star-shaped fortress lay on an exposed spit of land at the mouth of the Chesapeake Bay. The Army had occupied the massive brick battlements for hundreds of years, holding the ground even during the Civil War, when it formed an impregnable Union enclave in the midst of the Confederacy. But the long presence on the shores of the Chesapeake was coming to an end. The post, which had ceased being vital to the country's defense almost a century earlier, was slated for closing in a year or so. In the Army, change sometimes came slowly.

On this day, as a frigid wind swept in off the water, another sort of closure was happening on the parade grounds. One of the last U.S. officers to have served in Vietnam was retiring from the Army. As a lieutenant in 1972, Scott Wallace had been an advisor to South Vietnamese troops in the Mekong Delta. He had risen in the following decades through the ranks, eventually commanding troops during the invasion of Iraq, and he'd run Fort Leavenworth prior to Petraeus's arrival there. Now he was set to receive a proper four-star send-off, with a marching band and a thumping seventeen-gun salute fired by howitzers pointed out to sea.

General George Casey, as the Army chief, had flown in from Washington to preside. It was the kind of occasion Casey loved, the songs and ceremony recalling his childhood on posts around the world. In his black beret and camouflage fatigues, Casey beamed as he walked to the podium in the middle of the wide lawn. Seeing other officers he had served with for decades, some now retired, reminded him how much the Army had become his extended family. In the crowd he saw retired Army chief Carl Vuono, who had rescued Casey's career nearly twenty years earlier by getting him a job in the 1st Cav. It was a moment to look backward. Wallace's retirement after thirty-nine years in uniform meant that the Army was finally severing one of its last direct links to the war in Vietnam.

That conflict, Casey noted as he addressed the crowd, "was a formative experience both for Scott and for our Army." In its aftermath, the generals who ran the institution had asked, "Just how does this Army fight?" The answer they devised "took the Army out of the rice paddies of Vietnam and placed it on the western European battlefield against the Warsaw Pact." Casey had lived through that turbulent transformation as a young officer in Mainz and in Vicenza. He had stood guard in the barracks over his own men, including the drug addicts and the discipline cases that populated the ranks in those days as the Army withdrew from Southeast Asia and shifted to an all-volunteer force. And he had been part of rebuilding its strength, which still sent a surge of pride through him.

As Casey said goodbye to the last of the Vietnam generation, the Army was beginning to come home from Iraq after five years, facing the same questions about the future as it had in that earlier war. It had once rejected the idea that Vietnam had something to teach. No one thought it would repeat the same mistake after Iraq. But what lessons would it take? Casey's experiences had led him to some conclusions. One of the biggest lessons that he'd taken was that counterinsurgency warfare was far harder than he'd thought it could be. "As a division commander in Kosovo, I would have said that if I can do conventional war, I can do anything else," he often said as chief. "Now I know that isn't true." The Army absolutely couldn't lose its ability to wage counterinsurgency wars, he said.

But he worried that young Army officers, who had been schooled in Iraq and Afghanistan, were losing the skills that they'd need in future conventional battles, the sort that he and his generation had spent several decades mastering at the National Training Center. To best prepare the Army, he settled on the split-the-difference approach that reflected the way he had worked through most problems while in command. It was carefully reasoned, meticulously researched, and unlikely to require the major institutional changes that some counterinsurgency advocates demanded. Casey wanted to locate the middle point somewhere between counterinsurgency and conventional combat that would allow the military to react in whichever direction it had to in the future.

He found reassurance by examining Israel's 2006 war with Hezbollah in southern Lebanon. At first glance the Hezbollah forces didn't look too different from the insurgents in Iraq and Afghanistan. They operated in small cells and lived among the Lebanese people. But the Hezbollah fighters were far better armed and trained than the enemies the United States had fought. Over thirty-four days, the insurgents pounded the Israelis with sophisticated antitank guided weapons and cruise missiles. After the battle, senior Israeli commanders blamed their losses on their long tours in the West Bank and Gaza. The years of occupation duty, they argued, had caused their soldiers' conventional skills to atrophy and left them vulnerable to the disciplined and well-armed Hezbollah fighters. By 2009, the Pentagon had coined a new term to describe the Lebanon battle and others like it. They were "hybrid wars" that combined aspects of a conventional fight, counterinsurgency, and peacekeeping. Much as it had been for the last four decades, the Army was embroiled in a debate about what the next war was going to look like and what kind of military the United States would need to fight it. The truth was that there was no consensus, other than that the Army should not turn its back on Iraq.

John Abizaid's long experience in the Arab world gave him a different view than most about the changes the military needed to make. He'd retired from the Army and moved home to the Sierra Nevada, an hour's drive from Coleville, where he and Kathy had grown up. They loved the soaring, snowcapped peaks that surrounded their home. Abizaid also loved the fact that he was far from Washington, D.C., a place where he'd never felt entirely comfortable. He jokingly said he was living in "ungoverned space," a term the Pentagon applied to terrorist sanctuaries in Pakistan and Somalia.

Even in retirement, the Middle East and its problems still dominated his thoughts. He'd watched the conflicts between moderates and extremists, Shiites and Sunnis, Israelis and Palestinians unfold since his days at the University of Jordan in the late 1970s. It had taught him to take the long view of events in the region and to appreciate the limits of military power on its own to make lasting changes.

After his retirement, he tried to explain his ideas at universities, foreign policy think tanks, military bases, and even at the monthly Rotary Club luncheon in Gardnerville, a town about thirty miles from Coleville. The source of the instability in the Middle East, as Abizaid saw it, was the conflict between moderates and extremists within Islam. The United States couldn't decide this struggle. "I came to the conclusion a long time ago that you can't control the Middle East," he often said. But America could help its more moderate allies prevail. His solution amounted to an anti–Powell Doctrine for the Arab world. Rather than relying on military force to remake the Middle East, he wanted to send small teams of soldiers and civilians to work with allies to reform their economies and build competent local armies and police. "Throughout the region we need to quit being the primary military force and over time do less as we increase the capacity more and more of indigenous forces," he said.

If there was a model, it was one he had seen on his travels years earlier when he had come across a tiny band of British soldiers in the wilds of Oman, training and fighting with the Sultan's army. Britain had shed its empire and most of its global commitments, but it still pursued its interests where and how it could, with a clear-eyed sense of limits built up over centuries. The United States had far more resources and more places where it needed to be present, but it could learn from Britain's example, he thought.

The problem was finding soldiers who could put his ideas into practice. They had to be soldiers like John Abizaid. In his retirement he sat on the board that chose officers for the Olmsted Scholarship, the program that had first sent him to the Middle East. The program could produce officers who were culturally aware and comfortable in foreign lands, the qualities he thought were needed. The problem was that there weren't nearly enough of them. During the Cold War the Defense Department had trained tens of thousands of Sovietologists and nuclear strategists. The Olmsted program paid for only twenty-seven officers each year to study overseas. "Why not have 270 or 2,700?" Abizaid wondered.

His approach offered a plausible source for a segment of the military, but it was no panacea for the entire Army, a force of over a million active and reserve soldiers, few of whom had Abizaid's curiosity about historical and cultural forces shaping the places where they might be called on to fight. Abizaid recognized this.

But his unhappy experience in Iraq was a poignant example of a fact Abizaid had long warned about: generals didn't get to pick the wars they were asked to win. There was no guarantee that a future White House wouldn't send the Army into another misbegotten conflict or that a crisis wouldn't emerge requiring a large conventional ground force. The Army had to be ready for a whole range of contingencies—as Iraq had shown.

While Abizaid was talking about changes that would take decades, soldiers in Iraq had been forced to adapt as best they could. And though it had taken too long, they had done so. The best officers had worked tirelessly to understand the politics and culture of their areas. They brokered local cease-fires between warring Sunnis and Shiites, bought off sheikhs with reconstruction projects, and even rebuilt religious shrines if that was what it took to achieve even a tentative peace. The most curious among them pored over works of history and counterinsurgency theory from Vietnam and Algeria. The learning process had often been slow and costly. Many still lacked the kind of deep cultural understanding that Abizaid wanted. But, spurred on by dissidents in its ranks and painful battlefield failures, the Army had become a very competent counterinsurgency force.

It was Petraeus who both drove this change and benefited from it. A few days before he gave up command in Iraq several hundred soldiers gathered in Al Faw Palace for a party to say goodbye. The lights dimmed in the palace banquet hall and a highlight video, set to thumping rock music, began to play on a movie-theater-sized screen. Images of exhausted soldiers and wailing, grief-stricken Iraqis gave way to a clip of Petraeus testifying before the Senate Armed Services Committee. "The situation in Iraq is dire. The stakes are high. There are no easy choices, and the way ahead will be hard," he said in a flat monotone. "But hard is not hopeless." The music quickened. Soon the soldiers on the big screen were collaring insurgents, handing out school supplies, and cutting ribbons on new police stations and sewage-treatment plants.

When the lights came back on Petraeus stood atop a plywood riser. Although he would never admit it to Holly, he was sad to leave Iraq. His life there had settled into a comfortable rhythm. The daily battle update, the regular trips to visit his field commanders, and the weekly meetings with Maliki all had afforded him a feeling of control over the war that had dominated six years of his life. His new job as the top commander in the Middle East would give him a continuing role in Iraq. But it was clear that most of his attention was going to be consumed by the growing violence and instability in Afghanistan and Pakistan. In truth, the U.S. military's influence in Iraq was on the wane. Iraqi-led victories over Sadr's militia in Baghdad and Basra in the spring of 2007 had given Maliki, who only months earlier had been fighting for his political survival, a new swagger. Iraq was returning to real self-government, though where it would lead was uncertain.

The soldiers who gathered for Petraeus's farewell weren't really there to celebrate the gains in Iraq. They'd come to thank the general for what he'd done for them. In his nineteen months in command he'd imbued his troops—many of whom had begun to doubt whether victory was even possible—with a new resolve. He'd made the Army feel smart again, and convinced his brigades and battalions that they could prevail.

As custom dictated, his soldiers had brought gifts for their departing commander. The noncommissioned officers in the palace arranged with the Pentagon to have him named the Army's first honorary command sergeant major. It was an accolade freighted with irony. Petraeus's tendency toward micromanagement early in his career had often made him the scourge of his sergeants. Now they wanted to welcome him into their fraternity. Next Lieutenant General Lloyd Austin, Petraeus's deputy in Iraq, presented him with a replica of the "Iron Mike" statue that stands across the street from the Fort Bragg officers' club. The statue depicts a World War II–era paratrooper who has just alighted in enemy territory. His foot rests on a pile of rubble. He is fingering the trigger of his weapon. His helmet is unbuckled and slightly askew. For decades the type of fighting man the statue represented was the Army ideal, one that Petraeus had always aspired to. He turned the statue in his hands. "I have never received one of these, but it means an awful lot," he said, his voice breaking with emotion.

The embrace of his own army was important to Petraeus, but so was the regard of his hero Marcel Bigeard. They had kept up an occasional correspondence over the years. Now that the legendary French paratrooper was over ninety, the letters from France came less frequently and were written by an assistant. But Bigeard's sentiments were unmistakable. He had followed Petraeus's exploits in Iraq and now treated the younger American officer as an equal. One letter arrived on the anniversary of Dien Bien Phu, the French defeat in Indochina where Bigeard had been taken captive. He had come home to France years later determined to rebuild the spirit of the French paratroopers. He had not forgotten those days. "The last will of General Bigeard is to have his ashes spread over the Dien Bien Phu area," the letter said. It closed with these words to Petraeus: "I wish you all the best for your mission. I know how difficult it is. . . . Airborne, all the way."

He had begun as a skinny, hyperambitious lieutenant, the kind of officer who sat with a megaphone in the motor pool and instructed his sergeants on the proper way to grease an axle. He had grown into a general who, though still demanding, was far more comfortable with uncertainty and experimentation. His disparagers over the years had said he had risen by connections, but they had been rendered mute by his achievements. Now the Army that had once questioned his combat skills hung on his pronouncements and debated his ideas, even the old war horses from Vietnam. At gatherings of retired generals, Petraeus would listen respectfully as his predecessors urged him to go on the offense in Iraq, as if a flanking maneuver or a rising body count would finally end the war. Petraeus would gently remind them that winning in Iraq required killing the enemy, to be sure, but much more. Above all, it required patience. He was the most influential officer of his generation. In 2008, he had made a special trip back to the Pentagon to chair a promotion board to select the next group of one-star generals. These were the officers who would lead the Army for the next decade. Petraeus's panel went out of its way to reward soldiers who had proven themselves as innovators in Iraq. Colonel Sean McFarland, who had forged critical early alliances with Sunni tribal leaders in Anbar Province, made the list of forty new one-stars. So too did Colonel McMaster, whose approach to securing Tal Afar had prefigured the strategy Petraeus employed in Baghdad. Petraeus's panel ignored the misgivings of some of McMaster's former superiors in Iraq, who worried that he could be single-minded and stubborn, and focused on his battlefield performance.

The unorthodox ideas that Petraeus had championed years ago in Sosh now dominated high-level Pentagon strategy papers and policy speeches. "The U.S. military's ability to kick down the door must be matched by our ability to clean up the mess and even rebuild the house afterward," Defense Secretary Robert Gates opined. Gates's message was that the American way of war, built around quick battles and high-tech weapons, was giving way to a new reality in which economic development and improved governance were often more important than overwhelming force.

No one was sure how long Petraeus's ideas would endure. There was little institutional support in the Pentagon, defense industry, or Congress for the relatively low-tech weapons needed for wars such as those in Iraq and Afghanistan. Lawmakers wanted to focus on big, expensive projects that brought jobs to their districts.

Petraeus's vision for his Army also was hardly the palliative that the Powell Doctrine had been. At best, it promised more long wars whose considerable burdens would be borne by a military that accounted for less than one-half of 1 percent of American society. Even President Obama's plan to end the Iraq war reflected this sobering reality. "Let me say this as plainly as I can. By August thirty-first, 2010, our combat mission in Iraq will end," the president promised in a speech delivered in front of thousands of camouflage-clad Marines. He then went on to say that he was going to leave as many as 50,000 troops in Iraq through 2011 to advise Iraqi forces, kill terrorists, and provide security for military and civilian personnel involved in governance and reconstruction projects. These were essentially the same missions the military had performed in 2008 and 2009.

Only a few days later Obama dispatched 17,000 more soldiers and Marines to Afghanistan. As he had done in Iraq, Petraeus stressed that troops would have to live among the Afghan people, protect the population, and where possible win over reconcilable enemies. In Afghanistan, though, Petraeus faced a new set of problems. The country was larger than Iraq, more fractured, and heavily dependent on the cultivation of opium for its economic survival. The enemy had a safe haven in the ungoverned regions of Pakistan. The ongoing Iraq war and the global economic crisis meant that Petraeus would have to make do in Afghanistan with less reconstruction money, fewer troops, and smaller, more poorly equipped indigenous security forces. "Afghanistan is going to be the longest campaign of the long war," Petraeus predicted.

The test of whether Iraq had changed the Army permanently would not come in Afghanistan. It would come in the Pentagon, where the decisions were made about who got promoted, what equipment was bought, and how soldiers were trained. Few other officers would be as involved in those decisions as Pete Chiarelli, the Army's vice chief. He had been home from Iraq for a little over a year when a retired colonel named Gary Paxton, one of his old brigade commanders, stopped by his house for dinner. The two officers went back decades to Chiarelli's stint in Germany in the late 1980s. Paxton had taken command of Chiarelli's brigade just after the CAT competition. He had learned about the role that then Major Chiarelli had played in pushing the United States to victory in the contest and quickly snapped up the bright young officer to serve as his operations officer, the prime job for a major in a combat brigade.

Paxton was nothing like the brainy officers who inhabited the Sosh department. He was brash, loud, and tactless. Chiarelli never forgot how Paxton had addressed his troops at a Christmas tree lighting ceremony at Gelnhausen two decades before. "Everybody's going to get some time off," he said. "Some of you guys will go home and be with family, and some of you guys are single and are going to go downtown and get drunk and try to get laid." Chiarelli went rushing up to him after the speech. "Sir, you can't say that stuff anymore," he laughed. "Twenty percent of the people out here are females."

Despite their differences, Chiarelli admired Paxton immensely. He was the archetypal Cold Warrior, ready to face off against the Soviet Red Army, stationed only a few hundred miles from their base. Paxton had retired from the Army in the early 1990s and moved to Alaska, but he and Chiarelli and their families had kept in close touch. Their eldest sons had both served as best man at each other's wedding. Their wives spoke often. So when Paxton and his wife passed through Washington the Chiarellis invited them for dinner. Soon the talk turned to Iraq, where the violence had finally begun to fall. Only a few months earlier the war had seemed lost. Now there was at least a reasonable hope that it was salvageable.

"Well, what do you think about Iraq?" a delighted Paxton asked Chiarelli.

The progress under Petraeus had been "absolutely fantastic," Chiarelli replied, but unless there was matching economic and political progress in the coming months, the sectarian violence would spike as U.S. troops withdrew, and the gains could be transitory. Paxton listened, but Chiarelli could tell that he wasn't buying it. His old mentor, who had done a tour in Vietnam, was pretty sure he knew what had happened in Iraq: Petraeus had taken command and after years of dithering had finally ordered his troops to start punishing insurgents. Instead of behaving like some academic or city administrator, Paxton thought he'd acted like a soldier. "You know, Pete, the problem with you is that you just never were tough enough," Paxton said.

Chiarelli stared right at his former mentor. His voice tightened with anger. "Petraeus feels exactly the way I do," he growled. "I promise you that." Chiarelli carried the insult around with him for months. "I don't think I've ever been hurt quite that much," he recalled. "It just tore my heart out."

The testy exchange between the two old friends showed how much had changed since the first tanks crossed from Kuwait into southern Iraq in 2003. Then the Army had for years believed almost unquestioningly in the wisdom of the Powell Doctrine and in its ability to bludgeon just about any foe. Six years and many painful losses later, it had emerged from Iraq as a far more flexible, modest, and intellectually nimble force. Colonels, majors, and captains in Iraq and Afghanistan took risks and saw themselves as more than just combat officers. They understood that in today's wars building and brokering disputes were sometimes as important as killing the enemy.

It was that army that Chiarelli had wanted badly to lead in combat. Even after getting passed over for the Iraq command in 2007, he held out hope that President Bush would pick him to replace Petraeus the following year. Once again, it didn't happen. Although he had been on the short list, Bush gave the position to General Odierno, whose knowledge of the country was more current, senior White House officials reasoned. Unlike Chiarelli, who had presided with Casey over Iraq's descent into civil war, Odierno had a proven track record of success from having served as Petraeus's deputy. Fairly or not, Chiarelli and Casey would always be marked as the officers who had been in command when the place came apart.

When Chiarelli got his fourth star in the summer of 2008 and was named vice chief, he was an odd choice for the position, which didn't exactly lend itself to the pursuit of soaring strategic thoughts. He'd also be working directly for Casey. Ever since their tour together their relationship had been civil but strained.

Chiarelli didn't want to be a typical vice chief, stuck behind a desk administering the Army's far-flung posts and installations and fighting to save its weapons programs from the budget axe. He had to do those things, to be sure. But he also saw his job as making sure the military's penchant for order and discipline didn't cut off the argument and debate about what the Army had undergone in Iraq. One of his responsibilities was to talk to all of the new brigadier generals, who gathered several times a year in groups of about two dozen to think about the service's future and the role they would play in shaping it. At one of these meetings, at a conference center outside Washington just before Christmas in 2008, he ended his presentation with a quotation: " 'America's generals have repeated the mistakes of Vietnam in Iraq. . . . The intellectual and moral failures common to America's general officer corps in Vietnam and Iraq constitute a crisis in American generalship.' Does anyone know who wrote these words?" he asked.

"Paul Yingling," several officers in the small crowd replied. Lieutenant Colonel Paul Yingling's essay "A Failure in Generalship" had been published almost two years earlier, but his words still drew winces and groans from most senior Army officers. Since it appeared, Yingling's career had not gone smoothly. His artillery battalion had received orders to Iraq earlier that year. Because his troops were going to be guarding prisoners and not in combat, the Pentagon had decided to send the battalion but not Yingling or his staff officers. He had taken command of the battalion only a few months earlier, and now it was being ripped away from him. Many in the Army saw the move as punishment for his criticism of the generals.

When Chiarelli learned what was happening, he called Yingling at Fort Hood to offer his help. Although the two shared a connection to Sosh, they had never met. Petraeus, meanwhile, interceded from Baghdad. A few days later Yingling learned that the Army had changed its mind. He was going to be allowed to serve alongside his soldiers in Iraq. The fifteen-month deployment was Yingling's third in five years. He had volunteered for all three.

Chiarelli understood why some of the new one-star generals groaned when they saw Yingling's incendiary words. But he was also determined to change their mind-set. "Isn't this the kind of officer we want in our Army?" he asked. "He's passionate, intelligent, and engaged."

Iraq had forced massive changes to the Army's equipment, training, and strategy. But the most important legacy of the war had been cultural. The war had upended most of the service's basic assumptions about how it should fight, undermining the Powell Doctrine with its emphasis on short, intense wars but not replacing it with anything nearly so straightforward. Chiarelli wasn't sure he could predict what the next war would look like. But he knew what kind of officers would be needed. He wanted an officer corps that argued, debated, and took intellectual risks. Even that laudable goal was far from accepted within the Army.

1 **The helicopters descended onto the hilltop clearing:** This account relies on coverage of General Casey's press conference in the *New York Times* on June 30, 1970, "Last Combat Unit out of Cambodia After Two Months," and interviews with the elder Casey's daughters Joan Gettys, Winn Cullen, and Ann Bukawyn, who watched television coverage of the event.

2 **Casey climbed into the copilot seat of his Huey helicopter:** The details of Casey's disappearance are taken from *Incursion* by J. D. Coleman, a journalist and retired Army lieutenant colonel who served with Casey.

5 **That evening, the Caseys hosted a party at their house to celebrate:** The description of the party comes from interviews with George W. Casey Jr., Winn Cullen, and Casey's Georgetown University friends Christopher Muse and Ray O'Hara.

8 **As the funeral party gathered at Fort Myer's Old Post Chapel:** The account of the funeral and gathering at Quarters One came from interviews with the elder Casey's children and Sheila Casey. It also relies on news coverage in the *Washington Post.*

9 **After three days of battling a low-grade forest fire:** The biographical material on Abizaid and his family comes from interviews with him, Kathy Abizaid, Michael Krause, and Lieutenant General (Ret.) Karl Eikenberry, Abizaid's West Point roommate.

12 **The telephone calls came late at night:** The biographical material on Chiarelli and family relies on interviews with him, Beth Chiarelli, and Theresa Chiarelli.

14 **Rummaging in the garage one day as a teenager:** This account comes from interviews with Chiarelli and is also covered in *The Long Road Home: A Story of War and Family* by Martha Raddatz.

15 **As a kid Dave Petraeus used to sneak onto the West Point campus:** The account of Petraeus's time at West Point comes from interviews with Petraeus, Holly Petraeus, General (Ret.) William Knowlton, and fellow cadets Chris White, John Edgecombe, Dave Buto, and Reamer Argot.

19 **A few months after he arrived, a gang of soldiers tore through:** The account of Casey's time in Mainz and Vicenza was based on interviews with Casey, Lieutenant General Tom Metz, Ed Charo, E. K. Smith, Joseph Tallman, Jeff Jones, Jack O'Conner, L. H. "Bucky" Burruss, Jim Simms, Turner Scott, and Jeff Rock.

19 **"The price of Vietnam has been a terrible one":** General Michael's letter was
  quoted in *The Long Gray Line: The American Journey of West Point's Class of 1966*
  by Rick Atkinson.

22 **A few weeks earlier Lufthansa flight 181, bound for Frankfurt:** The description of
  the origins of Delta Force comes from *Delta Force: The Army's Elite Counterterrorism Unit by* Colonel (Ret.) Charlie A. Beckwith and Donald Knox.

24 **Some days Casey and the other soldiers started before dawn:** The description of
  Casey's Delta Force tryouts came from interviews with Casey and fellow participants L. H. "Bucky" Burruss and E. K. Smith.

CHAPTER TWO

27 **"Well, we have finally made it to the Hashemite Kingdom of Jordan":** All letters to
  the Olmsted Foundation were provided by General Abizaid and Kathy Abizaid.

27 **the seven other winners that year had all gone off to Europe:** Information on the
  other scholars came from the Olmsted Foundation website.

32 **Toward the end of his stay Abizaid decided to run the entire length of Jordan:**
  Some details of Abizaid's run came from an article in the *Jordan Times* that was
  published in 1980.

33 **"One of the most intelligent officers I have ever known:"** Abizaid's fitness reports
  were included in his application for the Olmsted Scholarship.

CHAPTER THREE

35 **The letter from a captain named David Petraeus:** The description of Petraeus's
  letter came from an interview with Brigadier General (Ret.) James Shelton.

36 **When, shortly after arriving, she heard a radio commercial:** The account of Petraeus's arrival at Fort Stewart came from Holly Petraeus. The description of the
  24th Infantry Division's readiness came from several sources, including interviews
  with Petraeus, Lt. Gen. (Ret.) George Stotser, Lt. Gen. (Ret.) Ed Soyster, and the
  Department of the Army Historical Summary for fiscal year 1980.

36 **A picture snapped that evening:** The account of the training exercise in France
  comes from Gen. Petraeus and from Rick Bursky, who served in the 509th and
  took the photograph.

37 **he had lobbied to come to Fort Stewart for one main reason:** Holly Petraeus and
  others described his interest in joining the Ranger battalion. Petraeus described

his interest in Bigeard and receiving the autographed picture as a Christmas present.

38 **So he began spending one day a week in the motor pool:** From interviews with Petraeus and Dan Grigson, a fellow company commander in the 24th Infantry Division.

39 **His success in the EIB competition "put Petraeus on the map":** The accounts of the basketball championship and the Expert Infantry Badge ceremony come from Petraeus, Shelton, and Col. (Ret.) George Wilkins.

40 **"We thought he was the best guy for the job":** From interview with Shelton.

40 **It was like the Fourth of July, only with real rockets:** From interview with Marty Gendron.

41 **"basically what we have is a hollow Army":** The account of Meyer's speech at Camp David comes from James Kitfield's *Prodigal Soldiers,* an excellent history of the Army from Vietnam to the 1991 Persian Gulf War.

41 **When a *New York Times* reporter showed up at Fort Stewart:** Shelton is quoted in the *New York Times,* September 24, 1980.

41 **"The difference between you and me, Dave":** From interview with Grigson.

42 **He wanted Petraeus to be his eyes and ears, to carry out sensitive assignments:** From interview with General (Ret.) John Galvin.

42 **"Sir, your April evaluation," read the cover sheet:** Document provided by Galvin.

43 **Their close relationship did not always go over well:** From interview with Lt. Gen. (Ret.) H. G. "Pete" Taylor.

44 **"Some people compared Petraeus to Massengale":** From interview with Martin Rollinson.

45 **For two weeks, he and Petraeus crisscrossed the battlefield:** From interviews with Taylor and Brigadier General (Ret.) Taft Ring.

47 **Hezbollah, the militant Shiite group:** For an account of Hezbollah's rise, see *Hezbollah* by Augustus Richard Norton.

48 **He and the four dozen or so other United Nations observers:** The accounts of Abizaid's time in Lebanon come from interviews with Abizaid and other members of the observer group: John Wagner, Larry Colvin, and Greg Von Wald.

49 **"War in southern Lebanon is difficult to imagine by common standards of reference":** Taken from a paper written by Abizaid entitled "In Defense of the Northern Border: Israel's Security Zone in Southern Lebanon." December 30, 1986. It was written for the Army's Command and General Staff College at Fort Leavenworth, Kansas.

49 **"There was no shortage of willing martyrs"**: Taken from Abizaid, "In Defense of the Northern Border."

50 **"Moderates in Amal, unable to deliver on promises"**: Taken from Abizaid, "In Defense of the Northern Border."

51 **Shortly after he returned, Thurman marched down**: This scene was recounted by Lt. Gen. (Ret.) Dan Christman, who was also in the office with Thurman and Miller.

CHAPTER FOUR

52 **Beth Chiarelli was just about to tee off**: From interviews with Beth Chiarelli and General Peter Chiarelli.

55 **they were joining a high-powered crowd**: From interviews with Beth Chiarelli and Peter Chiarelli, Brig. Gen. (Ret.) Lee Donne Olvey, and Jeffrey S. McKitrick.

56 **Chiarelli *was* a little intimidated**: From interview with Chiarelli.

57 **Throwing together freethinkers and ambitious young officers**: The history of the Social Sciences Department comes from *The Lincoln Brigade* by Capt. Martha S. H. VanDriel and from numerous interviews. Biographical material on Brig. Gen. George A. Lincoln came from interviews and from *Issues of National Security in the 1970's: Essays Presented to Colonel George A. Lincoln on His Sixtieth Birthday*.

59 **"I am going to take your file and I am going to keep it upside down"**: From interview with Chiarelli.

59 **"A member of the department is *always* a member of the department"**: From interviews with Olvey and McKitrick.

60 **Petraeus, who admired him immensely, decided to take the gamble**: From interviews with Petraeus and from "Beyond the Cloister," an article he wrote for *The American Interest* in July–August 2007 that recounts his experiences in graduate school.

61 **His foray into civilian graduate school had its humbling moments**: From interviews with Petraeus, John Duffield, and from "Beyond the Cloister."

61 **When Taylor arrived at West Point in the 1970s**: From an interview with William Taylor. Other details about the Social Sciences Department and Vietnam come from interviews with Petraeus, Chiarelli, Asa Clark, McKitrick, and Andrew Krepinevich.

63 **The two officers long had been on parallel intellectual paths**: From interviews with Petraeus and Krepinevich.

64 **The acclaim from outsiders made the Army even more defensive:** General (Ret.) Bruce Palmer Jr.'s review of *The Army and Vietnam* appeared in *Parameters,* Autumn 1988. The details of Krepinevich's treatment by the Army came from an interview with Krepinevich.

64 **Petraeus later referred to Krepinevich's treatment as "unsettling":** From Petraeus's dissertation, "The American Military and the Lessons of Vietnam: A Study of Military Influence and the Use of Force in the Post-Vietnam Era."

66 **After returning to West Point, Petraeus finished his dissertation:** From interviews with Petraeus and Galvin, and from Petraeus's dissertation.

66 **Olvey had to pull another officer out of graduate school:** From interviews with Olvey and William Sutey.

CHAPTER FIVE

68 **Lieutenant Ed Massar poked his helmet out of the turret:** The account of the Canadian Army Trophy competition comes from interviews with Chiarelli, Maj. Gen. (Ret.) Tom Griffin, John S. Luallin, Joe Schmalzel, John Menard, and Joe Weiss, as well as from archival video and Defense Department after-action reports.

70 **His Army was determined to win the trophy:** The account of the competition came from Luallin and others.

71 **the Chiarellis were still settling into their new life:** The description of the life in Gelnhausen came from Beth Chiarelli and her children, Peter and Erin.

71 **A few weeks after taking command, Powell came to Gelnhausen:** The description of the dinner at the officers' club came from Luallin, Schmalzel, and Menard. Powell's memories of Gelnhausen are described in his memoirs, *My American Journey.*

73 **"You have a problem," he warned Luallin:** From an interview with Luallin.

74 **Enraged, the younger Abrams summoned Lieutenant Joe Weiss, the maintenance officer:** From an interview with Weiss.

76 **It would only confuse them, he told his superior:** From interviews with Chiarelli and Luallin.

77 **"You took a hell of a chance," the officer said finally:** From an interview with Chiarelli.

77 **Powell allowed himself the general's prerogative of claiming credit:** From Powell's *My American Journey.*

77 **"Warning to the Warsaw Pact," it read:** From *Americans on Target,* Army Research Institute for the Behavioral and Social Sciences, August 1989.

78 **"Don't tell anybody, but by February fifteenth you guys will be out of here":** From interview with Beth Chiarelli.

79 **Vuono had come to rely so heavily on Petraeus:** From interview with Petraeus.

80 **He spent hours drafting forty-page playbooks that his troops could stuff into a pocket:** The account of Casey's leadership as a battalion commander is based on interviews with Dan Hampton, Johnny Parker, Bill Carter, and Tom Carrick.

82 **"The specter of Vietnam has been buried forever in the desert sands of the Arabian Peninsula":** This quote is from a radio address by the president to U.S. Armed Forces stationed in the Persian Gulf region, March 2, 1991.

82 **"Could you help this guy Casey out?":** From interviews with Gen. (Ret.) Carl Vuono and Gen. (Ret.) John Tilelli Jr.

CHAPTER SIX

85 **"I know you understand the rules of engagement":** This account of Operation Provide Comfort is developed from interviews with Abizaid and more than a dozen soldiers from his battalion and higher headquarters, including Chris Cavoli, Ron Kluber, Greg Brouillette, Chuck Cardinal, Sean Callahan, Kim Kadesch, Pete Johnson, and Gen. (Ret.) John Shalikashvili. Abizaid also described his experiences in a March 1993 article in *Military Review* entitled "Lessons for Peacekeepers."

90 **"We can't make a country out of that place":** From Powell's *My American Journey*.

90 **"We must recognize that peacekeeping is no job for amateurs":** This is taken from Abizaid's March 1993 article in *Military Review* entitled "Lessons for Peacekeepers."

91 **Most of the captains and majors now working for him had been to war:** This account of Petraeus's battalion command is drawn from interviews with Petraeus, Gen. (Ret.) Jack Keane, Fred Johnson, Andrew Lucke, Holly Petraeus, and Randy George, and from several published accounts of the shooting accident.

94 **"It made others joke about us, which pulled us together":** From interview with Petraeus.

95 **"Don't cut my LBE," he muttered. "I just got it to standard":** From interview with Fred Johnson.

98 **Several weeks later, Petraeus ran into Colonel Bob Killebrew:** The account of Petraeus's tour in Haiti is drawn from interview with Petraeus, Robert Killebrew, John Shissler, and Lt. Gen. (Ret.) Joe Kinzer.

100 "An environment conducive to political, social and economic development": From "Winning the Peace: Haiti, the U.S. and the U.N.," *Armed Forces Journal International,* April 1995.

100 These clunky terms reflected confused thinking: The definition of "Military Operations Other Than War" is taken from US Army Field Manual 100-23, *Peace Operations,* December 1994.

101 "Doctrinal voids exist at every level," Abizaid warned: From "Preparing for Peacekeeping" by John Abizaid and John Wood, *Special Warfare Magazine,* April 1994.

101 "On that day I think the two of them really didn't like each other": The quote was recounted in a conversation with an officer who is close to both Petraeus and Abizaid and served on their brigade staff in the 82nd Airborne Division.

102 The refugees were Muslims who had once lived in Dugi Dio: The account of the episode at Dugi Dio is drawn from an interview with Casey, Lt. Gen. (Ret.) William Nash, and from an October 11, 1996, article in the *The Talon,* a weekly newspaper published by Task Force Eagle in Bosnia.

105 "You want Abizaid?" he asked: The account of Abizaid's transfer to Task Force Eagle comes from Nash.

106 That morning, Chiarelli updated Clark on the timetable: The account of Chiarelli's and Casey's roles in the Kosovo War come from interviews with Chiarelli and Casey and from General Wesley Clark's memoirs, *Waging Modern War: Bosnia, Kosovo and the Future of Combat.*

109 "your chain of command is your chain of command": From an interview with Abizaid.

CHAPTER SEVEN

110 On the sixth day of the invasion of Iraq, Lieutenant General John Abizaid sat in: This account is based on detailed notes of the meeting taken by one of the participants and interviews with Abizaid and Paul Wolfowitz.

112 "Wouldn't it be wonderful if this place turns out to be something": This quote is taken from *In the Company of Soldiers* by Rick Atkinson, who was embedded with the 101st Airborne Division.

114 "We're in a long war here. I want to keep our guys from getting killed": Also taken from Atkinson, *In the Company of Soldiers.*

116 "You've got to get a force in here and give them some tanks": This quote is taken from *Cobra II* by Michael R. Gordon and Gen. Bernard E. Trainor.

118 **Less than a week after arriving, Petraeus stood in a former Baath Party reception hall:** The account of the election preparations relies on a detailed journal kept by Colonel Richard Hatch, interviews with Hatch and Jeanne Hull, and 101st Airborne Division memos.

120 **"At this time would the Shabaks please move to their delegation room":** From a National Public Radio segment entitled "Iraq Near Establishing Interim Government," May 5, 2003.

121 **"Have you done anything like this before?":** This exchange was taken from "Mosul Elects Council and Mayor," which aired on CNN on May 5, 2003.

122 **"Do you know how huge it is to have a combat patch?":** Quote from Atkinson, *In the Company of Soldiers.*

125 **"I have had enough of Washington":** This quote first appeared in *State of Denial* by Bob Woodward and was confirmed in an interview with Lt. Gen. (Ret.) Jerry Bates.

126 **Franks's send-off was the sort befitting a conquering hero:** An account of the goodbye ceremony appeared in the *Tampa Tribune* on July 8, 2003. General Franks's goodbye speech was transcribed on the U.S. Central Command website.

130 **A couple of days later Petraeus and Basso flew to Rabiya:** The account of the Rabiya trip relies on "A Mix of President . . . and Pope; Army General Given Reins to Remake Mosul" by Scott Wilson in the *Washington Post,* May 16, 2003.

134 **"Did you see the look on their faces?":** The account of this trip relies on notes taken at the time by Major General John Custer, who accompanied Abizaid.

135 **Two days later Bremer called Abizaid and told him the Kurds:** This account draws on notes of the conversation taken at the time by Abizaid's executive officer, Colonel Joseph Reynes, and Bremer's memoir, *My Year in Iraq.*

135 **"Over the last two weeks we've hit the weapons caches":** This quote is from an August 3, 2003, article in the *Washington Post* by Thomas E. Ricks, who was traveling with Abizaid.

136 **"There is no Arab army on earth that's less than 300,000 in a country the size of Iraq":** From notes taken by Custer, Abizaid's intelligence officer.

138 **"This guy could be what we've been looking for":** From notes taken by Custer.

139 **"Why aren't we digging more wells?":** This exchange is taken from *Frontline*'s 2003 documentary *Beyond Baghdad.*

140 **On a drizzly winter day in December a line of:** The account of the renunciation ceremony relies on interviews with participants along with accounts of the ceremony such as "Ex-Baathists Renounce Party Ties," which aired on National Public Radio on January 27, 2004, and Patrick Cockburn's *The Occupation War and Resistance in Iraq.*

143 **This was Chiarelli's new domain:** The account of Chiarelli's first few weeks in Baghdad comes from an interview with Chiarelli and from a personal journal he kept during that period.

146 **Chiarelli removed his gear and the two men sat in frayed chairs facing each other:** From interviews with Chiarelli and James Stephenson.

148 **The first reports came in a little before seven o'clock in the evening:** The account of the Sadr City battle comes from Martha Raddatz's book *The Long Road Home* and from interviews with Chiarelli, Robert Abrams, and Gary Volesky.

149 **"Terrorize your enemy," Sadr proclaimed following the newspaper closure:** Quoted in Patrick Coburn's *Muqtada Al-Sadr and the Fall of Iraq.*

151 **He went back inside and placed a call to General Eric Shinseki:** Chiarelli's call to Shinseki is recounted in Raddatz, *Long Road Home.*

151 **"Sir, why didn't we bring our tanks?":** Recounted in Raddatz, *Long Road Home.*

152 **Abizaid had argued for postponing the moves against Sadr:** From Sanchez's book *Wiser in Battle.*

153 **"If you are going to take Vienna, take fucking Vienna":** From Bing West's book *No True Glory.*

153 **At Sanchez's headquarters the mood was grim:** From interviews with Colonel Casey Haskins and Stephenson.

154 **Chiarelli worried, too:** From interviews with Chiarelli, Volesky, and Barrett Holmes as well as from T. Christian Miller's book *Blood Money.*

154 **"Do these people even want us here?" a frazzled Bush asked Abizaid:** From Brig. Gen. John Custer's notes of the meeting.

155 **He was ushered into the company's dining facility:** The account of the Bechtel meeting is drawn from interviews with Chiarelli, Stephenson, Col. Kendall Cox, and from Stephenson's book, *Losing the Golden Hour, An Insider's View of Iraq's Reconstruction.*

157 **"I'll give you money when you get the place secure":** From an interview with Chiarelli.

157 **It was a field trip of sorts, organized by Chiarelli:** The account of the meeting between USAID and 1st Cav comes from an interview with Kirkpatrick Day.

158 **"That young man, sir—Kirk Day—is a goddamned hero":** From Stephenson, *Losing the Golden Hour.*

159 **"What I'm getting is not what I require":** From notes taken by participants at the meeting.

159 **"We are blowing our window of opportunity":** From notes taken by participants at the meeting.

CHAPTER NINE

161 **"Okay, who's my counterinsurgency expert"?: asked General George Casey:** The account of Casey's first meeting is based on interviews with Casey, Maj. Gen. Steve Sergeant, and senior staff members at the meeting.

162 **Just three months before the invasion he assembled:** This is based on interviews with Casey and members of the fifty-eight-person team. An account of Casey's effort was also mentioned in *Cobra II* by Michael R. Gordon and General Bernard E. Trainor.

163 **On his way into Iraq, Casey had been told by officers in Kuwait:** This account is based on interviews with Casey and Col. (Ret.) Derek Harvey and a previous account in *The War Within* by Bob Woodward.

164 **Six months earlier, on Christmas Eve 2003:** This account is based on an interview with Ryan Casey.

165 **Casey was told to put together a short list:** The description of Casey's selection as commander in Iraq comes from interviews with Casey, Abizaid, and Sheila Casey.

170 **"There is a strategic opportunity for success":** From an e-mail from Casey to Abizaid.

171 **"he wants Casey to stop saying *um* so much":** From an interview with Brig. Gen. James Barclay.

172 **Petraeus had been promoted and sent back to Iraq:** *Newsweek,* July 5, 2005.

172 **"From now on, I'm your PAO," he told Petraeus:** From a participant in the meeting.

173 **The U.S. troops, backed by helicopters and fighter jets, did most of the heavy fighting:** The account of the Najaf battle comes from interviews with Casey, Petraeus, Lt. Gen. Tom Metz, and Barclay, and from numerous published accounts.

174 **"Frankly I didn't expect such a key success so early":** From an interview with Casey.

174 **Not all of Casey's subordinate commanders were as convinced:** The account of the meeting comes from notes taken by a participant.

175 "I am not going to listen to Chiarelli . . . bitch about the State Department": From an interview with Robert Earle and from Earle's book, *Nights in the Pink Motel: An American Strategist's Pursuit of Peace in Iraq.*

175 "Will Sadr or his lieutenants attack again?": Taken from "Winning the Peace: The Requirement for Full Spectrum Operations," by Maj. Gen. Peter W. Chiarelli and Maj. Patrick R. Michaelis, *Military Review,* July/August 2005.

176 In late September, Petraeus put down his thoughts: Petraeus's op-ed, entitled "Battling for Iraq," appeared in the *Washington Post* on September 24, 2004.

176 "They just walked out the gate and didn't come back": The interview with Maj. Dixon was conducted by the Army's Combat Studies Institute at Fort Leavenworth, Kansas, in October 2006.

177 One of the deserters was the battalion commander: This account is based on an interview with Maj. Jones conducted by the Army's Combat Studies Institute at Fort Leavenworth, Kansas, in November 2006.

178 In June Abizaid had assured Petraeus that he would get whatever he needed: The account of this meeting comes from interviews with several members of Petraeus's staff at the training command.

179 Petraeus's staff knew they had a problem: This account is based on an interview with Colonel Fred Kienle, who served on Petraeus's staff and helped oversee the Iraqi army training effort.

179 In late 2004, Brigadier General James Schwitters: This exchange is based on interviews with Petraeus's staff and interviews conducted by the Army's Combat Studies Institute at Fort Leavenworth, Kansas.

180 "I lost fifty-three soldiers in Mosul": Lieutenant Colonel Charlie Miller accompanied Petraeus on this trip and took detailed notes. The account is also based on interviews with Petraeus and his aide, Sadi Othman.

181 Ham suspected that Barhawi had been cooperating: This account is based on interviews with General Ham and his staff.

182 Abizaid knew things weren't going well: The account of this meeting is based on detailed notes of the meeting taken by one of the participants and interviews with all of the officers involved.

185 But Major Grant Doty, a slim, bespectacled strategist: This account is based on interviews of those present at the morning briefing and emails provided by Major Doty.

188 "What a historic day": This scene is constructed from notes taken that day by Miller.

CHAPTER TEN

190 **Defense Secretary Donald Rumsfeld was furious:** This account relies on detailed notes taken by several participants at the meeting.

192 **The president had reservations:** This account is based on interviews with Casey, Abizaid, and Col. James G. Rose, who all participated in the meeting. An account of the meeting is also in *The War Within* by Bob Woodward.

193 **As Casey studied his new orders:** Casey confided this worry to his wife, Sheila, only after returning to the United States.

194 **Petraeus led Luck's team through a three-hour briefing:** The account of this meeting is based on interviews with several of Petraeus's staff officers, who took detailed notes.

196 **Finally Petraeus demanded a meeting with Casey's chief of staff:** The account of this meeting is based on an interview with Maj. Gen. Donovan and notes taken at the time by Petraeus's staff.

197 **Iraq was a "troop sump":** This quote comes from Bob Woodward's *The War Within* and was confirmed by several of Casey's staff officers.

199 **The Army's official history of the conflict:** This passage is taken from *Certain Victory: The U.S. Army in the Gulf War* by Brigadier General Robert H. Scales.

199 **"You need to stop thinking strategically":** This exchange was recounted by officers on McMaster's staff.

200 **When the briefing was done:** This account is based on interviews with both McMaster and Casey.

201 **"We're managing this war, not fighting it":** This quote was recounted by several of McMaster's staff officers.

202 **The two visited thirty-one different units:** This account is based on interviews with Hix and Sepp as well as a review of their final report.

205 **Casey's small plane touched down:** This account is based on interviews with several staff officers who attended the meeting as well as interviews with Casey and McMaster.

207 **U.S. advisors complained:** The U.S. advisors' complaints about McMaster are chronicled in interviews conducted by the Army's Combat Studies Institute at Fort Leavenworth, Kansas, and in *Iroquois Warriors in Iraq* by Stephen E. Clay.

208 **Rumsfeld hit the roof:** The defense secretary's remarks were made in a Pentagon press conference and posted on the Defense Department's website.

208 **With Iraq collapsing into civil war, President Bush cited:** The quotes are taken from Bush's speech on March 20, 2006, in Cleveland, Ohio.

208 **An influential *New Yorker* article:** The article, entitled "The Lesson of Tal Afar," was written by George Packer and published on April 10, 2006.

208 **"I understand you are looking for a kidnapped boy":** This account is based on interviews with Gen. Horst and Gen. Casey. It also borrows from an interview with Horst that was conducted by *Frontline* for its documentary *Gangs of Iraq*.

CHAPTER ELEVEN

213 **Casey clambered out of one vehicle along with several aides:** This account of the meeting with Jabr and the handling of the Jediriyah incident is taken from interviews with Casey and other participants.

216 **In November, Senator John McCain went public with his criticism:** A transcript of McCain's speech is on his Senate website.

218 **The doctrine, which drove the Army for two decades:** This description borrows from Rick Atkinson's account of the impact of the AirLand Battle Doctrine in his book *The Long Gray Line*.

219 **The most radical aspect of the manual:** This idea is taken from Sarah Sewall's introduction to the counterinsurgency doctrine, which was later published by the University of Chicago Press. The idea is elaborated further in "Our War on Terror" by Samantha Power, which appeared in the *New York Times* on July 29, 2007.

221 **He had only been back from his first tour since March:** From an interview with Chiarelli.

222 **The biggest reservations came from military intelligence officers:** From an interview with Col. Marcus Kuiper.

222 **From his base in Tampa, Abizaid told his staff to shift surveillance drones:** From Brig. Gen. Custer's notes.

223 **Two days after the bombing, a worried Casey:** E-mail provided by U.S. military officer.

223 **Sometimes he sat in his office or his quarters at night:** From interviews with Casey and Maj. Tony Hale. Documents provided by Casey.

224 **As he sat on a folding chair listening, Chiarelli became annoyed:** The account of Chiarelli's visits to Samarra comes from interviews with Chiarelli and other participants.

225 **"Anytime you fight—anytime you fight—you always kill":** A video of Steele's speech is posted on YouTube.

226 **The pungent smell of manure wafted up from the ground:** One of the authors accompanied Chiarelli on his visit to Al Asad.

228 **A few minutes into the proceedings:** Parts of this account came from coverage in the *New York Times* of the public aspects of the proceedings, including "Iraqis Form Government with Crucial Posts Vacant," May 21, 2006, by Dexter Filkins and Richard A. Oppel Jr. It also relies on interviews with Casey and his staff.

228 **"One, he absolutely believes":** Bob Woodward in his book *The War Within* provided a similar account of Casey's initial description of Maliki to President Bush.

228 **"Excuse me, ma'am. Did you say forty-eight?"** From an interview with Casey and from Woodward's *The War Within*.

229 **After the meeting Rumsfeld shot him a snowflake:** From an interview with Casey.

230 **"We've got to get in to see Maliki":** From an interview with Chiarelli.

230 **Maliki studied it intently for several minutes:** From an interview with Chiarelli.

230 **Chiarelli's doubts about Maliki grew more acute over the course of the summer:** From an interview with an officer who saw the intelligence reports.

231 **Casey had been back from leave only a few hours:** This account of the deliberations at senior command levels in the latter half of 2006 is drawn from interviews with Casey, Chiarelli, and others involved, as well as from e-mails, meeting notes, and other documents written by participants.

233 **"Do you really want that job?" she asked him:** From an interview with Celeste Ward.

235 **Incensed, Thurman ripped off the Velcro patch that held his two stars:** The account of the episode comes from someone who was present. Chiarelli recalled in an interview the training film from his days as junior officer.

237 **several of Chiarelli's staff were so worried:** This account of Chiarelli's meeting with Steele comes from two officers on Chiarelli's staff.

237 **A soldier griped in the *Washington Times*:** From *Washington Times*, February 16, 2007.

238 **The graying men around the conference table:** The account of the Iraq Study Group visit to Baghdad comes from an interview with Chiarelli and from Woodward, *The War Within*.

239 **To Casey's surprise, Maliki admitted that he had ordered the raid:** From an e-mail describing the meeting provided by a U.S. officer.

240 **Abizaid happened to be in Baghdad when he got Casey's note:** Abizaid's visit to Iraq was reconstructed through interviews with Abizaid and from e-mails provided by a U.S. officer.

243 **As Hadley's team prepared to leave for the airport:** Hadley's visit to Iraq was described by Chiarelli, by an administration official who accompanied him, and in Woodward, *The War Within.*

244 **A few days later Hadley drafted a classified memo for Bush:** Hadley's memo to Bush was reprinted in the *New York Times* on November 29, 2006.

246 **Bush was planning on giving an Iraq speech before Christmas:** The White House meetings were reconstructed using notes taken by a participant.

248 **He had sent word ahead of time that he needed a few minutes with Casey:** From an interview with Casey.

248 **Chiarelli's last day in Iraq was spent waiting for a plane:** The account of Chiarelli's return from Iraq comes from interviews with Chiarelli, Brig. Gen. Don Campbell, and Beth Chiarelli.

CHAPTER TWELVE

251 **At 7:27 a.m. Casey took his place:** The account of this morning briefing is based on notes taken by a senior officer in the audience.

254 **Abizaid stepped up the lectern and did his best:** A video of the change-of-command ceremony is available on the Department of Defense website.

256 **The volatile Mashhadani castigated Obaidi:** The first account of the dinner came in *Tell Me How This Ends* by Linda Robinson, which provides a detailed account of Petraeus's strategy during the surge.

259 **"Good morning," Petraeus mumbled:** The authors attended several of Petraeus's morning briefings in 2007 and 2008. This account is built from their observations and detailed notes taken by Petraeus's staff officers.

262 **Fixing Tower 57, which was just one small piece:** This account is based on interviews with Petraeus, his staff, and officers from the Third Infantry Division, whose soldiers were responsible for helping to provide security for the Iraqi repair crews. It also borrows from an account of the repair mission that was written by Army journalists and posted on the Multi-National Force–Iraq website.

262 **"I've occasionally wondered if there is some sort of bad-news limit":** This quote first appeared in a September 2007 article by Brian Mockenhaupt in *Esquire* magazine.

263 **Days earlier Lieutenant Colonel Dale Kuehl:** This account is based on interviews with Kuehl and some of his staff officers. A more detailed account of his efforts appears in *Tell Me How This Ends* by Linda Robinson.

266 **Even before Petraeus set foot in the country:** Senior U.S. military officers learned of the Iraqis' doubts through intercepts of Iraqi cell phone conversations.

266 **"Everyone knows this. We've been talking about it for months":** This account is based on interviews with Petraeus and his senior staff members who attended the meeting. The meeting is also briefly covered in Bob Woodward's *The War Within*.

267 **He sat behind a desk wearing a black cavalry hat:** This account relies on interviews with Kuehl and Pinkerton. It also borrows some details from "Meet Abu Abed: The US's New Ally Against al Qaeda," which appeared in the *Guardian* newspaper on November 10, 2007.

272 **He opened with a searing seven-minute video:** This video was shot by Sean Smith of the *Guardian* newspaper and first appeared on the *Guardian*'s website in 2007.

277 **A few days after he had returned to Baghdad he met:** The account of this meeting is based on detailed notes taken by one of Petraeus's staff officers.

277 **"This is not a government of national unity":** The account of this meeting is based on detailed notes taken by one of Petraeus's staff officers.

278 **In September 2008 the last of the U.S. reinforcements:** The account of the Rakkasans in Iraq is based on personal observations from time one of the authors spent with the unit in 2008.

EPILOGUE

287 **His solution amounted to an anti-Powell Doctrine for the Arab world:** This phrase is taken from David Kilcullen's book *The Accidental Guerrilla,* which was published in the spring of 2009. Kilcullen advocates a similar premise.

287 **"Throughout the region we need to quit being the primary military force":** This quote appeared in a speech that Abizaid delivered at Dartmouth University in the fall of 2008. A video of his address is posted on the Dartmouth University website.

288 **"Why not have 270 or 2,7000?" Abizaid wondered:** Abizaid made this point in a public address at Fort Huachuca in Arizona in the summer of 2008.

289 **When the lights came back on Petraeus stood atop a plywood riser:** This account is based on personal observations by one of the authors who attended the ceremony.

Hundreds of people have generously given their time to help us with this book. None deserve greater thanks than the four generals at the heart of the effort, their spouses, and their children. John Abizaid, George Casey, Peter Chiarelli, and David Petraeus all discussed their careers in multiple, wide-ranging interviews and e-mail exchanges over the course of a year during which no question was off-limits. They shared with us personal papers that provided valuable insight into their lives and careers and helped us understand them as young officers and as the experienced commanders they became. They generously encouraged the men and women they served with over the years to subject themselves to interviews. And they patiently endured numerous follow-up questions and other intrusions during our research. The book would not have been possible without their assistance.

We would like to thank Kurt Campbell, Michele Flournoy, and John Nagl, at the Center for a New American Security, an inspiring national security think tank that gave us a place to work, along with encouragement, countless ideas, and support. Our book was shaped by hundreds of hallway conversations at CNAS with the dedicated people who have made it the most creative and influential think tank in Washington. They include Price Floyd, Derek Chollet, Nate Fick, Michael Zubrow, Shannon O'Reilly, Vikram Singh, Jim Miller, Nirav Patel, Shawn Brimley, Colin Kahl, Sharon Burke, and Andrew Exum. Kurt Campbell, in particular, immediately grasped the book we were trying to write and went to extraordinary lengths to help us.

We'd also like to say a special thanks to Alexander "Sandy" Cochran and Kelly Howard, who provided valuable insights on General Casey's tenure in Iraq. Major General John Custer, Lieutenant Colonel Charlie Miller, Colonel James Laufenburg, and Colonel Richard Hatch were particularly patient with us as we asked them to walk us through old journals and field notebooks. In each case they supplemented their notes with crucial recollections and invaluable insights. Colonel Steve Boylan helped us both set up reporting trips to Iraq. We also benefited from his deep knowledge of the U.S. military in Iraq, which grew out of his long tenure as a public affairs officer there. Colonel Michael Meese, who heads the Department of Social Sciences at West Point, helped us understand the critical role that Sosh plays in the life of the Army and, even more important, encouraged others in the somewhat secretive world of Sosh to talk about the department.

We'd also like to thank our friends and colleagues from our days at the *Wall Street*

Journal, especially our editors there, Jerry Seib and Alan Murray. In the years when we were there, the *Journal* was a journalistic jewel that encouraged deep inquiry and nuanced writing about the world, and we continually sought to emulate those standards in this project. We owe a huge debt of gratitude to our agent, Gail Ross, and her assistant, Howard Yoon, who helped us form the idea for this book and helped shepherd the project through to completion. Our editor, Rick Horgan, and his assistant, Nathan Roberson, at times seemed to understand what we were trying to say and then accomplished it better than we had. Their guidance was invaluable.

David's parents, Nancy Fuller and Stanley Cloud, and Greg's parents Michael and Elaine Jaffe, grasped what we were doing and why from the beginning and supported it with their love and time. Thanks to Stanley Cloud, whose comments on our proposal and the final manuscript were invaluable. Finally, we would like to thank our wives and children, who sustained us from the beginning to the end of this project and continue to do so. Both of us had spent long stretches away from the people we love the most even before we began. When we explained what we planned to do, Jennifer Cloud and Kristie Jaffe became the book's biggest supporters, banishing our doubts and worries about secondary matters. They and our children, Allison Jaffe, Matthew Jaffe, and Joey Cloud, endured our moodiness and our long hours away from them without complaint. They provided irreplaceable advice, encouragement, and love to two first-time authors as they discovered writing a book is considerably harder than daily journalism. They never lost faith in what we were doing, and, because of that, neither did we.

Greg Jaffe and David Cloud
Washington, D.C.
May 2009